SONS OF THE REVOLUTION

Sons of the Revolution

Radical Democrats
in France
1862–1914

Judith F. Stone

Louisiana State University Press
Baton Rouge and London

Copyright © 1996 by Louisiana State University Press
All rights reserved
Manufactured in the United States of America
First printing
05   04   03   02   01   00   99   98   97   96   5 4 3 2 1

Designer: Glynnis Weston
Typeface: Goudy
Typesetter: Impressions
Printer and binder: Thomson-Shore, Inc.

The author is grateful to Paul Baquiast for permission to quote from Camille Pelletan's "Mé-moires (inédites)," Eugène Pelletan's letter to Camille Pelletan of September, 1879, Mme Joséphine Pelletan's preface to Pelletan's "Mémoires," and Mme Bréchet's interview with Paul Baquiast, all excerpted from Baquiast's Mémoire de maîtrise d'histoire, Université de Paris IV, 1986.

An early version of Chapter VII was first published as "La République et La Patrie: The Radi-cals' Nationalism Under Attack," in *Nationhood and Nationalism in France: From Boulangism to the Great War, 1889–1918*, ed. Robert Tombs (New York: HarperCollins, 1991), copyright 1991 by HarperCollins Publishers.

Library of Congress Cataloging-in-Publication Data

Stone, Judith F., 1946—
    Sons of the Revolution : radical democrats in France, 1862–1914 /
Judith F. Stone.
        p.   cm.
    Includes bibliographical references and index.
    ISBN 0-8071-2020-0
    1. Pelletan, Camille, 1846–1915—Influence.   2. Legislators—
France—Biography.   3. France—History—Third Republic, 1870–1940.
4. Republicanism—France—History—19th century.   5. France.
Assemblée nationale (1871–1942)—History.   I. Title.
DC342.8.P35S76   1996
944.08'092—dc20   95–32092
                                                        CIP

To Stanley, once again

CONTENTS

ILLUSTRATIONS

ACKNOWLEDGMENTS

A community of intellectuals and a network of academic institutions support all scholarly and historical work. This study of France's democratic political culture is no different. It draws on the insights, knowledge, generosity, support, and resources of friends and colleagues. My work gained enormously from the criticism and suggestions of those who read the manuscript, generously giving their expertise and time. I owe special thanks to Leslie Page Moch, who graciously submitted the entire manuscript to her demanding standards and perceptive insights. Rachel Fuchs and Herman "Gene" Lebovics provided invaluable observations and suggestions as readers of the manuscript. A long list of French historians in North America offered comments and advice on portions of the research presented as conference papers. Without this support I could not have pursued this study, but responsibility for its arguments and conclusions remains entirely my own.

Historical research in France presents particular challenges, as well as enormous rewards. I am grateful to the Faculty Research and Creative Activities Fund of Western Michigan University and the Burnham-Macmillan Trust of the History Department of Western Michigan University for funding several research trips. In France my work was made possible by the rich resources of archives, libraries, and their staffs who provided assistance, particularly the Archives Nationales, the Bibliothèque Nationale, and the Archives Départementales of the Bouches-du-Rhône. I have been especially fortunate to have had the opportunity to discuss my interest in the political culture of the Third Republic with two French scholars in this field. Gérard Baal, who has recently completed an exhaustive study of the Radical party, offered invaluable suggestions. Paul Baquiast, a historian and descendant of Camille Pelletan, generously shared both family papers and his own insights. I owe special thanks to two Parisians, Annie Couëdel and Philibert Nicolas, who so often welcomed me to their city and made me feel at home in their *quartier* and their *maison*. Cynthia Running-Johnson, my friend and colleague, always responded with assistance and good humor to my many queries about French translation. My effort to understand things French has also been enormously aided by my mother, Joan Freudman, who made France her home for many years and has taught me that one can be a citizen of several lands.

The process of moving from research to actual publication is long, arduous, and sometimes frustrating. The consistent confidence and good cheer of Margaret Dalrymple, former assistant director and editor-in-chief at Louisiana State University Press, greatly eased that experience. Kelly Keglovitz, manager of Western Michigan University's Computer Help Desk, efficiently solved word processing problems that at first appeared insurmountable.

The final paragraph is always the most difficult to write. I could not have completed my work without the support, encouragement, and hot meals provided by my partner, Stanley Stamm. His demanding and thorough reading and rereading of the manuscript enabled me to improve it. He generously gave of his time and, more important, of his spirit. This book, as my first, is dedicated to him.

Abbreviations

AD/BR Archives Départmentales, Bouches-du-Rhône

AN Archives Nationales,
Paris

APP Archives de la Préfecture
de Police de Paris

Introduction

Radical republican party leader Camille Pelletan died in Paris on June 4, 1915. He considered himself, and was universally acknowledged to be, among the most loyal "sons of the Revolution." His obituary in the party newspaper identified him as "one of the figures most closely associated with the Third Republic, one of its founders, one of the regime's strongest supporters."[1] The two leading Radical premiers of the interwar period, Edouard Herriot and Edouard Daladier, honored Camille Pelletan as a worthy ancestor. In 1923 Daladier commemorated the anniversary of Pelletan's death at the Parisian cemetery of Père-Lachaise. The Herriot government erected a statue to Pelletan in Salon-de-Provence, the southern town that he had represented for thirty years. Pelletan's admirers and detractors correctly identified him with the Third Republic, which he and his colleagues viewed as the legitimate heir of the revolutions of 1789 and 1848.

In the last quarter of the nineteenth century, Pelletan and this regime represented both a political tradition and a new political enterprise. To establish a republic in a major European state in 1871 was an audacious departure, a result of complex circumstances that led the French to experiment once again with republicanism. This book reminds readers just how daring that innovation was. The conservative historian Daniel Halévy recognized the force of the Republic's central principle, universal suffrage, as "that awesome phenomenon, that enormous craving for power which threatened to destroy those states that did not learn how to curb it. Universal suffrage was indeed a formidable development; we are so accustomed to it that we have some difficulty in weighing its impact."[2] Much to the chagrin of its many opponents, the republican system of governing persisted beyond the 1870s. Radical republicans such as Pelletan were dedicated not

1. *Le Radical*, June 6, 1915.
2. Daniel Halévy, *The End of the Notables*, trans. Alain Silvera and June Guicharnaud, ed. Alain Silvera (1930; rpr., Middletown, Conn., 1974), 55.

only to the continuation of the Republic but also—and just as strongly—
to the creation of what they viewed as an authentic democratic state and
society. This history of Radical democrats views them from new perspectives, seeking to recapture the fluidity of a particular past before it became
fixed as history. I begin by returning to the youth of these men and the
early years of the regime to which they were committed, examining their
expectations, ideals, and hopes before the onset of compromise and old age.

Although I am concerned with the early, intransigent, and passionate
republicanism of the Radicals, I also investigate the causes of their current obscurity. At the end of the twentieth century, seventy years after
his statue was erected in Provence, Camille Pelletan is entirely forgotten,
the French Radical party has only a marginal political existence, and the
Third Republic is considered by many a confusing historical period most
vividly associated with its ignoble defeat in 1940. I examine the forces that
have effaced this man and his politics. This study probes important traditional political institutions—electoral politics, party organization, and
parliamentary proceedings—within the larger social and cultural contexts
that sustained Radical republicanism and were in turn affected by it. In addition to analyzing formal structures of political power, I explore how men
and women during the first half of the Third Republic perceived, shaped,
and experienced political life and ideas. Radical republicans were at the
very heart of the political world of the Belle Epoque. Most broadly, then,
this is a study of the political culture of democracy: its articulation by a
specific group of men in late nineteenth-century France, their efforts to
construct a democratic state and society, the obstacles they encountered,
and the reasons for their decline into obscurity.

The careers of Radical politicians during the early Third Republic and
the history of the regime itself demonstrate the persistent difficulties that
all political actors have encountered when attempting to establish a democratic state in a heterogeneous society composed of contending classes,
sharply distinguished genders, and diverse cultures. Lynn Hunt has observed that "from 1789 onward, supporters of the Revolution were engaged
in the great adventure of the modern Western social contract; they were
trying to replace deference and paternal authority with a new basis for political consent."[3] This experiment is still not concluded. In the second half

3. Lynn Hunt, *The Family Romance of the French Revolution* (Berkeley, 1992), 4.

of the nineteenth century French republicans searching for a viable democratic tradition and an effective new state organization faced three major paradoxes. The first was the tension between the legacy of parliamentarianism and the principles of universal suffrage. Early nineteenth-century advocates of parliamentary rule, legitimated by a constitution, excluded the overwhelming majority of male citizens from political participation, which in their view negated the possibility of sound government. The parliaments of the Bourbon Restoration and the July Monarchy were explicitly created to defend men of wealth and education against the unreasoning and dangerous demands of the masses. Property qualifications severely limited suffrage. Supporters of such parliaments assumed that they would function as arenas in which representatives of various interests from the economic and cultural elite could negotiate their differences. The Orléanist defenders of the July Monarchy never doubted that legitimate, rational political authority could exist only within such a narrowly defined realm of political activity. Ultimately the entire population and the nation would benefit from such leadership. This parliamentarianism of the *notables* differed dramatically from the intentions of republicans, who demanded "universal suffrage."

For republicans, genuine popular sovereignty required that all citizens participate in the exercise of political power. The ability of all to vote was the most obvious expression of such power. Only broad inclusion in the political process could provide legitimacy to the regime and ensure that state and nation functioned in harmony. A leading Radical politician defined democracy as "the system which makes the right to vote a natural right, based on the condition of being a human person and independent of the material, moral, economic or social circumstances in which that person exists."[4] This activist vision of political involvement imagined the equal distribution of political power among citizens. The primary emphasis was on the citizen and voter, not the representative and the legislature. The passionate commitment with which republicans proclaimed this principle derived in part from their efforts to counter and delegitimize the suspect elitist parliamentary system. They also perpetuated a tradition of the French Revolution that identified parliamentary politics with dangerously divisive factions and sought instead unity in the name of the public good.[5] The

4. Ferdinand Buisson, *Le Vote des femmes* (Paris, 1911), 306.
5. Lynn Hunt, *Politics, Culture, and Class in the French Revolution* (Berkeley, 1984), 3.

experience of the Second Republic reinforced this suspicion and this republican tradition. Democrats in 1850 were appalled when the legislature restricted male suffrage. Even more disturbing, this pivotal mid-century experience demonstrated how easily "universal suffrage" could be manipulated, ultimately leading to the betrayal of popular sovereignty. Universal male suffrage had returned the conservative legislature that voted to restrict the right to vote; universal male suffrage had elected a president who forcibly overthrew the Republic. Although universal suffrage remained an essential principle of republicanism, republicans regarded it as a powerful political force that did not automatically yield the results they expected. The expression of popular sovereignty had to be guarded from a variety of distorting influences if it were to voice what republicans understood as the authentic will of the people.

As the century progressed, republicans identified two powerful forces that interfered with the citizens' expression of their political views—the Catholic church and economic dependence. Previous regimes had bestowed special privileges on the church so republicans believed that a republic could easily dismantle these privileges and eliminate clerical power.[6] The striking inequalities of economic power posed a greater dilemma because for the most part they had not been created by the state. The republicans then confronted a second perplexing paradox between their concept of equal citizens exercising political power and the existence of social and economic hierarchies organized around powerful class distinctions. Alexis de Tocqueville, perhaps the most notable nineteenth-century defender of the elitist parliamentary tradition, tellingly observed, "It is a contradiction for the people to be simultaneously impoverished and sovereign" (Il est contradictoire que le peuple soit à la fois misérable et souverain).[7] With this quip Tocqueville was certain that he had exposed the essential impossibility and irrationality of democracy. The republicans, by contrast, though agreeing that such a condition was contradictory, were convinced

6. This brief reference to anticlericalism is not to diminish its significance for republicans and particularly for Radicals; on the contrary, it was one of the most important themes of their political lives. But anticlericalism posed no dilemmas for the Radicals, unlike economic inequality, which raised many.

7. Quoted in Ferdinand Buisson, *La Politique radicale. Etude sur les doctrines du Parti radical et radical-socialiste* (Paris, 1908), 218.

that their political and social programs would reduce, if not eliminate, the misery of the people. As the century progressed, however, and the category of the people merged ever more with that of the working class, the most committed republicans faced the dilemma of attempting to function within two essentially incompatible views of society. The demand for equal rights for all citizens emphasized different problems and solutions than the demand for an end to economic exploitation. The most militant republicans stood between the concepts of citizen and class, unwilling to repudiate either one.

As republicans attempted to incorporate the organizing working class into their older vision of equal citizens, they faced yet another paradox: the essential limits of their claims to universality. "Universal suffrage" meant male suffrage; "citizen" signified an adult man. Throughout this book "universal suffrage" appears in quotation marks to remind the reader that when republicans used this phrase, which they did repeatedly, they meant something else. This exclusion was no mere oversight to be corrected as the republic progressed. Early in the French tradition of republicanism, men made a conscious decision that popular political participation could succeed only if women were barred from it. Despite this choice, there always remained an awareness among republicans that such massive exclusion undermined the claims to universality and natural rights so critical to legitimating the democratic movement. Throughout the nineteenth century republicans were haunted by the "woman question." Many early republicans attempted to imagine the appropriate family and the appropriate republican mother who would fulfill the vital task of nurturing future citizens. Later the problematic issue of women's place in the republic became even more urgent as women themselves demanded full citizenship and the right to vote, directly challenging Radicals to fulfill their proclaimed commitment to "universal suffrage." The paradox of this universality, which required exclusion, was further heightened by symbolic representations of liberty and the republic itself as female figures. The reasons for such allegories are multiple, but certainly an important factor must be that women "were chosen to express the ideal of freedom because of their very distance from political liberty. Liberty was figured as female because women were not imagined as political actors. Yet the embodiment of political ideals by female figures also opened the door to a different vision."[8] By the end of the century, some Radical politicians recognized that the segregation of women created an enormous obstacle to the fulfillment of their democratic objectives.

In their attempt to establish a democratic state in the last quarter of the nineteenth century, republicans constantly encountered the contradictions embedded in their own principles, those relating to "universal suffrage," economic and social hierarchies, and gender distinctions. Although I emphasize efforts to overcome these contradictions, I do not reject the widely held view of the Third Republic as a political system based on a conservative bourgeois consensus. I do stress, however, that this outcome, to defend the existing social hierarchy, emerged only after repeated, bitter, and passionate conflicts that were never completely resolved through the entire existence of the Third Republic. The bourgeois consensus was constantly criticized and renegotiated. Not all supporters of the Third Republic, not even all its bourgeois supporters, universally applauded conservative efforts to preserve the social status quo. In fact, one of the most significant characteristics of French political life of this period was the heterogeneity of the bourgeoisie, a class sharply divided on political, social, and cultural issues.[9] This history argues that alternative visions of the Republic existed and some politicians made genuine efforts to realize them. An emancipatory, reformist program, which the aspirations of la République sociale still shaped, countered the policies of the conservative consensus. That most of this program failed to be implemented does not diminish the historical significance of those who attempted to formulate, promote, and enact it. Radicals were central to those efforts and the conflicts they engendered.

While examining Radical republicans from new perspectives, this book makes no effort to rehabilitate them. Their right-wing critics often identified serious flaws in their programs and their characters. The partial truth of these partisan attacks accounted for some of their persuasiveness. Especially astute was the conservative criticism of the slippery ground on which pol-

8. For the intense anxieties created by these tensions around the gender issue, see Hunt, *Family Romance*, 121–23, 152, quote on page 83.

9. For divisions within the republican middle class, see Philip G. Nord, "The Party of Conciliation and the Paris Commune," *French Historical Studies*, XV (Spring, 1987), 1–35. Nord earlier elaborated on this theme in his important book *Paris Shopkeepers and the Politics of Resentment* (Princeton, 1986).

itics, social climbing, and money converged and on which Radicals often floundered. This history moves beyond the numerous clichés surrounding the Radicals, but it also demonstrates the development and, in some cases, the importance of those same clichés. If I begin at a time of great expectations, before the Republic even existed, I observe the movement of these men and their aspirations from possibility and experimentation to electoral success and parliamentary power to immobility and bitter disappointment. In an inverse fashion, these sentiments paralleled the growth of their political organization and their electoral victories. We follow Pelletan and his cohort from a semilegal opposition group during the Second Empire to the largest political party in the Third Republic's Chamber of Deputies by 1910. In the process of this transformation they created a system of beliefs, rules of political behavior, symbols, and a rhetoric that have indelibly marked French politics.

The political culture of democracy in France is unthinkable without the imprint of Radical republicans. For this alone they merit considerable attention in the late twentieth century. Their history is especially instructive at a time when the rhetoric of democracy remains the most universally accepted language of politics and state legitimation, while at the same time it evokes increasing skepticism from citizens. It was the Radicals who, in the late nineteenth and early twentieth centuries, introduced the political categories and shaped the institutions that now seem synonymous with modern, representative states: citizen, equality, popular sovereignty, universal suffrage. Although some of these categories failed to become concrete social and political realities, the rhetoric itself has been an important force in shaping a specific political culture that played a dominant role in France from at least 1850 to 1950. Beginning as early as the 1860s intransigent promoters of democracy struggled to elaborate a viable democratic tradition and establish what they considered an authentic republican order.

A voluminous bibliography on radicalism exists, which is largely weighted toward a negative view of both the Radicals and the Third Republic. Neither the party nor the regime has emerged from contemporary accounts or historical studies as especially attractive or impressive. The pre–World War I decades were studded with often bewildering shifts of governments and political personnel, regularly interrupted by complicated and unsavory scandals. The Great War provided a moment of high drama but ended in an inconclusive victory that set the Republic and its dominant party, the Radicals, limping toward the disaster of yet another war, defeat, and national dismemberment. During the interwar period, conservative critics of the republican regime mixed historical and contemporary observations to demonstrate the moral corruption and, even worse, the mediocrity of the state and its leading defenders, the Radicals. They had no doubt that the national malaise was the consequence of republicanism and the legacy of men such as Pelletan. Many conservatives and those further to their right felt themselves suffering under a long and destructive "dictatorship" of the Radical party.[10] Daniel Halévy in particular has deeply shaped subsequent evaluations of the Third Republic and the Radical party. His 1930 study, *La Fin des notables*, charts the demise of the social and political conservative elite during the 1870s and its replacement by politicians committed to and dependent on universal male suffrage. While offering important insights, Halévy infused his analysis with a deep regret for the loss of France's talented and dedicated aristocratic leadership. Republicanism and republicans, in Halévy's view, were symptomatic of a long deterioration. He noted that already by the 1930s the first generation of these republicans had fallen into obscurity. In a more polemical work of 1934, *La République des comités*, Halévy explicitly stated his view of the Radicals' mediocrity that permeated the entire regime. As early as the 1890s they represented a "tradition a bit worn out by use" and "a school for cowardice." The Radicals' electoral triumphs of the early twentieth century coincided with the "classic age of parliamentary degeneracy." Halévy was convinced that during World War I "in their hearts they betrayed France." Perhaps most repulsive to Halévy, the Radicals were mediocre social climbers devoid of ideas who had attained positions of state power. Such visceral bitterness against the Radicals was not only a phenomenon of the interwar years. It often adopted the vocabulary of the Radicals' political opponents, simply adding a historical dimension. Paul Bosq, a centrist political commentator who described the various parliamentary groups in the 1890s, dismissed the Radicals as pure negation: "The balance sheet of the Radical party . . . is in one word: a

10. See, for example, Robert Cornilleau, *De Waldeck-Rousseau à Poincaré. Chronique d'une géneration (1898–1924)* (Paris, 1926), 64 and *passim*. Cornilleau was a proponent of social Catholicism and especially dismayed by the Radicals' anticlericalism.

mess. . . . They have squandered everything, wasted everything, destroyed everything."[11]

Conservative and right-wing criticisms of Radicals and the Third Republic have often reflected a deep suspicion of democratic government and universal suffrage. Even for those more sympathetic to democratic aspirations, a negative portrait emerges. Among French historians the "Hoffmann thesis" continues to influence the prevailing view of the Third Republic. Developing an explanation for change in post–World War II France, Stanley Hoffmann proposed that one important cause was a strong and widespread reaction against the society and, to a lesser degree, the politics of the Third Republic. Agreeing with the French sociologist Michel Crozier, Hoffmann characterized the Third Republic as a "blocked society." This world of stalemate prized stability, rested on a political and social alliance of the middle classes and peasantry, excluded the industrial working class, and retained an ambiguous attitude toward authority, both fearing and desiring it.[12] Though Hoffman did not specifically focus on the Radicals or their political policies, he made it clear that they personified these politics of stalemate.

Other historians have taken up and elaborated the socially conservative consensus which Hoffmann paints. In Sanford Elwitt's *Making of the Third Republic* and his later *Third Republic Defended* a similar republican conservatism emerges. Here it is explicitly linked with a cohesive and self-conscious bourgeoisie able to extend some concessions to a temporarily restive petite bourgeoisie and peasantry during the early Republic. The essential components of the political and social compact were set by the late 1880s, resting on agreements over railroads, schools, and tariffs. This conservative consensus among various strata of the bourgeoisie was then maintained throughout the Republic, once again excluding the working class. *The Third Republic Defended* addresses the adjustments required in this original conservative compact after the 1880s in response to changed so-

---

11. Commenting on the leading thinkers of the 1870s—Renan, Taine, and Flaubert—he stressed that all had portrayed the nineteenth century as a period of decline (Halévy, *End of the Notables*, 51); quotes *ibid.*, 3–5. Daniel Halévy, *La République des comités. Essai d'histoire contemporaine, 1895–1934* (Paris, 1934), 37–39, 107–108, 138; Paul Bosq, *Nos Chers Souverains, les opportunistes, les radicaux, la concentration, la droite, le dernier batteau* (Paris, 1898), 45.

12. Stanley Hoffmann, *In Search of France* (Cambridge, Mass., 1963), especially his essay "Paradoxes of the French Political Community."

cial and economic conditions following the Great Depression. Specifically, Elwitt examines the elaboration of reform policies intended to resolve the "social question" and the growing concern within the political elite about working-class activism. Elwitt insists on the irrelevance of most major political issues around the turn of the century. Significant decisions were not made during elections or in the legislature; rather, a broad bourgeois coalition of industrialists, academic social scientists, government administrators, and a few politicians formulated policy. Radicals and their fervent democratic aspirations play almost no role in either of these two major studies of the Third Republic. From Elwitt's perspective, republicanism functioned as an effective form of bourgeois class politics.[13]

Although the political polarization of the interwar years and the 1940 defeat still color much of the literature, a number of post-1945 works have focused more sympathetically on the institutions of the Radical party, established in 1901. More recently several new perspectives on the Third Republic have emerged which suggest new evaluations of the Radicals' role within that regime. Scholars now have available three indispensable general surveys of the period 1870–1914: Jean-Marie Mayeur's *Les Débuts de la Troisième République*, his *La Vie politique sous la Troisième République*, and Madeleine Rebérioux's *La République radicale?* The provocative question mark in Rebérioux's title implies a series of problems still to be answered about the Republic, the Radicals, and their relation to state power. More specialized studies of the Radicals have also appeared: Gérard Baal's massive *doctorat d'état* on the Radical party from 1901 to 1914, focusing on Emile Combes and identifying the sources of popular radicalism, and Serge

13. Sanford Elwitt, *The Making of the Third Republic: Class and Politics in France, 1868–1884* (Baton Rouge, 1975) and *The Third Republic Defended: Bourgeois Reform in France, 1880–1914* (Baton Rouge, 1986), quote on 18. A similar view of the Third Republic is expressed in Herman Lebovics, *The Alliance of Iron and Wheat in the Third French Republic, 1860–1914: Origins of the New Conservatism* (Baton Rouge, 1988). Judith F. Stone, *The Search for Social Peace: Reform Legislation in France, 1890–1914* (Albany, N.Y., 1985), offers an alternative view of social reform formulation and its supporters. Gary Cross also stresses the importance of the reformist coalition in *A Quest for Time: The Reduction of Work in Britain and France, 1840–1940* (Berkeley, 1990). Mary Lynn Stewart, from the perspective of gender-specific legislation, supports a more coercive view of reform legislation in *Women, Work, and the French State: Labour Protection and Social Patriarchy, 1879–1919* (Montreal, 1989).

Berstein's exhaustive studies of the party under Edouard Herriot's leadership during the interwar period. To some extent these works have overcome the opprobrium with which the Third Republic had been treated and have established the central role of the Radicals in this regime.[14]

The ongoing revisions of our understanding of the French Revolution have suggested new perspectives regarding those who claimed to be the heirs of 1789 and of nineteenth-century republicanism in general. François Furet, who has reinterpreted the history of the Revolution, has also been interested in tracing its historiography and the impact of that historiography and mythology on the origins of the Third Republic. Furet, together with several other perspicacious historians, has sought to restore the importance of the early Third Republic and to rehabilitate the contributions of moderate republicans, particularly those of Jules Ferry. He has argued that the Revolution left conflicting legacies. One, which the nineteenth-century historian Edgar Quinet propagated, required the repudiation of Jacobin terror and led to liberty and republican parliamentarianism. The second insisted that the revolutionary heritage was a "bloc" and that it led to the absolutist, intrusive, and bureaucratic state. Jules Ferry opted for the first reading of the Revolution and made that view an essential premise of the Third Republic. In the 1980s Furet urged his fellow citizens to recognize this particular democratic lineage, derived not from the dramatic episodes of 1789 and even less from the violence of 1793, but rather from the parliamentary compromises of the 1870s and 1880s, when a liberal, positivist, and pragmatic regime was established.[15]

14. See Albert Milhaud, *Histoire du radicalisme* (Paris, 1951); Daniel Bardonnet, *Evolution de la structure du Parti radical* (Paris, 1960); introducing a longer view is Jacques Kayser, *Les Grands Batailles du radicalisme dès origines aux portes du pouvoir, 1820–1901* (Paris, 1962). Jean-Marie Mayeur, *Les Débuts de la Troisième République, 1871–1898* (Paris, 1973) and *La Vie politique sous la Troisième République, 1870–1940* (Paris, 1984); Madeleine Rebérioux, *La République radicale? 1898–1914* (Paris, 1975); Gérard Baal, "Le Parti radical de 1901 à 1914" (Doctorat d'Etat, Université de Paris I, 1991); Serge Berstein, *Histoire du parti radical,* (2 vols.; Paris, 1980–82), Vol. I.

15. François Furet, ed., *Jules Ferry, fondateur de la République* (Paris, 1985), and François Furet, *La Gauche et la Révolution française au milieu du dix-neuvième siècle. Edgar Quinet et la question du jacobinisme, 1865–1870* (Paris, 1986). For an excellent critique of Furet's polarization, see Nord, "Party of Conciliation," 4–5.

Other recent commentators on the Third Republic have also subscribed to Furet's dichotomy of the revolutionary tradition and his preference for moderate republicanism. As early as 1968 Pierre Barral highlighted the indispensable role of Jules Ferry during the regime's creation and the shaping of its distinctive and successful republicanism. Claude Nicolet's 1982 study of the republican idea stressed the essential tension within republicanism between a conciliatory, opportunist sensibility and an intransigent, radical one. Nicolet located this divide as an internal fissure of the Radical party after its establishment in 1901. Although less hostile than Furet to the Radical tradition, Nicolet also argued that it was the empiricist, reformist tradition that enabled the Republic to function and survive. He too associated this moderate, opportunist republicanism with a reasonable, mature political tradition. The same year that Nicolet's work appeared, Odile Rudelle published her thesis on constitutional conflicts in the early Third Republic.[16] She too contrasted a mature parliamentary regime capable of practical compromises with an absolutist republicanism derived from revolutionary mythology and quixotically seeking to establish authentic popular rule. Rudelle astutely identified major functional and ideological dilemmas of the Third Republic: popular sovereignty embodied in "universal suffrage" was the indispensable mechanism that legitimated the regime, but it could not be easily translated into the governing methods of a parliamentary system based on interest groups and power negotiations. This tension exploded into a constitutional crisis in the late 1880s. Rudelle argues that republicans positively resolved this crisis in favor of pragmatic parliamentarianism.

For Daniel Halévy the Third Republic, "la Grande accusée," figured as a menacing invasion of the mediocre and banal masses.[17] In Stanley Hoffmann's analysis it was an obstacle to modernization. Contemporary French historians have charted the difficult but ultimately successful emergence of a mature republican state which in practice eschewed the utopian

16. Pierre Barral, ed., *Les Fondateurs de la Troisième République* (Paris, 1968); Claude Nicolet, *L'Idée républicaine en France, 1789–1924: Essai d'histoire critique* (Paris, 1982); Odile Rudelle, *La République absolue: Aux Origines de l'instabilité constitutionnelle de la France républicaine, 1870–1889* (Paris, 1982).

17. Maurice Agulhon's introduction in Jean Estèbe, *Les Ministres de la République, 1871–1914* (Paris, 1982).

aspirations of Jacobinism and established a liberal, empiricist parliamentary system. In this incarnation, the Third Republic becomes a reassuring model of reasonable, modern political behavior. The moderate republicans have been valiantly rescued from historical oblivion, but at the expense of their opponents, the Radicals. Despite the heuristic advantages of two competing models of republicanism, one that triumphs and the other that is eliminated, the Radicals cannot be so easily dismissed. They were essential participants in the construction of the Third Republic. Recent historians have demonstrated the importance of nineteenth-century republicanism and the establishment of the Third Republic. In too many cases, however, the Radical tradition and Radical politicians have been neglected. Their complex and protean political culture of left-wing radicalism, which Camille Pelletan personified, is the subject of this study.

What follows, however, is no biography. Rather, Camille Pelletan serves as an entry point into a particular political environment and sensibility.[18] Why this politician and not another? Primarily because his contemporaries saw him and he presented himself as the embodiment of radicalism. The Radical movement formed him, and he in turn shaped it.[19] His entire life was intimately associated with political developments, and for decades he served as a leader in the Chamber of Deputies. One of his obituaries noted that he "was involved in all the important events of the Third Republic."[20] Pelletan closely observed the Commune and the prolonged constitutional struggle of the 1870s; he was an actor in the Boulangist agitation, the Dreyfus Affair, and the creation of the Bloc des gauches. His particular position in these critical events often revealed perspectives different from those found in standard accounts. His career embraced journalism, electoral politics, parliamentary representation, the organization of the Radical party, and ministerial office.

I locate Camille Pelletan at the intersection of several distinct yet related contexts: familial, social, and cultural, as well as political and ideological. This point permits me to move beyond conventional political history and

18. There is one very laudatory biography, Tony Révillon, *Camille Pelletan, 1846–1915: Quarante-cinq années de lute pour la République* (Paris, 1930). Paul Baquiast is presently preparing a *doctorat d'état* on Eugène and Camille Pelletan.

19. *La Revue politique et parlementaire*, XXIII (1900), 632.

20. *Le Petit Provençal*, June 6, 1915.

draw on more recent methodological insights of the social sciences and humanities. My perspective rejects the older view that politics is an activity essentially dominated by rational calculation in a distinctly public arena. Politics can be more fruitfully studied as deeply embedded in a cultural context that shapes assumptions about political activity and aspirations about what politics ought to achieve. This perspective is especially valuable for France during the nineteenth century, when essential beliefs about authority and its legitimacy were challenged and were being reconstructed. Assumptions about and desires for authority and legitimacy were rooted in a matrix of symbols and rhetoric. Loyalties and traditions linked to family, region, religion, class, and occupation further strengthened these networks of assumptions and aspirations. More conscious processes such as education reinforced these complex webs of beliefs and values about political behavior. Gender, perhaps more than any other identity, affected political culture in nineteenth-century France. Politics on any level was assumed to be an exclusively masculine activity. Cultural beliefs about what was "natural," as well as the law itself, excluded women from official roles within the political system. To be female was to be defined as a nonpolitical being. Transgressions of this definition were deeply unsettling to most men, most politicians, and many women.[21]

I use the concept of political culture to focus on the efforts of a group of men in the second half of the nineteenth century who attempted to construct a distinctive vision and practice of democracy. Among the most interesting aspects of their efforts was the extent to which Radical politicians, and especially Camille Pelletan, vacillated between a search for legitimating traditions and a commitment to introduce emancipatory innovations. In addition, the impact of gender distinctions was especially powerful among Radicals. Few other political groups were more deeply marked by the masculine assumptions surrounding political activity. Yet their own political beliefs would not allow the Radicals to ignore the "woman question" and forced them to consider new relationships between women and politics. In the fluid world of mid-nineteenth-century radicalism, family operated as a powerful force connecting the private and personal world of the individual with the public, social, and political environments. Radi-

21. Hunt, *Politics, Culture, and Class,* 1–16.

cals well understood the significance of certain family ties. Two metaphors dominated their rhetoric and aspirations: one spoke of their commitments as loyal sons of revolutionary fathers and the other of their responsibilities to their peers as members of a republican brotherhood.

Culture provides a productive vantage point from which to analyze the development of radicalism; the Radicals themselves viewed their ostensibly political project as linked to a particular culture. They fervently believed in the cultural triumph of words, a triumph they believed was a unique French contribution to "civilization." The Radicals of Pelletan's circle strongly associated themselves with rhetoric and literature. They claimed to represent a realm in which words and reason, rather than blind obedience and violence, would resolve all social and political conflicts. They luxuriated in endless streams of words, both spoken and written. They never doubted that speeches and reading transformed individuals. Their own lives had been powerfully touched by the literary masters of the eighteenth and early nineteenth centuries. Nineteenth-century Paris provided a setting where writers, painters, journalists, and politicians mingled regularly, creating a rich interchange among those who identified themselves with innovation. The Radicals eagerly supported experiments in romanticism, realism, and impressionism. They declared themselves part of an emerging avant-garde modern culture. Their failure to retain this connection with modernity explains much about the limitations of the Radicals' political project.

Pelletan endlessly and obsessively reasserted his identity as a fervent "fils de la Révolution," who had inherited his republicanism from his well-known father, Eugène. The first chapter focuses on the Second Empire milieu of the senior Pelletan, who was a respected member of the opposition circles around Jules Michelet and Victor Hugo. Chapters I through IV are primarily organized as a chronological narrative, emphasizing the cultural contexts of emerging radicalism. This section culminates with the establishment of the Radical party in 1901. The remaining chapters shift to a more analytical and thematic approach. "Universal suffrage" is examined in the context of provincial, small-town electoral politics in Pelletan's southern district. The analysis of parliamentary representation charts the emergence of a new republican political elite in the Chamber of Deputies. It moves from the institutional power of deputies, located in parliamentary committees, to the deputies' social world. This Paris milieu inevitably pressured deputies to enhance the status and income of their successful, middle-class families. Later chapters explore the efforts to create a republican state during the Radical government of Emile Combes, 1902–1905, and the dilemmas this attempt created. Particular attention is given to Camille Pelletan's controversial role as minister of the navy. These chapters examine the bitterly debated questions of that era: Did Radicals have sufficient authority to govern? If they could govern, could they create a democratic state and society? I conclude with an analysis of the multiple attacks on Pelletan as minister and their relation to the larger failure of militant radicalism. I emphasize the divisions among Radicals which eventually altered their party. Considerable attention is given to the nationalist Right, whose cultural attack succeeded in transforming Radicals into a music hall joke. Throughout, I probe the same problem that constantly confronted the Radicals: is an authentic republican order viable; can democracy function not only as an ideology but as a governing system?

I THE FATHERS

The generation born in the 1810s, immediately after the Great Revolution and Napoleon's reign, reconstructed republicanism. These young bourgeois men, initially uncertain of their careers, arrived at maturity between the 1840s and 1860s; they were deeply affected by the romantic movement. They witnessed and participated in the Revolution of 1848; they struggled through the Second Empire. In the early 1830s some encountered republicanism, still a semiclandestine revolutionary sect with only a handful of followers. Among the literate urban public, the first Republic of 1792 was generally condemned as an anarchic, bloody Reign of Terror. More broadly the revolutionary Republic was largely forgotten or viewed as an episode preceding the glories and defeats of the Napoleonic Empire. By the mid-1860s these university-trained men of the bourgeoisie had refashioned the revolutionary and Jacobin legacies into the ideology and program of an embryonic legislative opposition. In turn, this ideology, program, and political practice would be passed on to the next generation, the leaders of the Third Republic. They would insist that this refashioned republicanism was the only appropriate ideology for the modern world and the only one that could legitimate the modern state.

The romantic generation stood between the momentous developments of the Revolution and the late nineteenth-century efforts of Third Republic politicians to construct a permanent regime. This transitional generation of the mid-century was acutely, often painfully, aware of coming after the "great events" of the late eighteenth and early nineteenth centuries. Nostalgia for a heroic past which they could never adequately emulate permeated their views of the Revolution. Their own possibilities were seen as more limited and prosaic. This sentiment was even more pronounced among the next generation, which often felt inadequate when compared to the heroes of 1789 and 1792 or to their own fathers of 1848 and 1852. Republicanism, the purported political system of the future, would always be suffused with nostalgia and a constant nagging doubt. The past provided models of inspiration, reminders of present limitations and failures, and lessons about the consequences of defeat. Eugène Pelletan, an emblematic member of this romantic generation, wrote of the importance of the revolutionary legacy for himself and his peers, "The Revolution . . . is our soul, our flesh, our nature."[1]

Nineteenth-century republicans worshiped their revolutionary ancestors, but they also believed that their generation could succeed where the revolutionary one had failed. By the 1850s republicans were convinced that their political program and practice must be distinguished from the heritage of revolutionary violence. In their reading of revolutionary history they identified violence and civil war as the causes of despotic rule. Some believed that Napoleon's empire was the consequence of the Terror.[2] The same Eugène Pelletan who lauded the Revolution also regretted that "the Terror . . . beheaded the Revolution's halo."[3] This republican generation, born in the 1810s, was dedicated to correcting and avoiding the Revolution's most serious error—the violence, repression, and civil strife of the Terror. They intended to hand on to their sons a political heritage that was the culmination of the great traditions of 1789 and 1792 but eschewed violence and would therefore be capable of forging a new permanent republican state and society.

Although republicanism was not an exclusively Parisian phenomenon, it was heavily influenced by developments in the capital. Between the 1830s and the 1860s Parisian political life was transformed several times, as was the city's demography, geography, culture, society, and economy. The Parisian population exploded in the first half of the nineteenth century. In 1831 it was a city of 780,000; by 1846 its population reached 1,050,000, having grown by almost one-third.[4] Although birth rates increased, most of this expansion was the result of migration to the capital. Louis Chevalier

1. Eugène Pelletan in *Les Droits de l'homme* (Paris, 1858), quoted in Edouard Petit, *Eugène Pelletan, 1813–1884. L'Homme et l'oeuvre d'après les documents inédits* (Paris, [1913]), 94.

2. This view in particular became identified with Edgar Quinet. For a discussion of the conflicting and competing interpretations of the Revolution see Furet, *La Gauche et la Révolution française*.

3. Petit, *Eugène Pelletan*, 91.

4. Pierre Sorlin, *La Société française*, vol. I, *1840–1914* (Paris, 1969), 104.

calculates that the peak immigration periods were between 1831 and 1836, when 112,047 newcomers entered the city, and between 1841 and 1846, when an additional 127,119 migrants came. Young working-class men dominated this influx, streaming to the metropolis with its promise of better paid employment. A smaller group of migrants to the capital were young bourgeois men seeking education, fortune, and fame.[5] These recent lycée graduates flocked to the university, especially to the law faculty, crowding into the student neighborhood of the Latin Quarter. They would be both the models of and the audience for the new romantic sensibility. When the students of the 1830s eventually graduated, in one fashion or another, many remained in Paris. Their highly competitive search for acclaim and lucrative careers shaped the legal and journalistic professions. Among these professionals could be found many future republican politicians. During the 1850s and 1860s the authoritarian regime of the Second Empire thoroughly redesigned central Paris. In these decades almost every resident confronted varying degrees of physical and cultural dislocation.

In addition to this constellation of demographic, social, cultural, and material change, contending political forces located in the capital dominated the nation. The dramatic Parisian events of the 1848 Revolution, the failure of the Second Republic, and the coup that established the Second Empire indelibly marked the republicanism that eventually emerged in the 1860s. This transformation of bourgeois urban life, especially that of Paris, and the feverish political activity of the mid-nineteenth-century capital were two important contexts that shaped the new republicanism.

In 1833 a young man of twenty from the Atlantic coast near Royan arrived in Paris. Eugène Pelletan had already completed two years of legal studies in Poitiers and intended to finish his degree in Paris, joining the capital's expanding community of "la jeunesse des écoles." Decades later his son Camille Pelletan would write that the move to Paris had transformed his father's life. The provincial Eugène found himself in a university and student milieu revitalized after centuries of intellectual somnolence and

5. Louis Chevalier, *Labouring Classes and Dangerous Classes in Paris During the First Half of the Nineteenth Century,* trans. Frank Jellinek (Princeton, 1973), 226–27. Accounts of such bourgeois migrations were standard in contemporary literature. Balzac, Stendhal, and Flaubert all had such figures in their fiction.

19

cultural marginality. Students, a few of their professors, and the permanent residents of the Paris Left Bank viewed themselves as crusaders, creating new forms and new subjects for poetry, the novel, history, and the visual arts. Camille Pelletan described his father's generation as "extraordinary." During the 1830s this cohort codified romanticism and elaborated the essentials of a bohemian life. These two closely connected cultural movements expressed the discontent of young bourgeois men with their own social class and its conventional notions of work, wealth, marriage, and social obligation. Their rebellion soon became a feature of masculine coming-of-age within bourgeois culture. It was expected that at least some university students would reject established norms and question accepted values. The financial constraints—usually temporary—experienced by Parisian students encouraged fantasies of revolt and utopia. The artist, especially the writer, assumed the role of social outcast and prophet. Language became an instrument to change the world. Looking back on this era, the younger Pelletan glorified "the bohemian life of the Left Bank . . . young people rich in dreams and hopes . . . poor in everything else . . . searching for an ideal with empty pockets."[6]

In this environment Eugène Pelletan soon abandoned law for journalism and literary criticism. He joined the young acolytes surrounding the leading romantic writers, Chateaubriand, Victor Hugo, George Sand, and Alphonse de Lamartine. Although their political sympathies differed widely, these artists all agreed that the writer had political responsibilities and could offer the nation political direction. More than many romantics, however, Eugène Pelletan held firmly to a belief in progress. While deeply touched by the romantic sensibility, he never repudiated the eighteenth-century rationalist tradition exemplified by Condorcet. His biographer would assert that progress was his religion. This faith was connected to Pelletan's devotion to the Revolution. He was "un fils de la Revolution." Eugène was convinced that the human and social progress initiated in 1789 would and must continue in the nineteenth century. During the 1840s he wrote a series of well-received articles which demonstrated the inevitabil-

6. Camille Pelletan, "Mémoires (inédites)," in Paul Baquiast, "Camille Pelletan (1846–1915). Esquisse de biographie" (Mémoire de maîtrise d'histoire, Université de Paris IV, 1986), 180–82, 194, quote on 184; Jerrold Seigel, *Bohemian Paris: Culture, Politics, and the Boundaries of Bourgeois Life, 1830–1930* (New York, 1986), 58.

ity of progress. In the early 1850s these were collected and published as *La Profession de foi au dix-neuvième siècle*. This melange of romanticism, a fervent belief in progress, and identification with the French Revolution drew Eugène Pelletan to one of the leading historians of the 1830s and 1840s, Jules Michelet.[7]

Eugène's son Camille recalled childhood visits to Michelet, whom he came to regard as "the greatest historian ever." This sentiment was not merely a personal, family recollection; it was shared by the larger circle of republicans. On the occasion of Michelet's death in February, 1874, one republican journalist noted that "Michelet's departure leaves a void in the nineteenth century. . . . [He was] the poet of history. He remade France. His *History of France* [was] a resurrection." Michelet's vision of France strongly affected Eugène Pelletan's republicanism, as well as that of his son. His multivolume *Histoire de France* demonstrated the emergence of the French nation and the French people. For Michelet national identity depended on the increasing unity of the "people," a process that was far from complete.[8]

Michelet insisted that the historical past was related to contemporary political issues. Together with his colleague at the Collège de France, Edgar Quinet, he mounted an energetic defense of the state-controlled university against clerical influence.[9] In general, Michelet regarded the church as a threat to the integrity and identity of France. His anticlericalism remained fundamental and intense. If religious education poorly prepared young men for the university, it became truly nefarious in its influence on women. His 1845 study *Du Prêtre, de la femme, de la famille* passionately denounced what he perceived as the priestly control of French women. "Our wives and our daughters are being brought up by our enemies. . . . The *enemies*

7. Camille Pelletan, "Mémoires (inédites)," in Baquiast, "Pelletan," 199; Petit, *Eugène Pelletan*, 24–29. His devotion to George Sand brought him a brief stint as tutor for her son, but he lost the position when Sand found Pelletan's declaration of love for her impossible.

8. Camille Pelletan, "Mémoires (inédites)," in Baquiast, "Pelletan," 249; Auguste Vacquerie, "Michelet obituary," *Le Rappel*, no. 1447, February 11, 1874. Between 1833 and 1844 Michelet had published six volumes of this massive work, bringing the development up to the Revolution. Eventually there would be seventeen volumes published between 1833 and 1867.

9. They wrote *Des Jésuites* (Paris, 1843), and Quinet lost his position at the Collège de France. During the Second Republic Quinet was elected to the Constituent and Legislative Assemblies and then in 1852 was exiled by Louis Napoleon.

of the modern spirit, of liberty and progress." Clerical influence pitted wives against husbands, completely disrupting the "natural" order and harmony of the "foyer familial." In contrast, the family should be an environment in which "a mother raises a child under paternal direction, until that moment when the greater mother, the nation, calls him for public education."[10] This work, which ran through three editions the year of its publication, brought together Michelet's central contemporary concerns: the nation and its defense against internal divisions whatever their source.

The church and its insidious divisive influences were not the only dangerous forces Michelet identified. He elaborated these contemporary concerns in one of his most popular texts, the 1846 *Le Peuple*. Its subject, like so much of Michelet's writing, was the nation, *la patrie*. This emotional address to contemporaries identified class, gender, and religion as the sources of dangerous alienation and division among the French. Michelet offered advice and hope for unity and strength to overcome such fundamental weaknesses. He promised that the study of history would promote a national resurrection. He stated clearly that the development and force of the nation was linked to the emergence and power of "le peuple." Michelet gave this term special force and prominence, but he left its definition open and frequently shifted its meanings. At one point he limited "the people" to the great mass of the French population who were workers and peasants. Later in the text "simple folk" constituted "the people." They might be "simple by nature or simple by education . . . children . . . peasants." At other times "le peuple" became synonymous with what others would call "les misérables," the "wretched of the earth." "All those who groan or suffer in silence, all who aspire and strive toward life, these are my people. . . . They are the People." Still more ambiguously and in language with strong Hegelian overtones, Michelet claimed that "the people" might be an ideal embodied in a great man. "The highest form of the People is rarely found among the people. . . . Its true essence, with its greatest force, is only in the man of genius; in him resides the great soul."[11]

The year after *Le Peuple* appeared, Michelet published the first volume of his study of the French Revolution. Together with the histories of Lamar-

10. Jules Michelet, *Du Prêtre, de la femme, de la famille* (Paris, 1845), 2, 286.
11. Jules Michelet, *Le Peuple* (1846; rpr. Paris, 1974), 154, 165, 195, 186.

tine and Louis Blanc, all published around 1847, this work restored the Republic of 1792 to a new stature. Michelet presented 1792 as the culmination of centuries of development, the heroic expression of "the people." The combination of the elusive concept of "the people" with this adulation of the Revolution ultimately brought Michelet to endorse democratic institutions.[12] By implication he supported republicanism, but he never explicitly declared himself a republican either in *Le Peuple* or in *L'Histoire de la Révolution*. *Le Peuple* never examined specific political institutions and ideologies. Its concerns remained more general: *la patrie* and *le peuple*, why they were weak and how to make them strong. Nonetheless, the republican movement would adopt Michelet's rich vision of "the people" with all its contradictions and its ambiguities. It became a pivotal concept in the republican lexicon.

For Michelet and his admirers "patrie" and "peuple" were the essential realities of nineteenth-century French experience. They suffered, however, from a debilitating lack of unity. Class, gender, and religion divided the nation. Such divisions were material and spiritual, affecting personal identity and happiness. National identity and individual identity were inextricably linked; family and nation depended upon each other. The modern world with its factory system and ever-increasing number of "misérables" threatened such organic connections.[13] In addition, the desire for upward social mobility created animosities, dislocations, and isolation, particularly among young bourgeois men aspiring to improve their status. Michelet never repudiated either the factory system or market competition, but he did believe that their negative consequences could be mitigated. Once values were correctly organized and the nation clearly became the individual's principal identity, then unity, productivity, and happiness would replace alienation, conflict, and insecurity.

Two institutions could serve this end. Most important was the ordered, patriarchal family in which mothers would prepare their children and par-

12. 1865 preface of Michelet, *Le Peuple*, 247.

13. *Ibid.*, 93, 96–101. The term *misérable* was already very much a part of the vocabulary in the 1840s when discussing the social question. Victor Hugo, then just sketching his major novel *Les Misérables*, used the term in the first draft written in the 1840s. Michelet's romantic critique of the factory system as causing workers' alienation was also very much in fashion. It parallels Marx's concerns at this time.

ticularly their sons for the larger world, all under their husbands' supervision. Second was a system of public education, which would further prepare boys for citizenship and patriotic devotion. Michelet's ultimate goal was to establish a profound, unbreakable union among the French. "The fatherland is actually that great friendship which contains all others. I love France, because it is France, and also because it is the country of those whom I love and have loved." Family and school would reinforce this devotion. Individual and nation would be mutually dependent, tied by powerful feelings much deeper than reason. In the closing pages of *Le Peuple* Michelet drew a series of emblems which would remain popular patriotic images into the next century. "The fatherland as legend: our two redemptions, the first by the holy Maid of Orléans, the second by the Revolution, the energy of '92, the miracle of our new flag and our young generals. . . . Even more noble the glory of our sovereign assemblies, the peaceful and truly humane genius of '89."[14] The conflation of nation and republic would become standard for the republicans of the next generation.

During the 1840s Eugène Pelletan and his peers eagerly embraced Michelet's critical analysis of the contemporary world and his vision of a new era of unity, purpose, and productivity. Michelet specifically addressed his work to the "young men" of the future. His vision, which connected the individual, the family, and the nation, must have been especially attractive to Eugène Pelletan, whose own family was full of conflict and sharply divided loyalties. Pelletan's parents, who had married during the Revolution, were from very different backgrounds. Eugène's biographer described the marriage as unhappy; elsewhere Eugène's father was characterized as "hard and nasty." He came from a Catholic family and was a landowner along the Atlantic coast, as well as the local notary and justice of the peace. His wife, Elizabeth-Jeanne, was the daughter of a Protestant pastor who in the last decades of the Ancien Régime had illegally preached his faith. Madam Pelletan was never close to her husband but adored her three sons. Eugène certainly remembered her as an excellent mother.[15] When each boy reached the age of twelve, his father sent him to a Catholic boarding school in Poitiers. Eugène despised his life there and was expelled after

14. Michelet, *Le Peuple*, 206–208, 199, 243.

15. *Ibid.*, 239; Petit, *Eugène Pelletan*, 5–7; Camille Pelletan, "Mémoires (inédites)," in Baquiast, "Pelletan," 189–90.

leading a student rebellion. By the time his secondary education was complete, Eugène had vehemently renounced Catholicism forever and espoused
deism. He was strongly attracted to his mother's Protestantism and would
write a laudatory biography of his grandfather, the clandestine pastor.[16]
The antipathy between father and son must have been especially strong,
for Eugène and a second brother were excluded from their father's will.
After their father's death in the 1840s, the disinherited brothers brought
suit against their father's designated heir, seeking what they viewed as their
legitimate inheritance.[17] Michelet's vision of national solidarity, nurturing
mothers, unified families, and patriotic faith must have had a special appeal
for Eugène Pelletan.

This appeal extended to a larger circle of students and recent graduates
attracted to Michelet's insistence that political issues were fundamentally
moral ones. The national resurrection he proposed depended on a moral
revival, particularly among the young professionals of the bourgeoisie. He
urged the university graduates of the 1840s to return to the standards of
virtue demanded by Jean-Jacques Rousseau and the Jacobins. For many
in Michelet's audience a future republic embodied a moral vision that
would eliminate corruption, sustain a serious civic life, and promote the
interests of productive citizens. This vision drew not only on Michelet's
writings and lectures but on a broader sentiment combining anticlericalism,
Protestant traditions, neo-Kantian philosophy, an ongoing reevaluation of
masculinity, and a search for more satisfying marriages.[18] Eugène Pelletan's
family history and his experience with the romanticism of Left Bank Paris in
the 1830s made him an ideal representative and promoter of this republican
morality. By 1844 he had already contributed to its didactic literature with
an anticlerical pamphlet, *Les Dogmes, le clergé et l'état*.[19]

16. Eugène Pelletan, *Le Pasteur au désert* (Paris, 1877); Petit, *Eugène Pelletan*, 12.

17. Camille Pelletan, "Mémoires (inédites)," in Baquiast, "Pelletan," 190.

18. Katherine Auspitz has characterized this emerging republican morality as one which
prized the work ethic, demanded self-control, and recognized the need to improve relations
between husbands and wives (*The Radical Bourgeoisie: The Ligue de l'Enseignement and the Origins
of the Third Republic, 1866–1885* [Cambridge, Mass., 1982], 31).

19. Eugène Pelletan's commitment to the traditions of both Rousseau and Michelet continued after the Third Republic was created. In 1878 he traveled to Geneva to speak at the
celebration of Rousseau's centenary (Police report, July 7, 1878, Eugène Pelletan, Ba 1216, APP).
The following decade he chaired the committee to erect an official statue at Michelet's tomb.

The mid-century upheavals of the 1848 Revolution and the Second Republic deeply marked this generation and profoundly affected the republicanism they would eventually reconstruct during the 1860s. The Paris revolution of February, 1848, linked republicanism firmly with the repudiation and demolition of the Orléanist dynasty and its limited constitutional monarchy. Throughout the 1840s there had been mounting criticism of the ability of the Orléanist parliament to govern and lead the nation. Republicans would long associate parliamentarianism and liberalism with the corrupt July Monarchy and the special moneyed interests that had dominated it. Immediately following the collapse of the monarchy, there was a euphoric outpouring of national solidarity and enthusiastic support for the new Republic. Appropriately, the romantic poet Alphonse de Lamartine and the republican opposition leader Alexandre Ledru-Rollin headed the popularly proclaimed provisional government. Lamartine had turned to history and politics in the 1840s. His 1847 study of the Girondins, like Michelet's work, revitalized interest in the Revolution and republicanism. By the late 1840s Lamartine had joined the republican opposition in the Chamber of Deputies, supporting Ledru-Rollin in the demand for an extension of suffrage. In 1847 Lamartine founded a newspaper to disseminate his political ideas. His collaborator in this short-lived effort was Eugène Pelletan, who had chosen journalism as his career.

Writing about the Second Republic soon after its fall, Eugène Pelletan passionately described what it had meant to its supporters. It was a "redemption. . . . To all peoples it declared: 'Peace'; to men it said 'Love.' . . . Let us proclaim it loudly . . . the Republic . . . is fraternity, unity and harmony." Eugène's son shared his father's enthusiasm for this brief regime. He would write, "Those nine or ten weeks in February and March were among the most productive for France, one could even say for Europe. . . . Universal suffrage [was introduced] which gradually became the principal political model for the entire world . . . the initiator of social reforms."[20]

In 1848 the thirty-five-year-old Eugène eagerly sought to be an active participant in this experiment. Refusing his friend Lamartine's offer of a position with the provisional government, he preferred instead to stand

20. Eugène Pelletan, *Histoire des Trois Journées de février de 1848*, quoted in Petit, *Eugène Pelletan*, 59; Camille Pelletan, *Victor Hugo. Homme politique* (Paris, 1907), 128.

for election in his native department of Charente-Inférieure. Both in the April, 1848, election for the Constituent Assembly and again in the May, 1849, election for the Legislative Assembly, Eugène Pelletan ran and lost. Eugène remained outside the legislative bodies of the new regime, expressing his enthusiastic support through journalism. The majority of the nine-hundred-member Constituent Assembly were moderate republicans who rejected both social revolution and monarchist reaction. Despite Pelletan's defeat, the April, 1848, election was essentially an endorsement of Lamartine's leadership.[21] This republican body of lawyers, doctors, and journalists was responsible for creating a new constitution and for addressing the deteriorating social and economic conditions of the capital and the nation.

In the spring of 1848 the Constituent Assembly became increasingly preoccupied with the need for social order. Between April and June, the representatives pressured the new Executive Committee to reduce the working-class presence in the capital. With mounting anxiety, the Constituent Assembly singled out the National Workshops as the source of revolutionary plots against the new Republic and demanded their dissolution. These workshops had been organized in March as a temporary and rather traditional response to the crisis of mass unemployment in the ever more crowded capital. Their original political purpose had been to contain revolutionary agitation, which they seemed to have accomplished. Three months later, the new Constituent Assembly viewed them very differently and insisted that the Executive Committee close them. On June 21 a decree was issued requiring all unemployed in the National Workshops to leave Paris immediately or, if they were under age twenty-five, to join the army. This act provoked the furor of the Paris working class. Both unemployed and employed took up arms against the republican government. After three days of fighting, the army and the National Guard broke through the barricades of the working-class neighborhoods and fiercely repressed the uprising. During these "June Days," fifteen thousand people were arrested and five thousand were sent to penal colonies in Algeria.[22] The Constituent Assembly placed Paris under a state of siege and replaced

21. Maurice Agulhon, *1848 ou l'apprentissage de la République, 1848–1852* (Paris, 1973), 55.

22. Even more than fifty years later, Camille Pelletan would describe the National Workshops as a "deplorable expedient" (*Victor Hugo*, 134), *ibid.*, 136; Agulhon, *1848*, 66–73.

the Executive Committee with the military man who led the repression, General Godefroy Cavaignac.

It was clear that the June Days marked the beginning of the end of the Second Republic. The December election for the president of the Republic demonstrated that rural voters repudiated the original architects of the Republic, rejecting Ledru-Rollin and even more thoroughly Lamartine. They also refused to endorse the military repression identified with General Cavaignac or a return to conservative royalism. Instead, they overwhelmingly supported Louis Napoleon Bonaparte, whose program was vague but whose name was renowned and who had little association with the Second Republic. The May, 1849, legislative elections created an assembly increasingly polarized between a strong representation of republican democratic-socialists and an equally strong party of "order."[23] By the spring of 1849 supporters of the Republic found themselves in the untenable position of defending the regime against both conservatives and revolutionaries. The egalitarian republican message terrified the Right. On the Left the Republic faced bitterly disenchanted former supporters, working-class revolutionaries who had taken up arms against the new regime in June, 1848.

The June Days and its immediate aftermath remained disturbing memories for republicans. In many respects this episode was even more difficult to assimilate into the republican vision of progress than the Commune of 1871. Moderate republicans often preferred to pass over the June Days in silence.[24] One description of Eugène Pelletan's political career commented that it had been overtaken by the "tumult of events and . . . the smoke of civil war." Republicans at the time and later explained that by the late spring of 1848 "the eloquence of Lamartine," which had calmed "the storms of the populace," was no longer adequate.[25] Left republicans usually agreed that something had to be done about the unemployed and that closing the National Workshops had been a crime, but even with hindsight they could offer no solutions. In contrast to this republican uneasiness about the past,

23. Agulhon, *1848*, 85, 91. Louis Napoleon received 5,400,000 votes, his closest competitor, Cavaignanc, had 1,400,000. The biggest loser was Lamartine with only 8,000 votes.

24. Petit's biography of Eugène does not mention June, 1848.

25. Camille Pelletan, "Mémoires (inédites)," in Baquiast, "Pelletan," 212, 210. Karl Marx was more dramatic. "The fireworks of Lamartine have turned into the war rockets of Cavaignac" (*Class Struggles in France, 1848–1850* [1850; rpr. New York, 1964], 57).

the bitter confrontation between the republican state and Parisian workers would serve as a powerful historical lesson for later socialists. Marx's dramatic study of the Second Republic, *Class Struggles in France, 1848–1850*, first published in 1850, fixed this particular scenario as a permanent and irrevocable feature of the "bourgeois" republic. Marx argued that during the June Days "the veil that shrouded the republic was torn to pieces."[26] He was convinced that republicans as bourgeois would inevitably stand on the opposite side of the barricade from the workers. The republicans, for their part, often repressed this disturbing scenario and repudiated the Marxist conclusions. For republicans, no matter how alarming the actions of "the people" might be in some circumstances, they remained critical to the creation of the republican state.

Among republicans Victor Hugo was one of the few to attempt to grapple with the June Days. His own experiences gave a special urgency to this effort. The Second Republic transformed his life and his art. The Revolution "turned upside down all [his] expectations and all [his] ideas." In the late 1840s Hugo had been the most renowned poet, dramatist, and novelist of France. The Académie Française had recently elected him a member and the king had designated him a peer of the July Monarchy. Orléanist aristocrats patronized this middle-aged, well-established literary figure. At first, Hugo opposed the 1848 Revolution. In March he ran for election on a platform of defeating "the danger from the Left"; Parisian voters rejected him.[27] In a June, 1848, by-election he again stood for the Constituent Assembly in a Paris district. This time he won on a moderate platform in which he stood "for the common people against the elite; for order against anarchy." That same year Hugo's two sons and his closest associates established a journal, *L'Evénement*, with the epigram, "Intense hatred of anarchy and deep love for the people." Although the poet had no official position on the paper, his influence was decisive. During the June Days he clearly endorsed the government's actions against the workers. Unlike most representatives, however, he visited the workers' barricades. Hugo

26. Camille Pelletan, *Victor Hugo*, 134–35; Marx, *Class Struggles*, 56.

27. Camille Pelletan, *Victor Hugo*, 117, 120. In 1845 Hugo was inducted into the Académie and named a Peer of France (André Maurois, *Olympio ou la vie de Victor Hugo* [Paris, 1954], 327–33). The voice of republicanism during the July Monarchy, *Le National*, was bitterly critical of Hugo and his romanticism (Camille Pelletan, *Victor Hugo*, 70).

strongly supported Louis Napoleon's bid for the presidency. By the spring of 1849, however, his position began to shift. He was ever more disillusioned with Bonaparte and particularly with the president's conciliatory moves toward the Catholic church. Hugo was elected to the Legislative Assembly in May and found himself drifting to the Left as he joined with republicans to oppose the increasing clerical influence in education.[28] Bonaparte's coup against the Republic in 1851 placed Hugo firmly in the opposition camp. During his self-imposed twenty-year exile he was able to speak forcefully for the republican opposition to imperial rule. These profound changes led Hugo to return to an unfinished manuscript, annotating the February, 1848, pages, "Here a French aristocrat was interrupted and now the man in exile continues."[29]

That manuscript eventually became Les Misérables and was not completed until 1862. Only after his flight from France did Hugo link the stories of working-class misery, legal inflexibility, and Christian redemption with political and social rebellion. After 1860 Hugo completed the work and devoted most of the fourth and fifth parts of the massive novel to a popular uprising set in the early 1830s. In this fiction he dramatically expressed the new attitudes of republicans following the events of 1848–1851. Armed insurrection, barricades, civil war, and class conflict were now vividly seen as the greatest threat to emancipatory politics and republicanism. Ideals of solidarity and pacification were replacing those of conflict and militancy. Yet at the same time, neither Hugo nor many republicans could bring themselves to repudiate entirely the older, heroic revolutionary tradition.

In a long digression set entirely outside the action of the novel, Hugo explored his own experiences and observations during the June Days of 1848. The dominant image was one of a grotesque confrontation of forces which "naturally" should be united. He called the uprising a "social disease. . . . the greatest street battle ever witnessed in history." He insisted that the insurrectionists were attacking the Republic and its most cherished princi-

28. Quoted in Maurois, Olympio, 346, 351; Camille Pelletan, Victor Hugo, 121. There were rumors that Hugo had hoped for a cabinet appointment as minister of education and was personally annoyed that this went to the clerical Frédéric Falloux.

29. Victor Hugo, Les Misérables (3 vols.; 1862; rpr. Paris, 1985), III, 540.

ples, "liberty, equality and fraternity, even . . . universal suffrage." He had no doubt about the necessity to defend the Republic, the justice of the repression, and the legitimacy of his own position. He carefully assembled the conventional words of disdain, disgust, and repulsion when describing those who rose against the Republic. They were the "rabble" bound and limited by their "anguish . . . despondency . . . [and] deprivation," wracked with "fever . . . pollution . . . ignorance . . . [and] darkness." Shockingly, these forces of the "mob" attempted to overthrow the legitimate power of "the people," the Republic, "the demos." In this first view Hugo associated himself, as he actually did in June, 1848, with the forces of order and repression. But in the novel a long "however" followed this description of the threatening "mob." Hugo then transformed the negative words of disdain into words of sympathy. While denouncing the madness of the "mob," he also recognized the "grandeur and magnificence" of those who have experienced abject misery. The ultimate symbol of this horror and grandeur was the barricade itself, which Hugo described as a breathtaking monster, a Cyclops, constructed by contemporary heroes comparable to Sisyphus and Job. The romantic poet stood in awe and admiration of this extraordinary heroic intrusion that halted everyday urban life. At the same time it was tragic because it was doomed. It was a "rebellion of the people against itself. . . . What was [the barricade] attacking in the name of the Revolution, if not the Revolution itself." [30]

In the end, the barricade and those defending it remained an "enigma" to the poet-observer. He returned to the side of order and attempted to justify himself. "The outrages of this crowd which has suffered and bleeds . . . are in effect popular coups d'état and must be suppressed. The man of integrity . . . precisely because he cares for this crowd fights it. But. . . . this is one of those unusual moments when, while doing one's duty, one feels uncomfortable and even wants to stop." [31] Such expressions of vacillation, evocations of duty and regret, difficulty in identifying who the "people" are and how they should be addressed all became recurring themes in republican discourse. But in the aftermath of the Second Republic, Hugo, from the

30. *Ibid.*, 223–27.
31. *Ibid.*, 224.

privileged position of artist in exile, was one of the few republicans to deal directly, if inconclusively, with the dilemmas raised by the workers' insurrection of June, 1848.[32]

Most republicans regarded the June Days as threatening memories, whose ambiguities and contradictions were best repressed or treated as fiction, but Louis Napoleon's coup against the Second Republic was a transforming event that paradoxically marked the origins of a new republican movement. Looking back to the mid-century, republicans pointed to the Bonapartist coup as a decisive moment when clear lines were drawn. Legality, justice, and democracy had stood firmly on the side of those deputies and other patriots who had rejected the illegal, immoral usurper. Republican deputies and Parisian journalists now joined a popular movement of peasants and workers opposed to the reprehensible, clerically dominated despot. The army and police brutally repressed their resistance. The republican opposition insisted that the coup and the regime it established were counter to nature, contradicting law, reason, and progress. In the immediate aftermath of the 1851 coup, republicans experienced both righteous outrage and paralyzing despair. "The crime had the insolence of a monstrous anachronism . . . something like the infamous atrocities of a Cesare Borgia . . . the destruction of legality by the very person who was supposed to guard it . . . arrests at dawn . . . representatives of the nation chased out at sword point . . . rage and . . . indignation . . . a desperate stupor . . . a choking disgust with this deadly shame."[33]

The events of the winter of 1851–1852 were more complex than remembered. The parliamentary opposition in Paris had consisted of Legitimists, Orléanists, and liberals, as well as staunch republicans. The objectives of

---

32. Flaubert also portrayed the June Days in *L'Education sentimentale*, published in 1869, only a few years after *Les Misérables*. Unlike Hugo, Flaubert remained an external observer of his characters' actions, though he too insisted on the ambiguity of the conflict. A secondary character, and the most sympathetic in the novel, fought against the workers and then reflected: "Perhaps he ought to have gone over to the other side and joined the smocks; for after all, they had been promised a great many things which had not been given to them. Their conquerors hated the Republic; and then they had been savagely treated! No doubt they were in the wrong, but not entirely; and the good fellow was tormented by the idea that he might have been fighting against a just cause" (Gustave Flaubert, *Sentimental Education*, trans. Robert Baldick [1869; rpr. New York, 1964], 333).

33. Camille Pelletan, "Mémoires (inédites)," in Baquiast, 213–14.

the Parisian politicians and the popular resisters, particularly those in the south, were far from identical.[34] In the immediate aftermath of the coup, republicanism as a viable political ideology and movement appeared to have been permanently eliminated. Two massively successful plebiscites in 1852 endorsed Bonaparte's actions; the Second Empire was declared in December, 1852, and, most important, favorable economic conditions returned. The seizure of political power seemed an unquestionable success, and the new authoritarian order was solidly established. These developments transformed the lives of Parisian and provincial republicans. They experienced deportation, exile, arrest, and harassment. In provincial Nantes the adolescent Georges Clemenceau witnessed the arrest and then release of his father. In Paris Eugène Pelletan was able to keep his name off the list of those republicans to be deported, but the events of 1851 profoundly altered him. In politics he had always been "mild and very moderate. . . . But the coup d'état marked him deeply with an implacable hatred, an unquenchable passion." Eugène's young family, which now included his wife and five children, suffered a significant material loss after 1852. Immediately before the coup, Eugène had been on the point of winning his suit against his father's will, which had disinherited him. After 1852 he lost the case; no court was willing to find in favor of an active republican.[35] Following the excitement, euphoria, and experimentation of the Second Republic, a chilling atmosphere descended on Paris intellectual life. Decades later Camille Pelletan described this new era. "Just like natural history, intellectual history . . . also has its ice ages. Prolific explosions of national genius are followed by long freezes. . . . New generations are born already old and withered. You might think that the life force itself was exhausted. . . . The era following the Second of December was such an intellectual ice age. . . . You would have imagined that the nation of '89 . . . had been annihilated, so thoroughly was the leaden silence of despotism accepted."[36]

Between 1848 and 1852 reemerging republicanism, the romantic generation, and their new morality were all severely tested and failed. The

34. Maurice Agulhon, *La République au village: Les Populations du Var de la Révolution à la Deuxième République* (Paris, 1979), 381–405.
35. Camille Pelletan, "Mémoires (inédites)," in Baquiast, "Pelletan," 215, 190.
36. Camille Pelletan, *Victor Hugo*, 276–77.

young men of Michelet's public did not create a viable regime or a resurgent nation. Fundamental republican beliefs had been shaken. During the 1850s and 1860s republicans struggled to identify the authentic "people" and to distinguish a genuine popular voice from that expressed in manipulated plebiscites. The central republican goal became the transformation of the authoritarian state into a republican one without civil war. There was also a growing recognition that this goal could be accomplished only when accompanied by an appropriate republican culture. The transmission of this culture in school and in the family would form republican citizens. This reexamination profoundly marked the young men who came of age during the Second Empire. It is hardly surprising that in the inhospitable atmosphere of Paris in the 1850s the initiative for this reevaluation came from those in exile. Nor is it surprising that Victor Hugo, protected by an international reputation and assured a large audience, would assume the leadership.

Hugo and his close associates constructed a new image for the writer. The "Grand Proscrit," the great exile, the poet-seer, laboring to redeem the nation and the Republic, replaced the worn image of the 1840s of the successful court poet. One biographer has suggested that this transformation occurred just in time to revive the writer's flagging inspiration and reputation. Camille Pelletan more generously wrote of Hugo's exile as the "environment [in which his] genius expanded. . . . A new life began for him, very disciplined, but of an incomparable intellectual grandeur."[37] Although Hugo was a recent convert to republicanism, most republicans accepted his claim to inspire the movement. His allegiance provided legitimation and stature to their opposition.

In December, 1851, Hugo crossed the border to Brussels. The following year, joined by family and associates, he moved to the British island of Jersey and then in 1855 to a villa on the neighboring Channel island of Guernsey, where the Hugo entourage remained until 1870. The house in Brussels was maintained, affording some members of the Hugo circle greater proximity to France. The exile was confining, and occasionally British officials harassed Hugo, but it was never uncomfortable and the poet never lacked

37. Maurois, *Olympio*, 385; Camille Pelletan, *Victor Hugo*, 242. Pelletan's biography was specifically intended to demonstrate Hugo's political influence, especially during the Second Empire.

financial resources.[38] Hugo's output, inspired by his furor against the Bonapartist regime and his new commitment to republicanism, was prodigious. Just arrived in Brussels, he published an account of the coup and the resistance, *Histoire d'un crime*. Simultaneously he composed an impassioned pamphlet, *Napoléon le petit*, which had an original printing of seventy thousand; many copies were smuggled into France. The pamphlet elaborated a theme Hugo had already introduced in one of his first opposition speeches in the Assembly in July, 1851. Louis Napoleon was a mediocre imitation of a previous era, a "usurper" in every sense. His ersatz regime was built on the basest motives. The regime and its self-proclaimed leader were ridiculed and lampooned. As a consequence of these publications, the Belgian government, under French pressure, insisted that Hugo leave Brussels in the summer of 1852.

The next year *Les Chatiments* appeared, a powerful collection of satiric poems continuing the attack on the regime. One historian has claimed that with this publication Hugo became the "patriarch and prophet of democracy."[39] Short, biting songs that could be easily memorized alternated with long contemplations of historical developments, which in turn were followed by bitter denunciations of specific politicians. The collection ended with the promise of a better future, the end of tyranny, and the establishment of "the universal Republic." Of course, the collection entered France illegally, thus offering publishers a lucrative incentive to reprint it, despite the dangers of censorship. In Camille Pelletan's recollection, Hugo's prose and poetry permeated the environment of Left Bank Paris in the late 1850s and 1860s. According to Pelletan, the major accomplishment of *Les Chatiments* was to create "a deep moat . . . between the young and the government." This educated elite would always, in the younger Pelletan's view,

---

38. Hugo's wife, Adèle, languishing under the restrictions of island exile, first traveled to Paris in 1858 and then made regular visits, spending more and more time in Paris and Brussels. She died in 1868. Camille Pelletan preferred a more dramatic version of Hugo's exile. "He arrived almost ruined . . . under constant surveillance . . . his plays forbidden . . . his new writings proscribed" (*ibid.*, 229). This image is belied by the fact that in 1862 Hugo received an unprecedented lump-sum payment of 250,000 francs for the delivery of his manuscript *Les Misérables* (James Smith Allen, *In the Public Eye: A History of Reading in Modern France, 1800–1940* [Princeton, 1991], 36).

39. Barral, ed., *Fondateurs de la Troisième République*, 11; Camille Pelletan likened them to the work of Juvenal in *Victor Hugo*, 246.

associate the Second Empire with "the idea of shame, crime and blood." From the very beginning of the Second Empire, then, Hugo provided the opposition with an unshakable conviction of moral and aesthetic superiority. As important, he constructed a language and satiric method by which to undermine the prestige of the imposing new empire.[40]

Hugo did not accomplish this political and cultural feat alone; his family and a dedicated circle of admirers, which increased along with his stature as the Grand Proscrit, supported his projects. Hugo insisted that a large family circle accompany him in exile. His oldest son, Charles, after serving a brief prison term, represented his father in Brussels and Paris and frequently traveled to the Channel islands.[41] The younger son, François-Victor, also served a brief prison term and was then cajoled and coerced to live with his parents on Guernsey. Hugo's wife, Adèle, assisted with the dissemination of his works on the Continent, although she was increasingly estranged from her husband and spent ever more time away from Guernsey. Juliette Drouet, Hugo's longtime mistress, provided total adulation, adoration, and secretarial services. She first visited Guernsey at Christmas, 1864, and after Adèle's death in 1868 was a more visible member of the Hugo circle. Hugo's youngest daughter, Adèle, seemed less willing to play her part and suffered most dramatically from this confined life. Finally she ran away only to decline into chronic madness. The able and devoted Auguste Vacquerie (1819–1895) and Paul Meurice (1820–1905), who had been associated with Hugo since the 1840s, vastly strengthened the somewhat problematic support of the immediate family. Near contemporaries of Hugo, they had been aspiring literary figures in the heyday of the romantic movement. Auguste Vacquerie's brother had married Léopoldine Hugo. The young couple had drowned in a boating accident in 1843, a family tragedy that had in-

40. Camille Pelletan, *Victor Hugo*, 258. François Furet, describing Edgar Quinet's feelings at the beginning of the Empire, notes that he "shared the sentiment which one finds throughout the literature of the period . . . in Marx and in Hugo. Quinet not only detested the Second Empire and its leader. He was ashamed of it . . . [it was] a dishonor" (*La Gauche et la Révolution française*, 29–30). In addition to these specifically political texts, Hugo wrote and published two major collections of lyric and epic poetry, *Contemplations* (1856) and *La Légende des siècles* (1859). Both were successful and further disseminated the Hugolian vocabulary and rhythms.

41. Charles married; he and his wife, Alice, had two children and resided primarily in Brussels until 1870.

spired Hugo for almost a decade. Ties of kinship and admiration linked Vacquerie, who was also a poet, playwright, and journalist, to the Hugo family. He voluntarily shared Hugo's exile and was especially devoted to Hugo's neglected and unhappy wife.[42] Paul Meurice served a most critical function. He remained in Paris during the Second Empire, editing Hugo's work and successfully managing his finances. A wide variety of fellow ex-iles—such as the young journalist Henri Rochefort—as well as curious visitors to Guernsey constantly expanded this inner circle.[43] Proponents of spiritualism, utopian socialism, republicanism, and women's rights all circulated in the Hugo orbit.

Among one of the most important of Paul Meurice's tasks was supervising the publication in Brussels of Hugo's long-awaited, much heralded epic novel Les Misérables. It appeared in 1862 after decades of creative labor. Hugo had first conceived the story of the convict and the bishop in the 1840s; he had composed much of the text between 1845 and 1848; and he had then returned to the manuscript in 1860, elaborating the larger historical context. In Brussels a huge banquet celebrated its publication. Its regulated sale in imperial France was a major political and literary event, one sign that the regime was becoming less authoritarian. Paul Meurice and Auguste Vacquerie, as well as Adèle and Charles Hugo, were on hand to promote and coordinate the reception of the novel. Stories were told of Parisian artisans and students forming associations to purchase copies to read aloud in their cercle d'amitié. Forty-eight thousand copies were sold within days of its appearance.[44] The novel's circulation contributed to the opposition's electoral victories in 1863, which marked a further relaxing of the repressive regime of the Second Empire. Camille Pelletan described Les Misérables as being met with an "explosion of admiration" that inspired the students of the 1860s to oppose the regime and support republicanism.[45]

42. Maurois, Olympio, 400.

43. Rochefort had visited Hugo at Guernsey. In the late 1860s his inflammatory journal La Lanterne provoked a series of serious criminal charges. Rochefort fled to Brussels in 1868 where the Hugo family welcomed him (Henri de Rochefort, Les Aventures de ma vie [5 vols.; Paris, 1896], I, 370–71, II, 17–19). See also Chapter III below.

44. Hugo, Les Misérables, III, 553–54.

45. Camille Pelletan, Victor Hugo, 283–86, 289; Camille Pelletan, "Mémoires (inédites)," in Baquiast, "Pelletan," 266.

The novel was a "modern epic," intended to prepare a new future. In its pages Hugo pronounced his magnificent, sonorous, and endless words on the social question, republicanism, revolution, gender relations, the family, and the future of France. Two central and interrelated themes dominate this massive fiction: the horror and pointlessness of class war and the urgent need to construct loving, healthy "intact" families. The novel's long climax portrays the death of young republicans and children of "the people" on the barricades. Although their motives and actions are heroic, such confrontations must be stopped at all costs. Frenchmen must cease to battle one another. The unnatural fratricide within the national family must be halted. Class war, an awesome experience in Hugo's literary universe, was only one manifestation of a much more profound despair within French society. Strife permeated even the most intimate relations, particularly those between men and women. The problem of dehumanization and isolation lay in the complex intersection of class, gender, politics, and individual identity. In some instances this experience was so devastating that the family became hopelessly corrupted and beyond salvation. Then the family itself bred degradation, viciousness, and death.[46] Yet the family might also be the source of overcoming this multiple despair. Such a family, centered around a *"femme simple, a woman of the people,"* would be the source of harmony, unity, and solidarity. The "natural," procreative, loving subordination of wives to husbands in the family was to be a model for all social relations and would also produce individuals capable of entering such relations. The authentic *femme simple* would instruct bourgeois men in the deeper values of life which lay outside the market and even outside politics.

Les Misérables offered the hope of a better republican future for all of France but only if such new, healthy, productive families could be established. The novel turns around the regenerative powers of the permanently childlike Cosette, the quintessential *femme simple*. She embodies metaphors of class and gender as the abandoned, illegitimate daughter of a woman who has been exploited as a seamstress, prostitute, and textile worker. At a dra-

---

46. Hugo, *Les Misérables*, III, 170. Throughout the novel the Thénardiers represented this counter family, which progressed from being in difficult circumstances, to a family of child abusers, criminals, and degenerates, to one in which parents sold and ultimately killed their own children. By the end of the novel the surviving Thénardier père has fled to the United States to become a slave dealer, thus finding an appropriate society to match his personal evil (*ibid.*, 524 and *passim*).

matic moment of gunfire on the barricades Hugo stops the action and shifts the scene to Cosette's awakening in a distant, calm neighborhood. Hugo emphasizes that "she knew nothing" of the armed conflict. Her perpetual ignorance is constantly underscored and portrayed as a great strength. Oblivious to the barricades, Cosette savors the quiet of the household and her dreams of love; she opens her shutter to the bright sunlight and contemplates a nest of swallows. "The mother is there, spreading her wings over her brood; the father comes and goes, bringing food and kisses in his beak. . . . Cosette thinks of Marius as she watches these birds, this family, this male and this female, this mother and her little ones."[47]

Hugo's long, didactic novel ends with the marriage of Cosette and Marius, two orphans reconciled to their own origins and embarked on the creation of a harmonious future. Cosette creates family peace and by extension a larger social and political reconciliation. Her ability to end conflict has little to do with rational persuasion and much to do with her instinctive "feminine" qualities to promote love and harmony. Again Hugo stresses her "ignorance." While understanding little, she alone recognizes and demonstrates that it is the banal acts of daily life, not political manifestos, that are truly significant. In the concluding epiphany of the novel she describes an idyllic family gathering set in a beautiful flowering garden where her husband and her guardian would eat the strawberries she had cultivated. "[And there] we'll all live in a republic where everyone will say 'tu.' " Cosette is the ideal wife instinctively able to enlighten her husband without abandoning her subordinate role.[48] In Les Misérables Hugo clearly identified the success of the future republic as dependent on the correspondence between the political and domestic realms. Class conflict, which posed one of the greatest dangers to a nascent republic, would be eliminated as class relations followed the new family model. Division would be transformed into a new harmony in which hierarchies would be accepted as reasonable and natural.

Paradoxically, the members of Hugo's circle were much more successful at creating "families" of peers than traditional conjugal families. They devoted most of their energies, affections, and loyalties to circles of like-minded

47. Ibid., 257, 260.
48. Ibid., 528, 468–70, 525–26.

men. Many were either bachelors or lived in highly unconventional marital arrangements, as did Hugo himself. Political and intellectual colleagues provided the sense of family much more than did wives. During the 1860s political journals were the focus of one such important circle of republican brothers, while at the same time functioning as the heart of the opposition. Hugo and his group had already experimented with journalism in the late 1840s. The enterprise had resulted in short prison terms for Hugo's sons and Paul Meurice during the last months of the Second Republic. The Hugos would be more successful with their second journal, created at the very end of the Empire. Like Hugo, republican journalists claimed the power of words over the imposing material force of the regime. They freely borrowed the style and vocabulary of the Grand Proscrit. They viewed themselves as part of the larger Left Bank literary and intellectual milieu hostile to Louis Napoleon in which the arts and politics were closely intertwined.

The most serious challenge that republican journalists faced in the 1860s came less from the imperial censor and judges, than from the transformation of newspapers themselves. Between 1850 and 1870 many journals began to shed their predominantly serious, explicitly political, and essentially bourgeois characteristics. *Le Figaro* first appeared in 1854 and became a daily in 1866. It appealed to a general audience and featured articles attractive to a sophisticated, Parisian taste. It was decidedly "nonpolitical," a clear advantage in the repressive atmosphere of the first decade of Louis Napoleon's regime. It rapidly established itself and became a permanent alternative to the traditional political press. Even more significant was the innovation of the "petite" press. *Le Petit Journal* in 1863 began this breakthrough by initiating a small format of only four pages and an even smaller price of five centimes or one sou. *Le Petit Journal* and its later competitor *Le Petit Parisien* relied largely on crime and scandal to attract a popular audience and often competed directly with the political, republican press. The circulation of these aggressively nonpolitical papers increased rapidly.[49] Contemptuous republican journalists described the "petite" press as petty in several ways. It never addressed "anything serious, it speaks only of the theater, the backstage and the back alleys; it traffics in scandal, sells the

49. Claude Bellanger, *et al.*, *Histoire générale de la presse française* (5 vols.; Paris, 1969–75), II, 298–300, 327–28.

reputations of married women . . . [and] holds a loaded gun to everyone's honor."[50] Significantly, and not surprisingly, republican journalists resisted these innovations in the newspaper industry. During the Second Empire the politically committed continued to staff the relatively small number of opposition papers. These journals remained much more traditional in format, retaining their serious tone and addressing a relatively small readership.

Among these republican journalists Eugène Pelletan established a widely respected reputation. Following Louis Napoleon's coup, he and his family continued to live in Paris in an internal quasi-exile. Under some hardship, Eugène Pelletan and his colleagues earned their livelihoods and expressed their convictions through the highly censored press of the Second Empire. Describing his father's experiences of the 1850s, his son Camille noted, "The life of a committed writer was atrocious, caught between the threats of the state and the concerns of the papers' financial backers." Eugène wrote for a wide variety of newspapers, not all of which were republican: Les Débats, La Presse, Le Siècle, L'Estafette, Le Courrier de Dimanche, and Le Courrier Républicain. His political views, however, prevented him from securing a permanent position.[51] In 1868 he and Emile Zola established the journal La Tribune; it folded within a few months. Family life for the Pelletans, now totaling seven, must have been precarious.

Conditions worsened when Eugène was imprisoned. Brief prison terms for infractions against the stringent but capriciously enforced press laws were a common experience for almost all republican journalists. Their cases were tried without a jury. Eugène was charged because he had written in the Courrier de Dimanche that Austrians enjoyed greater liberty than the French. He served three months in 1862 and was fined the not insignificant sum of 3,000 francs.[52] By the 1860s political prisoners were not badly treated as long as family and friends provided them with food and necessities. Parisians remained in the capital, housed in the Ste. Pélagie prison

50. Eugène Pelletan, La Nouvelle Babylone (Paris, 1862), 222.

51. Edouard Durranc, "Eugène Pelletan," La Justice, no. 4618, September 5, 1892; Camille Pelletan, "Mémoires (inédites)," in Baquiast, "Pelletan," 253–54; Camille Pelletan, Victor Hugo, 223.

52. Camille Pelletan, "Mémoires (inédites)," in Baquiast, "Pelletan," 267–68; Petit, Eugène Pelletan, 154–55.

located in the heart of the Latin Quarter.[53] Often these brief prison terms served to create or reinforce republican networks that developed into powerful political alliances during the Third Republic. Confined to the special political section of Ste. Pélagie, Eugène met and became lifelong friends with Auguste Scheurer-Kestner, a fellow Protestant who four decades later would lead the Dreyfusard struggle.[54] Similarly, during a six-month sentence in the same prison, a young journalist, Edouard Lockroy, met the republican activist Alfred Naquet through whom he was introduced to Paul Meurice and eventually to the rest of the Hugo circle.[55] During the Third Republic Naquet, a secularized Jew, would lead the parliamentary struggle for the legalization of divorce, and he would be prominent in the Boulangist movement. The most famous inmate of Ste. Pélagie was the veteran insurrectionist Auguste Blanqui. Young republicans such as Georges Clemenceau and Juliette Lamber Adam regularly visited him, demonstrating the continued fascination with revolutionary myths. Adam would soon be presiding over a social and political salon that was critical to the success of republicanism. Camille Pelletan described his father's imprisonment as a "joyous life. . . . a perpetual coming and going."[56]

By the end of the decade the liberalization of imperial rule was reflected in a less stringent application of press censorship and a marked increase in outspoken republican activity. A new crop of journals appeared. The young, inflammatory Henri Rochefort established *La Lanterne*. After its suspension, the Hugo family founded *Le Rappel*.

As the imperial regime went increasingly on the defensive, political opposition took on a more formal and institutional appearance. Following the Corps Législatif elections of 1857, a group of five republicans representing Paris and Lyons began transforming this previously powerless body into a forum of political debate. Soon after his release from prison, Eu-

---

53. Clemenceau, however, had very negative memories of his two and one-half months in prison in 1862, including that of a filthy bath which he refused to take (Gustave Geffroy, *Georges Clemenceau, sa vie, son oeuvre* [Paris, 1919], 23).

54. Camille Pelletan, "Mémoires (inédites)," in Baquiast, "Pelletan," 271.

55. Edouard Lockroy Papers, Don 24601, Bibliothèque Nationale, Paris.

56. Geffroy, *Clemenceau*, 53; Juliette Lamber Adam, *Mes Premières Armes littéraires et politiques* (Paris, 1894), 328–31; Camille Pelletan, "Mémoires (inédites)," in Baquiast, "Pelletan," 273.

gène Pelletan joined with fellow republicans to stand for legislative elections in 1863. Pelletan ran in the ninth electoral district of the Seine; his constituency was located largely in Parisian suburbs. The government contested his first victory, but Pelletan won the second ballot as well. The decision to participate in the imperial government, even as a critic, had not been easy. Pelletan, like all other candidates, had to swear his loyalty to the detested regime. His republican scruples were somewhat assuaged when Victor Hugo sent a congratulatory letter addressed to "my eloquent and dear *confrère*."[57]

In the next election of 1869, Eugène Pelletan joined an electoral list that included the most forceful opponents of the regime and future leaders of the Third Republic: Léon Gambetta, Emile Picard, Jules Ferry, Henri Rochefort, and Jules Simon.[58] His platform enumerated the classic republican demands: military reform; free, compulsory education; separation of church and state; and reduction of the state budget. He also addressed specific Parisian concerns: the suppression of the local city tax and the abolition of a military presence in the city. Pelletan reminded his electors that since 1863 he had been a voice in the Corps Législatif calling for greater liberty, the right to elect municipal councils, and the end to military adventures in Mexico and southeast Asia. The Parisian voters returned him to the legislature as part of the growing republican opposition. In this same election Pelletan also ran in a southern electoral district in the department of the Bouches-du-Rhône as part of a strategy to extend republican support beyond the large urban centers. His biographer considered this southern campaign more significant than the safer one conducted outside Paris. In the Midi, Pelletan addressed peasants and workers. Although he was defeated in 1869, Eugène Pelletan would be elected from this same region in 1871 to the National Assembly of the Third Republic. In 1881 his son Camille would successfully campaign in many of the same towns Eugène had first visited in 1869. Eugène Pelletan's electoral successes and participation as an important republican critic of the regime were logical outcomes of his journalistic activities. In addition to journalism and electoral politics, Pelletan also promoted the

---

57. Petit, *Eugène Pelletan*, 170–73.
58. *Le Rappel*, no. 16, May 19, 1869.

republican message through an extensive and well-attended series of public lectures.[59]

The republican press and supporters viewed their representatives as mounting a heroic struggle against a corrupt but powerful adversary. The politicians adopted postures inspired by Hugo's poetry and novels. According to one of their journals, the republicans in the Corps Législatif were "a handful of unarmed men—thinkers . . . writers . . . journalists, lawyers . . . workers—preaching the truth."[60] This unequal struggle pitted men whose only weapons were words against a usurper who had seized power by force. A less dramatic and less heroic image of the republican opposition was recorded in a police report of the 1870s. Describing Eugène Pelletan's career during the last decade of the Empire, it noted that everyone acknowledged him as a "good human being, charitable and sympathetic. . . . His extremely sentimental politics [earned him] the name of the enraged sheep."[61] By the late 1860s, Eugène Pelletan, now in his fifties, experienced both the sharp frustration and mounting hope of other republicans of his generation. On one hand, they viewed themselves as men of talent and ability blocked by a regime and its sycophants, whom they considered wasteful, corrupt, dangerous, and without merit. On the other hand, they were convinced that they and their political beliefs were gaining ever wider support from the "people" and would soon replace a decaying political order.

A visceral repulsion against the Bonapartist regime most vividly characterized these beliefs. A recent study of Edouard Manet's republican allegiances identified the essentials of opposition politics in the 1860s as "a disabused secularism, detestation of the Empire and a pro-Union posture in the American Civil War."[62] Louis Napoleon's willingness to permit the Catholic church massive influence in primary education, a continued and growing presence among secondary institutions, and even a voice within

59. Eugène Pelletan, Profession de foi in Ba 1216, APP; Petit, Eugène Pelletan, 203–204. The towns of Salon, Lançon, Grans, Saint-Chamas, and Istres would be the heart of Camille's Third Republic electoral district (Le Rappel, no. 14, May 17, 1869). For an example of his success see preface to Eugène Pelletan, La Femme au XIXᵉ siècle (Paris, 1869).

60. Le Rappel, no. 10, May 19, 1869.

61. Ba 1216, APP.

62. Philip G. Nord, "Manet and Radical Politics," Journal of Interdisciplinary History, XIX (Winter, 1989), 459.

the state university outraged republicans. Not only was this viewed as a major obstacle to the cultural and political emancipation of the "people," but it threatened the livelihoods of republican educators. Of equal significance, the low esteem given to secular education jeopardized the future training and careers of these republicans' sons. The strong pro-Union stance was part of a larger opposition to the activist imperial foreign policy, which ranged from the Crimea to the Italian peninsula to Mexico. Republicans denounced this policy as militarist, aggressive, a tragic waste of French lives and resources, and an international assault on legitimate aspirations of national liberation. Louis Napoleon's flirtation with the American Confederacy was viewed as another facet of this effort. The same year he stood for election, Eugène Pelletan composed a biting pamphlet, *Adresse au roi coton*. He denounced the abomination of slavery, praised the heroic action of John Brown, and even lauded the Orléanist princes who had joined the Union army. Pelletan reminded French readers of their revolutionary and republican heritage, which necessarily must align them with the "magnificent struggle" of their sister Republic.[63]

The alternative to this detested imperial regime was the promised peace and harmony of the future Republic. Its essence would be political equality made real through the process of universal male suffrage. The principle of "one man one vote" had to be distinguished, however, from Bonapartist plebiscites. In addition, the intense class conflicts and the flood of elections between 1848 and 1852 had challenged belief in the automatic virtues of universal male suffrage. Voters must be citizens who were genuinely independent, sufficiently educated to recognize their own interests. Regularly elected representatives, serving in institutions possessing real power, were the alternative to personal, authoritarian domination.[64] Republicans, however, had to demonstrate how they would create such a new order.

In the 1860s republicans stressed that their political principles must be grounded on broad moral and cultural values. The opulent display and adulation of titles during the Second Empire repelled them as much as

63. Eugène Pelletan, *Adresse au roi coton* (New York, 1863).

64. In 1858 Eugène Pelletan published his *Droits de l'homme* supporting this ideal of the independent rational individual. As important, in 1860 he published a historical novel *La Décadence de la monarchie française*, which, although set in the eighteenth century, was intended as a comment on all personal rule.

its repressive police network. A pivotal focus of this cultural conflict was the reconstruction of Paris under the direction of the imperial prefect of the Seine, Baron Georges Haussmann. Haussmannization, as the prefect's massive urban development projects have come to be called, has been widely analyzed, and historians' evaluations differ significantly.[65] Statistics attest to its enormous impact on the capital: 350,000 Parisians displaced; construction of boulevards to make up 20 percent of central Paris streets; 80 million francs for new sewer installations; vast extension of the city's boundaries, increasing its acreage 100 percent; a new outer ring of railroad stations; doubling the number of trees; modernization of the police force with new night patrols; the erection of public urinals on major boulevards; 2.5 billion francs spent on construction.[66]

Paris was transformed into an imposing imperial capital in which insurrections such as those of February and June, 1848, were thought to be impossible. Republicans were outraged. In *Les Misérables* Hugo prefaced the arrival of Jean Valjean and Cosette into Paris with a personal aside on the author's longing for this city, which he no longer knew. "Because of the demolitions and the reconstructions, the Paris of my youth, which I have enshrined in my memory, is now a Paris of another era." In response to the Bonapartist creation of a new imperial city, Hugo proceeded to construct or reconstruct the old Paris, "a precious illusion, in his fiction." This Paris, Hugo hoped, might have as powerful an effect on readers as Haussmann's projects. The old Paris recreated in the novel was "the holy ground made visible . . . the very form of France itself, one does not want to change anything about it, because one clings to the shape of the fatherland as to the face of one's mother."[67] Hugo's words transformed Haussmann's ostensible

65. See analyses and bibliographies in David H. Pinkney, *Napoleon III and the Rebuilding of Paris* (Princeton, 1958); Howard Saalman, *Haussmann: Paris Transformed* (New York, 1971); David Harvey, *Consciousness and the Urban Experience: Studies in the History and Theory of Capitalist Urbanization* (Baltimore, 1985); T. J. Clark, *The Painting of Modern Life: Paris in the Art of Manet and His Followers* (New York, 1984).

66. These are only the most striking changes (Clark, *Painting*, 37–38).

67. Hugo, *Les Misérables*, I, 455–56. This nostalgia for the loss of the old, authentic Paris is more complex than irate reactions to Haussmann's construction crews. Clark notes that such regrets were already expressed in the first half of the century, and Hugo himself had evoked similar sentiments in his 1831 novel *Notre Dame de Paris*. The republicans absorbed this romantic sense of permanent loss (Clark, *Painting*, 32–33).

modernization project into a desecration of the nation, a sacrilege, and an unnatural act of matricide.

In 1862, the same year *Les Misérables* appeared, Eugène Pelletan's *Nouvelle Babylone* directed a biting satire against Louis Napoleon's Paris. It met with considerable success. Pelletan combined republicanism, liberal Protestantism, romantic sentiment, anticlericalism, and an unshakable belief in progress.[68] He damned not only Haussmann's boulevards but implicitly the entire imperial society and state. Pelletan employed the literary device of a naive but intelligent provincial visiting the capital after a thirty-year absence. The character, like the author himself, spoke glowingly of the "good old days" of the 1830s, when he had studied in Paris and when the excitement of the romantic movement had stirred the Latin Quarter. The city of the 1860s appeared to have been ravaged. It was in total disarray, *boulversée*. Apartments, buildings, gardens, and neighborhoods had been ripped apart. The diagonals of the boulevards had uprooted a complex, organic world of long-established trades and attachments in well-defined communities. Without mentioning either the emperor or Haussmann, Pelletan depicted them as conquering generals coldly calculating their bombardments. The symmetry of Haussmann's much praised construction led Pelletan to compare him to a giant spider.[69] Pelletan rejected the claims that this urban transformation was creating economic opportunities, political stability, and cultural grandeur. The costs were too high and the actual gains transitory.

New values of luxury and idleness were replacing the traditional veneration and interdependence of home, family, and work. Spiritual discord, totally disrupting "la réligion de foyer," matched the material chaos. As the tour proceeded, this fictional voyage increasingly focused on the bourgeois family and women's roles. Wealthy, unproductive, and self-indulgent wives were parasites requiring the labor of poor women and devouring the wealth of their husbands. The children of such women could only grow up to be

68. Petit, *Eugène Pelletan*, 105. Artists' and intellectuals' despair about the transformation of Paris was widespread and not restricted to republicans. The elitist cultural critics Edmond and Jules de Goncourt entered the following in their journal November 18, 1860: "Our Paris, the Paris in which we were born . . . is disappearing. . . . The home is dying. Life is threatening to become public. . . . These new boulevards make one think of some Babylon of the future" (*Pages from the Goncourt Journal*, trans. and ed. Robert Baldick [New York, 1984], 53).

69. Eugène Pelletan, *Nouvelle Babylone*, 11, 330, 23, 38.

burdens on the state. They would never become productive citizens and patriots. Pelletan's itinerary moved from the rubble of demolition crews to the dissolution of morality and the family. He concluded his visit by calling on his readers "to save the family if we want to save the fatherland, because a nation is only the family enlarged. . . . [We must] regenerate man in the home."[70] This call for greater personal probity in the service of the nation, as well as his denunciation of luxury associated with women of the world, recalled Rousseau's message of simplicity, naturalness, and virtue. Like the eighteenth-century thinker, Pelletan had no doubt that a clear moral order in which women had a major role was essential for a future republic.

In the Rousseauean tradition equality and universal rights "naturally" belonged to men, who therefore were citizens. As Carol Blum has persuasively argued, Rousseau's most influential texts on education, *Emile* and *La Nouvelle Héloïse*, subordinated women to men and presented new educational models to reinforce that subordination. In Rousseauean political theory women were assigned the domestic sphere, responsible for rearing republican citizens, and were to defer to male authority.[71] During the Revolution and after, the republican promise of equality had both encouraged women's emancipation and excluded women from political participation. In 1793 the Jacobins had aggressively affirmed that citizens, the crucial republican category, were exclusively men.[72] The rhetoric of equality embraced equality before the law, equality of political participation for citizens, and equality of opportunities. While the Code Civil, implemented during the first Napoleonic Empire, guaranteed citizens legal equality, it relegated married women to the status of minors, barring them from participation in legal actions. Republicans could not imagine authentic individuals and citizenship without personal property, which guaranteed independence. They also accepted the legal restrictions making it impossible for married women

70. *Ibid.*, 23, 105–11, 299.

71. Carol Pateman, *The Disorder of Women: Democracy, Feminism, and Political Theory* (Stanford, 1989), 36, 19–21; Carol Blum, *Rousseau and the Republic of Virtue: The Language of Politics in the French Revolution* (Ithaca, N.Y., 1986), 122–23.

72. Joan Landes, *Women in the Public Sphere in the Age of the French Revolution* (Ithaca, N.Y., 1988); William H. Sewell, "Le Citoyen/la citoyenne: Activity, Passivity, and the Revolutionary Concept of Citizenship," in Colin Lucas, ed., *Political Culture of the French Revolution* (New York, 1988), 117–20.

to control property and, in effect, making it impossible for wives to function as fully independent individuals. The apparently universal republican principles of the public realm depended on the exclusion and subordination of women. Men were individuals and citizens, active in the state; women were mothers who produced and nurtured future citizens.

By the middle of the nineteenth century, republicans such as Pelletan, though still accepting the essential premises of the Rousseauean and Jacobin views, began to reexamine some of their consequences. Pelletan's critique of contemporary morality was never simply an endorsement for some lost domestic idyll. On the contrary, he asked, if women were entirely banished from the public sphere, could they ever adequately fulfill their domestic and civic function of republican motherhood? Could they possibly create republican families? Behind this renewed interest in the woman question at mid-century was an implicit uneasiness about the coexistence of seemingly contradictory principles—separate spheres and republican equality. If the family was to be the linchpin of a morality crucial to the success of a republic, it must be far removed from the avaricious, corrupt, and miserable marriages which Pelletan associated with imperial culture. Public and private decadence were one.[73] New cooperative marriages must reform and transform the family. Pelletan joined the issues of political transformation, anti-Bonapartism, domesticity, and the education of women.

Pelletan stressed the critical role of mothers in the creation of republicans and the republic. He called for a new set of relations between husband and wife, a new respect for mothers, and a new emphasis on the education of women. Mothers must be educators and transmitters of a particular moral vision. Two years after La Nouvelle Babylone he wrote La Charte au foyer, selecting a political metaphor for his title. Pelletan argued that equality between the separate spheres of the domestic world and the public realm would be possible once women's education was reformed. Women must have access to all forms of knowledge if they were to succeed in their "natural" duties as wives and mothers. He reiterated his earlier criticism: frivolous women were being ruined by boredom; they were entirely estranged from their husbands, and they were neglecting their sons, turning them into cal-

73. Eugène Pelletan, Nouvelle Babylone, 114–15.

culating egoists. The following year Pelletan's exploration of the condition of women went much further. His 1865 work *La Famille: La Mère* surveyed women's history from "the state of nature" to the present, including such topics as "Asian women, Athenian women, hetaera, medieval chivalry, and women during the Revolution." Not only were historical eras explored, but different stages of a woman's life history were analyzed: "the engaged young woman, the mother, and the separated woman." Again failed marriages, linked to the moral and political decadence of the Second Empire, were a major concern. Now Pelletan even endorsed divorce as a necessary evil to combat the greater evil of incompatible couples.[74] Despite his passionate public endorsement for republican mothers, however, he had little to say about his own wife. His son Camille also passed quickly over his mother. He did indicate that she "was an excellent soul full of tenderness and devotion to her husband and children."[75] Despite such perhaps formulaic praise, Camille mentioned his mother only once in his memoirs and never gave her name.

Throughout his survey of the female experience, Eugène Pelletan strained to reconcile his belief in progress with the historical realities of women's continuing subordination. The final chapter on "women as citizens" overflowed with contradictions. On one hand, Pelletan insisted that women shared with men the same essential quality of humanity, and therefore they must have access to all the rights and liberties inherent in humanness. On the other hand, he claimed that women could never truly have a profession; they could only master an "état," a trade. A few pages later, however, he admitted that once women worked for wages, they must be recognized as citizens. Implicit in this conclusion was the recognition that an exclusively domestic existence barred one from public life. But the public realm was also in need of reform. In fact, he stated that "the problem with politics is that it has been masculine. . . . There is a need for women's sentiments." Though apparently promoting marriages in which wives and husbands would be genuine companions, Pelletan also seemed to fear the consequences of such a reordering of the domestic order. He ended am-

74. Eugène Pelletan, *La Charte au foyer* (Paris, 1864), 20–22; Eugène Pelletan, *La Famille: La Mère* (Paris, 1865), 303. This work was intended to be the first part of three volumes on the family. The second and third were to deal with the father and child but were never completed.

75. Camille Pelletan, "Mémoires (inédites)," in Baquiast, "Pelletan," 206.

biguously by calling for the education of women so that "women may be what they ought to be."[76]

Despite, or perhaps because of, their contradictions, these works were extremely popular and led to well-attended public lectures which were then published.[77] In March, 1869, Pelletan, now representative for the Seine, spoke on woman in the nineteenth century to a Paris audience. He covered his usual themes: domesticity and the equality of separate spheres, the importance of mothers in raising good citizens (i.e., republicans), and the pressing need to reform women's education. On this occasion he included the Code Civil in his criticism, insisting that "women reason just like men" and therefore ought to be treated as full adults. Pelletan even speculated on the future possibility of extending not only civil rights but political rights to women. "She is part of society; I would not want to claim for her now *le droit de cité*, that is a question for the future, but I will say that she does not have the right to be uninterested in what happens in society."[78] Although Pelletan's audience certainly included women, his arguments were an effort to convince men of the urgent need to change educational institutions and women's civil status. He was especially eager to influence the new generation of university-trained young men. According to Pelletan, institutional reforms would transform women, making possible more compatible relations between husband and wife and a more tranquil, more moral, and happier family. Such families would support the reform efforts toward a new, parliamentary republican regime, which in turn would lend further support to harmonious domestic and social environments.

In 1862 Eugène Pelletan asserted: "Private virtue supports public virtue; the pride of the individual becomes the dignity of the citizen [and] the grandeur of the nation."[79] He did not invent this conviction, nor was he the sole or most important voice to insist that private and public lives were inextricably connected. This sentiment, together with the desire to reform these spheres, suffused the entire republican community in the 1860s. It motivated the growth of Masonic lodges, the movement of Libre Pensée, and the establishment of the Ligue de l'Enseignement. The theme of the

76. Eugène Pelletan, *La Famille*, 312, 315, 327, 335.
77. Petit, *Eugène Pelletan*, 129.
78. Eugène Pelletan, *La Femme au XIXe siècle*, 21, 31.
79. Eugène Pelletan, *Nouvelle Babylone*, 114–15.

relation between public and private reappeared almost obsessively in the literature of the period. As we have seen, Victor Hugo in Les Misérables made the regeneration of France dependent on the establishment of domestic love and order.[80] Like Eugène Pelletan, Hugo endorsed and even glorified the conventional assumption of separate spheres for men and women, but also like Pelletan, he viewed women's contribution to the larger community as essential and requiring greater freedom to be fulfilled properly. The Grand Proscrit viewed himself and others acclaimed him an advocate of women's emancipation. He and members of his circle actively endorsed and associated with those organizations demanding greater freedom for women. In an oft-quoted eulogy for a fellow exile, a woman utopian socialist, Hugo proclaimed the nineteenth century the era of women's rights.[81]

The certainty that republicanism required a close collaboration between the moral realm of the family and the public realm of politics also permeated the works of the influential historian Jules Michelet. After the destruction of the Second Republic and the imposition of Louis Napoleon's Empire, Michelet gave ever greater attention to the domestic sphere and particularly to the role of women. After being removed from his official positions at the Collège de France and the Archives Nationales, Michelet continued his multivolume history of France, but he also devoted more time to natural history, the study of religions, and the woman question. Michelet increasingly stressed issues of "secular morality," in which the conditions and the roles of women, their relations with men, and the reform of those relations figured prominently. His perception of women and his views on their appropriate conduct, however, were much less affirmative than either Pelletan's or Hugo's.[82]

Michelet had already argued forcefully that unnecessary divisions among the "people" led to unnatural enmity between classes and genders. The re-

80. Auspitz, Radical Bourgeoisie, 31, 61. If Hugo affirmed the possibility that personal and political relations could be redeemed, Flaubert despaired of any such future. Nonetheless, his masterpieces, Madame Bovary and L'Education sentimentale, relentlessly examined their interdependence.

81. The funeral took place in 1854 and the eulogy is quoted in Claire Goldberg Moses, French Feminism in the Nineteenth Century (Albany, N.Y., 1984), 149.

82. When Emile Zola reviewed Eugène Pelletan's study La Famille: La Mère he declared his preference for "Pelletan's more realistic version of woman as companion, than Michelet's deceptive portrait of woman as idol" (quoted in Petit, Eugène Pelletan, 128).

cent republican disasters and France's moral malaise reinforced this view.[83] Michelet, like Hugo and Pelletan, identified the absence of authentic republican mothers as a primary cause of current dilemmas. This persistent theme of women's roles, especially in what might be a reinvigorated republican France, was the central theme of two tracts, *L'Amour* (1858), and *La Femme* (1860), written specifically to refute the radical views of utopian socialists who had been critical of the family, marriage, and women's subordination in those institutions.[84] By the 1850s some republicans were coming to regard the revolutionary critique of the traditional home, like the call to armed insurrection, as a cause for the disastrous end of the Second Republic.

L'Amour and *La Femme* were widely read; in 1860 alone Hachette published three editions of *La Femme*. Both were marriage manuals addressed to the young men of France and especially to the circle of Left Bank students who followed Michelet's courses and frequented his soirées. They were intended for the next generation of republicans just reaching adulthood in the 1860s. Michelet argued that these bachelors had a patriotic and moral responsibility to establish families and republican households. There were two obstacles: the luxury, idleness, and clericalism that corrupted bourgeois women, and the abject misery that degraded working-class women. Michelet, who was supersensitive to conditions of alienation, opened *La Femme* with a description of these two alienated states. In the first, men and women were increasingly unable to communicate with one another; they had such fundamentally different life experiences that they appeared as two distinct peoples.[85] The second was that of the single, working-class woman, *l'ouvrière*, whose impoverished existence resulted in endless economic and sexual exploitation. These observations brought

83. Edgar Quinet, Michelet's colleague and collaborator of the 1840s and now an exile in Switzerland, also contemplated the failure of the Second Republic, but he identified the most serious problem as the inheritance of Jacobin authoritarianism. Michelet criticized Quinet's *Histoire de la Révolution*, published in 1865, less for its negative portrait of the Jacobins than for its failure to recognize the heroism of "the people" in arms during the First Republic (Furet, *La Gauche et la Révolution française*, 66–67, 104–109).

84. Jules Michelet, *La Femme* (Paris, 1860), preface.

85. *Ibid.*, 23. Eugène Pelletan bemoaned the same condition in *Nouvelle Babylone*, 111, and in *La Famille*, 265–81.

Michelet to the categorical conclusion that "woman cannot live without a man."[86]

Unquestionably, the issue of France's declining birth rate, which by mid-century was becoming a national preoccupation, as well as Michelet's personal obsession, provided a strong motive for this insistence that all women were destined to be wives and mothers. According to Michelet, physiology linked women more closely with nature than men, endowing them with unique nurturing abilities. He was convinced, for example, that all little girls naturally adored gardens and could instinctively raise masses of flowers. But *La Femme* was not simply a plea to increase the birth rate. It called specifically for a republican wife and mother, drawn from the "popular classes" or from those remaining bourgeois families that had not yet succumbed to moral corruption. Through proper training, such girls would become wives who could create a much needed haven for republican husbands and could supervise the indispensable moral training of their children. In Michelet's ideal, women were to sustain and nurture not only their own children but future generations and the future republic. Woman was destined to live "for others. . . . She is the cradle of the future, she is its school, still another cradle. In one word: She is the place of worship."[87]

This domestic and patriotic devotion was embodied in the nursing mother. Michelet's glorification of breast-feeding, similar to that found in Rousseau's earlier educational tracts, served as a practical call for improved infant care and as a powerful symbol of the fecund, harmonious family and state. Such mothers provided a forceful example of the expected, heroically silent sustenance which women must provide for the nation. Women must be trained from childhood to fulfill their nature, which was "to live for others" and to experience suffering.[88] This maternal image, with its undercurrent of eroticism and pain, so powerfully affected Michelet that he sometimes forgot his original intent, the promotion of republican households. He simply glorified the suffering, devoted, bare-breasted mother. In

86. Michelet, *La Femme*, 53, and title of chapter IV. Given Michelet's descriptions of women's exploitation, a more logical conclusion might have been that women could not live with men.

87. For Michelet's adoration of the child, see *ibid.*, 67, and for the cult of maternity see 96, 104, 121; see also 68, 120.

88. *Ibid.*, 118 and 268. One might ask why training is necessary to do what is natural.

La Femme he spent three delirious pages describing an Italian Renaissance painting that portrayed a young woman nursing a band of starving orphans. Rather than a paean to domesticity, Michelet here revealed the almost sensual rewards of public benevolence. Apparently, he failed to realize that this was a version of wet nursing which he, like Rousseau, condemned, and that it was something women could do successfully without men. For Michelet the painting captured "the intoxication of charity," which would be women's reward for their perpetual acts of sacrifice.[89]

Michelet's ultimate goal, however, was not public altruism but hierarchical domesticity. Near the end of the manual Michelet depicted his vision of perfect harmony: It is a cold snowy, winter Sunday; the family cozily gathers around the "flaming hearth where supper is warming." There is almost no sound, and "he, the man, takes advantage of this day to do what he likes. . . . [He reads.] He knows that she is behind him. She makes almost no noise, but does all that is necessary with a soft, undulating movement." She instructs the children with lessons drawn from nature; robins arriving on this winter day offer excellent examples of fraternity. In fact one did not have to listen to her exact words; simply her presence instructed. At the end of the day the children delight their father by singing the "Marseillaise" and a hymn to God. And over this patriotic apotheosis "she" blesses them all.[90]

Since the 1840s Michelet had viewed women not merely as symbols of the republic but as the means by which the republic would be made possible, a republic uniting the bourgeoisie and the "people." Both women and the working class had become estranged from the bourgeoisie, which in turn had grown egotistical, cold, and cynical. Bourgeois men rarely married until their late thirties and then sought loveless matches of convenience with wealthy, spoiled women. Michelet was convinced that the consequence was a physical degeneration of the population. Miserable marriages were wreaking havoc with the birth rate and with masculine vitality and political commitment. In the preface to *La Femme* he condemned modern novelists for their negative portraits of marriage, which he felt encouraged wives to

89. The painting, *The Intoxication of Charity* by Andreo del Sarto, was in the Louvre. See *ibid.*, 186–89.

90. *Ibid.*, 359–63.

have adulterous affairs.[91] The alternative to such despair should be neither infidelity nor the denunciation of marriage. Rather, the unhappy bourgeois bachelor must find a woman of the "people" who could be educated and transformed to suit her husband's needs. Michelet counseled, "The woman you ought to marry . . . should be simple and loving, without any final definition. . . . I like her best poor, alone, with few family ties. Her educational level is a very secondary issue." In fact, Michelet observed that "women of the people (who are not nearly as vulgar as the men . . .) listen to men [socially] above them. . . . [They express the] touching confidence of the people." Such marriages would constitute miniature republics in which alienation was overcome and roles appropriately assigned; in turn, these households would produce properly reared republican citizens and future republican mothers. Once this was accomplished, woman would provide a permanent celebration for man: "She would be [his] Sunday. . . . his joy, his freedom, his festival."[92]

By the late 1860s the essential elements of a revised republicanism were in place. The legacy of the Great Revolution and the Republic of 1792 was read to mean an independent, equal citizenry, steeped in a pervasive morality of civic and domestic virtue and enthusiastically participating in a state legitimated by universal male suffrage. To these essentials were added the experiences of the Second Republic and the Second Empire. Bourgeois republicans now clearly identified class divisions and, worst of all, class conflict as dangerous threats to the unity of the "people," which was an absolute necessity for the survival of a republican regime. The changing and expanding working class was seen as a vital element of that critical republican category, the "people," and, at the same time, as the source of

91. Ibid., preface. This might be a specific reference to Flaubert's Madame Bovary, which the imperial censor had brought to court on precisely these charges.

92. Ibid., 68–69, 209, 356–57. During the intense debate on the woman question in the 1860s, a few courageous and usually republican women challenged Michelet. Critics such as Jenny d'Héricourt condemned his deep misogyny and exposed Michelet's fierce attacks on women despite his apparent sympathy for women's plight. See Karen Offen, "A Nineteenth Century French Feminist Rediscovered: Jenny P. d'Héricourt, 1809–1875," Signs: Journal of Women in Culture and Society, XIII (Autumn, 1987), 144–58; Susan Groag Bell and Karen M. Offen, eds., Women, the Family and Freedom: The Debate in Documents (2 vols.; Stanford, 1983), I, 335, 342–49; see also Theodore Zeldin, France: Ambition and Love (Oxford, 1979), 293.

potential divisiveness and therefore danger. In addition, the major proponents of republicanism stressed its social, cultural, and moral dimensions. This political movement could be sustained and broadened only if the schools and the home promoted principles of equality and secularism.

Women were seen as the key to such republican moralizing. Here too, however, as with the working class, bourgeois republicans were ambivalent. Bourgeois women were viewed as easily corrupted and a source of luxury undermining manly republican virtues. Most seriously, many women throughout the social structure continued to be fiercely attached to a morality defined by the church. Finally, like all bourgeois men, republicans' attitudes toward women were colored by the growing concern over the declining French birth rate. Even in the late 1860s, when sympathy ran high for the embryonic women's movement, republicans offered women little more than a glorified position in the domestic sphere. These men were deeply, perhaps even obsessively, concerned about the condition of women, yet their most advanced program remained Eugène Pelletan's call for improved female education and reforms of the Code Civil. Female domesticity was the almost universally accepted ideal, although details might differ. For Michelet, as well as for Hugo and Eugène Pelletan, the "natural" hierarchy of the family served as their principal model for the "family" of the republican nation which they all sought to create.

The republican program for the working class was given much more prominence beginning in the 1860s, if only for the obvious reason that half of the working class had some access to the vote. By the end of the Second Empire republicans had a specific list of proposals intended to improve workers' conditions. During the 1869 campaign for the Corps Législatif, republicans from a Paris working-class constituency proposed a reform platform to their candidate, Léon Gambetta. That platform became known as the Belleville program and brought Gambetta electoral victory and national notoriety. The proposals summarized republican thought on the "social question" and combined political and cultural reforms with hopes for greater social and economic equality. It concluded by clearly identifying republican aspirations and priorities: "Economic reforms . . . while subordinate to the political transformation must constantly be examined from the perspective of justice and social equality. Only these principles can eliminate social antagonism and fully realize our motto, Liberty, Equality and Fraternity."[93] Victor Hugo in *Les Misérables* had already sketched a similar series of reforms. He called on republicans to "encourage the rich and protect the poor. . . . end misery by ending the unjust exploitation of the weak by the strong . . . improve workers' wages . . . introduce free and compulsory education . . . making knowledge the basis of your manliness . . . be both a strong people and a family of happy men, democratize property, not by abolishing it but by universalizing it, so that every citizen without exception might be a property owner . . . know how to generate wealth and how to distribute it. Then you will have both material and moral grandeur and you will deserve to be called France."[94] This genuine republican desire to improve workers' lives, thus creating greater equality and greater security for a republican regime, was fraught with contradictions. Hugo's diverse goals were much more difficult to implement in practice than in the romantic prose of the novel. The republicans' commitment to the equality of citizens would always be limited by their acceptance of social hierarchy.

Especially complicating the republicans' intentions to effect substantial social change was their equally strong commitment to avoid violent confrontations. The most important lesson they drew from the Second Republic and Bonaparte's coup was that violent class conflict had fundamentally weakened the new Republic, leaving it vulnerable to dictatorial takeover. In addition, during their long years of exile and harassment in the Second Empire, republicans had benefited from the contrast between their defense of constitutional order and legality and Louis Napoleon's usurpation and banditry. When they won elections to the imperial Corps Législatif, they were soon convinced of the value of electoral campaigns and opposition politics as means to propagate the republican message and to achieve real, if limited, political gains. The republican representatives and their supporters among artists, journalists, students, professionals, and workers imagined that these gains would continue to increase and that eventually they would be able to replace the decadent imperial structure. Although they had warned about the dangers of Bonapartist militarism, they were not prepared for the Franco-Prussian War or its consequences.

93. Quoted in Kayser, *Grandes Batailles*, 23–24.
94. Hugo, *Les Misérables*, II, 407–408.

By the late 1860s, not only had the central themes of a revised republicanism been delineated, but a generation of republican leaders had been formed. Romantics of the 1830s had become the parliamentary and journalistic voices of a confident, sober, nonrevolutionary republicanism. Eugène Pelletan certainly was representative of this opposition movement. He spoke for and to professionals, as well as small property-owning Parisians who were convinced that they would lead an inevitable political, moral, and national regeneration. The powerful visions of Michelet and Hugo inspired them to create a new national "family," joining the "people" and the educated bourgeois. Many of the men who had gathered around the republican banner at the end of the Empire had first arrived in Paris as ambitious parvenus, connected to "la jeunesse des écoles," and going on to make their careers as lawyers and journalists. By the 1860s political office complemented their other activities, often combining to promote upward mobility.[95] Even during the Second Empire distinctions existed within this fraternity of republicans. A left republicanism had already emerged, more committed to the moral and social dimension of a future republic, more concerned that the working class be included. But such distinctions were secondary; intractable opposition to the Second Empire united all republicans.

The validity of that opposition found no better confirmation than the Franco-Prussian War. On September 1, 1870, only six weeks after declaring war against Prussia, Louis Napoleon led himself and an army of one hundred thousand to abject defeat in northeastern France. The republican opposition had no choice but to act. They declared the Third Republic on September 4, 1870, and organized a doomed effort to continue the war against the invading Prussian armies. That same month the grueling siege of Paris began; in January, 1871, Paris surrendered and hostilities ceased. The republicanism of the 1860s indelibly marked both the new regime and those younger men who would govern the Republic from the 1880s to World War I. That next republican generation faced the task of coping with defeat and implementing the principles their fathers had elaborated in exile and in opposition.

95. Barral in his study *Fondateurs de la Troisième République* gives less attention to this group of republicans than to their more moderate, liberal republican colleagues led by Jules Ferry, whom he characterizes an "a team of notables with property, established wealth and social authority" (12–14).

II THE SONS

The republican opponents of the Second Empire had not anticipated that war—international and civil—would inaugurate the Third Republic. Nor had they anticipated that monarchists would control the Republic during most of its first decade, thus leaving their imprint on the new regime. The traditions of republican opposition, honed during the Empire, did not disappear with its collapse during the Franco-Prussian War. If anything, republicans were more threatened during the first decade of the Third Republic than they had been in the closing years of Bonaparte's reign. The new generation of republicans, young men in their twenties, whom Camille Pelletan so well represented, greeted the proclamation of the Republic on September 4, 1871, "with a joy which would turn the evening of that day of liberation into a festival of Liberty and the Nation." The very next day, however, they were confronted with "the most cruel disillusions."[1] Invasion, military defeat, and civil war formed the initial context of the Third Republic. Opponents and most supporters were convinced that this regime would be only a brief interlude leading to another, more authoritarian form of state. These predictions failed to materialize, the Republic persisted, and by the 1880s republicans were celebrating the definite establishment of the regime. Between 1871 and 1885 partisans of the Republic had to come to terms with its origins in a brutally suppressed civil war, the Paris Commune, and with its constitution, the creation of a monarchist assembly. In the process they formed resilient networks of journalists and parliamentarians.

Since its repression in May, 1871, the Paris Commune has been a mythic event for diverse political traditions. It remains difficult to disentangle its actual developments from its impact on political leg-

---

1. Camille Pelletan, *Victor Hugo*, 300.

end.[2] Parisian petit bourgeois and workers initiated the Commune as a violent protest against the proposed peace with the victorious Prussians and against the monarchist Assembly, which they perceived as a danger to the newly declared Republic. The Commune also expressed the frustration and desperation of Parisians who had been besieged for months. It ended as a bloody civil war pitting the military forces of the newly elected conservative National Assembly, then sitting in Versailles, against the Paris National Guard and irregular troops of the revolutionary municipal government, called the Commune. During the last week of May, "la semaine sanglante," the forces of Versailles killed twenty-five thousand Parisians, mostly artisans and workers, and took almost forty thousand prisoners.[3] For the majority of republicans who did not join the Commune, such as Camille Pelletan, its existence and destruction created several difficult issues.

Most republicans did not identify with the Commune because of lessons they had learned during the Second Republic and the Second Empire. Violence, civil war, and class war were all associated with the destruction of a republican government and the establishment of the authoritarian Bonapartist regime. Further, there was an even deeper horror of this particular civil war that divided citizens of the nation at the moment of military defeat when the foreign enemy was still occupying French territory. The republicans of Pelletan's circle, however, the men who would join with him in his journalistic efforts for the next twenty years, adamantly refused to repudiate the Communards. They were convinced that ultimate responsibility for the Commune lay with Adolphe Thiers's provisional government and the monarchist Assembly. From the beginning they sympathized deeply with the sentiments of affronted nationalism and ardent, popular republicanism which fueled the Commune.

---

2. For a range of interpretations on the Commune see Camille Pelletan, *Questions d'histoire. Le Comité central et la Commune* (Paris, 1879) and *La Semaine de mai* (Paris, 1880); Karl Marx, *The Civil War in France: The Paris Commune* (1871; rpr. New York, 1940); P. O. Lissagaray, *Histoire de la Commune de 1871* (1896; rpr. Paris, 1983); Georges Bourgin, *La Commune* (Paris, 1953); Stewart Edwards, *The Paris Commune, 1871* (London, 1971); Louis Greenberg, *Sisters of Liberty: Marseille, Lyon, Paris, and the Reaction to a Centralized State, 1868–1871* (Cambridge, Mass., 1971).

3. Edwards, *Paris Commune*, 346.

Some of these militant republicans, of whom Georges Clemenceau was one of the most prominent, actively sought to negotiate a truce between the revolutionary Paris government and the national provisional government. They literally stood between Versailles and the Communards. This party of conciliation, as they were called, shared the Communards' revolutionary heritage and their sentiment of outraged republican patriotism. In his examination of this party of conciliation, Philip Nord has made clear their sympathy for the Commune and their antipathy toward the National Assembly.[4] The republican elected officials who formed the Ligue d'Union républicain pour des droits de Paris, the retailers and manufacturers of the Union nationale de commerce et de l'industrie, and the Parisian Freemasons, while espousing many of the same attitudes as the Communards, ultimately rejected rebellion for fear of jeopardizing the new Republic and further weakening the just defeated nation.

Defense of the Republic and the nation motivated both the Communards and the republicans who sought to end the civil war. Examining the complex motives contained within the Commune brings into sharp relief the republicans' bitter sense of defeat and betrayal following the National Assembly's ratification of the armistice on March 1. Significantly, one of the journals identified as an important voice for the republican conciliators was the Hugos' *Le Rappel*. On May 22, the day following the Versailles army's assault on Paris, it published a poem by Victor Hugo denouncing the treaty. Whatever its literary merits, "After Having Read the Peace Treaty" clearly articulated hatred toward the Prussian enemy and desire for revenge.

> This is the pride of those who are in chains
> To have no other refuge from now on than hatred
> . . . Love the Germans? It will come; the day
> When by the right of victory one has the right to love
> . . . We will wait our turn . . .
> Let us have them at our feet, then we'll extend a hand.[5]

But though many of the younger Parisian republicans, led by patriarchs such as Hugo, shared the Communards' rejection of the peace and the

4. Nord, "Party of Conciliation."
5. *Le Rappel*, no. 708, May 22, 1871.

policies of the National Assembly, most also distanced themselves from the Commune. Again Hugo set the tone and rhetoric for this double critique of both the National Assembly and the Commune. One central theme of his enormously popular *Les Misérables* had been the denunciation of violence and fratricidal civil war. The famous barricade sequence of the novel was a long plea against such deadly confrontations. During the Commune itself, which Hugo observed from Brussels, he always decried the "insanities of both sides."[6] In a poem published in *Le Rappel* on May 7, Hugo condemned both the Versailles troops' bombardment of Paris, which endangered the Arc de Triomphe, and the Communards' demolition of the Vendôme column erected by Napoleon I. In this moment of divided loyalties he appealed to a higher patriotic commitment. Both monuments represented the victories of "this great People" which had been "the envy of the Teutons." He concluded in despair that the French were desecrating and destroying the memorials to their own dead. "We live in new and ominous times."[7]

Left-wing republicans did not merely express rhetorical criticism of the Communards. *Le Rappel* repudiated the Commune as anachronistic and sharply criticized its policies, which were becoming increasingly repressive as the political and military situation deteriorated. One editor of the journal, Victor Hugo's youngest son, François-Victor, noted that many "honest and committed patriots" had fallen into the serious error of seeking to repeat the past. Echoing Marx's denunciation of Louis Napoleon's coup d'état, the younger Hugo insisted that revolutionary imitations could only lead to tragedy and decadence.[8] François-Victor urged his readers to understand correctly the lessons of the Great Revolution, which should not simply be copied but should inspire genuine innovation. "Let us remember that our ancestors were innovators. . . . They were the offspring of their own inventions. . . . Let us follow their example by not imitating them." The younger Hugo urged a "new politics," one that would address "the great social and economic problem which our fathers did not resolve." More immediately, another editor soundly denounced the decision of the

6. Victor Hugo was in Brussels because of his eldest son's death and because it was a convenient time to leave Paris (Maurois, *Olympio*, 508–509).

7. *Le Rappel*, no. 693, May 7, 1871.

8. Karl Marx, *The Eighteenth of Brumaire of Louis Bonaparte* (1852; rpr. New York, 1963), 15–18. This fear of repeating the past appeared frequently in the later nineteenth century.

Commune's Committee of Public Safety to suppress ten journals and invoke martial law. In his view, this act showed the Commune to be no different than the conservative government of Versailles. "Look at the condition of freedom of the press in France in 1871 and under a regime that calls itself a Republic. France has two governments . . . but as far as the press is concerned they have the same policy. Versailles kills us and Paris beats us."[9]

Despite such criticisms, *Le Rappel* continued to publish and was one of the few non-Communard journals to appear in Paris through the week of brutal repression and desperate reprisals that ended the Commune. What was most evident in that last week was the helplessness of the would-be mediators. They offered little in the way of explanation or alternatives to the intense violence surrounding them. On May 22, *Le Rappel* published an article by Victor Hugo which seemed intent on piling up romantic clichés to avoid seeing the actual brutality in the streets. From Brussels Hugo even dared to conclude that eventually "fraternity" would emerge from this "sublime conflict." More appropriately, one of the editors in Paris admitted that there was nothing left but silence and a final plea for the beleaguered metropolis. "We are for Paris." In identifying with Paris, the editor Paul Meurice declared his sympathy with the Commune or at least with the victims of the Versailles army. Camille Pelletan, now a journalist at *Le Rappel*, strongly shared this view. His articles contained bitter attacks against the National Assembly at Versailles and against Adolphe Thiers, whom Camille portrayed as "a senile fossil of the old regime, a pitiful, stodgy little old man."[10] Thiers was the ultimate political survivor, an Orléanist who for that reason alone earned the disfavor of the republican Left. Following the total collapse of the Commune, Victor Hugo opened his Brussels house to refugees from Paris.[11] In November, after the publication of two articles criticizing the government's ferocious repres-

9. *Le Rappel*, no. 701, May 5, 1871; Auguste Vacquerie in *Le Rappel*, no. 706, May 20, 1871.

10. Victor Hugo in *Le Rappel*, no. 709, May 23, 1871; Paul Meurice, *ibid.*; Camille Pelletan in *Le Rappel*, no. 694, May 8, 1871.

11. Belgians, terrified by reports of the Commune, then attacked the house (Camille Pelletan, *Victor Hugo*, 320–21). Hugo at this time began an affair with one of the French refugees, an eighteen-year-old widow of a Communard (Maurois, *Olympio*, 510).

sion, a presidential decree suspended *Le Rappel*. It did not reappear until March, 1872.[12]

The circumstances of *Le Rappel* during and after the Commune were significant not merely as the record of certain republicans' attitudes in this critical period but because *Le Rappel*, together with other political journals, was instrumental in shaping the political ideology and culture of the new regime. In the period 1872–1914 politics and journalism remained as inextricably linked as they had been during the Second Empire. The influence of newspapers became even more powerful because they functioned as the major, if not the exclusive, means of mass communication in the parliamentary republic. They also functioned as important badges, identifying readers with particular political positions. Their number and circulation expanded significantly, the result of improved technologies of production and distribution, declining costs of individual copies, and rising rates of literacy.[13] Partisan political newspapers now had to compete with the very successful commercial press, "journaux de divertissement" such as *Le Figaro*, and the popularly priced "petite" press. Few political journals adopted new formats, and none could match the circulation of the large dailies, but they continued to articulate and shape the essential political debates of the period.

Le Rappel had its greatest influence during the 1870s. At the end of the decade its circulation stood close to forty thousand at a time when most republican journals welcomed a circulation of ten thousand.[14] Most of its readers were Parisian workers, artisans, small retailers, and students. It joined with other republican journals and politicians to develop a successful opposition to the conservative majority of the National Assembly. The imprimatur of Victor Hugo gave it unassailable anti-Bonapartist credentials. Although it had been critical of the Commune, it had even more strongly opposed the repressive actions of the Versailles Assembly. Finally, it was not closely tied to any one leading republican politician. Particularly after May, 1871, *Le Rappel* increased its following among Parisian workers and

12. Paul Meurice, *Le Rappel*'s editor, had already been arrested briefly by the Versailles troops (Ministère des Beaux Arts, Censor, *Le Rappel*, F18 407, AN).

13. Bellanger *et al.*, *Histoire générale de la presse française*, III, 138–40.

14. *Ibid.*, 225. Camille Pelletan in *Victor Hugo* gave circulation figures for the last year of the Empire, 1869, as one hundred thousand (297).

artisans because of its relatively low price of ten centimes and because the Communard journals had been repressed, many of their writers and editors imprisoned, exiled, or executed. Partly as a response to this readership, the paper led the campaign for Communard amnesty, serializing Camille Pelletan's sympathetic history of the Commune, and it also had one of the few regular columns reporting on the trade union movement, "Le Bulletin de Travail." *Le Rappel*, however, never intended to identify with a particular class. It explicitly appealed to that socially heterogeneous political category of Parisian republicans which associated students, young professionals, and small retailers, as well as artisans and workers. Ideologically the articles of *Le Rappel* called for the unity of the "people" as opposed to the interests of a particular class.

The journal had begun publication during the last year of the Second Empire, May 4, 1869, and was without question the Hugos' newspaper. It successfully imbued the emerging republicanism of the 1870s with the influential writer's political views and rhetorical style. Victor Hugo, still in exile in Guernsey, had no official position with the paper, but his influence was undeniable. One scholar of the press has called *Le Rappel* "the church of hugolian democracy."[15] It was, on a variety of levels, a family affair. This was not the first time that the extended Hugo clan had created a journal. *Le Rappel*'s establishment and original editorial board copied exactly the Hugo journal of 1848–1851, *L'Evénement*. Of course, it did not follow the earlier paper's political views, which could hardly be counted as republican. Victor Hugo inaugurated the new journal with an article addressed to the editors, "To My Sons." He concluded with a promise that as "a quiet old man" he would write no more for their journal; not surprisingly, Hugo failed to keep this promise. Through the 1870s he contributed articles and several political poems. Most important for building circulation, he permitted *Le Rappel* to serialize his latest works *L'Homme qui rit* in 1869 and *Mes Fils* in 1874. The Hugos' journal of 1869 was originally intended to speak for the republican opposition to the Empire and to promote republican candidates for the recently liberalized Corps Législatif. *Le Rappel* voiced humanitarian sentiments—often in excessive prose—opened its columns to all strains of republicanism, appealed to the working class, and was the most implacable

15. Bellanger *et al.*, *Histoire générale de la presse française*, III, 225.

opponent of Bonapartism. Its attacks on the imperial regime were composed with "a jubilant hatred."[16]

Hugo's enormous stature had deeply affected the members of his intimate circle who directed the daily functioning of the paper. In both 1848 and 1869 Hugo's sons, Charles and François-Victor, headed the editorial board. Neither seemed to have given decisive leadership to the paper. Both died prematurely: Charles in March, 1871, at the age of forty-five, at the very moment that the Commune began, and François-Victor two years later, also at forty-five. Both had served brief prison sentences for their political journalism during the Empire, but neither had established a distinctive career of his own. In a major biography of Victor Hugo his handsome eldest son is described as languid, lazy, and expensive to support.[17] François-Victor never married, was reputed to be a dandy, and, like his father, had a voracious sexual appetite. One might speculate that at least one motive in establishing these Hugo papers in 1848 and 1869 was to provide the "boys" with occupations. Although this younger Hugo generation seemed to offer an especially pathetic example, their circumstances reflected the more general dilemmas of many nineteenth-century young men of the bourgeoisie. These particular "fils de la Révolution" never managed to match their father's accomplishments, let alone the mythic deeds of revolutionary heroes.

If Charles and François-Victor were transitory figures on the editorial board, two other members of the Hugo household were much more permanent, Auguste Vacquerie and Paul Meurice. Almost until the end of the century these two men were the driving editorial force of *Le Rappel*. Correspondence between Vacquerie and Hugo in the late 1860s indicated that though Vacquerie was clearly in charge of the journal, he frequently requested Hugo's approval.[18] Vacquerie proved to be a demanding editor in chief, often difficult to deal with and abrasive.[19] Both he and

---

16. Camille Pelletan, *Victor Hugo*, 297.

17. Maurois, *Olympio*, 391. His friend Henri Rochefort described him as "the best-looking fellow one can imagine . . . a spoiled child . . . but good, friendly, and fun loving" (*Aventures de ma vie*, II, 17).

18. Victor Hugo, Manuscripts, March, 1868–August, 1869, NAF 24801, Bibliothèque Nationale, Paris.

19. Eugène Pelletan to Camille Pelletan, cited in Baquiast, "Pelletan," 387; also Camille Pelletan, *Victor Hugo*, 11.

Meurice, who venerated Hugo, followed the novelist's general political perspective.

At its founding the editorial board of Le Rappel also included Henri Rochefort, who at thirty-eight had recently established his reputation as the "enfant terrible" of the opposition press. Although the substance of the opposition and the nature of the regime would change over the decades, Rochefort would maintain a consistent stance as a vituperative, often slanderous critic of the "establishment." He was the ultimate nineteenth-century frondeur and a member of the Hugo inner circle. Rochefort would always articulate the most extreme views of republicanism, which, as we shall see, could threaten the Republic itself. Although he certainly exaggerated his intimacy with Victor Hugo, the poet unquestionably welcomed Rochefort as a fellow exile during the Empire and attempted to intercede for him after his arrest and imprisonment following the repression of the Commune. Rochefort was a guest in the Hugo home in Brussels and in Guernsey. That Hugo probably addressed him as "mon fils" corresponds to the Hugolian style. His friendship with Victor's sons seems consistent with other reports. During exile in Brussels they served as Rochefort's seconds in one of his many duels. His claim to be the godfather of Charles Hugo's son also seems plausible. In 1896, when Rochefort published his five-volume autobiography, his devotion to Hugo had not abated. He described "my admiration for the great poet who has written the most beautiful verses which rightfully glorify our language."[20]

In the late 1860s the brief publication of La Lanterne, which furiously attacked the Second Empire and Louis Napoleon Bonaparte, established Rochefort's reputation. The government seized the paper in 1868 for what it labeled as "offenses against the person of the Emperor, the incitement of hatred against the government." Rochefort would never be in good taste. These were all strong recommendations for including Rochefort in the new enterprise of Le Rappel. In Rochefort's version, he, the Hugos, Vacquerie, and Meurice formed the first editorial board of the journal named by Victor Hugo. This initial association was short-lived.[21] In 1869 and again

20. Rochefort, Aventures de ma vie, II, 16, 20, 45, IV, 352, II, 51.

21. Ibid., I, 370–71, II, 85. Maurois claims that Le Rappel was actually modeled after Rochefort's illegal version of La Lanterne (Olympio, 487). For a sample of Rochefort's contributions, see Le Rappel, no. 9, May 8, 1869.

during the Commune Rochefort launched his own paper. He was even more sympathetic to the Communards than were the journalists of *Le Rappel*, but he too cannot definitively be labeled a Communard. Such nuances did not interfere with the Versailles Assembly's desire to make an example of Rochefort. After the defeat of the Commune, Rochefort was condemned to deportation for life. Hugo's pleas throughout the early 1870s may have saved him from execution and certainly resulted in some improvement of his prison conditions. In 1872 *Le Rappel* serialized a novel Rochefort wrote while imprisoned, providing him with much needed cash.[22] Although no longer a major contributor to the journal, Rochefort continued to be part of the Hugo/*Le Rappel* circle through the 1870s and into the 1880s. *Le Rappel* editors often referred to Rochefort's case as a major example of the injustices of the Versailles Assembly. They applauded his escape from New Caledonia in 1874 and celebrated his legal return to Paris in 1880.[23]

Able younger journalists quickly filled the places left vacant by Charles, François-Victor, and Rochefort. Edouard Lockroy had been introduced to Paul Meurice through his prison companion, Alfred Naquet. He was invited to join *Le Rappel* at its foundation and by the early 1870s had become a member of the editorial board. Lockroy soon combined journalism with elected office. In 1871 he was among those republican representatives of Paris who had futilely struggled to conciliate the Assembly and the Communards. He resigned with other members of the far Left in protest over the peace terms. In 1873 he returned to the Chamber of Deputies as the republican representative from the Bouches-du-Rhône and in 1876 as deputy for the first district of Aix-en-Provence. In 1881 he was elected deputy from the popular eleventh Paris arrondissement. His position within the Hugo circle was also more firmly established when he married Charles Hugo's widow, Alice, in a civil ceremony in 1873 and began to present himself as the third son of the great poet. Kinship or legal ties might strengthen one's

22. Roger Lawrence Williams, *Henri Rochefort: Prince of the Gutter Press* (New York, 1966), 132.

23. The impressionist painter Edouard Manet, who had always been close to left-wing republicans, painted a canvas titled *L'Evasion de Rochefort*, at the time of his return in 1880-1881 (Musée d'Orsay, RF 4067). Even as late as 1895, when Rochefort had broken with many of his original comrades, *Le Rappel* gave his second return from exile extensive and sympathetic coverage (no. 9097, February 5, 1895).

attachment to the Hugo family, but they were by no means required. Eugène Pelletan's solid reputation as a journalist and republican, as well as his contacts with the Hugos, certainly recommended his twenty-four-year-old son, Camille, to the editors of *Le Rappel*.[24] He too joined the journal in the last months of the Empire. The young Pelletan had just completed his archival studies at the Ecole des Chartes, and his first assignment was to cover the opening of the Suez Canal and life in Egypt.[25] By the early 1870s Pelletan was also an editor. In fact, the government cited his articles and those of Lockroy as the cause of the journal's suspension in November, 1871.

In addition to the journalists associated with *Le Rappel* there were more obscure figures who served as general manager (*gérant*) and committed themselves financially to pay any government-imposed fines. One such individual was Albert Barbieux, who managed *Le Rappel* until 1872. The police report on him for that year indicated many doubts about his "political sentiments." A man of fifty, he had worked for the Compagnie du chemin de fer du Nord and now in Paris ran a not very successful business in foreign wines. He was involved in deals on the stock market and with publishing houses. He had been deported to Algeria in 1852 for his resistance to the Bonapartist coup, was eventually pardoned, and had close ties with Vacquerie, Meurice, Rochefort, and Charles Hugo. During the Second Empire his position as manager of *Le Rappel* had led to several prison sentences and fines. The report was a response to Barbieux's application to begin a new journal because publication of *Le Rappel* was suspended. He pleaded that his new journal would be "moderate." He finally received authorization in June, 1873, to publish *Le Ralliement*, which he sold three years later. After 1872 Barbieux moved on to other ventures. M. Pelleport, whose family had shared Victor Hugo's political views and the poet's exile in Jersey, then became managing editor. A lawyer of second or third rank and of limited re-

24.   Eugène Pelletan had been invited to both the wedding of Alice Hugo and Edouard Lockroy and the 1874 funeral of François-Victor Hugo the next year (Police report, Eugène Pelletan, Ba 1216, APP).

25.   Camille sympathized with the Egyptian peasants but viewed Europeanization as inevitable and ultimately as beneficial (*Le Rappel*, nos. 217–18, December 21–22, 1869). His father wrote to his son that the venerable Michelet had praised the young writer's articles (Eugène Pelletan letter, in Baquiast, "Pelletan," 385).

sources, Pelleport had spent his youth with Garibaldi in Italy.[26] These men with strong republican ties, some education, constrained fortunes, and an eagerness to experiment with different political and commercial ventures circulated on the outer fringes of the Hugo circle.

From the beginning, Le Rappel was the enterprise of the larger Hugo "family." New participants sometimes considered themselves members of this extended family even before joining the paper. The author of an obituary for François-Victor Hugo spoke of the large number of Hugo's "intellectual sons." Victor Hugo "has created a real intellectual family and those who are part of it will always regard the poet with a sort of filial piety. . . . Of all the men of genius Victor Hugo is perhaps the only one who has the gift to inspire along with . . . admiration, family intimacy."[27] To be Hugo's "son" was similar, on a somewhat more intimate and more intense level, to being "un fils de la Révolution." In the very first issue of Le Rappel Hugo addressed the editors as his "sons" and urged them to maintain their fraternal unanimity. He saluted them as "sons of the revolutionary changes of the nineteenth century." In his view, these "journalist-poets" incarnated the essence of the century that would be the triumph of "L'HOMME."[28]

During the 1870s and early 1880s the "family" that was created in the offices of Le Rappel was a republican brotherhood under the benevolent authority of the great literary patriarch. Writing in 1895, Camille Pelletan nostalgically recalled his first visit to the offices of Le Rappel. The year 1869 was an extraordinary time "charged with an electric atmosphere heavy with revolutionary storms. . . . [It was a time when] the constraints of rigid political categories were being broken. Life overflowed into the paper which, open to all points of view, gathered into the same phalanx Vacquerie, Meurice, Quinet, Louis Blanc, Rochefort, Pyat, and Lockroy, all under the brilliant guidance of the most powerful genius of this century."[29] Not only did narrow partisan categories break down in these dramatic moments, but so too did the boundaries between private and public. Public commitment and actions absorbed and energized these men's existence. In this context

---

26. Censor, Barbieux, F18 407, AN.
27. Francis Jenne, obituary of François-Victor Hugo, in Victor Hugo, Ba 884, APP.
28. Le Rappel, no. 1, May 2, 1869.
29. Le Rappel, no. 9119, February 27, 1895.

new, resilient ties of solidarity and fraternity were forged. Shared journalistic, literary, artistic, and political projects created new "families" with close bonds. These "families" offered emotional and financial support, as well as security, to the new generation. They provided public positions from which political careers could be launched. In addition, they eliminated or marginalized the diverting, disruptive, and demanding presence of women and children. In all likelihood, Pelletan was not even aware of the masculine exclusivity of this circle. Like most of his peers, his education had been shaped by the lycée and the men of his family. The university and bohemian circles which Camille frequented as a young man further reinforced the masculinism of this early formation. As he matured and became increasingly involved in politics, his milieu would be that of editorial rooms, Masonic lodges, and the Chamber of Deputies—all exclusively male environments. Such pervasive gender segregation reflected what men and most women accepted as the "natural" order of the public world.[30]

Of course, in the Hugo circle, the exclusion of women did not eliminate the "woman question" because the great patriarch championed the extension of legal rights to women. Although the woman question never dominated the columns of Le Rappel, the movement was commented on regularly. The earliest meetings of the Association pour le droit des femmes in 1869 were advertised in its back pages. One of the few lead articles to address women's issues appeared, significantly, in the midst of civil war. Auguste Vacquerie's front-page story for May 11, 1871, was titled "Women's Rights." In it he endorsed a proposal being debated in the English Parliament which called for women's suffrage. His article eloquently supported a concept of equality that would make no gender distinctions.[31] At the same time, however, the article was as much an effort to expose the contradictions of the left republicans' political opponents as a statement for women's

30. Robert Nye has provided a new perspective on the significance of the nineteenth-century gender system that rigidly segregated men and women. Nye examines the consequences of this system on bourgeois men, whose masculine identity became increasingly precarious as the century progressed. He offers especially useful insights into the construction of masculine identities among bourgeois republican men (Masculinity and Male Codes of Honor in Modern France [New York, 1993], 47–49, 128).

31. Le Rappel, no. 697, May 11, 1871.

rights. Later in the 1870s and 1880s, *Le Rappel* followed and endorsed the efforts of fellow left republican Alfred Naquet to legalize divorce. In this instance as well, the parliamentary debates were covered as much to gauge the growing far Left presence in the Chamber and the increasing success of anticlericalism as to report on women's rights. Nonetheless, Vacquerie's commitment to women's emancipation did not waver. In the early years of the Third Republic, Vacquerie joined Victor Hugo and Eugène Pelletan in promoting La Ligue française pour le droit des femmes. Hugo and Vacquerie served as honorary presidents. During the late 1880s and 1890s, when Vacquerie was editor in chief of *Le Rappel,* the articles on women's issues, though never numerous, were regular.[32] At his funeral in February, 1895, the militant socialist feminist Paule Mink would salute Vacquerie as "a resolute partisan of women's emancipation."[33]

Although the men of the *Rappel* circle recognized the campaign for women's rights, they always subordinated it to political issues they considered more important and pressing. Like Hugo, their sympathy for the women's movement did not interfere with their endorsement of domesticity and hierarchical gender relations. They never hesitated to accept as natural the exclusively masculine worlds of the university, the editorial room, and the political arena. Like all newspapers of the Left, *Le Rappel* always spoke of "universal suffrage" when it meant universal male suffrage. According to the accepted rhetoric of the day, "manliness" was an important, frequently noted positive attribute. In the newspaper's columns Radical politicians always spoke with a "masculine eloquence" (*éloquence virile*) and expressed "a manly faith" (*une foi virile*) in the Republic.

The Hugo "family" was centered at *Le Rappel,* but it extended well beyond the newspaper, hardly surprising considering the power of the Hugo influence. Between his final return to Paris in 1872 and his death in 1885, Hugo regularly held a large weekly salon and also entertained up to a dozen or more intimate friends at frequent dinners. In his biography of "le Maître," Pelletan described the large gatherings at the house on the Boulevard Elyau as ones where you met "the unknown . . . the most famous . . . men of all

32. See, for example, the endorsement of women's suffrage by Lucien Victor-Meunier, "La Cause des femmes," *Le Rappel,* no. 9104, February 12, 1895.

33. *Le Rappel,* no. 9115, February 23, 1895.

nationalities, celebrities . . . scientists . . . [and] ardent revolutionaries." Hugo "welcomed all, being sure to greet the most obscure novice. . . . [He was] animated, simple, loving a good laugh and free with his Gallic genius. . . . [But always he had] a certain grandeur."[34] Smaller dinners often brought together Hugo's republican political friends, Louis Blanc, Jules Simon, Léon Gambetta, and Georges Clemenceau. In May, 1877, the Hugo home became a meeting place for the republican opposition to monarchist attempts to undermine the Republic. During the 1870s Hugo was the undisputed patriarch of the Republic. In the opening issue of Le Rappel Victor Hugo characterized the younger generation that gravitated around him as "attending school in the morning and the theater in the evening."[35] These young bourgeois professionals with bohemian interests had been unhappy with the imperial regime, and they disdained the early governments of the Third Republic.

A group portrait by Henri Fantin-Latour, Coin de table (see p. 77), shown at the Paris Salon of 1872, reveals these young, aspiring men of the Hugo circle. Fantin-Latour was an accomplished portraitist who specialized in paintings of contemporary artists and still lifes. Here he depicts a gathering of young men after dinner. The individuals personify Hugo's characterization of combining the intellectual, the artistic, the professional, and the bohemian. Coin de table is superbly constructed, balancing contrasting lines and colors. The brilliant white of the tablecloth sets off the somber tones of the men's suits and the background. Five men are seated at the table, clearly divided into three on the left and two on the right. Three other men stand. The central standing figure, distinctively marked by his white shirt and his hand in the jacket, is the centerpiece of the painting around which the others are clustered. The figures are also divided between a core of five individuals—three standing flanked on either side by a seated man— who focus the viewer's attention on the central standing figure, and two somewhat isolated groups on the extreme left and the extreme right, who face outward away from the main party, almost with their backs toward one another. These various lines of cohesion and strain among the figures are balanced by the objects on the table, which Fantin called "pleasant

34. Camille Pelletan, Victor Hugo, 339.
35. Maurois, Olympio, 535–38; Le Rappel, no. 1, May 2, 1869.

things to paint. . . . fruits, flowers, etc."[36] Whether intended or not, the construction of the group portrait captured the tensions of solidarity and individualism of these young men seeking to make their mark.

The models for Fantin's *Coin de table* were habitués of overlapping groups whose larger ties connected them to the Hugo circle, militant republicanism, and the Parisian avant-garde.[37] The central figure of the canvas was thirty-three-year-old Emile Blémont, who in 1872 established a new literary journal, *La Renaissance littéraire et artistique*, intended to promote new poetry for the new era, although it survived for only two years. The two other standing men were Pierre Elzéar, twenty-three, and Jean Aicard, twenty-four, Blémont's collaborators on the new journal. Three other members of this artistic enterprise were seated from right to left: Camille Pelletan, twenty-six, Ernest d'Hervilly, thirty-three, and Léon Valade, thirty-one. The two figures on the far left form somewhat of a couple apart and would make major contributions to French poetry, Paul Verlaine, twenty-eight, and eighteen-year-old Arthur Rimbaud. Verlaine together with Valade was part of a group of poets who survived on their civil service positions with the Paris City Hall.[38] These poets of the City Hall had close ties with the creators of *La Renaissance*.

Writing soon after the last issue of his journal, Blémont explained the aim of its editors. "The day after our disasters, after the army's capitulation and the two sieges of Paris, a few young men, greatly troubled, but full of courage and hope, wanted to affirm the vitality of a new France, despite the skepticism of the rest of Europe." It is hardly surprising that Victor Hugo personally endorsed their efforts that blended art, national devotion, and

36.   One critic has suggested that the artist chose a neutral title to distance himself from his avant-garde and bohemian models (Luce Abélès, *Fantin-Latour: Coin de table. Verlaine, Rimbaud et les vilains bonshommes* [Paris, 1987], 5–6, 24–26, quote *ibid.*, 18). Fantin-Latour described an earlier conception of the painting which included a mythical female nude at the center.

37.   For a similar series of connecting networks linking republicans and the artistic avant-garde see Nord, "Manet and Radical Politics," 451–53.

38.   Camille's interest in poetry was academic and historic as well as artistic. His 1869 thesis for the Ecole des Chartes had been "De la forme et de la composition des chansons de geste." Already during the Second Empire the Paris municipal administration served as a refuge for a heterogeneous mix of writers with republican sympathies. Henri Rochefort had also been employed at the Hôtel de Ville.

commitment to the "new France." Despite his call for a new poetry, Blé-mont was an ardent admirer of Hugo's and soon became a close associate. The poets of La Renaissance, d'Hervilly, Valade, Blémont, and, of course, Pelletan all contributed in varying degrees to the Hugos' Le Rappel. In addition, these men were part of the larger bohemian culture. Most attended the monthly dinners of the Vilains Bonshommes, a social group that brought together artists, poets, musicians, journalists, and politicians. They met regularly from 1869 to 1873, with a hiatus during the Franco-Prussian War, at the Milles Colonnes restaurant located in the Palais Royal. It was here that the poets probably met Fantin-Latour. Blémont and Valade were principal organizers of these gatherings, Valade serving as the group's secretary. Valade apparently was uneasy with the success and recognition of the Bons-hommes. In late 1871 he organized a much less respectable circle to meet in a Left Bank hotel. This circle compiled a collection of poems, L'Album zutique, which parodied the Vilains Bonshommes, among other cultural institutions. Major participants in this more rowdy and irreverent circle were, in addition to Valade, Verlaine, Rimbaud, and Camille Pelletan.[39] Other participants would later perpetuate this style of the "blague," the joke, in the Montmartre cabarets of the 1880s.[40]

Fantin-Latour's group portrait of these men was not favorably received during the Salon of 1872. The jury hung it above another painting so that it was barely visible; there were some negative reviews, and most damaging of all, some critics ignored it. Like other contemporary painters, Fantin insisted on presenting modern figures engaged in daily activities depicted on the scale of historic canvases of the seventeenth and eighteenth centuries. One reviewer complained that the "epic and monumental proportions confer on the work an entirely inappropriate dignity. . . . These contemporaries painted by Fantin . . . deserve to decorate the walls of a living room."[41] Such negative assessments asked in effect why there should be any public, artistic representation of these young Parisian left republicans whom many regarded as "parvenus, lawyers without cases and journalists without futures, politicized during the Empire in the brasseries

39. Quoted in Abélès, Fantin-Latour, 23–24; see also ibid., 29, 26, 43, 22, 34–37.

40. See Seigel's discussion of such bohemian projects as the Hydropates and Le Chat Noir in Bohemian Paris, 37. See also Mariel Oberthür, Le Chat Noir, 1881–1897 (Paris, 1992).

41. Abélès, Fantin-Latour, 19, quote, 20.

Henri Fantin-Latour, *Coin de table*. Oil on canvas. 1872. Musée d'Orsay, Paris.
(Cliché des Musées Nationaux, Paris)

of the Latin Quarter."[42] Some critics, however, praised Fantin "for having the courage to portray life itself, contemporary life in its everyday settings." Jean Aicard, one of the models for the painting, wrote most perceptively in *La Renaissance littéraire et artistique*, "M. Fantin . . . has prepared . . . the most accurate and most valuable documents on the demeanor, the exterior, the habits of the men of our age. He is not put off by the rigid dress which we wear today. . . . We all know that the moral and intellectual tenor of an age suggests a particular look, a way of trimming one's beard and of wearing a suit; the spirit of an age is revealed in the smallest details. . . . Nineteenth-century physiognomies have been painted by M. Fantin in his *Coin de table*."[43] One of the great struggles for modern artists of this period was to discover the appropriate methods to represent their contemporary world.[44] Certainly in the 1870s young militant republicans, who frequented the same circles as avant-garde artists and writers, shared a sense that their mission was to construct a politics appropriate to the modern age and modern men. Ultimately the artists would be much more successful than republican politicians in liberating themselves from past traditions.

Le Rappel stood in the forefront of this effort to create a modern politics. The editors called for the elaboration of language, symbols, and settings appropriate to an authentic republic in the late nineteenth century. Victor Hugo had already anticipated these issues when in the first number of *Le Rappel* he had written, "We [have been] born of revolutionary changes, the sons of catastrophes which are really triumphs; to the rigid ceremony of tragedy, we prefer the pell-mell of the drama."[45] This manifesto of modernity was difficult to implement because those politicians whom *Le Rappel* editors considered antiquated tragedians still retained political power in the 1870s. Even more disturbing, the creators of the new republican drama had great difficulty agreeing on script, actors, or scenery. *Le Rappel* editors had criticized the Communards for their disastrous efforts to duplicate the revolutionary gestures and speech of 1793, but *Le Rappel* also looked to the Revolution to legitimate its republicanism. Throughout its existence, the

42. Mayeur, *Vie politique*, 18.

43. Abélès, *Fantin-Latour*, 21, 22.

44. T. J. Clark discusses this issue in regard to impressionism in *Painting of Modern Life*, 78, 172, 203.

45. *Le Rappel*, no. 1, May 2, 1869.

paper printed two dates on its masthead: one following the Gregorian calendar in which issue number 1614 appeared on August 11, 1874, and a second one following the revolutionary calendar in which the same issue, number 1614, was dated 25 Thermidor Year 82. This dependence on the past was repeated regularly in articles commemorating the great men and events of the revolutionary period, which was constantly culled for models and lessons.

This dual effort to forge a modern politics and simultaneously defend the revolutionary tradition reinforced *Le Rappel*'s leading position during the 1870s. Its excellent journalists further enhanced its success. In addition, the small numbers of competitors, a result of the draconian press censorship of this decade, strengthened its preeminence. In the first years of the Republic *Le Rappel* had strongly supported the Government of National Defense, endured the Prussian siege, denounced the conservative results of elections to the National Assembly, and called for the continuation of the war. The Hugo paper consistently and strongly opposed the Versailles Assembly and was sympathetic to the Communards, although critical of some of the revolutionaries' policies. It participated in the forefront of the two tasks on which all varieties of republicans agreed: the preservation of a republican regime, which the monarchist majority of the National Assembly threatened, and the wresting of parliamentary power from that conservative majority, which sat from 1871 to 1876.

In the parliamentary arena these tasks entailed a simultaneous defense of the regime and criticism of conservative governments requiring complex, sometimes apparently compromising and contradictory arguments. Outside the Assembly, the opposition press could present a clearer, more comprehensible and consistent republican message. And no journal was better placed to do this than *Le Rappel*. The paper's main focus and its readers' concerns were politics, especially the machinations of the National Assembly. Although all the editors contributed to this theme, young bohemian Camille Pelletan was awarded the task of composing the daily column covering the Assembly from May, 1873, to February, 1875. The column, "La Physionomie de la séance," established Pelletan's journalistic reputation. In 1875 the articles were collected in one volume, *Le Théâtre de Versailles*.[46]

46. Forty years later, in one of Pelletan's obituaries, a journalist would claim that he had created "a unique genre of scathing and witty accounts of parliamentary debates" (*Le Radical*, June 6, 1915).

The title suggested that the entire Assembly was out of touch with the contemporary world. In his reports Pelletan stressed four themes: artifice, the dead weight of the past, individual portraits, and an explanation of why such relics continued to wield political power.

Pelletan reinvigorated a well-established republican rhetorical device: the contrast between the natural, authentic, "manly" republican spirit and the artificial, feminized, corrupt anachronism of royalism. Throughout the daily, somewhat tedious reporting of Assembly politics, Pelletan constantly called attention to the location of the Assembly in the theater of the Palace of Versailles. As late as 1876, he reminded readers that this Assembly had from its beginning been associated with the stage, first the theater of Bordeaux and then, even more significantly, the theater of the Bourbon palace. To locate the new regime's first legislative body in this monument to royal absolutism, "that elegant, reckless, décolleté, sparkling, and witty monarchy of the eighteenth century,"[47] was an affront to the Republic and to Paris. Then to seat the deputies in the palace's theater underscored, at least to republicans, the vulnerability of the regime surrounded by the decor of aristocratic dissimulation. In such a setting, deputies could hardly be expected to conduct anything other than farces.[48]

Repeatedly Pelletan associated the Assembly with carnival and Mardi gras, the traditional riotous ritual that inverted values.[49] Budgetary debates were a carnival and masquerade.[50] Important Assembly sessions were performances that drew Parisian society, especially the women, whose "outfits . . . would variegate the balcony." Their distracting presence further reinforced the corrupting femininity that haunted the theater. Pelletan's first article described the Versailles theater as imbued with the maleficent spirits of its eighteenth-century patrons, three despised women of republi-

---

47. Camille Pelletan, *L'Assemblée au jour de jour. Du 24 mai 1873 au 25 février 1875. Théâtre de Versailles* (Paris, 1875), 6. There is considerable ambivalence in Pelletan's description of the rococo style. He both appreciated and disdained it. See also Debora L. Silverman on the rococo revival of the 1890s and the eventual designation of Versailles as historic monument (*Art Nouveau in Fin-de-Siècle France: Politics, Psychology and Style* [Berkeley, 1989], 8, 152).

48. Camille Pelletan, *L'Assemblée*, 5.

49. For examples see *ibid.*, 2 and 272.

50. *Le Rappel*, no. 1483, March 9, 1874. In his own parliamentary career Pelletan would become an expert on budgetary questions.

can demonology. "For four long years an important part of the history of France has been taking place in a playhouse planned for *la fille* Poisson, the marquise de Pompadour, completed for *la fille* Vaubernier, the comtesse Dubarry, and inaugurated by Marie-Antoinette of Austria."[51] The healthy, natural alternative to this artificial setting was Paris, "that magnificent Paris of the siege which accepted all its sufferings . . . with a manly (*virile*) faith . . . in those two sacred ideals which cannot be separated: the Fatherland and the Republic."[52]

But the monarchist Assembly was more dangerous than a farce or a carnival; it threatened to bury the living republic under the dead weight of the past. The metaphor of the dead returning to disrupt the progress of the living became central in Pelletan's description. In his view, the conservative majority, formerly the "liberals" of the 1850s and 1860s, "the little young men of the aristocracy, bored before they're old . . . the elated mystics. . . . and the village seigniors" were "all part of a perfectly preserved antediluvian fauna." He insisted that the traumatic events of 1870–1871 had acted like a great underwater typhoon, wrenching up these strange creatures from long forgotten seabeds and flinging them to the surface. Pelletan was certain that this Assembly was a "political musée de Cluny"; its members were "ghosts." In the closing days of the Assembly's existence, as it was finally promulgating the Republic's constitutional laws, Pelletan summed up its fundamental dynamic: "the fierce struggle of the Assembly against the principle of modern France. . . . The royalist crusade . . . presented the surprised and anxious nation with the spectacle of the past emerging from the grave to crush the present." The conflict within the Assembly was clearly marked out as the living struggling against the dead.[53] While the Assembly was primarily absorbed with constitutional issues, the dominant concerns of the later Radicals' politics were already taking form. The parliamentary far Left persistently raised the questions of budgetary allocation, equitable taxes, and the influence of financial interests on legislative decisions.[54]

---

51. Camille Pelletan, *L'Assemblée*, 4, 1. See Hunt, *Family Romance of the French Revolution*, 91–99, for an analysis of the republican tradition which associated women, the aristocracy (Marie Antoinette in particular), dissimulation, and corruption.

52. *Le Rappel*, January 2, 1876.

53. Camille Pelletan, *L'Assemblée*, iii–vi, 274, 3.

54. *Le Rappel*, no. 1407, January 2, 1874, and no. 1438, February 2, 1874.

During these serious political struggles, Pelletan delighted in satirizing the Assembly majority of outmoded provincials. In the midst of the important debate on the law regulating municipal mayors, Pelletan sketched the "physiognomy" of the under secretary speaking for the de Broglie government.[55] Numa Baragnon, a "second or third rate lawyer from Nîmes," is captured with the detail and cruelty of a Daumier caricature: "A half-dozen chins holding each other up, so loaded with grease that no fold separates one from the other . . . thus consigning the mouth to where one would look for the eyes . . . the rest of the face is . . . a balloon . . . carrying on its surface two large lips on which a huge mustache spills its black crescent, a large bulbous nose with turned-up nostrils, two great eyes. . . . Everything about him is large. . . . We can never see him without thinking of La Fontaine's frog. . . . I would define his oratorical style as specializing in killing flies with paving stones." The most reprehensible royalists were usually fat.[56] Ancient, emaciated ones were parodied, too, but usually less brutally.[57] More sinister than the royalists were the Bonapartists, who continued their allegiance to the detested Empire. Eugène Rouher, former imperial minister and now deputy, appeared as especially repugnant.[58] Occasionally Pelletan denounced all members of the Assembly, irrespective of political affiliations, as parasites failing to recognize the seriousness of their responsibilities, eager only to adjourn for vacation.[59] Interestingly, as the end of the Assembly approached, Pelletan the historian and poet could not resist one heroic depiction of an intransigent, doomed Legitimist, Gabriel de Belcastel, who denounced his fellow conservatives without principle, willing to accommodate to the Republic. "Raising his tall thin body to its full height at the rostrum, throwing back his bald head with its thick white beard, spanning the Assembly with his outstretched arms in the gesture of a prophet . . . he overflows with urgent appeals of desolation and anger. . . . The faith of another century prays, shouts, sobs and trembles in his voice;

55. The law intended to end the election of mayors and impose tighter centralized control through the prefects.

56. Camille Pelletan, L'Assemblée, 100–101. See also the description of M. de Lorgeril, ibid., 270.

57. For example, the Legitimist M. de Franclieu was "old, bald and stooped over . . . but at least he has some convictions" (Le Rappel, no. 1415, January 10, 1874).

58. Camille Pelletan, L'Assemblée, 163.

59. Le Rappel, no. 1493, March 9, 1874.

and one asks what curious circumstances brought this phantom from the grave, resembling a medieval preacher of the Crusades, before this crowd of bourgeois parliamentarians."[60]

A few deputies could be admired, however, as the number of republican representatives grew with each by-election. Pelletan contrasted these heroic portraits to the "antediluvian fauna of the majority." Léon Gambetta, the republican leader, assumed the grandeur of a mythic figure as he engaged in a titanic conflict with the Bonapartists. "Then M. Gambetta scales the rostrum, head high, the imperious brows, his breast full of passion and superb fire, overflowing with indignation; and with an absolute and proud gesture, with a voice reverberating like a fanfare and rending like thunder, he explodes that word '*misérables*' over the heads of the Bonapartists . . . a searing apostrophe, worthy of the Homeric wars." A few months later, Pelletan described Gambetta as "dominating [the crowd], he takes hold of it; this is *the orator* with the full meaning of that word." The essential virtues of a republican deputy were clearly delineated in the description of Pascal Duprat, who proposed that the Republic's Senate be elected by universal male suffrage. In Pelletan's view, Duprat was "vigorous and incisive with a restrained talent. He is a concise and frank orator. . . . with a strong, sober elegance . . . [and] a clarity in his exposition." The more prominent republican Henri Brisson shared similar positive attributes, being "serious, austere, energetic."[61] Republicans of his father's generation most impressed Pelletan. In the spring of 1874, he reported on Ledru-Rollin, the aged leader of the Second Republic, whom he now saw for the first time. "His arrival produced a lively commotion . . . the session . . . was interrupted. . . . It was fascinating to watch the men of the Right examining from a distance the lion of '48. . . . He carries his sixty-seven years vigorously. . . . He is large, compact, erect."[62]

60. Camille Pelletan, *L'Assemblée*, 276–77.
61. *Ibid.*, 165–66, 265, 259, 263.
62. *Le Rappel*, no. 1475, March 11, 1874. One can judge the degree to which these portraits were constructed by comparing this image with Pelletan's report of Ledru-Rollin in his biography of Hugo, where he wrote of Ledru in the 1870s, "He was out of breath; nothing was left" (Camille Pelletan, *Victor Hugo*, 154). This more negative view was corroborated by Joseph Reinach's observations in *Le "Conciones" français. L'Eloquence française depuis la Révolution jusqu'au nos jours. Textes de lecture, d'explication et d'analyse pour la classe première (lettres)* (Paris, 1893), xxv. Reinach identified the rhetorical style of 1848 as absurdly out of fashion by the 1870s.

A profound frustration with what he called "la politique de théâtre" inspired Pelletan's considerable ability to capture the atmosphere and the individuals of the Versailles Assembly. At moments his tone was close to despair as he contemplated the interminable delays in consolidating a republican Republic. He expressed his deep "desire to put an end to this provisional status." The temporary regime contradicted the concrete reality of the nation. "And this land which is France; this great nation . . . this people possessing liberty . . . wait."[63] The present Republic seemed a sham, barring genuine republicans from access to power and distorting the authentic will of the people. An important question was how this Assembly, which ought not to be, came to be elected. Pelletan was never able to answer that question satisfactorily. One explanation was the trauma of "l'année terrible." The experience of war, defeat, and civil war had so disrupted the normal course of events and the citizens' reason that they selected this anachronistic Assembly.[64] But there were new enemies to confront. The events of 1870–1871 could not explain the Bonapartist recovery. Their electoral support, like that of the republicans, was increasing in by-elections.[65] Even more sinister was the clerical revival. Pelletan reserved his most withering sarcasm and greatest disdain for the Catholic cult of the Sacred Heart and the clerical deputies' efforts to secure official recognition of this veneration of Jesus' heart. This anticlerical denunciation also foreshadowed an important Radical tactic aimed at disrupting the alliance between the political center and the royalist Right. Concern about clerical influence would always attract some moderate centrists to join with the Left.[66]

By 1875 Pelletan concluded that the royalist threat to restore a monarchy was a charade. Nonetheless, he still identified the Orléanists, the centrists, and the liberals of this Assembly as the greatest danger to a genuine republic, a danger that had not yet passed. These were the men who pursued "un politique de théâtre," who aimed to maintain their own power, and who would abandon principles to accomplish this end. Only one example was the Orléanists' ability to shed their Voltairean beliefs to gain the support

63. *Le Rappel*, no. 1670, October 8, 1874.
64. Camille Pelletan, *L'Assemblée*, iii.
65. *Le Rappel*, no. 1672, October 9, 1874.
66. Camille Pelletan, *L'Assemblée*, 58, 59. In describing the devotions of the seventeenth-century nun who had founded the order, Pelletan skirted the obscene (56–57).

of the clericals of the extreme Right. In Pelletan's view, the deputies of the center promised only a dangerously unstable, provisional state. They had never been able to choose between the opposing principles of tradition and the republic.[67]

Embedded in this critique of Orléanism was a much more serious critique of parliamentarianism itself. Orléanism was identified with the July Monarchy, a regime that had excluded most Frenchmen from political participation and whose interest-riddled parliamentary politics was notorious. No republican considered this tradition an appropriate model for the Third Republic. In large part, the disdain heaped on the 1871 National Assembly derived from its identification with Orléanists or former Orléanists who were so important in its majority. The Assembly appeared to revive all the vices of the July Monarchy legislature: duplicity, abandonment of principle, compromise with former enemies, deception of the electors, power brokering conducted behind closed doors. These sentiments would persist well after the demise of the 1871 Assembly as a strong antiparliamentarian strain in Radical rhetoric. Through the 1880s, when Pelletan and his colleagues were establishing their own parliamentary careers, Radicals would question the parliamentary institutions constructed in the 1870s. This first generation of Third Republican Radicals would never be entirely comfortable equating the genuine Republic and parliamentarianism.

The overwhelming paradox, however, was that this Assembly, which the republicans so abhorred, did, despite all the intentions of the conservative majority, consolidate the Third Republic. Camille Pelletan was especially sensitive to the irony of this unintended consequence. As he described the complex maneuvers that resulted in the constitutional laws of the Third Republic, he repeated his amazement that "this Assembly which had been called on to destroy the Republic, instead organized it." Or, "Thus the Republic was finally established by its very opponents."[68] Pelletan agreed with his contemporaries and subsequent historians that the republican state was finally accepted because it divided the politicians, and perhaps the population, the least.[69] The paradox was further heightened when the first majority

67. *Le Rappel*, no. 1417, January 12, 1874; no. 1701, November 6, 1874.

68. Camille Pelletan, *L'Assemblée*, 275, 278.

69. "Royalism is impossible, the Empire odious, presidential rule discredited; only the Republic remains" (*ibid.*, 244).

to endorse a constitutional law clearly indicating the republican form of state was a majority of one vote.[70] The monarchists had been defeated, but the republicans had made concessions. An intangible but important one was in their style, abandoning passionate rhetoric, refusing to be pro-voked, and maintaining an attitude of "calm" and "moderation."[71] More concretely, the republicans abandoned their principle of universal male suffrage and accepted a Senate elected by indirect and restricted suffrage, essentially by provincial notables. Pelletan endorsed this compromise with little enthusiasm.[72]

The dominant theme by late 1875 was that the republican victory was well deserved and inevitable. In the preface to the collection of his Assem-bly articles, Pelletan attempted to provide a heroic gloss on this protracted struggle. "It is this Assembly . . . which last February 25 in a memorable movement of wisdom and patriotism voted the Republic." Pelletan's daily reports, however, were shot through with uneasiness and discomfort about this apparent victory. He wrote of the Republic's creation: "There is not a crumb of the epic in all this: it is prosaic, calm and bourgeois. It was done quietly, without noise, practically without emotion: nonetheless I don't know any historical period when the invincible power of republican prin-ciples have been more forcefully demonstrated." From a young poet raised on Michelet and Hugo, this can only have been intended as mixed praise. He conceded that the constitution was far from ideal and that it created a "bizarre" Senate and neglected important issues. Nonetheless, Pelletan concluded that these limitations were necessary compromises for "a coun-try committed to live freely within the legal order, since we have learned the cost of violence and despotism. This defective constitution will be ap-proved. It is the only path to the definitive Republic." He recommended a way to swallow such a compromise: "The best advice in such cases is

70. This was the Wallon amendment on the election of the Republic's president (ibid., 253–54).

71. See Gambetta's speech urging moderation, Le Rappel, no. 1569, June 13, 1874, and Louis Blanc's similar speech, Le Rappel, no. 1686, October 19, 1874. Radicals would later criticize Gambetta for this position.

72. "Republicans, confident in the support of rural democracy, confident in the force of the Republic, have not backed away from a project whose irrationality is not their responsibility, but whose consequences do not frighten them" (Camille Pelletan, L'Assemblée, 269).

to drink quickly without looking."[73] It was never clear, however, who was swallowing what: the royalists a republic or the republicans a conservative regime. The Republic had been established, and the monarchists had been defeated. A strong suspicion that this republic was not really *his* undercut the genuine celebration in Pelletan's reports. In one of his last articles to appear in *Le Rappel* he asked how well this parliamentary system would be able to translate the will of the people: "One might wonder how it can be that with a parliamentary regime, that fine-tuned instrument so appropriate, so well balanced to protect national sovereignty, that France has not been able to enact her best known and most clearly expressed desires?"[74]

The Republic was not definitively established in 1875, however. Despite the enactment of constitutional laws and the election of a republican majority to the Chamber of Deputies in 1876, some royalists persisted in their efforts to restore a monarchy or at least to obstruct the functioning of a popularly elected legislature.[75] The conservative president of the Republic, General Maurice de MacMahon, used his constitutional prerogatives on May 16, 1877, when he dismissed the moderate republican government, dissolved the newly elected Chamber, and prepared for new elections. *Le Rappel* actively and successfully participated with other republican journals, associations, and politicians in Léon Gambetta's committee of defense against what was perceived as a possible royalist coup attempt. The Right, once again in control of the government, hoped to orchestrate the elections in the fall of 1877. They failed. Despite considerable administrative pressures on voters, the republicans maintained their majority.

Finally, then, a Republic governed by a republican parliamentary majority became the state. By the end of the 1870s most republicans agreed that they had at last accomplished their original goals: the preservation of the regime and the unseating of the conservatives from political power. Nonetheless, the process remained incomplete. The Republic had a series of constitutional laws, but its supporters ruefully admitted that politicians hostile to or suspicious of democratic principles had shaped the funda-

73. *Ibid.*, 278, 269.
74. *Le Rappel*, no. 3592, January 10, 1880; Mayeur, *Vie politique*, 34.
75. One sign of such harassment of republicans was the continuing difficulties faced by *Le Rappel*. In October, 1875, there were rumors of its impending suspension. As late as October, 1879, the paper was seized and fined 200 francs (Censor, *Le Rappel*, F18 407, AN).

mental structures of the state. Further, the state lacked any declaration of principle or basic rights. Nonetheless, by 1880 regular legislative elections had taken place, republican majorities were returned, and the National Assembly had left Versailles for Paris.[76]

Intensifying tensions among republicans and the clear emergence of a Radical group that sought to transform and revise this imperfect Republic marked the 1880s. The next chapter will examine the growth and initial crises of this new political group. To understand the Radicals' critique of a Republic they regarded as flawed, we must first clearly delineate the limits of their opposition. The extreme parliamentary Left of the late 1870s and early 1880s, though critical and often frustrated, shared and helped to create a deep and passionate commitment to the Republic. Because of the emotional nature of this commitment, it was much more clearly expressed outside daily parliamentary negotiations, administrative actions, or even electoral campaigns. We can best understand this republican fervor by examining attitudes and actions surrounding the Fourteenth of July national holiday, the amnesty for the imprisoned Communards, and the official celebrations for Victor Hugo. None of these events was independent of parliamentary action. With the exception of Hugo's eightieth birthday, all required legislative initiatives, but all aimed to carry politics beyond the narrow limits of the National Assembly and actively engage the citizens. All were intended to demonstrate the uniqueness of the republican state, which derived its legitimacy from the citizenry. Each celebration sought to reach back to a variety of supposedly ancient methods to commemorate what was perceived as a new political era, the age of the "people." Republicans dared to transform the crowd from a threatening source of political instability to the celebrant and sign of the state's legitimacy.

The demand that the Fourteenth of July be officially recognized as the national holiday had been an important issue for republicans since at least September, 1870. Such a holiday would manifest the historic ties between the Revolution and the Third Republic. It would proclaim that France had only one national tradition and that was the republican one. Throughout

76. Mayeur, *Vie politique*, 34. For a summary of why 1880 marks the beginning of the republican Republic, see also Maurice Agulhon, *Marianne au combat: L'Imagerie et la symbolique républicaines de 1789 à 1880* (Paris, 1979), 12.

the nineteenth century the semiclandestine republican circles, Masonic lodges, and artisans' associations had more or less surreptitiously celebrated the Fourteenth, as well as other revolutionary *journées*. There was a growing expectation that this anniversary of political opposition could now become official.[77] By the spring of 1880 republicans were exerting considerable pressure on the Chamber to enact the Fourteenth as a holiday, although there was some hesitation even among republicans. With the possible exception of the extreme Left, the thought of uncontrolled crowds in the streets, especially in the streets of Paris, made the entire political elite uneasy. During the 1880s a special committee of the Chamber of Deputies considered new legislation to add to the already existing laws which restricted public demonstrations.[78]

Throughout the spring of 1880, the Chamber hesitated. In May, Camille Pelletan, now writing for a new, more extreme newspaper, expressed the position of the far Left, rapidly becoming the more defined group of Radicals. A quote from Michelet opened his article, which demanded the Fourteenth as a national holiday. "Holidays! Give us holidays!" Concerned perhaps that Michelet might not be authoritative enough, he then cited Thucydides' description of Pericles' funeral oration, reminding the French legislators that Athens had been praised among Greek cities because "she had instituted holidays to lift the people's spirits above the gloom of everyday life." He reiterated the importance of such "solemn occasions" and offered as examples the revolutionary period itself and, most interesting, the Judeo-Christian tradition, which, according to Pelletan, well understood how the commemoration of "miraculous" events could reinforce popular unity and loyalty. The Fourteenth of July could evoke similar emotions, but it would be a distinctively modern, republican, and secular holiday on which the people would celebrate themselves. It would also be a holiday that linked the nation, the people, and their liberties. "The people would see and hear themselves, would recognize their youthful faith . . . and commune with their own spirit." This vision of merging audience and performer was pure

---

77. Examples of steadily more public celebration of this anniversary were reported by a police spy to the prefect of the Bouches-de-Rhône, 1880–81, Activités politiques, M6 3305, AD/BR. See also Christian Amalvi, "Le Quatorze Juillet. Du *Dies irae* à Jour de fête," in *La République* (Paris, 1984), 427, Vol. I of *Les Lieux de mémoire*, ed. Pierre Nora, 2 vols.

78. Steven Hause, *Hubertine Auclert: The French Suffragette* (New Haven, 1987), 79.

Rousseau. Pelletan was indignant that republicans should hesitate to consecrate this anniversary. He challenged the new republican majority to show itself worthy of its "magnificent struggle of the *16 mai*" and to dispel any thoughts that it was "ashamed of the great democracy in whose name it speaks."[79] Under such pressure and in search of appropriate symbols to commemorate the Republic, the Assembly finally adopted the Fourteenth of July as the national holiday on July 6, 1880.[80]

Concerns about order increased as the day of celebration approached. *Le Rappel* called for a "popular and peaceful holiday." It warned its readers to avoid clerical provocations.[81] In many departments prefects anxiously monitored local preparations of Radical republicans and socialists for the new national holiday. The fears of violence were entirely unfounded; expectations of popular enthusiasm were surpassed. By all accounts, the first official Bastille Day was a complete success. In the provinces left-wing republicans organized banquets, political speeches, concerts, and especially popular balls. Dancing was the most prevalent way to celebrate the new holiday.[82] In Paris the festivities fulfilled and exceeded all the desires of the Radical republicans.[83]

Pelletan's article for the Fourteenth was didactic, explaining and glorifying the significance of the holiday for the crowds celebrating it. The well-known engraving depicting the people's assault on the royal fortress accompanied the article. For Pelletan the Fourteenth, the taking of the Bastille, was the entrance of the "people" onto the historical scene. Its

79. Despite his enthusiasm, even Pelletan had some qualms about this proposed popular national holiday. Throughout the article he reiterated the need for a "fête sereine de la paix" (*La Justice*, no. 130, May 24, 1880).

80. Amalvi, "Quatorze Juillet," 421–72, provides a good analysis of the Bastille Day holiday. His study is especially useful on the ongoing conflict between republicans and royalists, as well as the degree to which le Quatorze Juillet was viewed as an affront to the church, but he largely ignores the tensions among republicans who were debating the holiday; his identification of the Fourteenth as a moderate holiday neglects more militant aspects of the celebrations.

81. *Le Rappel*, no. 3777, July 13, 1880.

82. Police reports, June–July, 1880, July 13, 1880, M6 3305, AD/BR. In Marseilles especially militant republicans organized a ceremony on July 17 in which the children of freethinkers were "baptized."

83. Charles Rearick, *Pleasures of the Belle Epoque: Entertainment and Festivity in Turn-of-the-Century France* (New Haven, 1985), 15–16.

commemoration indicated and guaranteed the march of historical progress which linked Athens, Rome, and the Great Revolution to the Third Republic. "And now all of a sudden, what was in the air? . . . here by a magnificent resurrection . . . the people emerge in their full stature, in their superhuman strength; the people as great as those of Athens and Rome. . . . The people are born. This is the great event of the Fourteenth of July."[84] The new national holiday would celebrate that historic moment of popular self-consciousness, permit the people of the present to regard their own political power, and glorify the nation. According to Pelletan, the nation could exist only when the people were sovereign.[85] Reporting on the Paris festivities, Pelletan was overwhelmed with emotion much as the streets were flooded with the tricolors. The day of flags and parades gave way to a night of illumination and dancing, "everywhere a serene joy." Through all the festivities Pelletan viewed it as a day in which "artistic genius, shared by an entire people," was expressed in the popular devotion to liberty and fatherland. Pelletan was inspired to grand hopes that the tradition of popular, patriotic festivals inaugurated by the Revolution would now be renewed and that this tradition would displace monarchist and Catholic devotions.[86]

For Camille Pelletan and his associates one of the most important signs that the first Fourteenth of July initiated a new political era was the successful enactment of a near universal amnesty for those Communards still imprisoned. Now, in Pelletan's view, "the sorrows for the past, for the invasion and for the civil war" were entirely behind them and "the wounds have been cauterized."[87] The effort to gain the amnesty had been more bitter and prolonged than the battle for the national holiday. Once again, the moderate republicans hesitated while the republicans of the far Left demanded immediate action. The final passage on July 13, 1880, came only hours before the celebrations for the first official Bastille

84. Ibid.

85. La Justice, no. 182, July 15, 1880.

86. The first Bastille Day inspired a sharp anti-Christian tirade from Pelletan: "For so long modern nations, like those ancient ones who had wept for Adonis, mourned the Galilean and celebrated his supposed resurrection. What we celebrate today is the resurrection of France; it is the human miracle of the taking of the Bastille" (La Justice, no. 183, July 16, 1880).

87. Ibid.

Day.[88] Many who had unsuccessfully sought to negotiate a settlement between the Communards and the Versailles Assembly in 1871 later sought to secure amnesty for those arrested and deported. Clemenceau and Lockroy were active in both campaigns. It was one of the few specific political issues that the aged Victor Hugo actively pursued.[89] One motive was concern for close associates and friends who had been branded as Communards and deported. Hugo, for example, had been seeking the release of Henri Rochefort since his arrest in 1871. Republican deputies from Paris represented districts that either had participated in or sympathized with the Commune. Finally, left republicans were struggling to create an appropriate relation to the past. The securing of amnesty was linked to issues of how republicans should remember and how they should forget so as to secure the stable future of the Third Republic.

Camille Pelletan made two important contributions to this amnesty campaign. Le Rappel and the newer, more militant La Justice published his histories of the Commune. Le Rappel serialized Les Questions d'histoire. Le Comité central et la Commune in 1878.[90] This study focused specifically on the goals, organization, and actions of the Communards. The second history, La Semaine de mai, examined the repression of the Commune in the last week of May, 1871, and appeared in La Justice in 1880.[91] The two studies differed in subject and tone, but they shared several recurring themes which echoed through all the republican Left's discussion of the Commune and the need for amnesty. Pelletan, a trained historian, insisted that his intention was to present an accurate portrait of the events of the spring of 1871 based on the evidence of witnesses and "authentic documents."[92] He stressed that

88. The bill passed the Chamber of Deputies June 23; the Senate rejected it July 5 and then passed it on July 11. For an example of the enthusiasm with which the amnesty and the first Quatorze Juillet were met, see Nord's discussion of Edouard Manet's reaction in "Manet and Radical Politics," 465–66.

89. Hugo, who was named a senator in 1876, spoke for amnesty in the Senate on May 22, 1876.

90. The seven-part series of "Les Questions d'histoire. Le Comité central et la Commune" began with Le Rappel, no. 3149, October 24, 1878, and ran through no. 3157, November 1, 1878. It was then published as a monograph in 1879 by Dreyfous.

91. This series was considerably longer, beginning with La Justice, no. 31, February 15, 1880, and ending after forty-five excerpts with no. 90, April 23, 1880.

92. Le Rappel, no. 3157, November 1, 1878.

those who had destroyed the Commune had created a distorted account that needed revision.[93] Overall, he presented the Commune as a movement of Parisians who were hardly revolutionaries and whose clearest objective was municipal liberty. Desperation, patriotism, and the circumstances of a terrifying year had driven the people of Paris and the Communards.[94] Pelletan suggested a kind of collective madness brought on by extreme deprivation.

These histories of Paris in the spring of 1871 attempted a delicate maneuver to integrate the Commune into republican tradition. In so doing, Pelletan ignored the fact that the Commune had severely destabilized the first months of the Third Republic. He also had little to say about the various revolutionary groups who continued to commemorate the uprising and maintained the original Communards' opposition to the Republic.[95] Rather, Pelletan insisted that the Commune's repression had no relation to the origins of the Third Republic because it was the work of Bonapartists. Further, he suggested that the motives and goals of the Communards could easily be absorbed into a left republican program because they were neither intrinsically revolutionary nor violent once removed from the pathological context of defeat and the National Assembly's provocations.

The actual events of the Commune might be diagnosed as a sickness, but Pelletan had to admit that he saw among them "magnificent gestures which elevate a people above itself." His descriptions often recalled Hugo's fictional portraits of rebellion and barricades. The violence in which the Commune ended was, according to Pelletan, largely provoked. The Thiers government, the Versailles Assembly, and especially the military officers

93. Camille Pelletan, *Questions d'histoire*, 4–5. He used the arrest records to demonstrate that the majority arrested were workers and artisans with no previous criminal record (*ibid.*, 104).

94. *Ibid.*, 68, 18, 157. This interpretation is not much different from those in more recent histories, which have removed the Commune from its place in Marxist mythology. See, for example, Edwards, *Paris Commune*.

95. The annual commemorations of the Commune with a cortege to Père-Lachaise Cemetery on March 18 were frequently tempestuous gatherings. See Patrick H. Hutton, *The Cult of the Revolutionary Tradition: The Blanquists in French Politics, 1864–1893* (Berkeley, 1981). See also discussion of Victor Hugo's funeral below. Significantly, in 1881 Marseilles Radicals decided to discontinue their celebrations of March 18 because they now had the official holiday of July 14 (Police report, March 18, 1881, M 6 3305, AD/BR).

had all welcomed an opportunity to crush an independent Paris, where there was such strong popular support for the Republic.[96] In *La Semaine de mai* he specifically attributed the harsh repression to Bonapartist generals seeking revenge against republicans and relieving their frustration over the humiliating defeat they had just suffered. This argument disengaged the creation of the Third Republic from the repression of the Commune. That episode could now be viewed as the final bloody signature of the detested Bonapartist regime.[97]

As always, left republicans' bitter denunciation of the devastating consequences of civil war balanced their sympathy for and attraction to the Communards. Civil strife and class war were mortal dangers to the Republic that would prepare the way for a monarchist restoration to which France had been perilously close throughout the 1870s. Pelletan, attempting to capture the horror of the dismemberment of the body politic, turned to the rich images and rhetoric of the family. He decried the unnatural destruction of civil war and its legacy of unending retribution. In his view, it was because of the "horrible cycle of blind repressions and violent uprisings. . . . Nothing has lasted in France. . . . [Every] repression is powerless, because it forgets the sons of its victims. . . . The republic must put an end to this detestable chain reaction." He evoked the image of the family, but now a monstrous one leading to the death of its members and threatening the Republic itself. This abnormal family was composed only of brothers bent on revenge, pledged to carry out an endless round of vendettas. Despite his sympathy for the Communards and despite the absence of evidence that these women existed, Pelletan included a description of *une pétroleuse*. In his account, a poet "reportedly saw . . . an old woman in an outlandish, motley dress holding close to her breast a bottle filled with kerosene and caressing it with a tenderness that was both grotesque and sinister." The unnaturalness of civil war transformed the family from the means to reproduce life into the means to perpetuate assassination; women, rather than being republican mothers nurturing their infant sons, became crones suckling destruction. Pelletan reminded

96. Camille Pelletan, *Questions d'histoire*, 21, 59; Camille Pelletan, *Semaine de Mai*, 263.

97. This linking of the Commune and the Second Empire had already appeared in Hugo's speeches of the 1870s.

his readers that "civil wars are deadly for the republic."[98] They must be abhorred as counter to its nature. Ultimately the Republic had been rescued
in the summer of 1871 by the republican victories in the provincial by-
elections, "universal suffrage," a force much more powerful than violence
in Pelletan's view.[99]

Only full amnesty would end this deadly cycle of repression, revenge,
and further repression, instituting instead a new era of fraternal reconciliation. A full amnesty would remove the Commune from political debate and
end its ability to generate future deadly conflicts. Hugo had already defined
amnesty as political forgetting, "l'oubli dans la politique."[100] Once amnesty
was granted, the Commune could safely become what it ought to be, a historical event that could provide edifying lessons, the most important being
the grave dangers of civil war.[101] The past would thus cease to have political
relevance but could be remembered as historically instructive. Such distinctions between the dangerous memories of politics and the edifying lessons
of history were somewhat paradoxical coming from the spokesmen of left
republicanism. These "fils de la Révolution" required a highly politicized
history to make their positions and their rhetoric intelligible. In effect, the
amnesty, enacted on July 13, 1880, like the Fourteenth of July celebration,
played the didactic role of instructing citizens how to behave in the new,
permanent Third Republic. The historical lessons drawn from 1789 and
1871 were meant to underscore the need to preserve the Republic. Only
the Republic could fulfill the genuine aspirations of the people: stability,
equality before the law, and just reforms, regularly enacted.[102]

The amnesty and especially the Fourteenth of July were intended as
more than edifying history lessons. They celebrated the new Republic.
The amnesty asserted the Republic's political confidence, its ability to include all sons of the Revolution, while preserving its political stability.
The Fourteenth linked the regime to a heroic historical tradition, permitted "le peuple" to celebrate themselves, and demonstrated the Republic's
accord with its citizens, who could throng the streets as peaceful, festive

98. Camille Pelletan, *Questions d'histoire*, 184–86, 166, 178.
99. Camille Pelletan, *Semaine de Mai*, 407.
100. Hugo's Senate speech of 1876 quoted in *Le Rappel*, no. 3759, June 25, 1880.
101. Camille Pelletan, *Semaine de Mai*, 405–406.
102. Camille Pelletan, *Questions d'histoire*, 186–87.

crowds. Left-wing republicans were convinced of the persuasive power of such festivals and hoped to multiply them. Intensely conscious of classical and revolutionary models, as well as royalist and Catholic countermodels, republicans sought to revive and create their own cult of great men. No one better personified the ideal republican hero than Victor Hugo, patriarch of the regime. By the late 1870s he had attained the status of an icon. A popular, inexpensive, three-page biography described him as "strong and solid like an oak. White beard, ruddy complexion, a thick head of hair on a vast curved forehead, thoughtful, yet playful blue eyes, energetic neck, large shoulders: this is the man. He is unique, at once much younger and much older than you think."[103]

With the approach of Hugo's eightieth birthday, several left republican newspapers, including *Le Rappel* and Rochefort's new *L'Intransigeant*, decided to organize a popular celebration. They were joined by the Masonic Order of the Grand Orient.[104] The municipal council of Paris endorsed this proposal, and the Chamber, led by the Ferry government, added its support.[105] A gathering of Parisian journalists and artists elected the members of the organizing committee. It included Hugo's close collaborators Vacquerie and Meurice, who probably were most directly involved in the actual plans. An honorary committee was also formed and gathered an impressive, if eclectic, collection of international and French luminaries: the insurrectionary Italian patriot Garibaldi; the romantic English poet Algernon Swinburne; the president of the Third Republic; Ferdinand de Lesseps, heroic engineer of the Suez Canal; Louis Blanc, socialist veteran of the Second Republic; the romantic composer Charles Gounod; the elitist

---

103. Amalvi's, "Quatorze Juillet," 427, argues that the left republicans were absolutely correct in their evaluations of the Fourteenth. The most celebrated heroes of the Third Republic were much less likely to be military leaders than writers or scientists, secular saints rather than Roman conquerors. See Anver Ben-Amos, "Les Funérailles de Victor Hugo," in *La République* (Paris, 1984), 517–18, Vol. I of *Les Lieux de mémoire*, ed. Pierre Nora, 2 vols.; Felicien Champsaur, *Victor Hugo, les hommes d'aujourd'hui* (Paris, 1878).

104. In January, 1881, Blanqui's funeral drew a crowd of two hundred thousand; some of these participants certainly also participated in Hugo's funeral four years later (Hutton, *Cult of the Revolutionary Tradition*, 122–24).

105. On the municipal council, Tony Révillon, future Radical deputy, strongly supported this celebration because Hugo had been among the first to call for amnesty (*La Vérité*, February 19, 1881).

literary commentator Edmond de Goncourt; Ernest Renan, the positivist anticlerical; and the recently amnestied Henri Rochefort. La Compagnie du chemin de fer du Nord discounted its fares to Paris for the event, and a department store on the rue de Rivoli, Le Bon Diable, distributed souvenir cards with Hugo's portrait.[106] The celebration was a great success. On February 27, 1881, a crowd of approximately three hundred thousand marched from the Arc de Triomphe down the Avenue d'Eylau, a portion of which had been temporarily renamed Avenue Victor Hugo, to the poet's home. There Hugo stood with his grandchildren throughout the day to receive his admirers.[107] The presence of the children was important. Hugo had recently completed a popular collection of poems, L'Art d'être grand-père, celebrating the innocence of childhood. Rows of schoolchildren marched in the procession, and many lycées declared an "amnesty" on all punishments in honor of Hugo's birthday.[108]

Camille Pelletan viewed this festivity as unique in history, revealing the originality of the Republic and the French. "Rome knew its celebrations of Force; to Paris belongs the celebrations of the Idea . . . it is to this great genius that an entire people offers tributes which a Caesar might envy."[109] The adulation, especially within the republican left wing, was enthusiastic but not unanimous. A small group of Revolutionary Socialists in the fifteenth arrondissement viewed the festivities as serving the ends of the bourgeois government. They attacked Hugo's works as démodé and opposed to scientific and materialist principles. They urged workers not to participate. But this was the minority voice on the extreme Left. A conservative newspaper, Le Salut public, denounced the holiday as the "height of insanity . . . an appalling arrogance . . . [revealing] the rottenness of the civilization about which you are so proud. . . . [It was] pornographic that the 1881 ramblings of a senile Olympio should be raised to the level of a pope."[110] Such criticisms were overwhelmed by the crowds, which like those for the celebration of July Fourteenth mixed petit bourgeois, white-collar workers,

106. Victor Hugo, Ba 884, APP.

107. In the twentieth century one of the large boulevards off the Place de l'Etoile was permanently named Avenue Victor Hugo.

108. La Justice, no. 411, March 1, 1881.

109. Ibid.

110. Victor Hugo, Ba 884, APP.

artisans, and industrial workers. The police reports emphasized the festive, holiday mood of the participants. The slightly amazed, constantly repeated description of the holiday demeanor of the crowds suggests the deep anxiety within the government and the police about the consequences of large numbers of Parisians in the streets.[111] Similar municipal celebrations of Hugo's birthday occurred throughout France.[112]

This birthday fete was a dress rehearsal for the even more grandiose commemoration of Hugo's death at the age of eighty-three on May 22, 1885. His funeral became the occasion for one of the largest public festivities of the Republic in the pre-1914 period. It also closed the brief period celebrating the establishment of the Republic, taking place five months before elections in which a vituperative conflict between moderate and Radical republicans would dominate. The day following the poet's death, the moderate republican government immediately proposed a state funeral, which received near unanimous endorsement in the Chamber.[113] At the same time, Radical deputies and journalists, as well as the Paris municipal council, called for the "désacralisation" of the Pantheon and Hugo's burial in that monument. The far Left's efforts to repossess the Pantheon had been a standard demand since 1876. For them, the Pantheon was weighted with history and symbols. The detested Louis Napoleon reconverted this structure, which the Revolution had dedicated to the "great men of the nation," to a church. As *Le Rappel* explained, "It was the day after the criminal December coup that Louis Bonaparte with his still bloody hand offered it to the Catholic clergy."[114] To undo what the Second Empire had done, what could be a more fitting memorial to Hugo's long and triumphant struggle with *Napoléon le petit*?[115] Such a ceremony would also advance the anticlerical campaign which the Radicals were seriously pursuing in their effort to transform French culture. To reopen the Pantheon and bury Hugo there would lend grandeur to one of the most important acts that

111. The police reports also establish the "populaire" nature of this crowd: "Lots of employees and workers . . . in their Sunday best . . . overcrowded tramways . . . invaded by picnic baskets" (Police report, February 27, 1881, Victor Hugo, Ba 884, APP).

112. *Le Petit Provençal*, February 14–28, 1881.

113. The vote was 415 for and 3 abstentions from royalist deputies.

114. *Le Rappel*, no. 5554, May 25, 1885.

115. *Le Rappel*, no. 5559, May 29, 1885.

freethinkers chose to make, secular funerals.[116] Moderates had rejected the Radicals' earlier attempts to transform the Pantheon. Now the Radicals heaped scorn on "soi-disant" republicans, who hesitated to use the occasion of Hugo's death to "repossess the monument in the name of France."[117] Hugo's close collaborator Auguste Vacquerie admonished the Assembly: "The Parliament will never have a better opportunity to restore to the great men [of the nation] what the assassin of the Parliament gave to the chaplains."[118] The government conceded and issued a decree for the "désaffection de Panthéon" on May 27.

Hugo's death occurred at a moment of mounting tension among republicans, of increasing agitation and militancy among the small socialist groups, and of intensifying economic hardship for the working class. The funeral celebration itself reflected none of this, being the great apotheosis of Hugo, the Republic, and the nation. Anxieties did surround the planning for the funeral. The government and the official organizing committee feared revolutionary demonstrations and the eruption of violence. These fears became near panic when violence occurred during the May 24 commemoration of the Commune. All reports indicated that the police initiated the violence when they decided to seize the participants' red flags. Radical republicans joined the outrage of the Blanquists, anarchists, and socialists and voiced concern about police provocation during Hugo's funeral.[119] The Radicals dismissed fears about revolutionary violence and urged the government to accept groups carrying red flags in the funeral procession.[120] The moderates abandoned an effort to enact legislation against "seditious emblems," but

116. During the 1870s and 1880s, when secular funerals were strong statements of anticlerical and antireligious commitments, the church actively campaigned to regain "lost souls" on their deathbeds. The archbishop of Paris attempted to visit Victor Hugo just days before his death; the dying man refused the request (*Le Rappel*, no. 5550, May 21, 1885, and *L'Intransigeant*, May 23, 1885).

117. *La Justice*, no. 1958, May 25, 1885.

118. *Le Rappel*, no. 5556, May 27 1885; similar denunciations appeared in *L'Intransigeant*.

119. See *La Justice*, no. 1958 and no. 1959, May 25 and 26, 1885; *Le Rappel*, no. 5556, May 27, 1885; *L'Intransigeant*, May 26, 1885. Rochefort's paper called the attack "La Journée sanglante."

120. Vacquerie in *Le Rappel*, May 28, 1885, and Camille Pelletan in *La Justice*, no. 1964, May 31, 1885, argued that a flag was only "a scrap of cloth. A scrap of cloth that has value only if what it symbolizes has value." They asked for a return to common sense.

on the day of the funeral the police carried out their orders to seize any flags other than the tricolor. The revolutionaries avoided confrontation, and in the end only seventeen red flags were confiscated without incident.[121]

The paranoia persisted, however. The director of l'Ecole nationale des arts décoratives imagined that "anarchists" would occupy the basement of the Musée Cluny and threaten the collection.[122] He expressed the general bourgeois fear of working-class crowds in the streets on holiday. The organizing committee intentionally avoided a Sunday funeral to limit workers' attendance. Further, to allay the concerns about crowd control, the government insisted on a route of march that would avoid the more popular neighborhoods of the east and move as directly as possible from the Arc de Triomphe to the Pantheon through the affluent Saint-Germain neighborhood.[123] Despite Radical protests, the direct itinerary was followed.

These underlying tensions did not disturb what Le Rappel identified as "the funeral joy" and Camille Pelletan called a "funeral celebration."[124] The ceremony began the evening of May 31, when the unadorned coffin of the indigent, which Hugo had stipulated in his will, was transported to lie in state under the Arc de Triomphe. The coffin, representing the great man's ties to les misérables, was engulfed by an enormous, ornate catafalque designed by Charles Garnier, the architect who had completed the Paris Opera. Heavy black crepe embroidered with silver tears draped the Arc. Encircling the Place de l'Etoile were huge standards of more funeral cloth and placards with quotations from Hugo's works. Torches and electricity, which the Edison Company donated, illuminated this elaborate decor.[125] Through the night battalions of schoolboys and mounted troops of the Republican Guard stood watch over this gigantic structure. Even in an adulatory article, the art critic Gustave Geffroy could not fail to note "the lack of taste . . .

121. Police report, Victor Hugo, June 1, 1885, Ba 884, APP.

122. Ibid., May 30, 1885.

123. Ernest Vauquelin's article "Un Scandale" in Rochefort's L'Intransigeant, May 31, 1885, denounced the government's stupidity for this plan and also noted that this absurd route would "cause the city's central commercial neighborhoods to lose incalculable sums."

124. Le Rappel, June 3, 1885, and La Justice, no. 1966, June 2, 1885.

125. The expenses certainly outran the original allocation of 20,000 francs. In August, 1885, the Chamber allocated an additional 81,932 francs to cover total expenses of 99,376 francs. Bills were still being presented in September of that year (Funérailles de Victor Hugo, F1c I 187B, AN).

the rushed creation" of this republican funeral splendor. In addition to these official decorations there were throngs of vendors selling souvenirs of Hugo, photographs, and a *Histoire populaire*. Some entrepreneurs brought ladders and rented time. The crowd at the Arc during the evening of May 31 averaged about ten thousand.[126]

The next day, Monday, June 1, the Republican Guard began the procession, which included a regiment of cuirassiers, military bands, eleven wagons of wreaths, student battalions, the hearse itself followed by family and friends, and then delegation after delegation from every conceivable organization in France and throughout the world.[127] It took six hours for the procession to reach the Pantheon, and when it did contingents still remained at the Arc de Triomphe waiting their turn to march. At least two hundred thousand people formed the cortege, and as many as two million lined the route. There were speeches, but no one seemed to pay them much attention. The spectacle was the crowd, which in a very real sense regarded itself, as well as the display of republican pomp and republican kitsch. The remarkable event of the day was the absence of almost all incidents: almost no arrests, no violence. What surprised the police most was that "the crowd did not seem hostile to our officers." Pelletan commented that "the orderliness was truly miraculous."[128] The constant refrain of the republican press was the diversity and unanimity of the crowd. Gustave Geffroy wrote, "The entire humanity of this end of the century marched past yesterday. . . . They came from all the streets of the city, from all the cities of France, from all the countries of Europe. Bourgeois, workers, artists. Classes mingled, opinions joined."[129]

Pierre Nora's important collection *Les Lieux de mémoire* includes an analysis of Hugo's funeral. The author, Avner Ben-Amos, identifies the two essential elements of this massive ceremony: "a powerful demonstration simultaneously against the Right and against the extreme Left, a test

126. *La Justice*, no. 1965, June 1, 1885; Police reports, Victor Hugo, Ba 884, APP.

127. Funérailles de Victor Hugo, F1c I 188, AN; *Le Rappel*, June 3, 1885.

128. Police report, Victor Hugo, Ba 884, APP; *La Justice*, no. 1966, June 2, 1885. The most violent incident occurred when members of the crowd threw stones at an aristocratic residence on the rue Boche because the owners had placed broken glass on top of the wall to prevent anyone from sitting there to observe the funeral (Police report, June 1, 1885, Ba 884, APP).

129. *La Justice*, no. 1965, June 1, 1885.

of republican coherence and stability," and the overwhelming presence of the "crowd."[130] Ben-Amos associates this crowd with the fundamental modernity of the ceremony, a modernity full of ambiguities as the massive presence of the crowd linked aspects of egalitarianism, popular sovereignty, democracy, nationalism, and the irrationality of the masses. There can be no doubt that the adulation that was directed toward Hugo, as the embodiment of French genius and unity, was an extremely volatile and complex sentiment. Only a few years later a similar adulation would be transferred to others who were less safely dead, such as General Georges Boulanger. Ben-Amos, however, overemphasizes the nationalist character of the ceremony, especially in his discussion of the "inspirational" role Hugo's funeral had for the nationalist Maurice Barrès, as recounted in his novel *Les Déracinés*, and for Paul Déroulède, the leader of the Ligue des Patriotes.

In his search for the roots of extreme nationalism, Ben-Amos neglects the distinctions among the republicans. There is no question that for moderate and Radical republicans, as well as for most of those who called themselves socialists, Hugo's funeral was fundamentally a moment of unity and celebration. But it was also one of disagreement and conflicting experiences. Views differed on the nature of the ceremony, who ought to view it, and who could be included as bona fide mourners. Republicans varied in their commitment to anticlericalism. Certainly in 1885 republicans did not all agree on who might legitimately be considered "un fils de la Révolution."

The republican Left, which had been coalescing around the label *Radical*, had their own reading of this funeral celebration to glorify a figure whom they considered one of their own. They viewed the ceremony as the ultimate triumph of Hugo over both Bonapartes, the triumph of ideas over military combat. Of the flashy light show at the Arc de Triomphe Gustave Geffroy wrote, "The names of the generals and the battles inscribed in stone disappear—one sees only the eloquent words written on the improvised shields, words . . . words. . . . The slaughter of the battlefield is conquered by the written page. . . . Whatever the future may hold, there will have been one day in our history which condemned the Sword and glorified the Book." In Camille Pelletan's account of the funeral march, it was the gigantic, anonymous crowd and the city that triumphed over past civilizations

130. Ben-Amos, "Funérailles," 474, 513.

and their great men. The crowds were a natural force, joining with the River Seine. Paris was an active presence in the ceremony, providing "an incredible setting for this celebration of Genius and Glory—I am talking about springtime Paris in all its dazzling magnificence." Its monuments—the Arc de Triomphe, Notre Dame, the Pantheon—became icons for the writers' words. The day was a triumph surpassing those of Rome, dedicated to "the greatest of rebels."[131] Both Geffroy and Pelletan ignored the ways such a glorification of Hugo's words threatened to empty them of meaning, leaving only graphic designs on placards. They also ignored the militarization of the ceremony.[132] Nonetheless, they captured its key elements, the diverse crowd and the Republic's need to create a new type of hero, for a new type of state.[133] The Radical republicans' version of that new hero and new state differed from those of the moderates. In the Paris of 1885 the Radical version of this republican ritual had considerable influence. It existed in complex relation to those of the moderate republicans, the nationalists, and the socialists. Their distinct experiences of Hugo's funeral were emblematic of issues that both separated and united them. It was particularly in their conflict with moderate republicans during the critical 1880s that the Radicals developed their own political identity.

131. Geffroy and Camille Pelletan, La Justice, no. 1966, June 2, 1885. Celebrations of Victor Hugo's popular, republican accomplishments continued well after his death. To cite just one example, the small Provençal town of Salon was still celebrating his birth in 1902 (Le Petit Provençal, March 1, 1902, and Le Progrès de Salon, February 19, 1902).

132. Ben-Amos, "Funérailles," 509.

133. Ben-Amos brilliantly highlights these democratic aspects of the ceremony by concluding his essay with a quote from Friedrich Nietzsche, then visiting Nice. Nietzsche was appalled by this display of the democratic mass society, which he regarded as "stupid and vulgar . . . a veritable orgy of bad taste and blissful self-satisfaction" (ibid., 516).

III CREATING A RADICAL IDENTITY

The Third Republic took definitive shape during the 1880s. A less than perfect set of constitutional laws confirmed its legitimacy; invented rituals celebrated its existence; legislative elections returned a majority of proclaimed republicans to the Chamber of Deputies. The new generation of republicans from the previous decade was now rapidly approaching maturity. A minority of these republicans sought to define their own republicanism as distinct from that of their fathers' generation but continuing to embrace the central lesson of that older generation—the need to avoid violent confrontations and revolutionary activity. They identified themselves as Radicals, thoroughgoing republicans.[1] In their view the republican victory remained painfully incomplete, the work of the Great Revolution yet unfinished. A republican program still had to be elaborated and implemented. There was now a new urgency that such a program address changing social and economic conditions, specifically modern industrial forms of oppression and inequality. The new Radical group announced, "Heirs of the heroic generation of democracy and proud of our inheritance . . . we are of our time."[2]

The 1880s was a decade of significant political change—the establishment of an apparently permanent republican regime—and of major economic and social changes. Industrialization and ever larger market economies continued to transform France. At the same time, an international slowing of economic growth was reflected in declining prices, profits, and, in some industries, employment. Long-term industrial development

1. The term *Radical* first appeared in the 1830s and was borrowed from the English. In 1869 Léon Gambetta had used it during his campaign in the working-class Paris neighborhood of Belleville. By the late 1870s the extreme republican Left adopted it specifically to distinguish themselves from moderate republicans, whom they labeled Opportunists. See Barral, ed., *Fondateurs de la Troisième République*, 334.

2. "A nos lecteurs," *La Justice*, no. 1, January 16, 1880.

and the expansion of the industrial working class, as well as the conjunctural difficulties of low wages and unemployment were all alarming social problems.[3] They were also political ones. Not only were members of the political elite calling on the state to respond to these destabilizing conditions, but, more significant, male workers as enfranchised citizens could now register some of their views. This was truly the radical and experimental edge of republicanism in the late nineteenth century.

That electoral power was in the hands of men without property still terrified the established elites and exhilarated the politically adventurous, like the Radicals. In the early 1880s, when socialist political parties were just beginning to organize, the Radicals took up the issues of the working class. They had always realized the centrality to the republican enterprise of the male worker who was also a voter. On one hand, the Republic had to demonstrate its ability to respond to working-class needs, and on the other, it had to contain demands from that same working class. The Republic must both reconcile the working class to a regime that claimed to transcend class and control class conflict.[4] To do this required an activist state, which the Radicals were committed to instituting. The Radicals represented a new energetic party of the Left to which all "authentic" republicans were invited to flock.

From the Radicals' perspective not only was the republican project far from complete, but its own promoters, corrupted by parliamentary success, were now threatening it. While governing republicans were permitting political divisions to blur, Radicals insisted on drawing sharply defined political boundaries. "We embrace frankness in ideas and in deeds."[5]

3. Historians have long debated the significance of the economic downturn of the 1880s, which some have labeled the Great Depression. See François Caron and Jean Bouvier, "Les Indices majeurs," in L'Ere industrielle et la société d'aujourd'hui (siècle 1880–1980) (Paris, 1979), 128–37, Vol. IV of Histoire économique et sociale de la France, ed. Fernand Braudel and Ernest Labrousse, 4 vols.; Jean Bouvier, "Mouvement ouvrier et conjoncture économique," Mouvement social, XLVIII (July–September, 1964), 3–30; Maurice Levy-Leboyer, "La Croissance économique en France au XIXe siècle: Résultats préliminaires," Annales: Economies, sociétés, civilisations, XXIII (1968), 788–807; François Crouzet, "Essai de construction d'un indice annuel de la production industrielle française au XIXe siècle," Annales: Economies, sociétés, civilisations, XXV (1970), 56–99; Lebovics, Alliance of Iron and Wheat in the Third French Republic, 38–45.

4. La Justice, no. 141, June 4, 1880.

5. "A nos lecteurs," La Justice, no. 1, January 16, 1880.

Camille Pelletan as a young journalist. Portrait
photograph, Atelier Nadar, 1880.
(Phot. Bibl. Nat., Paris)

They strengthened and made more pointed their ideological opposition
to monarchists and Bonapartists. Even more important was their criticism
of the governing republicans, whom Henri Rochefort derisively labeled as
Opportunists.[6] The compromises, hesitations, and refusal to act on the part
of these moderates had prompted the Radicals to create and then distance
themselves first from the republicanism of Léon Gambetta, the republican
leader of the 1870s, and later from that of Jules Ferry, who headed governments in 1880–1881 and 1883–1885. Radicals identified the Opportunists
with "the eternal race of the bourgeoisie of the 1830s . . . Orléanists yesterday, the center Left today." They defined themselves as the antithesis
of opportunism, "implacable adversaries of that doctrine which abandons
everything in order not to compromise what remains."[7]

The Radicals' attitude toward the Opportunists combined feelings of
frustration, deception, and, perhaps, thwarted personal ambition, which

6.   Barral, ed., *Fondateurs de la Troisème République*, 333.
7.   "A nos lecteurs," *La Justice*, no. 1, January 16, 1880.

Camille Pelletan often bitingly expressed. During the 1870s his writings in *Le Rappel* had always been colored by a nostalgia for a lost, more heroic republican past that seemed impossible to recover, let alone surpass. In 1874 *Le Rappel* mourned the death of the romantic republican historian Jules Michelet as an "irretrievable loss," noting the increasing number of great men who were dying and the absence of any comparable figures to take their place.[8] This sense of loss fueled Camille's rage and desire. Neither the opportunist Republic of Gambetta nor the even more moderate one of Ferry met his expectations. To mark the new year in 1880 he wrote, "Once again a year falls away into the past! Finally the Republic has come. . . . And its arrival has been marked by an overwhelming nothingness . . . a total deception."[9] This sense of immobility and regret could no longer be contained in the columns of *Le Rappel,* which increasingly prided itself on its acceptance of the full range of republican views. Pelletan, however, articulated a sensibility deeply dissatisfied with the compromises necessary to secure the regime and impatient for that authentic republic, one that would act, intervene, and reform. By early 1880 he left the editorial board and ceased writing for *Le Rappel.* A few years later he would characterize this period as a "time [when] the struggles seemed over. Most of the [republican] leaders had passed the age of militancy . . . they thought about peacefully enjoying their victory so painfully won. . . . Nothing was repudiated; but one might put it off or even evade it! . . . Little by little corruption set in."[10] Pelletan and his associates denounced the Opportunists for reducing their commitment to authentic republicanism to mere rhetoric. The younger men insisted that words must ultimately become acts.

Camille Pelletan's departure from *Le Rappel* coincided with the sharpening divisions among republicans. Paradoxically, the incipient Radicals were in many ways even more dedicated to words than the republicans they criticized. For them, words had been and would continue to be an essential element of the republican project. They proudly proclaimed that "our century which has been so rich in great and noble spirits, has not had

---

8. *Le Rappel,* no. 1447, February 11, 1874.

9. *Le Rappel,* no. 3584, January 2, 1880.

10. Camille Pelletan, *Georges Clemenceau, célébrités contemporaines* (Paris, 1883), 28–29; see also *La Justice,* no. 59, March 14, 1880.

one important writer who did not employ his work to advance social regeneration and reorganization . . . Victor Hugo . . . Michelet . . . Proudhon, Louis Blanc, Quinet, Chateaubriand and Lamartine. . . . It is our task to struggle against political [evils] and to create new institutions." A new political group, willing to launch a new, aggressive journal, was needed to fulfill this desire for authenticity, to hone the appropriate words, and to end the enervating equivocation that characterized the moderate republicans in power. "[The only problem posed] is to prove that legality as well as equality is not necessarily incapable of progress."[11]

In the fall of 1879, Camille contemplated leaving the well-established *Le Rappel* to join a first-term deputy from Paris, Georges Clemenceau, in a new journal and new political enterprise. His father, Eugène, counseled against such a change in a letter dated September 27, 1879. Eugène was now a venerable figure: one of the founders of the Third Republic, member of the 1870–1871 provisional government of national defense, representative, and then senator for the Bouches-du-Rhône. Caution and moderation, which the Radicals so despised among the Opportunists, characterized the concerns of the elder Pelletan. Ideology and politics were not his priority; his son's career was. His father reminded the fiery Camille that it was foolish to give up what he had for the promise of greater renown. He stressed the considerable reputation Camille had acquired over the last ten years writing for *Le Rappel* with its large and secure readership. It was a position that Camille had "conquered at sword point." Eugène cited his own experience with fickle Parisian readers and reminded his son how quickly a journalist could be forgotten. Eugène pleaded that these considerations should enable Camille to ignore *Le Rappel*'s editor, Auguste Vacquerie, who occasionally interfered with columnists and whom everyone disliked because he was "a miser and a cold fish" (un ladre et un pisse-froid). The enormous popularity of Camille's columns in *Le Rappel* would guarantee his victory in the upcoming 1881 elections for the Chamber of Deputies.[12]

Eugène saw only uncertainty and danger in the proposed new journal. Georges Clemenceau had offered Pelletan the position of "principal editor" while retaining for himself ultimate control as "political director."

11. *La Justice*, no. 3383, April 9, 1889; "A nos lecteurs," *La Justice*, no. 1, January 16, 1880.

12. Eugène Pelletan to Camille Pelletan, September 27, 1879, in Baquiast, "Pelletan," 386–88.

To Camille's father, taking such a position was "gambling your future on someone else's hand." In addition, the highly respectable Eugène was uneasy about the entourage that surrounded Clemenceau. He found them "charming, pleasant, but mysterious and mixed up with the world of finance." He also wondered how sound the paper's financial backing was.[13] "Could a new journal succeed in the already overcrowded public arena?" demanded Eugène. And finally, in the letter's last paragraph, the republican patriarch got down to politics. To remain with *Le Rappel* would assure Camille the "sympathy of Gambetta . . . and the Left as a whole, without requiring that he identify with a particular leader or group; [to join] Clemenceau would immediately categorize him."[14] The son's response no longer exists, but it is likely that in 1880 Camille Pelletan, like Georges Clemenceau, felt pressed to take a stand and wanted very much to be categorized as distinct from the republican majority with their carefully calculated politics of survival and success. Camille disregarded his father's advice and resigned from *Le Rappel*, leaving behind the patriarchal circle of the Hugos. He took up his position as principal editor of Clemenceau's new paper, *La Justice*, in January, 1880.

Yet the younger Pelletan never completely broke with the older generation either on a personal or a political level. The two Pelletans had serious political and cultural differences, of which only the most important example was Eugène's support for Thiers's repression of the Commune.[15] Nonetheless, Camille continued to respect his father's achievements. Camille also maintained amicable ties with the editors of *Le Rappel* and certainly never questioned the theoretical and rhetorical legacies of Michelet and Hugo. More generally, though they remained acrimonious critics of republican

13. He had good reason for concern. Cornelius Herz, who would figure prominently in the Panama scandal of the early 1890s, financed *La Justice* between 1881 and 1883 (Bellanger *et al.*, *Histoire générale de la presse française*, III, 367).

14. Eugène Pelletan to Camille Pelletan, September 27, 1879, in Baquiast, "Pelletan," 388.

15. Apparently Eugène had objected to Camille's sympathetic history of the Commune, *La Semaine de mai* (Joséphine Pelletan, née Dénise, preface to Camille Pelletan, "Mémoires [inédites]," in Baquiast, "Pelletan," 164). Camille also disagreed with his father's views on secondary education, which had been imposed on him as an adolescent (*ibid.*, 255–56). There must also have been tension about Camille's unconventional lifestyle. Nevertheless, the expression of veneration by the son for the republican father remained powerful. Eugène died in 1884, four years after Camille had joined *La Justice*.

moderates and the constitutional framework of the regime, the majority of Radicals were staunchly committed to the regime itself. This complex position was already obvious in attitudes toward the Commune and during the amnesty debate. Even at their most militant, Radicals were always aware of the delicacy of their project, the articulation of a distinct left-wing republicanism. Separation from the larger republican circle was also often a personally wrenching and dislocating project. Writing about Clemenceau in the early 1880s Pelletan observed, "In the beginning the task was especially unrewarding and difficult . . . to attack the republicans, but not to lose the correct democratic perspective . . . to break with yesterday's friends, to expose oneself to abuse, to state troublesome truths, to struggle against the majority . . . while it would have been so easy and so profitable to follow it."[16] Such calls for essential change would have to be balanced against the Radicals' commitment to the defense of the regime.

Especially in the early 1880s, Radicals insisted on their differences with moderate republicans. Not only did they have distinct programs, but the Radicals claimed a style and outlook that distinguished them from other republican politicians. They would establish an authentic, dedicated republicanism that would rise above politics. In the Chamber they called themselves *l'extrême gauche radicale*. They prided themselves on the abrasive terms *irreconcilables* or *intransigents* and were proud of their reputation for pointed, aggressive political attack. They constantly reiterated this theme of their integrity and authenticity as opposed to their opponents, who hid their real intentions. Indeed, what distinguished Clemenceau's oratorical style was its directness, brusqueness, and frankness. Camille Pelletan lauded these characteristics as signs of an authentic republican rather than a politician. This concern with authenticity would continue through the decade, and it reflected the Radicals' suspicion of politicians, whom they simultaneously sought to join and denounce. In an 1883 campaign biography, Camille Pelletan presented his new collaborator, Georges Clemenceau, as the model Radical: "The word of M. Clemenceau is naked. . . . His speeches are like fencing. . . . In debate, he is unlike anyone else. He makes no attempt at rhetoric. . . . Many orators have something of the actor about them . . . but M. Clemenceau has nothing of this. On the rostrum you have the man

16. Camille Pelletan, *Georges Clemenceau*, 29–30.

himself."[17] Pelletan had long called for an end to the dissemblance he had observed in the Versailles Assembly and even more discouragingly in the republican-dominated Chamber. The Radicals claimed that they would introduce a new public authenticity. Through the 1880s and beyond, their favorite metaphor was the tearing off of masks—*arracher les masques, à bas les masques*—revealing duplicities beneath the proper public surface. An especially treacherous deception was the Opportunists' failure to produce political and social change. They denounced the existing Republic as sterile, incapable of generating meaningful laws, particularly failing to enact social reforms. Preceding the 1881 elections, Pelletan characterized the "politics of the last three years [as one] of expedients . . . adjournments . . . [and] miscarriages . . . leaving the Republic the institutions of the monarchy and . . . not daring to struggle for reforms." In contrast to this demoralizing state, the Radicals promised that they would ensure a rich, productive republic, a state of plenitude and fecundity, one capable of nourishing all its sons.[18]

Collaborating with Georges Clemenceau, Camille Pelletan would lead these efforts both as editor of *La Justice* and as a deputy of the Chamber's newly organized far Left. The press and the Chamber of Deputies remained for the Radicals the principal means of disseminating their position. These two arenas of activity were closely interconnected, but soon, and somewhat paradoxically, parliamentary actions created the agenda for

17. *La Justice*, no. 139, June 3, 1880; no. 17, February 1, 1880; Camille Pelletan, *Georges Clemenceau*, 5–7. See also Nye, *Masculinity and Male Codes of Honor*, 184–92, for an insightful discussion on relations among fencing, political rhetoric, and masculinity. Unfortunately, Nye's analysis of Clemenceau is brief.

18. *La Justice*, no. 584, August 21, 1881. While using a rhetoric dominated by images of the nurturing Republic, Radicals tended to ignore early reform legislation that designated women and children as its client population, even though Radical politicians were often deeply involved in the development and passage of such legislation. In the public discourse on social reform Radicals addressed an audience of male working-class citizens. For an important analysis of the relation between early gender-specific legislation and the elaboration of welfare state policies, see Rachel Fuchs, *Abandoned Children: Foundlings and Child Welfare in Nineteenth-Century France* (Albany, N.Y., 1984), and *Poor and Pregnant in Paris: Strategies for Survival in the Nineteenth Century* (New Brunswick, N.J., 1992); Stewart, *Women, Work, and the French State*; Elinor Accampo, Rachel Fuchs, and Mary Lynn Stewart, eds., *Gender and the Politics of Social Reform: France, 1870–1914* (Baltimore, 1995).

journalistic concerns.[19] The press, however, had the critical task of creating and maintaining broad political constituencies. By and large, journalism during the first half of the Third Republic admirably accomplished this task, as the number of journals and their subscribers grew enormously. Between 1870 and 1880 Parisian newspapers doubled both their number and the number of daily copies, and between 1880 and 1910 the number of daily copies published in Paris once again more than doubled. Expansion of the provincial press was even more rapid. The Radical leaders, Clemenceau and Pelletan, divided their energies between the Chamber and their newspaper. Clemenceau, Radical deputy since 1876, directed the Chamber's small extreme Left group, while retaining final control of *La Justice*. Pelletan was responsible for the daily editing of *La Justice*, which was the public voice of these deputies.[20]

Only a year after its establishment, *La Justice*, along with the rest of the French press, entered a new era of legal relations with the state. The republican Republic, turning its back on past regimes, enacted the most liberal press law in all of Europe in 1880.[21] With an appropriate sense of history, republicans in the Senate chose now Senator Eugène Pelletan to read out the new law immediately before its passage. All government restrictions, dating from the Empire to the early years of the Third Republic, were abolished. To establish a new journal the director was required simply to notify the minister of the interior. Cash security against the possibility of future fines was no longer necessary. Freedom of the press was nearly complete. The new law further stimulated the ever-increasing number of publications. In this environment, *La Justice* had to carve out a distinct space.

Eugène Pelletan had been correct when he had warned his son about the intense rivalry the new paper would encounter. Not only were there more

19. Pierre Guiral and Guy Thuillier, *La Vie quotidienne des députés en France de 1871 à 1914* (Paris, 1980), 184–86.

20. Bellanger *et al.*, *Histoire generale de la presse française*, III, 137–38, 367–68; Camille Pelletan, *Georges Clemenceau*, 30. The initial investment for the journal came from Clemenceau's father and represented an advance on his future inheritance (David Robin Watson, *Georges Clemenceau, a Political Biography* [London, 1974], 68–69).

21. The law had been originally proposed by the far Left deputy Alfred Naquet in 1876. Historians of the press often refer to the period 1881–1914 as the "golden age" of French journalism in part because of this law (Bellanger *et al.*, *Histoire générale de la presse française*, III, 22–23).

newspapers than ten years earlier, but competition for republican readers was especially fierce. The obvious political rival of *La Justice* was the principal organ of the Opportunists, *La République française*, edited by Léon Gambetta's political lieutenant, Joseph Reinach.[22] On occasion there were exchanges of opposing opinions between the two journals. More often, *La Justice* and *La République française* would fling bitter denunciations at one another, especially in the early years of the decade. A more comradely competition characterized the relationship between *La Justice* and *Le Rappel*. Though hoping to surpass the circulation of *Le Rappel*, *La Justice* never matched the older paper's success; the readership of *La Justice* remained at about ten thousand through the 1880s, compared with *Le Rappel*'s thirty thousand.[23] This limited circulation was comparable to that of other sectarian journals. *La Justice*, like *Le Rappel*, had the relatively low price of ten centimes, but neither could reduce its cost to the one sou (five centimes) of the mass circulation "petit" press. Another initially comradely competitor was *L'Intransigeant*, founded the same year as *La Justice*. Henri Rochefort, ardent republican, newly amnestied and riotous bohemian, launched this his third daily, *L'Intransigeant*, on the first official July Fourteenth. At first, *La Justice* viewed Rochefort sympathetically as the incarnation of "Paris populaire" and anti-Bonapartism. *L'Intransigeant* had several advantages the *Justice* group could never match: Rochefort's considerable journalistic experience and skill, his established popularity and notoriety, and his independence from the Chamber of Deputies. More consistently than the Radicals at *La Justice*, Rochefort articulated a profound disgust with the regime. With a circulation often above thirty thousand, Rochefort captured a much larger audience than *La Justice* and even took readers from *Le Rappel*.[24]

22. See, for example, *La Justice*, no. 15, January 30, 1880.

23. Bellanger et al., *Histoire générale de la presse française*, III, 367. During the 1880s *Le Rappel* lost readers, declining from a readership of 33,535 in 1880 to 22,500 in 1910. Some of the initial loss was owing to Pelletan's departure (*ibid.*, 225, 296).

24. *La Justice*, no. 154, June 17, 1880. Like *Le Rappel*, *L'Intransigeant* printed two dates on its masthead, the standard Gregorian one and the revolutionary one. Like Eugène Pelletan, Rochefort had been a member of the republican government of national defense in 1870–71. Within months he resigned from the position. In 1885 he was elected to the Chamber representing Paris and again soon resigned in disgust. The peak circulation of sixty thousand occurred soon after 1886, when the price was reduced to five centimes. After that there was considerable fluctuation (Bellanger et al., *Histoire générale de la presse française*, III, 227, 341).

All these journals provided news items for one another. Each newspaper devoted significant space to commenting, criticizing, and sometimes reprinting articles from its rivals. Although in the early 1880s the journals of the extreme Left had fairly amicable contacts, by the end of the decade divisions and disputes became vicious.

Like the rest of the republican press of the period, *La Justice* focused on politics and the issues of the Chamber of Deputies in particular, reporting the political activity of the new Radical group. The newspaper frequently reprinted Clemenceau's most important parliamentary speeches. Close Clemenceau associates Stephen Pichon, Georges Laguerre, Charles Laisant, and Edouard Durranc joined Pelletan, who was responsible for the daily lead column. Pelletan, Laguerre, Laisant, and Pichon were also members of Clemenceau's Radical group in the Chamber. The paper attracted the young left-wing lawyer Alexandre Millerand and Charles Longuet, militant labor theorist and Karl Marx's son-in-law.[25] Although politics dominated, columns on art and literature and serialized novels reflected the editors' interest in broader cultural questions. The art critic Gustave Geffroy, who promoted the impressionists, was an important member of the Clemenceau inner circle.[26] The editors certainly viewed themselves not simply as political radicals but also as participants within a larger cultural avant-garde. On the occasion of Gustave Flaubert's death in May, 1880, Pelletan attempted, unsuccessfully, to bring this deeply antipolitical novelist into the Radical orbit. "He was very firm on all religious issues. Mysticism had few adversaries more resolute." The following day, Geffroy offered a better-informed and sensitive obituary in which he described the central theme of Flaubert's *L'Education sentimental* as "the alternation between the grand dream of the past and the reality of the present."[27]

The general atmosphere in the editorial rooms of *La Justice* was, as Eugène Pelletan had predicted, not entirely respectable. Perhaps it was precisely this quality that attracted Camille Pelletan, in hope of asserting his bohemian identity against his father's serious, secular Protestantism. The editors and associates of *La Justice* frequented those aggressively male-dominated worlds of the boulevard, the café, and the theater. David Watson

25. For the relation between Longuet and Clemenceau, see Watson, *Clemenceau*, 85.

26. For only one example see *La Justice*, no. 2970, March 2, 1888.

27. *La Justice*, no. 116, May 10, 1880; no. 117, May 11, 1880.

in his biography of Clemenceau describes this milieu as populated by "adventurers of all types, whose origins were often obscure, and whose way of life did not accord with bourgeois conventions." They were bohemian certainly, but also thoroughly bourgeois. From many accounts, Clemenceau and Pelletan formed the ideal bohemian pair, the former an impeccably elegant "man-about-town," the latter disheveled and reportedly often inebriated. Clemenceau, separated from his American wife, Mary Plummer, was in regular attendance at the stage doors of the Opera and the theaters of the boulevards.[28] He eagerly engaged in the aristocratic fashion of dueling and had established a fearsome reputation. For his part, Pelletan lived openly and flamboyantly with a woman of "questionable morality." This "free union," which began in the early 1870s, lasted for thirty years and, at least according to gossip, Pelletan did not demand monogamy from his companion.[29] This highly unorthodox domestic life must have been a bitter disappointment to his moralistic father, as well as a pointed rejection of Michelet's dictum that republican bachelors must marry and create republican families. In his memoirs written near the end of his life in 1913, Camille Pelletan best captured the attitude of this republican circle toward women. He continued to puzzle over an old comrade from his bohemian days, Léon Valade, who liked to spend time with women. "He adored women, not at all with a robust, conquering physical passion . . . but with a sort of curious tenderness for everything about them and for all those complications of feminine nature. He preferred their company, scrutinizing their fleeting impressions, exploring their most superficial moods, and deciphering their most secret impressions."[30] An interest in women, other than a "conquering physical passion," seemed incomprehensible to Pelletan. Whether married or not, the men of *La Justice* acted as if they were without conventional families.

Not only were their private lives incidental to their much more demanding public activities, but their sexual relations were often transitory encounters. These sophisticated Parisians might be best characterized as

28. Watson, *Clemenceau*, 136, 33.

29. Mme. Bréchet, Interview by Paul Baquiast in "Pelletan," 374.

30. Camille Pelletan, "Mémoires (inédites)," in Baquiast, "Pelletan," 332. Valade was one of the diners in Fantin-Latour, *Coin de table*, oil on canvas, 1872, Musée d'Orsay, Paris. See Chapter II.

"morally marginal bourgeois."[31] Their apparent distance from bourgeois conventions meant their disengagement from marriage, wives, and children. They had reached maturity in the 1880s and 1890s during a period of ever more rigid segregation between bourgeois men and women. Unlike the previous generation of Victor Hugo and Eugène Pelletan, who had hoped to transform public life by infusing it with the morality of the healthy family, the next generation reinforced that element of French republicanism which sharply separated public and private functions. For the Radical circle around *La Justice*, the public world consumed the private sphere. Even more intensely than the editorial group at the Hugos' *Rappel*, the men of *La Justice* struggled to create a new kind of family in which women occupied the most marginal of roles. Authenticity, sincerity, and friendship were sought in intense relations of male camaraderie which bonded those who fought for the just political cause. In an embarrassingly laudatory biography of Clemenceau, written after World War I, Gustave Geffroy powerfully evoked the ambiance at *La Justice*. "[It] was a unique newspaper . . . because of the perfect camaraderie and even profound friendship which united its collaborators. One might say that we formed a real family, and Clemenceau adopted us all." Those on the editorial board shared late nights in "some modest restaurant," Sundays in the country "like good Parisians," and holidays such as Christmas Eve at Camille Pelletan's on the avenue de l'Observatoire, "an open party of poets, writers, artists . . . Camille reciting the poetry of Hugo, Baudelaire, Gautier. Oh! yes, those were good times!"[32]

On the surface, the contributors to *La Justice* energetically promoted the essentially rationalist and optimistic Radical objectives, which could be summarized as an effort to "improve political and social conditions through the increasingly complete development of the individual."[33] These

31. This category is used by Maurice Agulhon in his study of village political and cultural life in the Var in the mid-century, *La République au village*, 254–57, but it seems applicable here as well.

32. Geffroy, *Clemenceau*, 55–57. In his recent biography, *Clemenceau* (Paris, 1988), Jean-Baptiste Duroselle evokes a similar atmosphere at *La Justice*, citing Geffroy's biography. Geffroy's sketch parallels T. J. Clark's description of the emergence of modern leisure among the Parisian petite bourgeois of this era (*Painting of Modern Life*, 147–54).

33. *La Justice*, no. 15, January 30, 1880.

goals proudly perpetuated the Enlightenment tradition and argued for the inevitable fulfillment of progress. Polemics and a taste for biting verbal confrontations characterized the tone of *La Justice* and shaped the parliamentary speeches of its contributors. These were ambitious men energetically seeking to impose their presence on the public arena. Edouard Manet captured this force of personality in his 1880 unfinished portrait of Clemenceau. Nonetheless, despite the strongly articulated goals and the contributors' apparent intensity and self-assurance, a dissonant chord was often sounded in many of the paper's columns, jarring against the prevalent tone of progress and clear direction. Writers in *La Justice* expressed a bitter, sometimes acerbic disappointment and frustration directed most obviously at the moderate republicans who controlled the Chamber but also at the regime itself.

This pervasive disappointment went beyond immediate political issues. A shared fear that they were the epigones of an irretrievably lost past permeated their comments on present conditions. Within the editorial circle of *La Justice*, Edmond Durranc quipped both cynically and nostalgically, "Ah how beautiful the Republic was during the Empire."[34] There was an underlying uncertainty about the actual possibilities of political success. These ambitious political journalists, plagued by doubts, seemed to have modeled themselves on the flawed characters of Flaubert's *L'Education sentimental*. When Gustave Geffroy characterized that novel as "the miscarriage of all hopes," one wonders if he applied the description to sentiments held by those within his own circle. These men combined a sense of frustration, disappointment, cynicism, and uncertainty with ambition, arrogance, energy, and confidence. They loudly proclaimed that, supported by the will of the people, they could remake the Republic. Perhaps they hoped to convince themselves of this assertion.

The Radicals claimed to offer their constituents, the readers of *La Justice*, and ultimately all "true sons of the revolution" an authentic, thoroughgoing republican program, ensuring a genuine Republic. Republicanism had to be more than simply a change of political personnel, even if the new political class was now drawn from "les nouvelles couches sociales." The precise character of the regime, however, remained elusive. As Camille Pelletan

---

34. Quoted in Raymond Manevy, *La Presse de la Troisième République* (Paris, 1955), 81.

explained in one of the first issues of *La Justice:* "If the aim of republican politics is not simply to replace one man with another, an emperor with a president . . . but rather to improve political and social conditions by the ever more complete development of the individual, then the very principle of the Republic . . . must be . . . liberty."[35] Such a program incorporated what by the 1880s had already become the standard republican planks: universal male suffrage, civil liberties, separation of church and state, free, compulsory, and secular education, and the end of monopolies and financial privileges.[36] The Radicals read these issues in a way quite distinct from that of their moderate colleagues.

In the summer of 1881 Camille Pelletan presented himself and a Radical platform to the electors of the tenth Paris arrondissement. He began with a call for revision of the constitution, emphasizing the need for a single chamber elected by "universal suffrage." The treaty between the French state and the Vatican, the 1801 Concordat, had to be repealed and divorce made legal. Military service should be reduced from five to three years and made compulsory for all men, thus ending the exemption of priests. Pelletan called for absolute liberty of the press, meetings, and associations. To extend popular sovereignty judges should be elected. Education must become free, compulsory, and secular to fulfill its democratic and egalitarian purpose. Even though the Revolution had abolished classes, it was still necessary to fight against their vestiges. Legal reform could not be expected to address all problems, but the law should support the weak rather than the strong. Legal reforms could shorten the working day, protect the rights of employees in large enterprises, and provide greater equality among those engaged in the economic struggle. Reform of the taxes that unduly burdened the poor, review of the credit structure, and improvement of public assistance would all create greater equality. Finally, Pelletan stressed that peace must be viewed as the greatest glory of a free people.[37] Three persistent themes dominated this program and were given an especially Radical reading:

35. *La Justice*, no. 15, January 30, 1880. Charles-Ange Laisant made almost the same claim in his *L'Anarchie bourgeoise. (La politique contemporaine)* (Paris, 1887), 187. This book was based on an article published in 1884 in a small journal, *La République radicale*.

36. *La Justice*, no. 206, August 8, 1880. This was very similar to Gambetta's old Belleville program.

37. *La Justice*, no. 581, August 18, 1881.

anticlericalism, universal male suffrage, and sympathetic support for "the weak, the employees of large companies, the poor," in sum, workers. These concerns would remain essential issues for Camille Pelletan and left-wing Radicals for the next three decades.

The Radicals were often accused of manipulating anticlericalism to avoid the more fundamental "social question." Most contemporaries, however, were, like the Radicals, convinced that relations between church and state were central questions. Few would dissent from the observation that the church was officially hostile to republicanism until the 1890s and openly supported opponents of the regime. French republicans, especially the Radicals, were certain that the Catholic church obstructed progress and the development of a modern state and society. To create loyal citizens with republican families, the Republic had to wage a cultural campaign against Catholicism, especially in the realm of education.[38] In a series of *La Justice* articles in 1880 Pelletan stridently attacked the church and especially any Catholic activities outside narrowly defined religious functions. He viewed the effort to create associations of Catholic workers as a "vast conspiracy against modern society." Just as Michelet had observed earlier, church activities insidiously aimed to construct "a holy spy ring within the family, through the priest and the wife."[39] The aims of the church were the same as they had been for centuries: to defend, reinforce, and extend its power and control. Radicals perceived a primitive "backwardness" of faith that repulsed them. The passionate expression of religious devotion that experienced a powerful revival at the end of the nineteenth century appalled them as the archaic remnant of some barbaric age.[40] They saw only ignorant masses, composed largely of women, who were the dupes of a cynical clergy. The immense popularity of pilgrimages to Lourdes called forth bitter denunciation from Pelletan. He spoke of "sad farces . . . and the most terrible barbarism." Concluding with the worst condemnation he could imagine, Pelletan pointed out that French men and especially French

38. During the 1870s Bismarck also viewed the Catholic church as a threat to the forging of a national identity within the newly created German Empire.

39. *La Justice*, no. 150, June 13, 1880. He cites Michelet as a reference.

40. Adrien Dansette, *Histoire religieuse de la France contemporaine de la Révolution à la Troisième République* (2 vols.; Paris, 1948–51), I, 439–47; Gabriel Le Bras, *Etudes de sociologie religieuse* (2 vols.; Paris, 1955), I, 301–305.

women were behaving no differently "than Africans . . . [participating] in a savage swindle."[41]

Anticlericalism aroused such passion among Radicals because they viewed the issue as a cultural struggle in defense of universal male suffrage. Catholic institutions and beliefs were regarded as obstacles to genuine popular sovereignty, limiting the citizens' ability to act autonomously. Triumphant "universal suffrage" was a major theme in the political columns of La Justice. The essence of the republican project remained popular sovereignty. It was only through the constant renewal of the people's right to vote that the Republic retained its legitimacy and superiority over all other organizations of the state. Popular sovereignty was both the means and the end. Throughout the nineteenth century, republicans portrayed popular sovereignty as the dormant giant that would finally be aroused and sweep clean the French state. The genuine voice of the people would tear the masks from the false republicans and "arouse those who slept." During the 1880s Radicals constantly warned Opportunists to take care, prenez-garde, for soon they would experience the retribution of genuine "universal suffrage, [the judgment] of working-class and rural democracy."[42]

Repeatedly the journalists of La Justice and the deputies of the extreme Left identified obstacles that blocked the historic inevitability of authentic democracy and that they intended to dismantle. In addition to Catholicism and possibly as important were the compromised institutions and structures of the Republic itself. The Radicals were far from comfortable with the existing parliamentary organization. They viewed parliament and parliamentary politics, not without reason, as the state organization appropriate to the liberal bourgeois elites of the Orléanist monarchy. They disdained the constitutional laws of the Third Republic because these liberal Orléanists who still possessed so much influence during the 1870s had been their authors. Much of their bitterness toward the Opportunists resulted from the fact that these erstwhile republicans had compromised with and supported the Orléanist-designed state.[43] There can be no question that one aim of the

41. La Justice, no. 225, August 27, 1880.

42. La Justice, no. 106, April 30, 1880; no. 17, February 1, 1880.

43. In the spring of 1881 the Radicals of La Justice broke definitively with Gambetta on the issue of his support for the existing constitutional laws. It was hardly surprising that Gambetta would continue to support laws he had been instrumental in enacting. See La Justice, no. 495, May 24; no. 499, May 28; no. 565, August 2, 1881.

complex constitutional negotiations of the 1870s had been to contain, if not vitiate, the impact of universal male suffrage which elected the Chamber of Deputies. The Radicals claimed that the existing parliamentary structure and the electoral mechanism were tainted by "those rotting Assemblies of the July Monarchy, those Assemblies hostile to the most minimal reform, discredited by venality and intrigue." The Radicals protested this condition and sought a fundamental transformation through their campaign for constitutional revision. One reason for Radical support of the government of Charles Floquet, 1888–1889, was the hope that they could pressure this republican premier to endorse a bill for such revision. As late as 1893 a lead article in *La Justice* continued to call for the "restitution of French democracy . . . by finally permitting universal suffrage to prevail. On the day when national sovereignty will be assured, on that day only will the country be safe from scandals, crises and revolutions."[44]

Writing in the early 1880s before he had broken with the Radicals, the future Boulangist leader Charles Laisant perfectly expressed this perspective. He described the parliamentary milieu as one of "torrents of words thrown to the wind, following already agreed on formulas which are only for show and decoration . . . for the deputy all issues are reduced to maneuvers in search of a ministerial position." Continuing a theme Pelletan had established in his 1870s articles on the National Assembly, Laisant tied parliamentarianism to the July Monarchy. He accused the Orléanists of being a political party "without principles, without faith, with no perspective for the future, without patriotism." In the early nineteenth century they had instituted the parliamentary regime, "a method of governing based exclusively on egoism and hypocrisy." Laisant's rhetoric linked antiparliamentarianism with assumptions of national and "racial" character. Parliamentarianism was "borrowed from the English aristocracy and here in France has been connected to universal suffrage since 1848, a bizarre and monstrous pairing . . . by its very nature incompatible." He denounced parliamentarianism as a foreign import that "does not become our race at all."[45]

During the 1880s, the revision of the constitution became the Radicals' primary political demand. The presidency and the Senate, vestiges of

44. *La Justice*, no. 490, May 19, 1881; no. 197, July 30, 1880; no. 3320, February 15, 1889; no. 4751, January 16, 1893.
45. Laisant, *Anarchie bourgeoise*, 219–20, 52, 199, 230.

monarchical regimes, must be abolished. In addition, the electoral system of small, single-member districts, *scrutin d'arrondissement*, which favored local personalities and local issues, had to be replaced.[46] The state administration required decentralization; judges should be elected; deputies should be liable to popular recall; and a popular vote should ratify the constitution.[47] The editors of *La Justice*, speaking for the extreme Left of the Chamber, launched the campaign to revise the constitution and thus create that genuine republican Republic they so desired. In a rare article in June 1881, Clemenceau explained that every specific reform depended on the transformation of the constitution. "Do you want to be liberated from Catholic domination? Do you want to achieve democratic reforms? . . . Let me not even go that far. Do you want everyone in France to know how to read? Then we must begin with revision."[48] In 1883 three key editorial board members of *La Justice*, Camille Pelletan, Charles Laisant, and Georges Laguerre, actively participated in the formation of the Ligue Républicaine pour la révision des lois constitutionnelles. The actual impact of this extraparliamentary pressure group on the Chamber is difficult to gauge, but twenty-one Paris newspapers and fifty-eight provincial papers endorsed the Ligue.[49]

Through the 1880s the revisionist campaign accelerated. Before the legislative elections of 1885 the electoral law was changed. The new *scrutin de liste* system organized much larger voting districts and introduced ballots for party lists, rather than for individuals. The deputies of the extreme Left and *La Justice* had long been campaigning for this arrangement, which they viewed as a means to raise national political issues during legislative elections. Clemenceau and Pelletan attributed the Radical gains and the Opportunist losses in the 1885 elections to this "reformed" electoral

---

46. In their view, the small electoral district of the arrondissement had "limited the political consequences of the vote and increased corruption" (*La Justice*, no. 490, May 23, 1881).

47. Camille Pelletan, Profession de foi, 10ᵉ arrondissement, Paris and 2ᵉ circonscription, Aix-en-Provence, 1881, and Georges Clemenceau, Profession de foi, 1881, cited in Leslie Derfler, *The Third French Republic, 1870–1940* (Princeton, 1966), 121–23; Mayeur, *Vie politique*, 89–90.

48. *La Justice*, no. 514, June 12, 1881.

49. The republican moderate Auguste Scheurer-Kestner remarked that the members of the Ligue were "*déclassés*, malcontents, fishers in troubled waters, Bonapartists, clericals, monarchists, Caesareans" (quoted in Watson, *Clemenceau*, 82).

method. They consistently sought to retain the departmental lists and bitterly denounced Opportunists and those Radicals who intended to reinstate the single-member district for the 1889 elections.[50]

The campaign for constitutional revision must be seen in the larger context of the Radicals' efforts to implement and secure universal male suffrage. They recognized a serious tension between popular democracy and parliamentarianism. Whereas parliamentarianism emphasized the deliberations of deputies, the Radicals preferred to stress the action of citizens. Their attempts to accommodate these two traditions were central to the dilemmas of radicalism. Parliamentarianism remained a dubious, alien tradition, but Radicals often failed to offer a clear definition of popular sovereignty.

From the outset, the Radicals and especially Camille Pelletan were well aware that their commitment to "universal suffrage" excluded half the adult population, French women. A small group of consistent Radicals, including Camille, did support the extension of women's political rights, but even they were extremely cautious on the suffrage issue before 1900.[51] The exclusion of women from political activity, however, had implications beyond even female disfranchisement. Women were denied the full rights of citizens on the grounds of their "nature." This not only undermined the legitimating claims of "universal suffrage" as a natural right, but it also raised potential questions about certain categories of men. Republican ideology had long argued that female nature barred women from independence and autonomy, thus making it impossible for women to act in the public sphere. The entire political elite accepted this proposition. How, then, could working-class men, who also lacked independence and autonomy, exercise their rights freely? Radicals at least argued that the limits of workers' autonomy were not the result of their nature but rather the consequence of their economic situation. (A few would later apply this logic to women as well.) This question of the authenticity of male workers' votes

50. *La Justice*, no. 187, July 20, 1880; no. 3146, August 27, 1888; no. 3261, December 18, 1888. In the 1885 election, however, and possibly for the same reasons, the antirepublican Right also made significant gains.

51. In 1895 the Groupe parlémentaire de defense des droits de la femme was organized; Pelletan was a member, but the group was largely inactive. See Steven Hause and Anne Kenney, *Women's Suffrage and Social Politics in the Third Republic* (Princeton, 1984), 98–99. For early links between Radicals and feminists, see Hause, *Hubertine Auclert*, 33–34, 71, 74–75, 83.

became especially acute in the 1880s, a period of considerable economic dislocation.

The Radicals viewed a broadly defined working class, including industrial, artisanal, and agricultural workers, as an essential element of popular support for the Republic. They also recognized the danger to the Republic if workers could not be assured some realm of independence. The established liberal critique of democracy had always stressed the absurdity and dangers of awarding political participation to men without property. The Radicals intended to refute this argument in practice and to build a constituency for themselves among workers. The first generation of Radicals had no doubt that the Republic could be made only with working-class support. These politicians were not so far from the *république sociale* of 1848, fraught with its ambiguities, but certain that the Republic must have a social dimension and must address economic and social issues affecting workers.

La Justice identified the "social question" as another serious obstacle to the creation of an authentic Republic. Although many workers would increasingly gravitate toward the still embryonic socialist parties of the 1880s, the Radicals continued to view them as a central concern. Their major question remained whether male workers, even those working in factories, could become genuine republican citizens. Radicals replied yes, but only on the condition that workers (or for that matter any dependent social group) could achieve some form of autonomy. They must be able to operate freely in the political arena. In effect, once the worker achieved this independence his identity as worker would be subordinate to that of citizen, joined together with the other citizens of the Republic.

Following the example of *Le Rappel* and other left journals, *La Justice* had a regular column on the last page devoted to "le travail." In its first issue the editors of *La Justice* elaborated the essential Radical program concerning the working class, one in which contradictions would always abound.[52] The Radical Republic would assure the worker property and therefore independence. In addition, it would see that "to whomever works

52. Interestingly, in Pelletan's unpublished memoirs written in 1913, he recounted his first visit to an industrial site sometime in the 1870s. The Creuzot steel mill which he toured was clearly foreign territory to the young republican. It was a place of wonder, "this triumph of modern science," and awesome power. The force of the machines obscured any observation of the workers (Camille Pelletan, "Mémoires [inédites]," in Baquiast, "Pelletan," 334).

would go the entire product of his labor. Such is the problem which modern society must resolve." Radical politics would "reconcile Capital and Labor—these two *frères ennemis* . . . [creating] a practical socialism . . . [and] resolving the most serious task of the Republic . . . rallying all citizens in one indissoluble union [*faisceaux*]." Radicals always remained firmly committed to this eventual union of labor and capital under their political direction, but especially in the 1880s their inclination was to suspect that capital was subverting their republican objectives. In 1886 Pelletan asked rhetorically, "What attitude ought a republican government to adopt when a conflict breaks out between workers and their employers?" In his view the government was responsible for protecting those who lacked power. Some Radicals went even further than Pelletan. Charles Laisant denounced the bourgeoisie in his scathing publication *L'Anarchie bourgeoise*. He identified democracy exclusively with labor and insisted that the Republic was only a means to achieve social reform. Like Pelletan, he insisted that the extremity of modern inequality required authentic republicans "to associate themselves with the demands of the [outcasts], to lead them."[53]

Pelletan soon acquired a parliamentary reputation as the spokesman for Radical suspicion of large finance capital. In the Chamber he criticized government relations with the Banque de France, subsidies to private railroads, and fiscal policies that benefited large investors. A permanent theme in Pelletan's articles and his parliamentary addresses was *la féodalité financière*. This provocative slogan was frequently heard within extreme Left circles.[54] It enabled Pelletan to politicize an essentially economic reality, the power of large capital. Having created a parallel between aristocratic privilege and contemporary economic privileges, Pelletan could then argue that legislative action would remove or at least limit such privileges. Of primary concern were those institutions directly dependent on legislative approval for their economic activities—the central bank, the railroads, mines, and, of course, the state budget. Pelletan urged that the Chamber exert greater control in all these areas. He demanded banking policies to

53. *La Justice*, no. 1, January 16, 1880; no. 2468, October 17, 1886; Laisant, *Anarchie bourgeoise*, 115, 135, 184.

54. Rochefort constantly used this term. For its use among the Blanquists, see Hutton, *Cult of the Revolutionary Tradition*, 138.

extend credit to small borrowers, called on the state to redeem the major rail lines, and insisted on a balanced budget. All this would reduce the special privileges of the financially powerful, the *féodalité financière*. Like many of his colleagues on the extreme Left of the 1880s, Pelletan tended to focus on finance capital and often on Jewish financiers. Especially in his condemnation of the Banque de France, Pelletan was most indignant about the privileges accorded to the Rothschilds. In the early 1890s, when the charter for the Banque de France was to be renewed, Pelletan argued for the exclusion of Edmond de Rothschild on the grounds that he was not really French. These various efforts to reduce economic privileges granted by the state would ultimately provide the Republic with sound revenue that could support "programs of social emancipation."[55] The principal budgetary solution to the deficit was the progressive income tax, a reformed tax structure that incorporated both principles of fiscal soundness and egalitarian social policies. Pelletan's authority on these issues grew as his position on the Chamber Budget Committee became, in practice, permanent and as his financial expertise was repeatedly demonstrated.

These permanent aspects of the Radical program—a balanced budget, tax reform, extension of credit, greater state control of the banking system, a state-run rail system—were linked during the 1880s to support for unions and even strikes.[56] Labor militancy accompanied economic depression. Through the 1880s labor issues began to occupy more space in the columns of *La Justice*. Lead articles alternated parliamentary questions with firsthand accounts of strike activity. From its inception, *La Justice* took the position that the organization of workers into unions would enhance their bargaining power, as well as foster independent republican citizens. In addition, unions might enable employers and workers to negotiate on a more equal footing, thus eventually creating economic and social peace. Although Radicals regretted the occurrence of strikes and the social conflict they caused, they accepted them as unavoidable given "the economic dis-

55. Baal, "Parti radical," 49. Between 1893 and 1895 Pelletan repeatedly endorsed bills calling for the exclusion of Rothschild. On revenue-producing measures, see *La Justice*, no. 4630, September 17, 1892; no. 2271, April 3, 1886.

56. For a general discussion see Leo Loubère, "Les Radicaux d'extrême gauche en France et les rapports entre patrons et ouvriers, 1871–1900," *Revue d'histoire économique et sociale*, LXII (1964), 89–103.

order in which we live."[57] Further, both in the columns of *La Justice* and in the Chamber the Radicals urged governments to adopt an impartial stance in the case of strikes and to abandon the policies of the 1870s when "the Orléanist Republic favored the privileged class."[58]

In 1886 the miners' strike in the southern coal field centered at Decazeville aroused the entire nation. Pelletan, Stephen Pichon, and the young attorney Alexandre Millerand covered the Decazeville strike for *La Justice*. Although the violence of the strikers, which ended in the murder of a company engineer, was condemned, Millerand in a lead article insisted that the causes of such violence, namely the intransigence of the company, must be eliminated. Throughout the spring there were almost daily articles on Decazeville.[59] Pelletan persisted in criticizing the Freycinet government for sending troops to control the miners, although the Radical deputies never repudiated the government in the Chamber. In March *La Justice* opened a subscription for the Decazeville workers. Of course, *La Justice* was not alone in this activity and joined with other far left journals and the incipient socialist movement.[60] Although independent socialists such as Emile Basly were beginning to speak in the Chamber for French miners, Radicals remained convinced in 1886 that they had an important role in representing workers' demands to the parliamentary body.

By the early 1890s they were no longer so certain, but the editorial board of *La Justice* continued to lend its support to the distinctly more political strike of another group of southern miners in Carmaux. Pelletan and Pichon covered the struggle, which had been provoked when the aristocratic management of the mines fired a socialist worker and union activist because he had been devoting too many hours to his new political position of mayor.[61] This quickly escalated into a national issue; parliamentary debates

57. Stone, *Search for Social Peace*, 139–59; *La Justice*, no. 118, May 12, 1880.

58. Stephen Pichon used this phrase when covering northern textile strikes (*La Justice*, no. 127, May 21, 1880).

59. *La Justice*, no. 2206, January 28, 1886; see also no. 2274 and no. 2279, April 6 and 11, 1886.

60. Donald Reid, *The Miners of Decazeville: A Genealogy of Deindustrialization* (Cambridge, Mass., 1985), 91–106. Reid too quickly dismisses the contribution of the Radicals to the national campaign of support for the miners.

61. *La Justice*, nos. 4656–76, October 13–November 2, 1892.

pitted the owners, the Marquis de Solages and the Baron Reille, who also served as deputies for the region, against the independent socialist deputy, Alexandre Millerand, seconded by Pelletan and Clemenceau. In addition, the state inevitably took an interest in miners' strikes because of the special relations between the state and the mining companies. Pelletan was an ardent supporter of the workers' demands that their fired comrade be reinstated and permitted to carry on his elected responsibilities without interference. The workers requested that Pelletan and Clemenceau, together with Millerand, represent their case to the government when finally, after weeks of management's refusal to negotiate, government arbitration was accepted.[62]

The strike of the Carmaux miners demonstrated precisely why the Radicals had to focus their attention on the working class and why, in Pelletan's view, workers had much to gain from a genuine Republic. For Pelletan, management's original dismissal of a worker for political activity and its subsequent refusal to negotiate were blatant attacks on the most central political principle of republicanism, the unobstructed expression of "universal suffrage." When government arbitration was finally accepted ten weeks later, Pelletan applauded the appropriateness of a republican government interceding between workers and their employers to assure that "the workers' votes remained independent of employers' pressure."[63] Pelletan described his visit to a rain-drenched Carmaux, carrying the government arbitration decision, as a genuine revelation and education. The striking workers of Carmaux became in Pelletan's article the embodiment of authentic republican virtue and solidarity. This tableau was one he was sure would have deeply moved any republican who had seen it. The strikers belonged to a tradition that "linked the honor of the French fatherland to a fearless devotion . . . to the ideal of justice and progress, the democratic legacy to the present generation." Their solidarity and willingness to defend democratic rights, despite significant economic sacrifices, led Pelletan to promote the Carmaux strikers as model republicans.[64] Amazingly, in Pelletan's account of the strike, the miners' actions served to repudiate

62. *La Justice*, no. 4662, October 19, 1892.

63. *Ibid.* For the strike in general see Harvey Goldberg, *The Life of Jean Jaurès* (Madison, 1968), 102–105.

64. *La Justice*, no. 4676, November 2, 1892.

assumptions that society was governed by class conflict based on material interests. In his view, the strikers were defending republican political liberties. He pledged his loyalty to the workers' flag. But clearly Pelletan and his fellow Radicals remained outsiders, sympathetic observers of the struggle. At best, they could only promote republican intervention between capital and labor, both of which were essential elements of the Republic, even if the workers might have greater needs.

By the early 1890s, while Radicals continued to appeal to workers and to integrate working-class objectives into their rhetoric, they essentially stood on the sidelines. In the coming decades as working-class constituencies increasingly supported socialist representatives, Radical support for working-class militancy would become less automatic. But the link between Radicals such as Pelletan and the working class and its increasingly militant representatives would never be severed. Given these future developments, it was especially significant that in 1893 independent socialist Jean Jaurès won the special by-election in Carmaux.[65] Radicals never abandoned these concerns about economic issues, the "social question," and class relations, all of which clearly emerged in the 1880s and deepened in subsequent decades. Rather, these issues were at the heart of fundamental ambiguities in the Radical political commitment to citizens' equality and popular sovereignty. Such questions challenged Radicals to define the appropriate social context for their authentic Republic. At the same time, working-class demands and labor reforms would never be easily or fully integrated into a doctrine which believed that "the Revolution had destroyed all classes; it only remains to remove their last vestiges."[66] Defense of class interests would always contradict a doctrine whose ultimate goal was the absorption of all classes into the Republic of equal citizens.

This Radical program, centered on popular sovereignty, expressed through universal male suffrage, and seeking to integrate the working class into the Republic, was severely tested during the 1880s. Between 1887 and 1890 General Georges Boulanger, minister of war in the 1886 Freycinet government, headed a strikingly heterogeneous movement of opposition.

65. Goldberg, *Life of Jaurès*, 105–107.
66. Camille Pelletan, Profession de foi, X^e arrondissement, Paris, 1881, in *La Justice*, no. 581, August 18, 1881.

The Boulangist movement tapped various sources of intense discontent with the existing moderate republican regime. Moderate governments perceived this powerful, if extremely heterodox, alliance as a serious threat to the state. The debate on the actual or ultimate political intentions of the Boulangist movement continues unabated.[67] There can be little question that the movement's motives, goals, and even strategy were ambiguous and shifting. It attracted militant working-class and socialist support in Paris and the Nord, as well as royalist, conservative, and antirepublican voters in less industrialized southern departments such as the Dordogne and the Aude. Financial support came from such disparate sources as the royalist pretender and local Parisian committees of revolutionary Blanquists.[68]

Clearly Boulangism expressed several distinct strands of discontent with the existing regime. An important unintended consequence of this sometimes farcical, occasionally sinister political episode was to restructure Third Republic politics. According to William Irvine, the royalists' hope for a monarchical restoration was permanently shattered after their devastating experience with Boulangism. After 1889 the conservative and reactionary impulses contained in royalism would alternate between a new conservative politics that accepted the Republic and the strident new Right, which launched chauvinist, anti-Semitic, and populist appeals. According to Patrick Hutton, the organization of revolutionary Blanquists also came to an end during its involvement with the Boulangists. It too was fractured; Edouard Vaillant led one wing to Marxist socialism and parliamentary reforms, while another moved toward nationalism

67. Some of the more recent and important contributions to that debate are Hutton, *Cult of the Revolutionary Tradition*; William D. Irvine, *The Boulanger Affair Reconsidered: Royalism, Boulangism, and the Origins of the Radical Right in France* (Oxford, 1989); Jacques Néré, "La Crise économique de 1882 et le mouvement boulangiste" (Doctorat d'Etat, Université de Paris I, 1959) and *Le Boulangisme et la presse* (Paris, 1964); Zeev Sternhell, *La Droite révolutionnaire. Les Origines françaises du fascisme, 1885–1914* (Paris, 1978); and Rudelle, *République absolue*.

68. Jacques Néré in particular has stressed the socialist and working-class base of Boulanger's support in the industrialized Nord. William Irvine has demonstrated the critical importance of royalist financial and electoral support in the south (*Boulanger Affair*, 104–106). For royalists see *ibid.*, 137–41; for Blanquist support see Hutton, *Cult of the Revolutionary Tradition*, 13–14, 144–50.

and protofascism.[69] Zeev Sternhell, who recognizes the Radical republican roots of the Boulangist movement, stresses its critical role in the origins of French and later European fascism. In the late nineteenth century Boulangism, especially in the rhetoric of one of its most able spokesmen, Maurice Barrès, was the first political movement specifically to connect nationalism and socialism in an ideologically explosive combination.[70]

Although considerable attention has been given to the relations between Boulangism and the Right and between Boulangism and the working class, less attention has been given to the connections between Boulangism and its most immediate progenitors, the Radicals of the 1880s.[71] The Boulangist experience transformed Radicalism as it did the other political traditions. The Radicals in effect created Boulangism and were also the political group with which the Boulangists most obviously competed. The only concrete political demand of the Boulangists, constitutional revision, was taken directly from the Radical program. Much of the personnel who formed the inner circle around the dashing general had been drawn from the political group at *La Justice*. Georges Laguerre and Charles Laisant, Radical deputies and contributors to *La Justice*, simply brought over the program, methods, and some of the supporters of La Ligue Républicaine pour la révision des lois constitutionnelles into the Boulangist camp. These intransigent Radicals viewed the Boulangist movement as the continuation of their demand for revision and their search for an authentic Republic. The Boulangist movement permitted some Radicals to act on their bitter disillusionment with existing republican politics.[72] The well-attended salon of Marguerite Durand, wife of Georges Laguerre, served as the informal headquarters of the Boulangist movement. Laguerre, Laisant, and

69. Irvine, *Boulanger Affair*, 154; Hutton, *Cult of the Revolutionary Tradition*, 150–51; Sternhell, *Droite révolutionnaire*, 50–53. For a somewhat different view of the relation between the Blanquists and the Boulanger movement see Joylon Howorth, *Edouard Vaillant: La Création de l'unité socialiste en France* (Paris, 1982), 62–63.

70. Sternhell, *Droite révolutionnaire*, 41–44, 64–65, 75–76.

71. Correcting this lacuna, Philip Nord's study of Parisian shopkeepers provides useful insights about an important constituency that moved from radicalism to Boulangism and then to more moderate conservatism. Of Boulangists themselves he stresses their political ambiguity. See especially *Paris Shopkeepers*, 349. In addition, Odile Rudelle clearly identifies the central political tenets of the Boulangist movement with the Radicals (*République absolue*, 207, 284–85).

72. Laisant, *Anarchie bourgeoise*, 94.

Durand, joined by other prominent Radicals such as Alfred Naquet, established a new Boulangist journal in 1888, *La Presse*.[73] Charles Laisant was an especially accomplished journalist. Not only had he been a member of the editorial board of *La Justice*, but he had also served as the director of the mass circulation *Le Petit Parisien*, which eventually endorsed the Boulangist movement.[74] Naquet and Henri Rochefort, both early associates of Clemenceau and Pelletan, became key advisers to the general.

Most striking, it was Clemenceau himself who, according to all commentators, had lobbied in early 1886 for the appointment of a genuinely republican general as minister of war, namely Georges Boulanger. Clemenceau's influence in the Chamber had increased as a result of the 1885 elections. The Radicals' revisionist campaign, their relentless criticism of the Opportunists, and the new departmental voting had brought them some electoral gains and added to their parliamentary representation. The price, however, was the revival of the antirepublican Right and new tensions among the Radicals themselves.[75] The dramatic recovery of the royalist Right concerned Clemenceau and Pelletan, but they intended to strengthen their own improved parliamentary position. They moderated their opposition to the Opportunists both in the Chamber and in the columns of *La Justice* and were willing to support a government of republican concentration. In January, 1886, Pelletan described the cabinet of Charles de Freycinet, which contained three Radical ministers, as "one of conciliation, [and] republican concentration." He further admitted that the "Radicals who had arrived at power could not immediately carry out all of the reforms for which we have struggled." Ironically, such accommodation alarmed the more intransigent members of the *Justice* circle, but it also brought Boulanger into Freycinet's government.[76] The Opportunists lacked a clear majority and could govern

73. Bellanger *et al.*, *Histoire générale de la presse française*, III, 340.

74. By the late 1880s *Le Petit Parisien* had a circulation of over one hundred thousand (*ibid.*, 219–20).

75. Watson, *Clemenceau*, 104. The Radicals increased their proportion of seats in the Chamber from 14 to 19 percent and the proportion of moderate republicans declined from 69 to 44 percent, but the Right more than doubled its percentage of seats, from 17 to 36. In addition, there was some question as to whether Radical strength in the Chamber overrepresented their popular vote. This alignment of political forces resulted in extreme government instability (*ibid.*, Appendix IV, 422).

76. *La Justice*, no. 2186, January 8, 1886.

only with the support of the extreme Left. Hence Clemenceau's call for a republican minister of war was met. There was a shortage of generals who had the necessary qualifications. Boulanger, relatively young, good looking, and veteran of several battles, seemed an excellent choice.

Throughout 1886 and early 1887 Pelletan, writing in *La Justice*, made clear his support for the general. His enthusiasm suggested a larger Radical strategy of expanding influence in the Freycinet government and thereby gaining greater republican control over the military. Although this strategy badly misfired in the case of Boulanger, it underscores a persistent Radical concern to republicanize the military services, which were major institutional supports for antirepublican sentiment. Beyond reforms to democratize and eliminate clerical influence in the army, Boulanger's ministerial position also stirred hopes that military, nationalist fervor could be joined to republican ardor, thus reviving the revolutionary mythology of the nation in arms. Pelletan applauded Boulanger's decision to reintroduce a military parade as part of the ceremony for the still very new national July Fourteenth holiday. Pelletan found the popular acclamation the general received at the 1886 Paris celebration most gratifying. "The Fourteenth of July has celebrated both the Republic and the army. . . . The national holiday has become a part of popular custom. . . . The Republic has rekindled . . . a genuine military spirit . . . a profound and passionate feeling for the nation." A few days later Pelletan was still explaining the popular enthusiasm for the general and the army as the expression of democratic sentiments. In the late summer of 1887 Pelletan continued to defend Boulanger and endorse his bellicose comments on French relations with imperial Germany. Pelletan reminded the readers that the "German Empire born in violence, menaces all Europe." In his view, Boulanger was only asserting that "the French Republic has the right to maintain its place in Europe."[77]

Ultimately some of the Radical leadership, most notably Clemenceau and Pelletan, as well as most of the Radical electorate outside Paris, rejected the Boulangist movement by the summer of 1888. Earlier that year Boulangists had challenged Radicals to demonstrate the seriousness of their

77. *La Justice*, no. 2373, July 14, 1886 (the music hall song "En revenant de la revue," which became the general's anthem, referred to this parade); no. 2375, July 16, 1888; no. 2759, August 5, 1887.

own demand for constitutional revision. Radicals had long been denouncing the existing regime as an obstacle to popular sovereignty. Boulangists asked if they were willing to act on these claims. Clemenceau and Pelletan sharply rebuffed the Boulangist challenge. Considering their attitudes toward the Commune and generally toward civil war, their response to the Boulangist movement was not surprising. Clemenceau and Pelletan never doubted that the first priority must be the defense of the existing republican regime, despite all its flaws. Already in the fall of 1886 Pelletan wrote that "if radicalism has one raison d'être it is precisely to exclude any use of force, demanding instead peaceful reforms. . . . Otherwise we have revolutions for a few months . . . and then reaction for several years. . . . The greatest benefit of a Republic based on universal suffrage has been to save France from these ominous alternatives."[78] Only the regular workings of "universal suffrage" brought both progressive change and stability. The Radicals continued to view themselves as staunchly opposed to the moderate republicans, but they would never oppose the Republic. Unlike the Boulangists, the Radicals' call for revision was intended to reform, never to overthrow. After the summer of 1888, they muted their revisionist stance and joined some Opportunists in the campaign against Boulangism, but they did not abandon their demand for constitutional revision. As late as 1889 they still had hopes that a more thoroughly republican government would be able to institute fundamental legal changes. By the end of the Boulangist experience, however, the Radicals had shifted their emphasis from revision to republican defense. For some time they attempted to maintain both these seemingly contradictory positions toward the republican state. In the end, they always gave preference to defense, but the call for structural reform was never entirely abandoned.

As the Boulangist movement boisterously entered the electoral arena through a series of by-elections in the summer of 1887, Clemenceau and Pelletan grew increasingly alarmed. Nonetheless, they still resisted a complete break. In a March 8, 1888, article Pelletan analyzed a series of by-elections won by the general. He persisted in associating Boulanger's victories with the continued growth of radicalism, but he also voiced some reservations about the movement as a whole. Boulanger's success was the re-

78. *La Justice*, no. 2425, September 4, 1886.

sult of an ever-expanding Radical majority and the concomitant decline of both Opportunist and royalist support. The underlying cause of this political realignment was "the sterility of parliamentary action . . . the miserable miscarriages of the government and the Chamber, the humiliation of the democratic idea." But he also conceded that among those who endorsed this Radical soldier there might be some who were in danger of slipping into "the impotent dream of a strong man." Soon after Pelletan declared that *La Justice* was neither Boulangist nor anti-Boulangist. He admitted without regret that *La Justice* had strongly supported the republican minister of war. Now, however, while avoiding a direct attack on Boulanger, Pelletan viewed the movement around him as dubious. He criticized his old comrade Henri Rochefort for his wild enthusiasm, which too readily spoke of war and politicized the army. Still, Pelletan maintained that the Radicals' principal opponent remained the Opportunists. But Pelletan had to admit that the closest supporters gathered around Boulanger also seemed to constitute a danger. "They staff all the sinister coups in history." The only response to this potentially dangerous situation was, as always, "resolutely republican politics."[79]

By the late summer of 1888 the Radicals broke completely with the Boulangists. Now the Radicals faced the difficult task of explaining how their protégé, their former colleagues, elements of their electorate, and portions of their program were becoming serious threats to the Republic. Further, they had to find a new political position so as to increase their distance from the Boulangists and still maintain their differences with the Opportunists. That summer Pelletan began attacking Boulanger's lack of authenticity. Evoking his metaphor for the National Assembly of the 1870s, Pelletan described Boulanger's somewhat farcical debut in the Chamber of Deputies as an unsuccessful theatrical performance in which the general had arrived with his own claque. Boulanger's populist language masked his real loyalties to "monarchists and clericals."[80] The Boulangist movement had fallen into one of the conditions Radicals most denounced, "l'équivoque." By the fall of 1888 Pelletan linked Boulanger with Bonapartists. Former Radicals were excoriated for their association with this

79. *La Justice*, no. 2976, March 8, 1888; no. 2979, March 11, 1888.

80. *La Justice*, no. 3016, no. 3103, no. 3110, no. 3142, April 17, July 13, July 20, August 21, 1888.

latest version of a plebiscitory dictatorial threat. Pelletan specifically noted that Boulanger's electoral support in provincial by-elections came from Bonapartist committees and voters. *La Justice* pilloried Boulangism as the "resurrection of Bonapartism" and was confident that once its true affiliation had been exposed no one would any longer be deceived. In contrast to such dangerously politicized generals as Bonaparte and Boulanger, Pelletan praised the republican revolutionary tradition of "our fathers in the Convention" and their loyal generals "Hoche, Marceau, Kléber, Jourdan . . . who remained subordinate to the law." In the December 2, 1888, issue, commemorating the anniversary of republican resistance to Louis Napoleon's coup, these associations were made even more explicit. Boulanger was linked to the military defeat at Sedan. Like royalists and Opportunists, the Boulangists were warned to "prenez-y garde," for now that they were exposed they would no longer be able to "dupe the Radical and socialist masses." Universal suffrage would inevitably unseat them.[81]

But was that enough? A nagging uncertainty about the inherent "rationality" of the voter plagued the most fervent supporters of radicalism. In the Radical creed "universal suffrage" always expressed the popular will, and this expression was the exclusive legitimation of political authority. Necessarily, Radicals believed that an electorate with some education and emancipated from private interests must support a fully republicanized republic. The Boulangist movement reminded the Radicals that this scenario was not necessarily inevitable. Again the Radicals identified the dual status of citizen and worker as problematic and under some conditions incompatible. Workers' economic vulnerability, often very acute in the 1880s, made them easy objects of political manipulation. In the summer of 1888, the linking of working-class economic grievances and the Boulangist movement especially alarmed Pelletan.[82]

The year of the centenary of the French Revolution opened with a crushing defeat for the Radicals. Parisian voters, and especially those in the

81. *La Justice*, no. 3009, April 10, 1888 (Irvine's study corroborates this); no. 3009, April 10, 1888; no. 2981, March 13, 1888 ("prenez-y garde" became a standard rhetorical device in republican criticism of Boulanger); no. 3245, December 2, 1888; no. 3246, December 3, 1888.

82. He wrote, "Workers strike when they feel they are being exploited by their bosses. That's normal. Let them be careful not to fall under a worse exploitation: that of men who want to be the bosses of all of France and limit our republican freedoms" (*La Justice*, no. 3128, August 7, 1888).

popular Radical neighborhoods, overwhelmingly voted for Boulanger, defeating a Radical candidate. *La Justice* did not hide its despair or anxiety for the future. Pelletan rebuked those who had deserted the Republic and predicted the dangers of instability and political conflict, but he could offer no explanation for this "failure" of "universal suffrage."[83] Despite their beliefs, the Radicals had no mechanism to guarantee that universal suffrage would automatically support the Republic. Confronted by a political movement, which they admitted had successfully mobilized Radical and working-class constituents and which they believed would destroy republican institutions, the Radicals could only offer defense of the status quo. Though they gave republican defense the first priority, even aligning themselves with some Opportunists, they continued to insist that only an actively republican program of legislation would eliminate the sources of popular discontent.

Although their faith in universal suffrage was shaken, the Radicals consistently maintained their support for the departmental voting method, the *scrutin de liste*, and opposed the Opportunists' major strategy against Boulangism, the return to the single-member voting district. According to the Radicals, the causes of the Boulangist threat were not to be found in universal suffrage, but rather in the "political skepticism" encouraged by "the spectacle of men achieving power only to do the opposite of what they had declared the day before." Significantly, Boulangists of Radical origin shared the same analysis of the causes of political discontent, "compromised parliamentarianism." In a perspicacious article in the fall of 1888 Pelletan wrote, "The danger for the nation's representatives is not violence in the streets or in the barracks: it is to be discredited; it is to be the object of laughter." A return to the *scrutin d'arrondissement* would again confirm popular disdain for parliamentary action and would reinforce rather than reduce citizen discontent. In addition, Pelletan directly accused the Opportunists of using this crisis to revive their flagging political fortunes.[84]

As part of their effort to promote the anti-Boulangist position Radicals participated in a broad alliance of republicans from "Progressistes to so-

---

83. *La Justice*, no. 3302, January 28, 1889, and Rochefort, *Aventures de ma vie*, V, 156.

84. *La Justice*, no. 3261, December 18, 1888; Rochefort, *Aventures de ma vie*, V, 131; *La Justice*, no. 3210, October 26, 1888; no. 3152, August 31, 1888. Irvine corroborates Pelletan's contention that the change in electoral size was not the most important element in the decline of the Boulangist movement (*Boulanger Affair*, 126).

cialists." Its existence demonstrated a recurring theme in modern French politics, republican solidarity and republican defense. In the spring of 1888 Radicals and socialists, especially Jean Allemane and his followers, organized La Société pour les droits de l'homme et du citoyen to rally all "fils de la Révolution." The society would counter Boulangism *and* support constitutional revision. The original organizing committee consisted of Allemane, Paul Brousse, Clemenceau, Pelletan, Pichon, Arthur Ranc, Tony Révillon, and Paul Strauss. The aim was not only to "oppose the menace of a dictatorship . . . [but also] to emphasize a politics of the Left."[85]

The Radicals were especially strong supporters of this call to unity among all true "sons of the Revolution" because the Boulangist movement had so badly disrupted their own ranks. The intensity of the diatribes between Radicals and Boulangists resulted in part from the bitter sense of personal betrayal and abandonment among former political comrades. The Pelletan/Clemenceau group insisted that they had remained what they had always been, Radicals opposed to reaction and Opportunism, supporters of republican reforms. The Boulangists had compromised, undermined, and finally repudiated this creed. The June 9, 1888, issue of *La Justice* published a letter from former associate Georges Laisant with Pelletan's reply. Laisant asserted that his republican political beliefs had remained consistent and that they were entirely compatible with his ardent commitment to the Boulangist movement. The letter was strewn with assertions of patriotism and devotion to "the person of General Boulanger." From Laisant's perspective, Pelletan and Clemenceau had "abandoned all that they had sworn to uphold." He also admitted that "it was not easy for me to separate from men to whom I had become accustomed over the years to give my support [*sympathie*] and esteem." Nonetheless, Laisant accused Pelletan of being "a political dilettante." Pelletan responded with even greater disdain. He accused Laisant and the Boulangist movement of operating in that reprehensible condition of the "équivoque." Laisant had evaded his questions about the relations between the Boulangists and the royalists. The Boulangists were seeking a dictatorship, "the caesarean solution." Pelletan imagined what must be the feelings of those former Radicals, now Boulangists. "Yes you [are a Boulangist], you will remain that; and that is

85. *La Justice*, no. 3053, May 24, 1888; no. 3060, May 31, 1888.

precisely what so exasperates you. And full of a bitter bile (against yourself, against the miserable situation which you no longer have the power to change) you thunder against your friends of yesterday."[86] Once again themes of loss and regret deeply marked Radical rhetoric.

This rhetorical pathos, combined with righteous indignation, dominated a series of articles in which Pelletan addressed Henri Rochefort in the spring and summer of 1888. Although only a few years his senior, Rochefort had been among the political activists and popular journalists whom Pelletan had greatly admired and with whom he had had close contacts through the Hugo–*Le Rappel* circle. These articles to Rochefort intertwined the personal and the political. Pelletan identified Rochefort as the most significant Radical in the Boulanger camp, giving it enormous legitimacy among Radical and socialist voters. Rochefort's support was the principal means by which the Boulangist movement "masked" its dictatorial, Bonapartist aims.[87] As early as 1886 Pelletan had accused Rochefort of slipping rapidly into the camp of plebiscitory dictatorship. In March, 1888, Pelletan opened his articles to Rochefort with the address "notre ami," and asked if he really thought it prudent "to mix the sword with politics." Following a series of Boulangist electoral victories in the southwest in which Bonapartist organizational and voting support had been crucial, Pelletan bitterly attacked Rochefort. He confronted his former ally with his past opposition to the Second Empire. He quoted Rochefort to Rochefort. Two days later, the lead column was addressed to Henri Rochefort, and Pelletan's plea that he should not abandon past loyalties became even more explicit. He reminded Rochefort that "the hatred of caesarism made you what you are." Perhaps in desperation, Pelletan evoked both Michelet and Hugo to bring Rochefort to his senses. "O Rochefort! You have read the *Chatiments*; you know them by heart." Pelletan concluded on a melancholy note: "It is sad," a great man fallen so low. The next article, with mounting frustration, called on Rochefort to open his eyes but then concluded with ironic sorrow that the

86. Pichon and Millerand articles in *La Justice*, no. 2987 and no. 3136, March 19 and August 15, 1888; no. 3069, June 9, 1888. There was a similarly bitter and biting article on Naquet, *La Justice*, no. 3028, April 29, 1888.

87. See Sternhell on Rochefort's importance (*Droite révolutionnaire*, 44, 47–48). He gives the circulation of *L'Intransigeant* as two hundred thousand.

relation between Rochefort and Boulanger was one of love and "let's not speak of it any longer, for love is blind."[88]

After a long silence, Rochefort replied to Pelletan's attack in several articles in his paper *L'Intransigeant*. He jubilantly accepted his excommunication from the Radical fold: "You claim to exclude us from your Republic. So be it! We will bar you from ours." He decried the Radicals in the Chamber for having abandoned the authentic republican ideal and being enthralled by an "Orléanist parliamentary regime." After these articles he refused temporarily to engage in further harangues with his former allies. In two final articles of May and July, 1888, Pelletan returned to this dispute and mourned the "demise" of the old, the authentic Henri Rochefort. "Being used to rehabilitate the Empire . . . I have known many tragic deaths, but none like this. *De Profundis!*" And finally, "*Bonsoir* Rochefort. Now it is over. What is the use of speaking with you? The author of the *Lanterne* is dead." The article closed with one last final *hélas*: "Oh! the Rochefort of other times!"[89]

Although Pelletan's dismissal of Rochefort and the Boulangist movement in the summer of 1888 was essentially wishful thinking, the following year did see the end of the Boulanger Affair. The Radicals contributed little to its dismantling. There is no single explanation for the Boulangist defeats in the general legislative elections in the fall of 1889.[90] Critical factors that must be included are the energetic and repressive actions of the new, authoritarian minister of the interior, Ernest Constans, against the Boulangist leaders; the absence of the popular General Boulanger, who had fled to Brussels fearing arrest; the new law of July, 1889, forbidding multiple candidacies; the prefects' careful control and orchestration of the elections under Constans' supervision; possibly the return to the smaller single-member constituency; finally, the very nebulousness of the movement itself, which included both "the renegades of advanced republicanism [and socialism]

88. *La Justice*, no. 2297, January 27, 1886; no. 2981, March 13, 1888; no. 3009, April 10, 1888; no. 3011, April 12, 1888; no. 3013, April 14, 1888. See Chapter IX for Rochefort citing Hugo to Pelletan.

89. *L'Intransigeant*, no. 2836, April 19, 1888; no. 2838, April 21, 1888; *La Justice*, no. 3049, May 20, 1888; no. 3094, July 4, 1888.

90. For differing views see Hutton, *Cult of the Revolutionary Tradition*; Irvine, *Boulanger Affair*; and Sternhell, *Droite révolutionnaire*.

and reactionaries." Few of these developments were the work of Radicals. On the contrary, Radicals maintained a constant criticism of Constans' undemocratic policies. They did, however, campaign strenuously as the only authentic republican, reformist alternative to Boulangism. The news of Boulanger's flight in April, 1889, permitted Pelletan to exercise his invective against the cowardly actions of Boulanger. Writing in *La Justice*, Pelletan heralded the end of the Boulangist dream and nightmare, revealing the anxiety the movement had evoked and the relief that it seemed at an end.[91] Following the elections of 1889, Pelletan analyzed the results as having one indisputable message—the end of Boulangism. Although this development was certainly welcomed, it was reported with little jubilation. Opportunism had recovered, and Radicalism was in disarray.[92] "But this adventure of [Boulangism] has broken the ranks of French democracy. The present is characterized by two facts: the necessity to advance, a more imperious necessity than ever; and the dispersion of those who feel this need most strongly. . . . Those who ought to form the majority of republican progress are today paralyzed."[93]

This disarray resulted from conflicting reformulations of the Radical program, especially universal male suffrage and the defense of republican order. During the 1880s, republicans of the extreme Left had for the first time been in a position to establish a coherent political identity within a relatively stable parliamentary regime. For the Radicals the Boulanger Affair was the stage on which differing self-definitions were fully elaborated and dramatized. After 1885, both those Radicals who were opposed to the Boulangist movement and those who were drawn to it reevaluated their faith in "universal suffrage" as the automatic mechanism to create the true Republic. The Clemenceau-Pelletan group, now established in the Chamber, began to rely as much on the workings of parliamentary politics as on the force of the popular vote. The constellation of parliamentary forces

91. *La Justice*, no. 3541, September 24, 1889; no. 3368, April 4, 1888.

92. Although the percentage of seats in the Chamber changed relatively little between the elections of 1885 and 1889, the Radicals lost their advantages to both moderate republicans on their Right and socialists on their Left. In 1885 they controlled 19 percent of the Chamber. In 1889 that had slipped to 16 percent. Socialist, moderate, and Right percentages increased by one point between 1885 and 1889 (Watson, *Clemenceau*, Appendix IV, 422).

93. *La Justice*, no. 3541, September 24, 1889.

after 1885 gave the deputies of the extreme Left a new leverage which the leadership had little intention of abandoning. The intransigents, however, impatient and ever more repulsed by their perception of parliamentary decay and corruption, began to search for an energetic leader to mobilize the people. In contrast, Pelletan could write without hesitation that, despite all its admitted problems, the elected parliament was the only legitimate political power, and it alone "must preserve political authority."[94] Those politicians who retained the label *Radical* were reassessing their original disdain of this supposedly Orléanist institution. Increasingly they emphasized that only parliamentary representation could express popular sovereignty, based on universal male suffrage.

The issue of where sovereignty was actually located was also connected to the question of republican order. The 1880s did see the establishment of a republican order, although disagreement continued, and continues among historians, as to its precise nature.[95] The decade also marked transformations of both the Right and the Left. The Radicals attempted to situate themselves in this new landscape. By the end of the decade they were clear that there was no alternative but to support the new Republican order. They regarded those who threatened the Republic as dangerous, counter-revolutionary subversives. Yet they found it difficult to jettison entirely their rhetoric of opposition to and criticism of the state, which had been an essential part of their identity. Many within this first generation of Third Republic Radicals would always feel somewhat ill at ease with their role as the defenders of order. Yet at the same time Radicals continued to stress the egalitarian promise of republicanism, a promise that remained potentially disruptive of the social and parliamentary order they had come to accept. At the end of the 1880s, the Radicals balanced precariously between order and disorder, between authority and its critique. It was an awkward position for those seeking political power.

But in late 1889, Radicals, now more of a clearly defined political presence than at the beginning of the decade, could momentarily enjoy the defeat of Boulangism and celebrate the centenary of the Revolution. The Paris Universal Exposition marked this historic occasion, as well as the per-

94. *La Justice*, no. 2981, March 13, 1888.
95. See especially Elwitt, *Making of the Third Republic*.

manence of the Third Republic. Radicals were eager to promote it. The Eiffel Tower had become the controversial symbol of this festival, and Radicals were ready to make it their own. The tower was promoted by the Radical minister of commerce in Freycinet's government, Edouard Lockroy, and intended to announce a new age of science, industry, and class cooperation. The Radicals defended it against critics.[96] In an article on the opening of the Exposition, Pelletan characterized the tower as "a most overwhelming vision of the power of the human spirit armed with science. . . . The colossal sincerity of this scientific work astounds the imagination . . . it is that which it must be because it makes no effort to hide itself."[97] For Pelletan it embodied that elusive goal of Radicalism, authenticity. *La Justice* reported the July Fourteenth celebrations of 1889 as one of the most animated and joyous in many years. The exposition increased everyone's enthusiasm and offered a "spectacle of the [country's] productive vigor." The tone was optimistic, for certainly the people would inevitably triumph. "They have universal suffrage; they have the necessary liberties. All that is needed is will and patience. It is because of that [the people] remain peaceful in their power and that they celebrate the memories of their ancestors with the cry of Vive la République!"[98] But it is impossible not to hear in these enthusiastic descriptions of popular devotion to the Republic the voices of those who protest too much. The Boulanger Affair had badly shaken the Radicals' confidence in "le peuple," especially the people of Paris, and in "universal suffrage." During the next decade Radicals would have to elaborate further their new identification of the Republic with parliamentarianism and republican order.

96. Miriam R. Levin, "The Eiffel Tower Revisited," *French Review*, LXII (May, 1989), 1052–64, and Silverman, *Art Nouveau in Fin-de-Siècle France*, 1–9, 284–89.

97. *La Justice*, no. 3400, May 7, 1889.

98. Millerand in *La Justice*, no. 3470, July 15, 1889.

IV DEFENSE OF THE REPUBLIC
1892–1902

The Boulangist crisis had badly split the original Radical group and damaged their ideological coherence. Those, like Clemenceau and Pelletan,
who had rejected the extremist version of opposition to Opportunism,
found themselves burdened with a confusing program that simultaneously
defended and critiqued moderate governments. The Radicals' defense of the
Republic and parliamentarianism, which the Boulangists attacked, sharply
contrasted with their reputation as militant outsiders. Increasingly these
former young men of café meeting rooms came to be seen as comfortably
established, middle-aged journalists, editors, and deputies. The Radicals'
own faith in the central tenet of their ideology, "universal suffrage," had
been severely tried when former strongholds, such as the popular neighborhoods of Paris, rejected Radical candidates and voted for Boulangists.
Those who continued to adhere to the label *Radical* in the 1890s desperately needed to redefine their relations to the parliamentary regime and
the "people." This redefinition took place in the midst of continuing political crises which eventually exploded in 1898 in yet another dramatic
event, the Dreyfus Affair, whose significance at least matched that of the
Boulangist episode. Between 1892 and 1902 the Radicals would accomplish an impressive and surprising revival. The causes of this successful
restoration were less the result of any well-laid Radical strategy than the
outcome of fortuitous circumstances and the intransigence of antirepublican forces. During that decade Radicals transformed themselves from a
declining parliamentary orientation into the only organized nonsocialist
party in France. They would profit enormously from the political polarization created by the Dreyfus Affair, which most Radicals long ignored. In
1892–1893 they appeared as a group of political has-beens; in 1902 they
were poised to gain control of the Chamber and the government.

Scandals, shocking revelations of offensive deeds, were and still are an
element of most political systems. In modern representative systems the

power of scandal to damage careers and parties is considerably amplified. The Third Republic, characterized by universal male suffrage, the formation of a new political elite, and an increasingly commercialized culture, was especially prone to scandals. The history of the Republic has often been written as a litany of such scandals—from the Wilson Affair to the Stavisky scandal. Such familiarity has sometimes led historians to ignore the significance of the recurring themes of these republican scandals. It is useful to ask why the regime was so vulnerable throughout its history to accusations of corruption. The dangerous nexus of a new political elite and money was dramatically exposed during the Panama Affair. Contemporaries and historians agreed that the defeated Boulangist leaders initiated this scandal in the early 1890s, intending to compromise the republican government and moderate republicans.[1] In the process, the Boulangists further disorganized the Radicals, particularly through their success in eliminating the Radical leader Georges Clemenceau from office.

The Panama Affair came in the aftermath of the bankruptcy of the Compagnie universelle du canal interocéanique de Panama, which had attracted the investments of small property owners. The project to build a canal linking the Atlantic and the Pacific had been discussed during the 1870s, when it gained the support and involvement of two important men: Ferdinand de Lesseps, the organizer of the Suez Canal and successful entrepreneur who already owned the Panama Railroad, and Gustave Eiffel, the heroic engineer of the republican tower. De Lesseps and his son Charles became directors of the company, and Eiffel maintained close connections. Throughout the 1880s the company raised considerable capital with a well-organized and expensive publicity campaign in which the entire Parisian press participated.[2] In addition, several parliamentary bills permitting the company to raise capital through the issue of bonds (*obligations à lots*) furthered the apparently endless search for funds. Financing was still insufficient, however, and not even half the hoped-for 720 mil-

---

1. For two major studies of the Panama Affair see Adrien Dansette, *Les Affaires de Panama* (Paris, 1934), and Jean Bouvier, *Les Deux Scandales de Panama* (Paris, 1964).

2. *La Justice* carried regular advertisements for shares in the Panama company. More important, there were occasional articles on the company and the project, although less frequently in *La Justice* than in other Paris newspapers (Bellanger *et al.*, *Histoire générale de la presse française*, III, 268).

lion francs was secured in 1888; the company collapsed in 1889. In the long sorting-out process that followed, it became clear that the major costs had been incurred in debt servicing and the Parisian publicity campaign. Kohn-Reinach & Cie handled most of the advertising, which amounted to 22 million francs. The Baron Jacques de Reinach, head of this financial house, frequently employed the services of one Cornelius Herz, an assiduous entrepreneur and a man with infinite contacts.[3]

Financiers, journalists, editors, and parliamentarians all profited from the largesse of the Panama Canal company, and this was common knowledge among the Parisian political elite before and after the company's bankruptcy. Jean Bouvier in his study of the scandal has insisted that the more serious and significant scandal was barely discussed at the time— the practices of French financial institutions, particularly the new banks, which extended business credit. According to Bouvier, the bankers benefited the most from the manipulations of the Panama shares and bonds. They processed the sales and received a comfortable commission on all purchases (5.67%). There was little public debate immediately after 1889, and the role of the banks and the journalists was never carefully scrutinized. Not until the fall of 1892, several months before the next legislative elections, did denunciations of corruption emerge, and then they were directed almost exclusively at parliamentarians and particularly moderate republicans. Edouard Drumont, former Boulangist and leading anti-Semite, published a series of exposés in his newspaper, *La Libre Parole*, and the claims were taken up in the Chamber, where another former Boulangist charged that more than one hundred deputies had been bribed. Eventually only twenty-six deputies were formally accused and only one found guilty. A parliamentary investigation and the courts exonerated the parliamentarians. Camille Pelletan was a member of the inquiry, headed by Henri Brisson, another leading Radical. Prominent moderate republican Maurice Rouvier and Radical Charles Floquet denied personal corruption but admitted to using money from the Panama company against the Boulangists. Rouvier withdrew from politics for a time, and Floquet was defeated in the next election. The directors of the Panama Canal company, including

3. Bouvier, *Deux Scandales de Panama*, 74–106. In 1904 a new French company sold its concessions in Central America to the United States, which proceeded with canal construction.

Charles de Lesseps and Eiffel, were initially condemned to short prison sentences but then acquitted by spring, 1893. The investors' suits against bankers and financiers came to nothing.[4]

Bouvier argues that this scandal did not expose any serious weaknesses in the political system and simply reiterated already established themes of antiparliamentarianism and authoritarianism.[5] This conclusion underestimates the extraordinary ability of former Boulangists to manipulate the scandal and their success in justifying their own critique of the Republic and especially of the Chamber. Even though the Boulangist press had been as enthusiastic about Panama as any other and had shared in the company's handouts, in 1892–1893 the Boulangists reshaped the scandal into an exclusively political issue and attacked the government and parliament. The decisions of the courts to exonerate almost all those charged and especially the conclusion of the Chamber committee of inquiry that no substantial evidence existed against any deputies only confirmed the equation of politics and corruption. Thus the antiparliamentary discourse was once again legitimated only a few years after its proponents appeared to have been defeated. If anything, its ever stronger association with the growing anti-Semitic movement, which identified Jewish financiers as a major source of parliamentary corruption, provided powerful reinforcement.

The former Boulangists also used the Panama scandal against Georges Clemenceau. They spectacularly demolished the career of the Radical leader, preventing him from gaining any advantage from the Boulangist exposé of the Opportunists. The Boulangists returned to long-standing questions about Clemenceau's relations with Cornelius Herz, who was not only a disreputable financial middleman but a Jew who fulfilled every anti-Semite's fantasies. Herz had been an early financial backer of *La Justice*, but Clemenceau soon ended that relation when he bought back the shares in 1885. Herz accepted a considerable loss in this transaction. A year later, in the midst of attacking Jules Ferry, Clemenceau felt compelled to explain his dealings with the already notorious Herz.[6] Not surprisingly, the Herz connection resurfaced during the Boulanger Affair. Former associate Georges

---

4. *Ibid.*, 118, 203, 188.
5. *Ibid.*, 200.
6. *La Justice*, no. 2514, December 2, 1886; Watson, *Clemenceau*, 70.

Laguerre accused *La Justice* of accepting support from unscrupulous business associates. Clemenceau ridiculed these claims and referred readers to his 1886 article.[7] Significantly, the Boulangists, who had their own connections to Herz, did not pursue the issue. Four years later, the Herz question dramatically reappeared. Amazingly, Clemenceau seemed relatively unconcerned about his earlier contact with the now infamous Cornelius Herz. He believed that he could manipulate the Panama scandal for his own ends. During the fall of 1892, Clemenceau had been indirectly encouraging Baron de Reinach to supply information to *La Libre Parole* so as to damage Clemenceau's moderate opponents. The desperate baron was attempting to stop the press denunciations against him; the reckless Clemenceau was, like the Boulangists, hoping to destroy the Opportunists.[8] Instead, the complicated network of scandals trapped Clemenceau. By late November, 1892, his presence during discussions between the Baron de Reinach and Cornelius Herz implicated him in the scandal. That same night the baron killed himself. The next month, Paul Déroulède, head of the Ligue des Patriotes and Boulangist deputy, denounced Clemenceau as the patron, promoter, and friend of Cornelius Herz to whose other infamies Déroulède added that of foreign agent. Further, he declared that Clemenceau too was in the pay of an unnamed foreign power. Clemenceau, in one of his famous parliamentary confrontations, accused Déroulède of lying and then fought an inconclusive, faintly ridiculous duel with the nationalist leader.[9]

Camille Pelletan, writing in *La Justice*, defended his colleague and collaborator. He insisted that no one had dared link Clemenceau to the corruption promoted by the Panama Canal company because there was no connection. All the innuendoes were a diversion from the real task, which was to illuminate the truth behind this latest scandal. He regretted the current political atmosphere of "undefined suspicions easily explained, alas, by too many abuses. What is absolutely necessary is to bring everything to light."[10]

7. *La Justice*, no. 3144, August 23, 1888.

8. Watson, *Clemenceau*, 125; Bouvier, *Deux Scandales de Panama*, 149.

9. *La Justice*, no. 4717, December 13, 1892; no. 4724, December 20, 1892; no. 4725, December 21, 1892. During the duel the two exchanged six shots without injury to either one; it was considered a loss for Clemenceau (Duroselle, *Clemenceau*, 281–83).

10. *La Justice*, no. 4725, December 21, 1892. See also Pelletan's earlier calls for light, *ibid.*, no. 4696, November 23, 1892.

The light both Pelletan and his colleague Stephen Pichon adamantly called for failed either to explain the intricacies of the Panama dealings or to vindicate Clemenceau. How accurate or inaccurate the claims were against Clemenceau and Herz made little difference. The association of the two was enough to damn the powerful and disliked Clemenceau.[11]

The following year, during a bitter reelection campaign in the southern department of the Var, Clemenceau was pitted against a well-organized local opposition. Diverse interests united behind one exclusive objective: the defeat of the Radical leader. Local and national funds financed a journal, L'Anti-Clemenciste. The continuing campaign of the nationalist and right-wing Paris press against the Radicals reinforced this intense local opposition. Rochefort's L'Intransigeant eagerly joined the battle. One article damned Pelletan by association with Clemenceau and Clemenceau by association with Herz. Pelletan was "that lieutenant whose captain was the insolent presenter of the pious chevalier Herz, that spy and corrupter!"[12] In this bitter local and national atmosphere, Clemenceau failed to win a majority in the first round and was defeated in the second, when local socialists refused to endorse him.

Although the August–September, 1893, elections registered a shift to the Left, most significantly the socialist Left, Clemenceau's defeat was a shock and a serious loss for the Radicals. Pelletan responded with the standard rhetoric used to explain and negate electoral failure. The election had been stolen through manipulation and intrigue; the authentic will of the people had been distorted. Now the task of all genuine republicans was "to raise high the banner of French democracy, getting away from the intrigues, the machinations, the defamations."[13] The Radical group was far from its heady days of opposition and electoral victories of the early 1880s. A shaken Clemenceau now focused his energy exclusively on journalism, taking on the position of editor in chief as well as political director of La Justice. The staff of the journal was reduced. Pelletan resigned only

11. The contemporary journalist Paul Bosq, though recognizing Clemenceau's strengths, insisted that he was viewed as tyrant and detested by the entire Chamber. Bosq characterized him as an "intelligent cannibal" who stood only for "negation" (Nos Chers Souverains, 58–60).

12. "Marchand d'Orvietan," L'Intransigeant, June 14, 1893.

13. La Justice, no. 4982, September 4, 1893.

a month after the elections. The October 2, 1893, issue of *La Justice* announced Clemenceau's new position and offered no explanation for the changes.[14] Relations between the two men cooled but were never completely broken despite serious political differences in the future.[15] By 1895 Clemenceau abandoned the directorship of *La Justice* and as an isolated former deputy with a tarnished reputation became a free-lance journalist. Pelletan continued his well-established journalistic career, contributing to major Radical papers. He also inherited the leadership of the more militant Radicals in the Chamber, who in 1893 adopted the label of Radical-socialists. The right-wing press luxuriated in lampooning them all and ridiculing the Radical bid for political leadership. "Poor Pelletan, he was so delighted with Clemenceau's defeat!—Finally, he exclaimed, raising his fist to heaven: 'He won't be here anymore to overshadow me; I'll no longer appear as his satellite. I'll shine with my own light. It's my turn to be the sun, pulling into my orbit a mass of stars colored in all the shades of red.' Not at all, poor guy! . . . The humbled Pelletan creeps in after Millerand and Jaurès crying 'Don't leave me!' "[16]

How much did Clemenceau's departure from the Chamber or the Panama scandal really matter in the development and redefinition of left-wing radicalism? In the case of Clemenceau, it clearly deprived the group of a forceful and talented leader, but it also eliminated a domineering personality who had difficulty sharing power. His biographer David Watson identifies the 1893 defeat with the end of Clemenceau's ambitions to head a "dynamic, reforming republican party."[17] When a Radical party eventually formed, Clemenceau was not among its leaders, and his relation with the party remained at best ambivalent. Clemenceau's efforts to affect

14. Interestingly, in this period of political and journalistic difficulties *La Justice* devoted much more attention than in the past to the woman question, perhaps in hope of attracting new readers. See *La Justice*, no. 4559, July 8; no. 4589, August 7, 1892; no. 4743, January 8; no. 4863, May 8, 1893.

15. Clemenceau, who was a senator in 1902, would support Camille Pelletan as minister of the navy, but Pelletan would lead Radicals opposed to Clemenceau's policies as premier in 1906–1909. However, Clemenceau attended Pelletan's funeral in June, 1915. For partial information on the two men's split of 1893, see Duroselle, *Clemenceau*, 315–16, 402.

16. *Le Siècle*, July 18, 1895.

17. Watson, *Clemenceau*, 131.

French politics after 1893 abandoned any reliance on party strength and stressed the force of his individual personality. Yet the temporary efface-ment of Clemenceau did not eliminate the Radicals from parliamentary or national politics, despite all the fervent wishes of the Right. Radicals did, however, have to contend with the much besmirched image of the Re-public, the increasingly hostile attitude toward politicians, and their own continuing disarray.

During the Panama Affair politicians and the parliamentary system were made responsible for a scandal that originated in financial and business cir-cles and was furthered by an extraordinarily venal press. Ultimately no one was held accountable for the swindle, neither politicians, nor the press, nor the company directors, but the republican system was seriously tainted.[18] In 1893, echoing Pelletan's pessimistic sentiments of more than a decade earlier, Stephen Pichon began his New Year's Day article with profound regrets, "sad end and sad beginning of the year." In his view, everything had been in place for a clear and definitive confrontation between "democracy and reaction," especially considering the lines drawn during the Carmaux miners' strike. But the Panama scandals had changed all that. "They . . . upset the political opposition, disorganized the parties, and radically altered the electoral strategy."[19] At the core of this disturbing scandal had been the connection between money and politics, an underlying problem that would persistently plague Radical politicians. Without question, the Panama scan-dal had confirmed that entrepreneurs could influence political decisions and that politicians gave priority to their personal, particular interests over those of the community, the nation. In the late nineteenth century the sym-bolic archetype for this apparently threatening moral inversion of private gain over public good was the modern Jew, the quintessential individual bereft of national identity.

Among many biographical sketches of Cornelius Herz that appeared at the time, one included in a 1912 popular study of the Third Republic is of particular interest. The author was a British journalist who claimed both French and British parents and who was extremely sympathetic to the Republic. His explicit intention was to promote the French parliamentary

---

18. Mayeur, *Débuts de la Troisième République*, 207.
19. *La Justice*, no. 4736, January 1, 1893.

system. Nonetheless, his brief biographical sketch of Herz almost immediately evokes the fascination and repulsion this figure had for the public. "[Herz] was born at Besançon in 1845, but his father was a Bavarian, and Cornelius was taken to the United States . . . and naturalized as an American citizen. . . . He tried various callings . . . practiced medicine without a diploma in San Francisco, and became an agent in France for Thomas Alva Edison. . . . He managed to found . . . both an electric light and a telephone company. . . . [He] posed so successfully as a scientist . . . that the Legion of Honour was conferred on him. Yet, all the while, he was merely a charlatan—one of the first rank. . . . The truth is that Herz had a certain gift of assimilation, and was expert both in sucking the brains of those with whom he came in contact, and draining their purses."[20] Read one way, this purported Herz biography was an exemplary tale of upward social mobility, from obscurity to wealth, public recognition, and association with men of renown. Another reading made it a repulsive account of deception and fraud that bordered on the monstrous destruction of the innocent and the genuinely productive. Many in the 1890s found it comforting to believe that these characteristics were unique to Jews and not shared by prominent men such as de Lesseps or Eiffel. If French politicians behaved in a similar manner, it could be attributed to their association with and infection by men such as Herz.

Radicals themselves had often made similar assertions. Their recurring difficulty in explaining electoral losses, such as Clemenceau's in 1893, encouraged them to search for the conspiratorial actions of nefarious "corrupters" who bought citizens' votes and undermined authentic "universal suffrage." The well-established Radical tradition of attacking "la féodalité financière" made them highly sensitive to the issue of the distorting effects of money on politics. Radicals then were among the few politicians willing to consider the dilemmas of political corruption within the larger context of relations between a representative government, a capitalist economy, and a class society, although this consideration frequently slipped into a populist and nationalist anti-Semitism. Or it remained entirely rhetorical as Radical deputies themselves increasingly experienced pressures for

20. Alfred Ernest Vizetelly, *Republican France, 1870–1912: Her Presidents, Statesmen, Policy, Vicissitudes and Social Life* (Boston, 1913), 357–58.

greater personal income to accompany political success and to maintain a secure bourgeois lifestyle.

Following the 1893 elections the Radicals were in a considerably weaker position than they had been for some time. Although their electoral support had increased and their number in the Chamber had been slightly enlarged, they had lost their most dynamic leader, they had failed to defend the Republic against charges of corruption, and they were increasingly perceived as implicated in that corruption rather than an instrument to eliminate it. They had not clearly elaborated their vision of a democratic state in a democratic society. Most alarming for them, they were faced for the first time with a parliamentary challenge from the Left. The new socialist presence in the Chamber offered an alternative vision of state and society. Finally, the Radicals lost their leverage in republican parliamentary majorities. The moderate republicans turned more often to the Right, aligning themselves with conservatives and even Catholics, who ostensibly were reconciled to the Republic. The moderates' willingness to compromise the anticlerical position outraged Radicals.[21] Even before the 1893 elections, sensing their vulnerability, parliamentary Radicals formally organized and took on the label Radical-socialist. Pelletan assumed the leadership of the group and until the end of the 1890s was its president.

The Radicals' electoral manifesto of 1893 stressed a continuing hostility to former royalists, who had now "rallied" to the Republic, and a reaffirmation of their commitment to serious social reform. The centerpiece of the Radical-socialist reform program was the long-announced progressive income tax. Their electoral statement four years later reiterated the same themes and especially stressed their efforts on behalf of "attempted reforms, especially those that addressed workers' issues." In addition, the Radical-socialist group delicately explained its relations with the socialists. This relationship would be a major preoccupation for the next two decades. Radicals passionately defended individual private property, called for the creation of public services, and repudiated collectivism. At the same time, they recognized the collectivists as dedicated democrats and therefore "did not hesitate, while all the while maintaining their own position, to enter an alliance with the socialists . . . in order to unite all the forces of

21. Baal, "Parti radical," 11.

democracy against the reactionaries."[22] The Radical-socialist group never represented all Radicals but by 1898 did include 74 deputies. (These 74 were part of a larger Radical contingent of 178 within the 585 total number of deputies.) It also expressed an effort to establish a Radical identity as the party of reform and one sympathetic to workers, if no longer their exclusive spokesman.

This Radical-socialist group continued the positions that had already been enunciated in the pages of La Justice following the May Day shooting at Fourmies in 1891 and the bitter Carmaux strike the following year. They were critical of employers' actions, sympathetic to workers, although condemning violence, and anxious to introduce government arbitration. They were especially outraged when the government intervened militarily on behalf of employers.[23] Among Pelletan's last articles in La Justice was a series denouncing the government closing of the Paris labor exchange, La Bourse du travail. In the midst of working-class activity and militancy the republican government identified these worker-run centers as havens for subversion. On May 1, 1893, the republican government shut down the Bourse; two months later troops occupied it. In the press Pelletan accused the government of seeking to provoke a riot so it could use further repressive force. In the Chamber he denounced the government for being more tolerant toward unauthorized religious orders than toward working-class organizations.[24]

Such actions were a preview of an increasingly hostile government attitude toward working-class activity and organizations. Between 1892 and 1894 a series of individual anarchist attacks, most notoriously the assassination of the president of the Republic, Sadi Carnot, in June, 1894, resulted in legislation limiting press and speech. These laws, which their opponents

22. "Manifeste du groupe républicain radical-socialiste de la Chambre des députés," July 28, 1893, and "Manifeste du groupe radical-socialiste de la Chambre des députés," March 30, 1898, in Kayser, Grandes Batailles, 338–47.

23. For Radicals' general attitude on strikes and trade unions, see Leo Loubère, "Left-Wing Radicals, Strikes and the Military, 1880–1907," French Historical Studies, III (1963), 93–105; Loubère, "The French Left-Wing Radicals: Their Views on Trade-Unionism, 1870–1898," International Review of Social History, VII (1962), 203–30; Stone, Search for Social Peace, chap. 6.

24. La Justice, no. 4923, July 7, 1893; see also no. 4924, July 8, 1893; no. 4925, July 9, 1893; no. 4926, July 10, 1893; Annales de l'Assemblée nationale, Chambre des députés, Débats, February 10, 1894, p. 232.

labeled *les lois scélérates*, were often used to harass working-class organizations and restrict socialist newspapers. Pelletan delivered one of the major parliamentary speeches denouncing these laws, although he did not have the support either of all Radical-socialists or of all Radicals. Referring to the recent scandal, Pelletan denounced supporters of the press laws as "Panamistes," seeking to revenge themselves against the journals that had denounced them. More important, he viewed the repressive legislation as a means to control not only the socialist press and organizations but the Radicals as well. In his view, it was the work of the new political reaction which now dominated the Chamber.[25]

The political drift toward a republican center allied with new conservatives in the name of social order was briefly interrupted by the all-Radical government of Léon Bourgeois from November, 1895 to April, 1896. Bourgeois promoted his concept of *solidarité*, which was intended to guarantee social peace and eliminate class conflict. Among Radicals Bourgeois sat with the more moderate *gauche radicale* and had little affinity for Pelletan's rhetoric or his commitment to alliances with the socialists.[26] But like all Radicals, Bourgeois believed that the republican state required a reformed society. One of the first acts of his new government was to reverse earlier executive decisions and reopen the Paris Bourse du travail. Responding to the request of the Paris municipal council, which was dominated by socialists and Radicals, the premier acted to demonstrate the Radicals' confidence in Parisian workers and the government's willingness to associate with their demands. Bourgeois promised the open hand, *la main tendue*, toward workers and general social reform. The survival of the government depended on a very slim parliamentary majority made up of the Radical groups, a small number of moderate republicans uncomfortable with the deepening conciliation toward the church, and the small cluster of socialist deputies. Specifically, Bourgeois's government proposed a progressive income tax as the initial and fundamental reform from which all others would proceed. Radicals had promised this reform for almost three decades.

---

25. Chambre des députés, *Débats*, June–July 28, 1894, esp. 1106, 1112; see also Bellanger et al., *Histoire générale de la presse française*, III, 247. Pelletan first abstained on the vote and then on a second reading voted against the laws with 163 other deputies.

26. Baal, "Parti radical," 11; Stone, *Search for Social Peace*, 26–27.

On March 26, 1896, the Radical finance minister, Paul Doumer, submitted the government proposal for fiscal reform.[27] The deputies never had an opportunity to vote on it, probably much to their relief, but by a bare majority of four votes, the Chamber did pass a confidence measure which explicitly stated its resolution "to replace the personal property tax . . . with a general tax on income."[28] The Senate majority, however, was adamant in its opposition to the tax reform. Less than a month later the Senate demonstrated its lack of confidence in the Radical government and its fiscal reform by withholding funds until Bourgeois resigned. The senators demanded "a constitutional ministry having the confidence of both Chambers."[29] Even the colonial campaign in Madagascar was threatened with delay to end this experiment in Radical government. Once the Senate opposition was clear, Bourgeois resigned with embarrassing haste. Apparently this political conciliator was relieved to step down from a position that required endless confrontations.

There were others, however, who were less willing to abandon the struggle for fiscal reform, Radical government, and the limitation of senatorial power. Several Radicals were furious at Bourgeois for having refused to engage in a constitutional struggle. Throughout the spring, Camille Pelletan addressed crowds of workers, small shopkeepers, and civil servants denouncing the undemocratic actions of the Senate and calling for renewed efforts to implement the income tax. In most instances he shared the platform with his socialist colleagues. Immediately following the Senate's overthrow of the Bourgeois government, a joint socialist and Radical Comité d'action organized a large rally in Paris at the Tivoli-Vauxhall auditorium. Pelletan joined Jaurès and others addressing a crowd of several thousand.[30] In May he addressed twelve hundred trade unionists—half of

27. Soon after the Bourgeois government fell, Doumer was appointed governor general of Indochina by the conservative Méline government. After his return to France, he would be one of the principal opponents to Pelletan and his brand of radicalism. See Chapter VIII.

28. Chambre des députés, *Débats*, March 26, 1896, pp. 822–23.

29. Quoted in Maurice Hamburger, *Léon Bourgeois, 1851–1925. La Politique radicale-socialiste, la doctrine de la solidarité, l'arbitrage internationale et la Société des Nations* (Paris, 1932), 195.

30. "Paris contre le Sénat. Le Meeting du Tivoli. Le Reveil du peuple," *La Petite République*, April 26, 1896; Baal, "Parti radical," 18. Both *La Petite République* and *La Dépêche* of Toulouse reported attendance of ten thousand.

them railroad workers—and continued his denunciations of the Senate and the urgent need for a strong reform government.[31] As much as Bourgeois seemed to welcome the end of his contentious position as head of a Radical government, so did Pelletan seem to welcome his return to the role of opposition leader and the reemergence of the traditional Radical demand to revise the constitution, eliminating the undemocratic Senate.[32]

This opposition intensified when Jules Méline succeeded Bourgeois as premier. Méline had long been a leader of the republican moderates and had served as minister of agriculture in Jules Ferry's government of 1883–1885. He was the architect of the protectionist legislation of 1892. Of all republican politicians of the 1890s he was the most explicit about the advantages of joining with former monarchists and clericals in coalitions of social defense against working-class militancy and Radical reform efforts. Méline had initially been selected as premier to calm the anxieties within the bourgeoisie concerning the Radical proposal for fiscal reform. Daniel Halévy identified Méline's ministry as the most serious threat to the Radicals.[33] All the leading Radicals eagerly engaged in polemics with Méline and his supporters. Not surprisingly, Camille Pelletan was among the most ardent. Speaking in the industrial city of St. Etienne soon after the July Fourteenth holiday of 1897, Pelletan called for a "war to the death with this reactionary government" and the alliances of all authentic republicans—socialists, Radicals, and even moderates, if "there were any republicans left among them," he quipped. He decried the political direction of the Republic, which in his view had become "worse than the monarchy."[34] As the 1898 elections approached, the rhetoric became even more heated. Addressing an audience of almost a thousand in Nantes, Pel-

31. Police report, Saintes, May 9, 1896, in Ministère de l'Intérieur, Notes de la Police de l'Intérieur, Dossier Camille Pelletan, MI 25359, AN.

32. For a fuller analysis of the Bourgeois government see Hamburger, *Bourgeois*, and, particularly for its relation to reform efforts, see Stone, *Search for Social Peace*, chap. 3.

33. Halévy, *République des comités*, 34. For a sense of this new conservative alliance see Marcel Fournier, "L'Organisation du parti progressiste," *Revue politique et parlementaire*, XIV (1897), 235–47, and, for a more recent analysis, Lebovics, *Alliance of Iron and Wheat in the Third French Republic*, 160–65.

34. Police report, St. Etienne, July 18, 1897, in Dossier Pelletan, MI 25359, AN.

letan excoriated the government, which he described as subservient to high finance, particularly the Rothschilds, and as the "lackey of the pope."[35]

The Chamber too became a forum to attack the government and its conservative majority. In a debate on railroad policy in late 1896, the Radical Left had an opportunity to reiterate its demand that the state purchase the lines and the need for reduced transportation rates to promote industry and commerce, an issue about which the government was supposedly concerned. Pelletan in particular attacked the high rates of the Compagnie du Nord and its special discounts to foreign customers that enabled them to circumvent the disadvantages of Méline's protectionism. The government was accused of ignoring the railroad company's persistent violations of the customs regulations, making a sham of its own most lauded policies. During the 1897 Chamber debate on the naval budget, Pelletan and Méline clashed directly. Pelletan announced, "I am going to submit once again that perpetual indictment against the navy which the Chamber has heard for twenty years." This year the government's unwillingness to discipline the admiralty further exacerbated the waste, lack of preparedness, and absence of parliamentary control. In a general political atmosphere suffused with thickening patriotic rhetoric, Pelletan concluded his criticism of the navy and the government with a call to national duty. The Chamber was urged "to do your duty toward the French nation by demanding that the vices of the navy be corrected." Méline, after conceding that the government would study the charges of inadequate preparation, turned on Pelletan and questioned his motives and his loyalty. He denounced what he recognized as "purely political objectives" behind these criticisms. Méline admonished that genuine "patriots would avoid pessimism."[36]

Despite increasingly militant and left-wing rhetoric, Radicals of the late 1890s were floundering. Once again they felt that their electoral gains had been stolen from them. The Radical-socialist manifesto for the 1898 elections characterized the entire decade as one in which "reactionary and clerical forces . . . have exerted an ever more noticeable influence on the

35. This April 7, 1898, meeting was organized by the socialist federation of Nantes. See Police report, *ibid.*

36. Chambre des députés, *Débats*, December 5, 1896, pp. 873–79, December 14, 1896, pp. 1129, 1141–42, 1146, 1178.

government's politics." The only advantage in this politically deplorable situation was that now political choices were clear. Radicals claimed that after almost two years of the Méline ministry, "two politics are clearly facing one another: The reactionary politics of conservatism and clericalism, and the politics of democratic and social progress." The manifesto closed cautiously hoping that the nation would endorse democratic progress and would support Radicals in their effort to accomplish those long-deferred reforms necessary to "direct the Republic definitively toward democracy."[37] The difficulty was that unless the parliamentary composition changed drastically, Radicals could not forge the powerful majority necessary to support reforms, as the fragility and brevity of the Bourgeois experiment had demonstrated. In addition, they were facing new criticism from the socialists on their Left, which made the more moderate Radicals particularly uncomfortable. It was not at all clear that Radicals could agree among themselves on what reforms were essential for a democratic platform. Finally, there were doubts about whether the anticlerical strategy being used against the Méline ministry could generate a program of governing or even unite the opposition. The 1898 elections shifted the Chamber slightly to the Left and undermined Méline's majority, but the new government led by the Radical Henri Brisson hardly seemed to possess the dynamic leadership needed to create a democratic Republic. Failing to respond to the mounting pressure of the Dreyfus crisis, it proved ineffectual and drifted toward the political center.

This Radical uncertainty corresponded to a more general political and cultural atmosphere in which the traditional republican associations and loyalties seemed to have lost their coherence. Most striking was the transformation of nationalist sentiment during the final years of the nineteenth century. Trends begun during the Boulangist movement accelerated in the 1890s, enabling both republican conservatives of the Méline variety and the far Right to identify with a nationalist resurgence. A principal objective of the several conservative and moderate republican governments of the 1890s had been the strengthening of the army and the improvement of France's international position. They accomplished both. De Freycinet, holding the position of minister of war through several governments from

---

37. Manifeste du Groupe Radical-socialiste de la Chambre des députés, March, 1898, in Kayser, *Grandes Batailles*, 346–47.

1888 to 1892, reorganized and expanded the army. He instituted a three-year draft in 1889, which shifted the emphasis to a conscript force while still maintaining the prestige of the professional army and modernizing its equipment. The government presented the alliance with czarist Russia as a dramatic diplomatic breakthrough. Tentatively concluded in the summer of 1891, secretly confirmed the following year, and finally fully approved in January, 1894, this foreign policy achievement reorganized international diplomacy. The aligning of the Republic with the most autocratic state in Europe, one that had long been a target of Radical denunciations, astonished the world.[38]

The Russian alliance was the consequence of domestic political developments which the Radicals decried and another element transforming popular attitudes in directions the Radicals feared. By the time the first accords were signed, French investment banks were already heavily committed to Russian loans. The role of financial institutions was critical in initiating and then sustaining this diplomatic innovation. As significant for the Radicals was the changing tenor of urban popular sentiments and new attitudes within the political and cultural elites. An outpouring of popular enthusiasm greeted the new military alliance, and many among the cultural elite were eager to legitimate these new international ties. The December, 1893, visit of the Russian fleet to Toulon was the occasion of a series of grand festivities on the Côte d'Azur. The visit three years later of Czar Nicholas II and Czarina Alexandra officially and publicly sealed the new alliance. A jubilant reception of over a million Parisians welcomed them.[39] The monarchs joined the premier, Jules Méline, in dedicating the new bridge spanning the Seine named for the czar's father, Alexander III, one of the most reactionary Russian rulers of the nineteenth century. Debora Silverman, in a provocative study of French Art Nouveau, has suggested that the very style of the bridge, the ornate, luxuriant rococo revival that

---

38. *La Justice*, no. 427, March 17, 1881. Pelletan was outraged when the Chamber declared an official mourning for Czar Alexander II following his assassination. Twenty-four years later, Pelletan, sharing the platform with Ferdinand Buisson, another prominent Radical, fervently denounced the czarist government's repression of the 1905 Revolution (Camille Pelletan, *La Révolution en Russie. Discours*. Société des amis du peuple russe et des peuples annexés [Paris, 1905]).

39. Jean Denis Bredin, *L'Affaire* (Paris, 1983), 156–57.

flourished at the end of the century, was a means to join the two apparently different political cultures.[40]

For the Radicals these new assertions of national, military, and diplomatic strength presented a serious dilemma. Fervent nationalism had always been a central element of the revolutionary inheritance. Radicals prided themselves that their fathers had been the strongest defenders of France against the Prussians in 1870–1871. They had always been eager to defend the army and wanted desperately to republicanize it. At the same time, they were suspicious of militarism, particularly when it promoted an aristocratic elitism and showed a fondness for the church. By the late 1890s, then, the Radicals often seemed poorly equipped to confront a changing political climate whose ultimate direction remained unclear. The new republican conservatism of Méline placed the Radicals in the opposition. But they had difficulty defining the content of that opposition because new forces on the Left challenged their traditional stance as social reformers and representatives of the "people," and a reorganized Right assailed their claims to defend the nation and the Republic.

The Dreyfus Affair resolved the political quandary in which the Radicals found themselves. Ultimately the affair permitted the Radicals to identify a clear threat to the Republic and to present themselves convincingly as the only reliable defenders of the state and republican ideals. By 1899 and even more so in 1902, this strategy mobilized powerful electoral support determined to create a more genuinely republican Republic. When the Radicals took up this task and this identity as republican defenders in 1899, they adopted it with all sincerity, never doubting that they alone were equipped to fulfill this responsibility. Yet there was much irony in the political benefits the Radicals reaped from the Dreyfus Affair. As has been well documented, the entire political elite of the 1890s, with the exception of such extreme anti-Semites as Edouard Drumont, refused to admit that there was any Dreyfus Affair. The Radicals, like the socialists, accepted the military court's condemnation of Captain Alfred Dreyfus for espionage in late 1894 and gave the case little attention. Clemenceau's January 7, 1895, article in La Justice, "La Dégradation du Traître," was typical. Covering the military ritual that stripped Dreyfus of his rank, the report sympathized with

40. Silverman, Art Nouveau in Fin-de-Siècle France, 159.

the anti-Dreyfusard crowd, which Clemenceau described as "calm." Unlike Clemenceau, the right-wing nationalist Maurice Barrès in his account, "La Parade du Judas," recorded the cries of "death to the Jews . . . death to Judas." Both articles left no doubt that a dangerous spy had been convicted and properly punished.[41]

Generally ignoring the efforts of the Dreyfus family to reopen the case, most deputies refused to admit the possibility of error or worse on the part of the military. Not until 1898 were the politicians forced to admit that a controversy existed and that it stirred intense passions outside the Chamber of Deputies. Most deputies, like Méline, hoped to keep the affair out of the August–September elections. The Radical political leaders continued to maintain a considerable distance from those few maverick politicians who were beginning to take up the Dreyfusard cause. At the local level occasional Radicals took up the anti-Semitic crusade against Dreyfus.[42] The affair was the latest episode in the development of a significant, modern anti-Semitic movement that originated in the 1880s. This phenomenon was not limited to France but had even more virulent expressions in other European states.[43] The Boulanger Affair, the prolific polemics of Edouard Drumont, and the Panama scandal all contributed to the specifically French expression of the assumption that Jews were the cause of a whole range of social, economic, and cultural difficulties. Jean Bredin, the most recent historian of the Dreyfus Affair, attributes the persuasiveness of this new anti-Semitism to its contradictory but powerful mix of "counter-revolutionary thought, Catholic tradition, and a populist, socialist-tinged anti-capitalism." During the height of the affair in early 1898, anti-Jewish riots occurred in Nantes, Nancy, Rennes, Bordeaux, Epinal, Bar-le-Duc, Marseilles, and, of course, Paris. Thousands were involved in attacks on Jewish stores, homes, and synagogues. In Algeria there was a series of at-

41. *La Justice*, no. 5470, January 7, 1895; Maurice Barrès cited in Bredin, *L'Affaire*, 12. For unanimity on Dreyfus' guilt in 1894–95, see *ibid.*, 100.

42. Kayser, *Grandes Batailles*, 260; Nancy Fitch, "Mass Culture, Mass Parliamentary Politics, and Modern Anti-Semitism: The Dreyfus Affair in Rural France," *American Historical Review*, XCVII (February, 1992), 73–76.

43. For the originality and importance of French anti-Semitism see Sternhell, *Droite révolutionnaire*.

tacks against the large Jewish community.[44] In an excellent study, Nancy Fitch has demonstrated that violent hatred against Jews was not limited to urban areas but became an important issue in several rural campaigns during the 1898 elections. This efflorescence of anti-Semitism posed particular problems for many Radicals.[45]

This was especially the case for Camille Pelletan, leader of the Radical left wing. Anti-Jewish sentiment ran deep among Radicals because many linked it to their most fervent anticlerical beliefs. For Pelletan one of the obvious negatives of Christianity was its connection with Judaism. He frequently belittled Christian beliefs as nothing more than "mementos of a Jewish myth."[46] Even more clearly, Pelletan shared that anticapitalist sentiment that often identified "la féodalité financière" with Jews. He had called for the abrogation of the 1870 decree which automatically conferred French citizenship on the entire Jewish community of Algeria. The Rothschilds and their dominant influence among the regents of the Bank of France had long infuriated him. In the mid-1890s he proposed that the Rothschilds be excluded from the governing body of the Bank of France because of their international connections. Pelletan insisted that the Rothschilds had betrayed France in 1870 when they refused to extend credit to Gambetta in his effort to maintain an army against the Prussians.[47] His attacks on the Rothschilds brought him to the attention of Edouard Drumont. The police files on Drumont document a series of meetings between the two men in June and July, 1895. Both opposed the moderate government of Alexandre Ribot, and both were exploring strategies to upset the coalesc-

44. Bredin, L'Affaire, 35, 266–67.

45. Fitch, "Mass Culture," 57–58, 92–93. This position is contested in Michael Burns, *Rural Society and French Politics: Boulangism and the Dreyfus Affair, 1886–1900* (Princeton, 1984). Significantly, Clemenceau, one of the most important leaders of the Dreyfusard movement, rarely discussed anti-Semitism. His biographer Duroselle surveyed Clemenceau's Dreyfusard articles and found that out of a total of 655 articles only 5 had the word *Jew* in the title (*Clemenceau*, 452–53).

46. *La Justice*, no. 548, July 10, 1881.

47. For an example of Pelletan's attack on Rothschild, see *Le Progrès du Loiret. Organe démocratique et républicain*, June 18, 1899; for Pelletan's general hostility to Jewish bankers, see his article on the German banker Bleichroder, Bismarck's close associate, *La Justice*, no. 559, July 27, 1881. See also Baal on Radicals and anti-Semitism and Pelletan in particular ("Parti radical," 49–51).

ing of conservative republicanism. The police reporter never determined the exact nature of the Drumont-Pelletan meetings but speculated that the two came together because they had already been in contact over matters concerning railroad companies. In addition, the report suggested that Pelletan might be serving as an intermediary between Drumont and certain non-Marxist socialists in an effort to develop "a parallel campaign against the government."[48] The discussions ended badly, and by September, 1895, Drumont's *Libre Parole* was accusing Pelletan of having been in the pay of the very railroad companies he so often denounced.[49]

Much like his flirtation with Drumont, Pelletan's stance on anti-Semitism and the Dreyfus Affair vacillated.[50] He long hesitated to take a position and appeared distinctly uncomfortable with the prospect of defending the Jewish captain. Like most of his parliamentary colleagues, Pelletan ignored the case for four years. After 1898 that tactic was increasingly untenable. The actions of the small group of Dreyfusards and the vociferous challenges of nationalists and anti-Semites forced Pelletan and other deputies to formulate a position. In January, 1898, Emile Zola's article "J'Accuse," appeared in Clemenceau's paper, *L'Aurore*. Clemenceau, whose views had changed dramatically since 1895, disseminated this passionate attack on the government and the army General Staff, initiating the public and political Dreyfus Affair.[51] In August, 1898, Colonel Hubert Henry of army intelligence and chief among Dreyfus's accusers was arrested. His suicide convinced some that the Dreyfusard claim of an army conspiracy

48. Police reports, June 1 and July, 8, 1895, in Ministère de l'Intérieur, Notes de la Police de l'Intérieur, Dossier Edouard Drumont, MI 25320, AN. These were brought to my attention by Bertrand Joly, conservator at the Archives Nationales, who is preparing a study of Paul Déroulède.

49. *La Libre Parole*, September 9, 21, 1895.

50. Pelletan was always aware that there were obvious contradictions between anti-Semitism and republican beliefs. In an 1889 article attacking the Rothschilds, Pelletan explicitly denied any sympathy for anti-Semitism: "Never . . . have we been in any way disposed toward a return to the past that is called anti-Semitism. One of the honors of 1789 is to have given to members of the Jewish community their legitimate human rights" (*La Justice*, no. 3424, May 30, 1889).

51. Clemenceau's role in the Dreyfusard movement was critical. His was motivated both by a commitment to individual justice and an acute sense of how to upset the conservative consensus of the 1890s. Throughout he operated as an individual and parliamentary outsider. See Watson, *Clemenceau*, 145–49; Duroselle, *Clemenceau*, 436–44.

at the highest levels might have merit. It began to seem possible that an innocent man had been accused, condemned, and incarcerated. Yet Pelletan still hesitated to be drawn into a case which he still saw as a diversion manipulated by conservative republicans. Before the April, 1898, elections Pelletan continued to attack Méline as a conservative linked to Catholic interests and also tied to the private firms of the Haute Banque dominated by the "cosmopolitan" Rothschilds, who, like the clericals, threatened the Republic. In Nantes a few days later he renewed these charges against Méline.[52] His campaign statement was unique in its emphasis on local issues. He stressed his success in defending the interests of his constituents and in delivering material benefits to his electors. The short description of his national policies underscored his patriotism and his concern for military preparedness. He again alluded to his attempt to remove the Rothschilds from among the regents of the Bank of France. "I unsuccessfully called for the Chamber to remove the key to our military treasury from [the control of] international high finance."[53] Though he was violently opposed to the Méline government, he did not distinguish himself clearly from the anti-Dreyfusards.

A year later and at the height of a serious government crisis as the consequence of the Dreyfus Affair, Pelletan's attitude had changed. In a long speech before an audience of fifteen hundred in Orléans, just south of Paris, Pelletan began to delineate his position on the affair. Most important was to expose the enemies of the Republic. They were "high finance [*la Haute Banque*], the Church, clericalism." He did not retract any of his criticism directed against Jews associated with high finance. "What we object to among too great a number of Jews, is this financial situation which makes them in reality masters of France." At the same time he insisted that the anti-Semites were merely another group of clericals and that no true "son of the Revolution" could agree with them. "We do not object to Jews in general, we are too much sons of '89 to admit of original sin and that men are unworthy because of their birth." But he promised that he would continue to attack those "cosmopolitan Jews [*juifs internationaux*] who threatened the existence of the French nation." He stressed that only the Radicals

52. Police reports, Romilly sur Seine, April 5, 1898, and Nantes, April 7, 1898, in Dossier Pelletan, MI 25359, AN.
53. Camille Pelletan, "Profession de foi," May 5, 1898, *ibid.*

could be counted on to do this. For despite all their anti-Semitic ravings the clericals would always do the bidding of high finance. The clericals and nationalists had deceived some citizens by capitalizing on anti-Semitism. The only authentic patriots remained the Radicals, who alone were willing to defend both the "material blood and soil of France" and the ideal France of liberty and equality. A month later, in July, 1899, addressing the Lyons Bourse du travail, Pelletan became even more explicit about the need to defend the seriously endangered Republic against the "agents of reaction." He was repeatedly interrupted and shouted down; the police identified the disrupters as Blanquists and anarchists, as well as self-proclaimed anti-Semites. The following year the intense confrontations generated by the affair were diminishing and the political coalition of vindicated Dreyfusards was taking more definitive shape. Pelletan now evoked three somewhat modified enemies of the Republic—plutocracy, clericalism, and militarism. Perhaps protesting too much, he reiterated, that "he is not . . . an enemy of the Jews, but he has fought the association of Jewish financiers . . . he is above all a patriot." He ended major addresses in Perpignan and Dijon with calls to "a union of all republican parties to save the Republic and the French nation."[54] Pelletan never became a committed Dreyfusard, as some of his Radical colleagues did, but like them he concluded that the anti-Dreyfusards—the nationalists, the clericals, and the anti-Semites— were a serious threat to the Republic he hoped to construct.[55] The affair provided an opportunity to demonstrate to the electorate that Radicals were the inevitable and most qualified leaders of the Republic.

The insistence of the army General Staff and its political supporters that the civilian government could not question military justice and the

54. *Le Progrès du Loiret. Organe démocratique et républicain*, June 18, 1899; Police reports, June 18, 1899, July 3, 1899, Police report on speech to two thousand, Perpignan, May 16, 1900, and Police report on meeting of twenty-five hundred Comité d'étudiants républicain, Dijon, April 1, 1900, in Dossier Pelletan, MI 25359, AN.

55. Henry's suicide finally convinced Pelletan of Dreyfus' innocence, according to his laudatory biography by Révillon, *Camille Pelletan*, 130; Bredin notes that Pelletan and other Radicals still viewed Dreyfus as guilty until after the elections of 1898 (*L'Affaire*, 282); Clemenceau's biographer David Watson claims that the Radicals essentially remained anti-Dreyfusard up to the time of Dreyfus' second trial in the late summer of 1899 (*Clemenceau*, 147); Gérard Baal notes the explicitly racist anti-Semitism of the influential editor of Radical *La Dépêche* of Toulouse, Arthur Huc ("Parti radical," 51).

decision of militant Catholics, particularly the Assumptionist order, to take up the cause of the army forced even a reluctant Pelletan to become a nominal Dreyfusard. By 1900 the clericals, nationalists, and anti-Semites who had proclaimed Dreyfus's guilt were politically on the defensive, even though the 1899 military retrial again condemned Dreyfus, but "extenuating circumstances" reduced the sentence.[56] The moderate senator René Waldeck-Rousseau formed an energetic government of republican defense in June, 1899. Inadvertently but inevitably Radicals gained ever greater influence in the parliamentary majority. The well-established Radical agenda—centered on the need to republicanize the state, especially the military services, and on the need to control, if not disestablish, the Catholic church—was vindicated. It no longer appeared an extreme partisan platform, but rather urgently needed state policy. The alternate political direction which Catholic moderates and republican conservatives had attempted to follow during the 1890s—the formation of a conservative center—was discredited. Méline's initial success in marginalizing the Radicals was reversed.

Despite his position as head of this left-leaning republican coalition, Waldeck-Rousseau had no intention of abandoning his moderate goals and his objective to restore political stability. Throughout his government of republican defense he concentrated on restraining the enthusiasm of his own majority, particularly in their efforts to reform the army and the fiscal system.[57] Pelletan was never a strong supporter of Waldeck-Rousseau and constantly criticized the premier's past and current moderate inclinations.[58] Joining most of the socialists, Pelletan abstained during the first vote of confidence for the Waldeck-Rousseau government. But like many other Radicals, his commitment grew as the new government began to move against

56. The new republican government of René Waldeck-Rousseau then pardoned Dreyfus and in November issued a general amnesty for everyone involved in the affair. Many committed Dreyfusards, Clemenceau in particular, viewed this conclusion as a betrayal of their efforts. They had sought an unambiguous reversal of the original condemnation and the prosecution of those in the military who had perpetrated this injustice (Bredin, L'Affaire, 395–402).

57. Pierre Sorlin, Waldeck-Rousseau (Paris, 1966), 449–50; Baal, "Parti radical," 75–76. For a more positive view of Waldeck-Rousseau's government see Bredin, L'Affaire, 363–66.

58. Police report, February, 1901, in Police générale, Situation politique, 1899–1905, F7 12553, AN.

the church and the unauthorized Catholic orders. During the debate on the government-proposed Law on Associations, Pelletan argued passionately for the expulsion of the orders. In one especially inspired oration he turned the claims of the nationalists and clericals upside down. "Piety has never penetrated very deeply into the French race. No other country has always been more rebellious against the power of the clergy; no other country has better maintained, in the face of the highest, the most moving and most majestic religious concepts, its indefinable freedom to laugh which the genius of our writers have made into the most powerful weapon for emancipation in the world. . . . A different worship . . . the entirely worldly religion of civil sovereignty . . . that is our history; that is our national character."[59] The Radicals' continuing ability to claim the patriotic fervor as their own and to invest the post-Dreyfusard political agenda with passion gave them a particular advantage in the ensuing political and electoral confrontations.

But passion and rhetoric alone were not sufficient in the new political climate of 1901. Parliamentary power was within their grasp but still eluded the Radicals. The head of government was a man who only four years earlier had pledged himself to form a conservative coalition to defeat radicalism. Nationalists and clericals, though now less aggressive, had not disappeared. Although they had little influence in either the Chamber or the Senate and had lost much credibility, the nationalists increased their popularity in the politically and culturally important capital. In 1900 they temporarily gained control of the Paris municipal council with a smashing defeat of Parisian Radicals.[60] Furthermore, the church and the army, though shaken, still retained enormous power and what the Radicals saw as great privileges. Radicals were determined to capitalize on their unexpected prominence following the Dreyfus Affair and transform it into a

59. Chambre des députés, *Débats*, March 11, 1901, pp. 885–86. The Michelet and Rousseauean mix of nationalism and anticlericalism is especially strong.

60. Radicals and socialists had an overwhelming majority on the council in 1896 and took strong Dreyfusard positions. In 1900 thirty seats went to nationalists largely supported by a middle-class constituency. In 1904 the coalition of socialists and Radicals regained a majority, which they maintained until 1909. These changing majorities after 1900 were the result of small shifts among mostly lower-middle-class voters. See David Robin Watson, "The Nationalist Movement in Paris, 1900–1906," in *The Right in France, 1890–1919*, ed. David Shapiro (Carbondale, 1962), 49–84.

permanent position of political preeminence that would bring them control of the state. They sought an unambiguous popular endorsement in the next legislative election, and to that end they organized a political party.

Analyses of the Parti républicain radical et Radical-socialiste, which was inaugurated on June 23, 1901, have always stressed its weak structure and lack of genuine discipline. I, too, will explore these fundamental obstacles to party effectiveness. We should not forget, however, that among nonsocialists only the Radicals possessed any party structure. To the right of the Radicals, politics remained a highly individualistic affair in which requests for intermittent electoral support were followed by intricate negotiations among shifting groups in the Chamber. The Radicals intended to change this traditional form of political behavior. They sought to tie local Radical committees to national politics more permanently and more securely. It was precisely this development which Daniel Halévy charted with such dismay in his 1934 study *La République des comités*. Yet at the same time that Radicals introduced greater structure, an increasingly national perspective, and a role for local militants, they did not jettison the older, individualistic political traditions. The official name of the party—Républicain radical et Radical-socialiste—made clear that this was not a powerful union but rather the alliance (perhaps even temporary) of at least two preexisting, distinct parliamentary affiliations. There was also never any question about the essential function of the Radical party; its purpose was to win elections.

According to most reports, the initiative for the inaugural party congress came from leaders of Parisian Radical organizations who may have been especially sensitive to the need to maintain and enlarge the strategy of republican defense. By 1895 two Paris-based groups, the Comité central d'action républicaine and the Association pour les réformes républicaines, had joined forces under the name Comité d'action pour les réformes républicaines.[61] This umbrella group brought together youth associations, Masonic lodges, Radical newspapers, local committees, and some deputies. It had been active between 1896 and 1898 in directing opposition to Méline's conservative concentration. This committee issued the invitation in April, 1901, to the inaugural congress. The influential Comité républicain

61. For an 1894 appeal for concerted electoral and parliamentary action see "Appel de l'Association pour les réformes républicaines," in Kayser, *Grandes Batailles*, 350–51.

du commerce et de l'industrie, headed by the president of the jewelry manufacturers' association and a principal source of Radical campaign financing, supported the appeal. The critical endorsement of the Masonic Lodges of the Grand Orient further strengthened the invitation. The Masonic organization viewed this new attempt at political organization as an extension of its own efforts to organize Radical and republican opinion in support of the Waldeck-Rousseau government. For the July Fourteenth celebration of 1900 the Grand Orient had brought together a range of Radical groups in a successful demonstration of republican loyalty. This Parisian, but not parliamentary, call met an enthusiastic response in the provinces among local Radical committees, newspapers, and provincial Masonic lodges. Significant pressure for a national organization existed at the local level. When the 1,132 delegates to the congress assembled, they represented 476 local Radical committees, 155 Masonic lodges, 215 newspapers, 849 departmental and municipal officeholders, 78 senators, and 201 deputies. This was an impressive display of the breadth and depth radicalism had attained.[62]

From its initiation, the core element of the Radical party was the local committee in which deputies, departmental and municipal officials, and citizens came together to promote the Radical cause and candidates. Individual membership in the Radical party was possible but unusual. Citizens adhered to the party primarily through local committees. In 1901, 476 committees had responded to the invitation; by 1903, 600 were affiliated with the party and two years later the number stood at 912.[63] A few Radical departmental federations existed before the formation of the party, and more were established after 1901. The Seine and Rhône federations were the largest. Departmental federations had grown to twenty in number before 1914 and influenced the shaping of electoral alliances. In addition, regional organizations began to appear, such as the Federation of the Southeast established in 1907. But because most political life occurred either at the local level of the arrondissement and the Radical committee or at the national level in the Chamber, these intermediate structures had only limited influence on the direction of the party. In addition, those federations

62. Rebérioux, *La République Radicale?*, 51–53; Berstein, *Histoire du parti radical*, I, 38–41.
63. In 1908 approximately eight hundred committees had joined the party. The drop between 1905 and 1908 may reflect conflicts among Radicals which are analyzed in a later chapter. See Bardonnet, *Evolution de la structure du parti radical*, 43.

that did exist anxiously protected their autonomy from the central party organization. Often they served as vehicles to protest what they perceived as an excess of centralization.

The annual congress, which met in a different city for four days, usually in October, established the official program and direction of the party. Approximately eight hundred delegates attended, and, whether or not it influenced the actions of Radical deputies, it did serve as a critically important ritual, annually reconfirming Radical beliefs and commitment. The party never established a definitive procedure for the selection of delegates, thus giving occasion for disputes over credentials. The congresses voted for the party program and heard a variety of special reports. They elected, usually unanimously, the Executive Committee and the party president, who inevitably was a parliamentarian, the post often given as a reward for an arduous defense of the Radical cause in the parliamentary arena.[64] The Executive Committee had responsibility for implementing the party program, directing the party between congresses, establishing the agenda for the next congress, maintaining party discipline, and approving locally selected candidates. Despite its ostensible importance, the Executive Committee had only limited power, partly because of its unwieldy size of several hundred, but even more because its own members, especially those holding elected office, resisted any form of centralized organization. The Executive Committee clearly was not intended to handle day-to-day issues. It designated a much smaller (first seventeen, then thirty-three members) Bureau du comité executif, which occasionally attempted to impose direction, usually with limited results.

The principal dilemma facing the party was to establish clearly the relation between the party and elected officials who affiliated with it. Radical deputies had been operating for decades before the existence of the Radical party. Parliamentarians had considerable influence on and in the Executive Committee from the founding of the party; after 1909 they were designated as "membres de droit," inevitably dominating that body. This automatic inclusion of Radical deputies and senators guaranteed the unreasonable size

64. Combes was president in 1905–1906 and again in 1910–13, Pelletan in 1906–1907, and Joseph Caillaux in 1913–14, when he defeated the elderly Pelletan.

of the Executive Committee.[65] Initially many of the parliamentarians were wary of this new organization, which they suspected of threatening their independence. Clemenceau, already an outsider among Radical politicians, first because of his absence from the National Assembly for almost eight years following the Panama scandal, and second because of his prominent position within the Dreyfusard movement, always maintained his distance from the party. Significantly, he never attended any party congress, including the inaugural one. When he served as premier in 1906–1909, the party Bureau du comité executif condemned his policies. By 1909 he let his largely nominal affiliation with the Radical party lapse. Although Clemenceau's case was extreme, it indicated the difficulties of reconciling party organization with the already established power of individual Radical politicians.

Camille Pelletan was also initially suspicious of the party, fearing that more moderate Radicals such as Léon Bourgeois intended to use it to control the direction of radicalism. Unlike Clemenceau, Pelletan's response was to plunge into party activity and establish his left-wing radicalism as an undeniable force within local committees, at congresses, and in the governing bodies of the party. In 1906 the annual congress elected him president. Most Radical parliamentarians soon recognized the advantages the party offered without placing many restrictions on their activity. Often they energetically participated in the party because, from the beginning, it constantly reiterated the privileged position of elected representatives.

Despite efforts to establish party discipline, Radical deputies essentially remained autonomous, often deviating dramatically from the party program. The party had few effective mechanisms for disciplining members. The 1906 congress, for example, was preoccupied with questions of discipline.[66] Militants were outraged that nominal Radical deputies had led the attack on a Radical government. Yet only in 1910 did the party demand that deputies who were members must adhere exclusively to parliamentary groups affiliated with the Radical party. It was not until the following year that Radical deputies finally formed a Groupe du parti in the Chamber and insisted that all deputies who were members of the party must belong

65. The Executive Committee continued to expand. In 1904, there were 475 members; by 1910, 680 (Bardonnet, *Evolution de la structure du parti radical*, 93, 99–100).

66. See Chapter VIII for greater detail.

only to this group. Even then the effort was not entirely successful.[67] Most important, the party never succeeded in imposing voting discipline on Radical deputies. Often this battle over discipline was fought among Radical deputies themselves with parliamentary leaders frequently taking opposing stands. During the 1906 congress Pelletan, about to be elected party president, spoke both for and against increased discipline. He agreed that the Executive Committee needed to have greater authority over deputies, but he insisted that the Radical party must not adopt the socialists' insistence on orthodoxy. It was one of the few occasions that Pelletan used the socialists as a negative example. He concluded, "As for me, whatever program you may establish, if it includes an article which I would consider bad, I would fight against it and I would expect that you would exclude me from the party."[68] Without question, this lack of discipline, combined with the almost exclusive focus on the parliament and the tremendous influence of parliamentarians within the party, limited the ability of the Radical party to implement its programs. Nonetheless, these characteristics, particularly the prominence of the deputy, were the result of the Radicals' primary concern with electoral victories, which in turn was the result of their central ideological commitment to "universal suffrage." No one ever apologized for the fact that the purpose of the party was to build electoral support. Elections and voting were the essential responsibilities of citizens to the Republic and the nation.

The spring of 1901 appeared to many, particularly to grass-roots Radicals, the appropriate moment to take the unusual step in French politics of forming a structured party with some life outside the parliament. They were inspired by the specifically Radical sentiments of fear for the security of the Republic and hope that finally they would implement the authentic republican Republic. Since 1896 Radicals had been unable to counter the ever stronger drift toward a conservative construction of state and society. The Dreyfus Affair revealed the intensity of persistent antirepublican sentiment within the church and, most alarming for Radicals, within the army and among its civilian supporters. Radicals were fundamentally convinced

67. Bardonnet, *Evolution de la structure du parti radical*, 153.

68. Le Parti républicain radical et radical-socialiste, 6ᵉ *Congrès*, tenu à Lille, October, 1906, pp. 197–99.

that the genuine Republic was in danger and that only they could both save and create it. At the party's inaugural congress Camille Pelletan was given the task of expressing this renewed commitment to republican defense and creation. Although initially a bit wary of the efforts to organize a party, he not only served on the organizing committee but eagerly accepted his role of providing oratorical inspiration to the delegates. He would elaborate this role for the rest of his life.

Like so many of his later speeches, Pelletan's party declaration delivered on the closing day of the congress was strewn with clichés, but these clichés revealed deeply held Radical beliefs and the desired direction of the party. The delegates, whom Pelletan described as "a crowd of good citizens coming here from every corner of France," warmly received the speech. The urgent need for "all sons of the Revolution" to mount an effective republican defense against a devious enemy with many faces explained the purpose of this gathering. Such a defense had been a continuous theme throughout nineteenth-century French republicanism. But defense alone would not be effective. "The best means to defend the Republic is to render it republican." Five major areas of public, economic, and cultural life called out for such republicanization. Secular culture must be firmly established and clerical privileges ended. The republican state must control "large speculation" and "great capital." In addition, a public sector of the economy would organize both social services and defense interests. Third, long-awaited social reforms must be enacted. Their essential principle would be to defend "the inviolable right of each human being to the product of his labor." Of greatest urgency among these reforms were old age pensions. Fourth, republicanization required fiscal reforms, especially the introduction of the progressive income tax, which would introduce principles of equality into an archaic tax structure. Finally, the state itself at all levels and in every office of every ministry must become thoroughly and truly republican.[69]

Pelletan assured the delegates that this program of defense and republican reforms would be endorsed and supported by "universal suffrage . . . in total possession of itself and its legitimate authority . . . [in] the fullness of its sovereignty." He was confident that the assembled Radicals and their

69. Camille Pelletan, "Déclaration du Parti républicain radical et radical-socialiste," 1er Congrès, tenu à Paris, June 23, 1901, quoted in Buisson, La Politique radicale, 288–92.

program spoke to and for "the great masses of democracy, the millions of unknown . . . the true founders of the Republic." Never once in the speech did Pelletan mention the creation of a Radical party. Rather, he called for a defensive "union of republicans of all varieties against clericalism, against authoritarian enterprises, against the power of money, for the cause of social justice." This coalition was principally intended to win the 1902 legislative elections, but it promised that such electoral victory would engender a new fruitfulness, a new abundance, a new productivity in the Republic and in the nation.[70]

With this still somewhat tentative step toward greater organization the Radicals definitively accepted the republican state as it existed, while continuing to prescribe a series of reforms. Once again, with considerable fanfare, they also reconfirmed their commitment to "universal suffrage" and their dependency on electoral victory as the legitimation of their bid to govern. The Republic and popular sovereignty were threatened and must be defended. Only Radicals could succeed in these tasks. The next chapter examines the Radical principle of "universal suffrage" and the practice of electoral politics by focusing on Camille Pelletan's jurisdiction in the Bouches-du-Rhône.

70. *Ibid.*

V ELECTORAL POLITICS IN THE PROVINCES

The men who formed the Radical party had a clear conception of what constituted the fundamental core of the Republic. Commemorating the fourth anniversary of the then embryonic regime, Camille Pelletan stated that "universal suffrage" both had created the Republic and was its "essence."[1] Eight years later, once again celebrating the declaration of the Republic, Pelletan reiterated the centrality of "universal suffrage" and stressed that this institution had permitted "France to tear itself away from those grim alternatives . . . a few months of revolution . . . and then years of reaction."[2] According to the Radicals, "universal suffrage" was becoming "the leading political principle throughout the world."[3] "Universal suffrage" supported the Republic's claim to a superior legitimacy, resting on the will of the people. "Universal suffrage" was intended to divide political power equally among all citizens and to implement concretely popular sovereignty. Radicals thus viewed the institution of "universal suffrage" as the fulfillment of a long series of political struggles: the Revolution had experimented with "universal suffrage"; it had been tragically betrayed during the Second Republic; and finally with the Third Republic during the 1880s it had triumphed. The defense of "universal suffrage" was a fundamental tenet of the Radical creed. Only the unobstructed exercise of the vote could create an independent citizen, eager to participate in the political life of the nation.

Universal male suffrage was the necessary guarantee of a democratic government that would in turn protect and expand the interests of the voters, "the people." It was never declared as an end in itself. Pelletan and other Radicals argued that the principal justification of the Republic was its ability to provide voters not only with a voice but with an element of

1. *Le Rappel*, no. 1639, September 5, 1874.
2. *La Justice*, no. 2425, September 4, 1886.
3. Camille Pelletan, *Victor Hugo*, 128.

effective political power. Radicals always understood such power to be the ability of individual citizens to elect national representatives whom they could then hold accountable. In the 1880s, as radicalism was defining itself, the militant Radical Charles Laisant declared "universal suffrage as the means to achieve a more just distribution of well being." He linked "universal suffrage" to the very meaning of French national identity, "the only expedient left to France to accomplish her civilizing work and to recover possession of herself." Most Radicals endorsed Laisant's three fundamental, interrelated beliefs: "the Republic, universal suffrage and patriotism."[4]

Ferdinand Buisson, a leading Radical deputy from Paris, provided an excellent definition of "universal suffrage": "[The very essence of universal suffrage] consists precisely in acknowledging that the right to vote . . . no longer belongs to a particular category of citizens, determined by property qualifications, but belongs to the totality of all adult citizens. Fiction, perhaps. Simple convention, you say. But it is the soul of the regime. Democracy is the system which makes the right to vote a natural right, based on the condition of being a human person, and independent of the material, moral, economic or social circumstances in which that person exists."[5] In 1911 Buisson offered this argument to legitimate his unusual support for the extension of votes to women. The Radical commitment to "universal suffrage," however, had always been ambiguous. From its initial implementation most Radicals accepted "universal" to mean exclusively men. For decades Radicals chose to view the exclusion of women from political life as compatible with the claims of "universal suffrage" and popular sovereignty.

Buisson's belated recognition of this contradiction was not widely shared in the Radical party. Much more common were the assumptions expressed during the 1881 Christmas season by a left-wing Marseilles newspaper sympathetic to radicalism, *Le Petit Provençale*. "Christmas—Now's not the time for politics. . . . Ah well! yes it's Christmas. . . . Time for mothers and children to speak. . . . The family recovers its rights, the wife is queen of the

---

4. Laisant, *Anarchie bourgeoise*, vii, 73, 312.

5. Buisson, *Vote des femmes*, 306. Buisson was responding to decades of increasing agitation on the part of women for civil and political rights. Even he added qualifications and stressed the need for gradual change.

hearth."[6] Women and politics had to remain in two separate realms with their distinct seasons and activities. Even the force of a burgeoning suffrage movement would not succeed in dislodging this assumption. The exclusion of half the population from a supposedly universal principle contributed to an underlying incoherence in the Radicals' democratic rhetoric. This massive exclusion in the midst of supposed universality always left open the possibility that further exclusions might be found and accepted.[7]

Although most Radicals refused to address or even publicly recognize the denial of voting rights to women, they nonetheless decried other conditions that they viewed as distorting "universal suffrage." Since the beginning of the Republic they had argued that constitutional structures placed sharp constraints on the practice of universal male suffrage. It functioned only every four years to elect national representatives to the Chamber of Deputies and local representatives to the municipal councils, whose powers were limited by the central administration. Radicals insisted that popular sovereignty, expressed through the vote, be extended to other institutions of the Republic such as the judiciary. Many of the components of the Radicals' program were, at least in part, efforts to eliminate obstacles to the exercise of the vote. These barriers ranged from the ideological power of the Catholic church, to the preponderance of local notables in the indirect elections for the Senate, to the economic influence of large employers and great wealth.

Such obstacles could interfere with and distort the authentic expression of the popular will. Radicals had great difficulty imagining a legitimate opposition because they represented the Republic and therefore the people. It was almost impossible for them to admit that an electoral rejection of their program and candidates could be anything other than some sort of conspiracy, a deception of the electorate. Though passionately committed

6. *Le Petit Provençal*, December 25, 1881.

7. See Chapter VIII for a fuller discussion of the tension between the growing demands for women's suffrage and the Radicals. In addition, republican patriotism occasionally slipped into chauvinistic calls to redefine French citizenship along lines other than birth and naturalization. Calls to expel or exclude groups designated as "un-French" were frequent in the overlapping circles of Radicals and extreme nationalists during the 1880s and 1890s. The royal pretenders, royalists in general, and, with increasing frequency, Jewish financiers and even all Jews were denounced (Vizetelly, *Republican France*, 278).

to the expression of popular sovereignty, they struggled to explain why the exercise of the vote did not consistently or automatically result in their triumph. Usually they fell back on the inadequacy of the electorate and the perfidy of their opponents, who too easily "cheated democracy by persuading people to act against their own interests."[8] The distortion of universal suffrage might also be the result of unscrupulous candidates, some even calling themselves republicans or Radicals, who presented one platform during the election campaign, only to abandon their commitments once they entered parliament.

The Radicals' concern with the integrity of "universal suffrage" went beyond accusations of manipulation and deception. They identified structural problems inhibiting popular sovereignty. Especially in the 1870s and 1880s they carried on a vociferous campaign to dismantle the small-district, single-member electoral system—the *scrutin d'arrondissement*, which the conservative Assembly had enacted in 1875. They sought to introduce an electoral system of voting on a department-wide basis for lists of candidates. They hoped that this reform would encourage clearer party affiliations and programmatic campaigns. Immediately before the summer elections of 1881, Camille Pelletan denounced the existing *scrutin d'arrondissement* as "circumscribing the real political significance of the vote and increasing corruption." He urged "the abolition of this village ballot [*le scrutin de clocher*] in order to create an independent Chamber."[9]

Partly as a result of this Radical pressure, the voting law was changed in 1885 and the departmental list system was used in the next election. The results only partially fulfilled the Radicals' expectations. They welcomed the decline in the number of Opportunists and the increase in Radical strength, but royalists and Bonapartists also made surprising gains. This fragmented political situation contributed to the Boulangist movement. The Opportunists soon demanded a return to the single-member *scrutin d'arrondissement* as protection against Boulangist candidates in the elections of 1889. Despite their fierce opposition to Boulangism, the Radicals consistently rejected this strategy. Contrary to most views, they claimed that only the departmental *scrutin de liste* would expose the reactionary connections

8. Laisant, *Anarchie bourgeoise*, 266.
9. *La Justice*, no. 187, July 20, 1880; no. 490, May 19, 1881.

of the Boulangists.[10] Pelletan reiterated his concerns about local pressures on voters and his deep anxieties that such manipulation would exacerbate the greatest threat of all, growing "political skepticism . . . which undermines the reputation of national representation."[11] This Radical argument failed to convince the panicked Opportunists. It also failed to convince many Radicals, who were severely shaken by the rapidly growing popularity of the Boulangist movement and its apparent willingness to question the very foundations of the republican regime. For example, Marseilles Radicals had never wanted to abandon the single-member electoral district, which reinforced local, personal allegiances.[12] In 1889 the electoral system returned to the *scrutin d'arrondissement*, which remained in effect until 1919.

By the early twentieth century, when the question of the electoral system again became an issue, the majority of Radicals were in very different circumstances. Chastened by the Boulangist experience, their faith in the automatic nature of "universal suffrage" diminished, and as the principal beneficiaries of the parliamentary system, Radicals overwhelmingly supported the *scrutin d'arrondissement* against the sharp criticisms of conservatives and Socialists. Despite this ultimately self-serving transformation, the Radicals had in the early decades of the Republic raised important issues about the workings of popular sovereignty. They grappled with the tensions between the legitimating principle of "universal suffrage" and the difficulties of devising a mechanism to express the popular will accurately. Yet they were often hard-pressed to demonstrate that the act of voting actually translated the voters' choices into authentic political power and effective action.

Examining the specifics of local electoral politics, a series of Camille Pelletan's campaigns in the second district of Aix-en-Provence in the far southern department of the Bouches-du-Rhône permits us to evaluate the

10. The shift to the *scrutin d'arrondissement* was probably not the most significant factor in the defeat of Boulangists. More important was the manipulation and control of the elections exerted by the minister of the interior, coupled with the chaos of the Boulangist movement. See Chapter III.

11. *La Justice*, no. 3261, December 10, 1888.

12. Police report to prefect, June 11, 1885, Activités politiques, M6 3305, AD/BR.

results of this much prized popular sovereignty. By the turn of the century a distinct stereotype of the provincial supporter of radicalism existed, one "rooted among the rural people of the Midi." In his seminal sociocultural study of mid-century republicanism, *La République au village*, Maurice Agulhon recognizes the value of this conventional image. While amplifying and adding nuances, he essentially accepts the "very ancient assumption which explains the republican spirit of the southerner by his taste for politics, which itself is the consequence of sociability inherent in communal . . . or municipal life."[13]

Agulhon's classic study emphasizes the specifically southern context of this political persuasion. He underscores the social and cultural traditions of Provence, a region in which the distinctions between urban and rural, between bourgeois and "populaire," were much less rigid than in the North. Sociability was critical to the cultural, social, and economic existence of Provençal villages and small towns. The *chambrée* or *cercle* was a "grouping of men whose purpose was to meet in the evening, after work, for shared recreation, cards, conversation, etc." Agulhon locates the origin of Provençal democratic culture within this network of acquaintances, neighbors, co-workers, and friends at the points of contact between groups within the bourgeoisie and those whom he identifies as the "people"—artisans, factory workers, and peasants. Democratic convictions were elaborated in this milieu, which linked "the poorest village or small town bourgeois . . . with artisans, the avant-garde of the people." One mid-nineteenth-century observer harshly characterized this strata of the bourgeoisie as "a petite bourgeois youth, idle, intellectual, dissolute, free-thinking, and sociable." Often these young men were disdainfully viewed as "village bohemians, failed university students, physicians without patients, sons of wealthy peasants who, having grown weary of demanding urban careers, had retired from business and were squandering their papas' investments." Agulhon labels this politically significant social strata as "the morally marginal bourgeois."[14]

By 1870, however, the economic structures of this world had begun to change. Certainly the Radical elector would continue to be located in the

13. Agulhon, *La République au village*, 289, 13–14.
14. *Ibid.*, 219, 255–56. Despite Agulhon's claims for the specificity of the South, the social location and aspirations of these young men were not so far removed from those of the young Parisians who established a Radical identity in the 1870s and 1880s.

intersection between the bourgeoisie and the "people," but that intersection, in Provence as elsewhere, was being transformed during the late nineteenth century. The economy of Provence, which included the six departments of the southeast, was divided between the stagnating, rural Alpine interior and the developing coastal areas.[15] There was, however, considerable interaction between these two different economic worlds. To some degree, coastal developments destabilized the more traditional agricultural economy of the highland interior and contributed to its underdevelopment. Most obviously, the more prosperous economy of the coast and especially the burgeoning cities of Marseilles, Nice, and Toulon stimulated the rural exodus from Alpine valleys.[16] Those who remained behind found that the internal composition of their villages had been altered. Long-established rural manufacturing, which had supported artisans and provided seasonal work for peasant families, declined sharply. Inhabitants of highland villages were faced with ever fewer options, forced to rely more exclusively on an archaic polyculture, or leave.

On the coast the ancient Mediterranean commercial tradition was expanding and being reorganized, shifting to new products, new modes of transportation, and new markets. Traditional agricultural towns—particularly those with access to water for irrigation and with access to the insatiable northern markets via the Paris-Lyons-Marseilles railroad—shifted from commercial polyculture to highly specialized, market-oriented monocultures. Where vineyards did not monopolize the land, relatively new fruit orchards and vegetable farming did, often displacing older agricultural products such as olives and wheat. Economic development was striking in the far South, but it rested on a narrow base of agricultural consumer products. Wine production was the most important and among the most volatile. In the 1870s winegrowers experienced a devastating insect blight, phylloxera, which destroyed 25 percent of all French vines. The value of the 1887–1889 harvests was less than half that of 1871–1875. Wine pro-

15.   The six departments were the Hautes Alpes, the Basses Alpes (now called Les Alpes de Haute Provence), the Vaucluse, the Bouches-du-Rhône, the Var, and the Alpes Maritimes.

16.   Half of all migrants to Marseilles at the turn of the century originated from the surrounding region. See Christian Gras, "Les Disparités économiques régionales," in L'Ere industrielle et la société d'aujourd'hui (siècle 1880–1980) (Paris, 1979), 332–33, Vol. IV of Histoire économique et sociale de la France, ed. Braudel and Labrousse, 4 vols.

duction recovered by 1900 after considerable new investment and further specialization. Then overproduction in the first decade of the twentieth century sharply reduced prices. Provence was not as dramatically dislocated as Languedoc farther west, but here too the most lucrative sector of commercial agriculture suffered.[17]

The metropolis of Marseilles promoted the commercialization of agriculture in Provence, which transformed the economy of the coastal region through its demand for labor, the stimulus of its market, and its opportunities as an entrepôt linked to international trade. The port was among the fastest growing of French cities, doubling its population between 1872 and 1911, when it stood at 551,000. It was the largest port in France and in the entire Mediterranean, stimulating the development of adjacent, subsidiary industries. Marseilles firms led the world in the processing of agricultural oils (*oléagineux*), employing one hundred thousand workers in 1900. Increased productivity in Marseilles spurred communities surrounding the city. Marine construction expanded with two naval dockyards, one at La Ciotat east of Marseilles and the other at the home port of the Mediterranean fleet, Toulon. In the midst of these new activities traditional small-scale coastal fishing continued.[18]

While the South was developing a distinctive economy in the late nineteenth century, its democratic tradition also evolved. In his study *Radicalism in Mediterranean France*, Leo Loubère explores this cultural-political milieu and documents the dramatic success of Radical candidates between 1885 and 1906. He includes both the coastal departments of Provence and the departments west of the Rhône. During these years, which were critical in the ideological definition and organizational development of radicalism, deputies from the South were a dominant force among Radicals. The far South had the highest proportion of Radical deputies in relation to the number of electors between 1885 and 1893. In addition, between 1889 and 1906 the largest number of Radical deputies represented constituencies from the Midi méditerranné. Beginning with the 1906 legislative election, however, this identification of radicalism with the Midi began to decline. Loubère attributes both the rise of radicalism and its subsequent stagnation

17. Pierre Barral, "Le Monde agricole," *ibid.*, 379–88; Charles K. Warner, *The Winegrowers of France and the Government Since 1875* (New York, 1960).

18. Gras, "Les Disparités économiques régionales," 331–33.

to the unique small town culture of the region and to the economic domination of wine production. Small and medium property ownership, the desire for government intervention to aid economic development, and democratic traditions all combined to make vineyard owners and their workers ideal Radical electors. But in 1906–1907, when a government that was perceived as Radical and when a Chamber dominated by Radicals failed to address the severe dislocation of wine overproduction and price collapse, both owners and workers turned to the Socialist party.[19]

A more structural perspective of the region's economic transformation between 1870 and 1910 and its impact on political allegiances is offered by Tony Judt in his study of socialism in the Var. He proposes a conjunctural transformation which in the Var connected rural deindustrialization, the rise of the wine monoculture, population decline, and the increasing homogeneity of villages of small propertied peasants. Judt contends that all of these factors supported left-wing sentiment in Provence and were the basis for the important political shift away from the Radicals of the 1880s and 1890s to the Socialists of the early twentieth century. This change marked a significant rupture in political tradition and was not simply the next phase of a continuous left-wing identity, reaching back to 1848. In the Var those who voted for Radicals in the last decade of the nineteenth century and those who voted for Socialists in the early twentieth century were not the same individuals. Socialist support came from highland villages that had been abandoned by artisans and the petite bourgeoisie. New voters among these hard-pressed small propertied peasants, who were willing to explore collectivist solutions to their problems endorsed Socialists; Radicals maintained their strength in urban centers and the coastal towns.[20]

By the 1880s much had changed in Provence since the mid-century and much would change again by the early twentieth century. These transformations of the economic structure inevitably altered social relations: highland peasants were now more isolated and their livelihoods more pre-

19. Leo Loubère, *Radicalism in Mediterranean France: Its Rise and Decline, 1848–1914* (Albany, N.Y., 1974), 176, 180, 6, 106–107, 130, 148–51, 161. Until the 1880s Paris and the department of the Seine elected the largest number of Radical deputies with the Midi méditerranné having the second largest group.

20. Tony Judt, *Socialism in Provence, 1871–1914: A Study in the Origins of the Modern French Left* (New York, 1979), 23, 27, 33, 44, 91, 121, 114, 143, 153, 226.

carious; a larger and more proletarian working class emerged in urban centers; within towns and cities a salaried service sector, perhaps connected to the traditional petite bourgeoisie, flourished; many small and medium property owners producing wine, fruits, and vegetables were dependent on national and even international markets. Clearly these changes affected the complex intersection between the bourgeoisie and the "people," that critical meeting place for the development of a democratic culture. In addition to new economic developments, the very success of the Radicals in the Midi also affected Provençal sociability. Increasingly southern clubs became more explicitly political, linked to specific programs and politicians. This dense constellation of change necessarily transformed assumptions about who belonged to the category of the "people" and also altered expectations about appropriate relations between bourgeois and nonbourgeois citizens.

Throughout the pre-1914 period Radicals continued to present their supporters as members of that elusive social identity, "le peuple," inhabiting that amorphous intraclass milieu that linked the lower strata of the bourgeoisie and the working class. This claim was both a fiction and a reality. There was also a more important identity for Radical supporters, however, that of citizens, men defined by their political functions, who were theoretically all equal and exercising their rights. By stressing the importance of citizens and their rights, especially the right to vote, the Radicals avoided some of the difficult issues surrounding the shifting social conditions of the "people." At the same time they implicitly underscored once again the exclusively masculine nature of their political world. Well-established traditions of Mediterranean culture further reinforced such republican gender segregation. Men and women were not only tied to distinct patterns of work and family responsibilities, but most leisure activities were also sharply separated. Women were excluded from the politically critical environment of sociability. Leisure outside the home, providing an opportunity to discuss and act on political issues, was the exclusive purview of men. This gender segregation certainly influenced the republican and later Radical circles and committees of the late nineteenth century. Since the mid-nineteenth century, however, a small number of women did participate in democratic political activity. Their presence was much more likely when significant numbers of women worked outside the home and had begun to organize on the job. Their appearance and the extent of their involvement often occurred during especially militant and critical situations such as the armed marches to defend the Second Republic.[21]

During the Third Republic, despite persistent obstacles, a small number of Provençal women took part in left-wing politics. Police informants viewed their presence as an indicator of extreme militancy. To cite one example, in 1881 a Marseilles police spy provided the prefect with a detailed description of a local Radical *cercle*. Noteworthy was the presence of three unaccompanied women, as well as two other women who were identified as the "concubines" of their male companions. Even more alarming, these women demanded to be admitted to the Radical group but received only the status of honorary members. The attention given this episode signifies that it was unusual, but it also demonstrates just how seriously crossings of the gender boundaries were taken. In Marseilles proponents of women's emancipation found an audience. A year before the incident reported above, Paule Mink, socialist, feminist, and former Communard, presented a series of lectures sponsored by both socialist groups and Radical circles.[22] In the first years of the twentieth century, the major left-wing paper of Marseilles, which appealed to both Radicals and socialists, occasionally carried a column by "une Marseillaise," reporting on developments in the expanding women's movement.[23] An interesting shift in Provençal political culture was the occasional combining of political meetings with family gatherings and entertainment. As early as the 1880s, Radical groups organized lectures, soirées, and even bingo contests to appeal to mixed audiences.[24]

Yet these efforts to include women and women's issues in the political life of Radical circles were the exception. Much more typical was Radical men's outrage, as well as that of the police observers, when women attempted to voice political opinions. Women's political participation was especially condemned during the conflict surrounding the church in the first years of the twentieth century. It was clear, for example, that a woman in male dress denouncing religion to a mixed audience of two hundred in the fishing

21. Agulhon, *La République au village*, 233, 321–29.
22. Police reports to prefect, July 17, 1881, May and June, 1880, M6 3305, AD/BR.
23. See, for example, *Le Petit Provençal*, January 12, 1902, and June 18, 1906.
24. Police report to prefect, December 24, 1881, M6 3305, AD/BR.

town of Martigues deeply shocked the police reporter.[25] A contributor to a small town Provençal paper, *Le Progrès de Salon*, worked himself into a frenzy when reporting on the activities of clerical women organizing to defend the church. He concluded his article with an appeal, not to fellow republicans or anticlericals, but to all men to defend their exclusive political realm. "There is no man, worthy of the name, who is not outraged by such an intrusion."[26] While exclusion and separation along gender lines characterized southern Radical politics, even here women remained a disturbing presence and could not simply be ignored. Women's demands would become more vocal in the 1910s as the suffrage debate intensified.

In addition to the distinctions of class and gender, another difference, that of region, often threatened to divide candidates from their constituencies. The issue of a candidate from outside the local district and especially one from Paris figured frequently in electoral campaigns. Most southern elected officials were natives of the region. Loubère notes that the "average Radical deputy" from the Midi was a local man, often a professional, usually a lawyer, doctor, or merchant. Whatever their occupation, all had investments in vineyards and were personally knowledgeable about viticulture. Usually they had risen through the ranks of municipal and departmental politics. A dense network of associations on the regional, departmental, and local levels supported them.[27] Although many deputies began in local politics, once they secured a legislative career in the Chamber they became national politicians, members of the Parisian political elite. Then, whatever the deputy's origins, he always faced the possibility of being criticized as an outsider. Camille Pelletan was from his first campaign in 1881 an *exotique*, an outsider hoping to expand Radical influence in the Bouches-du-Rhône. He was not the only outsider "parachuted" into Provence. Deputies with considerable national prestige, like Pelletan, could afford a certain degree of neglect toward their districts, but such neglect could not continue indefinitely. All incumbents were vulnerable to the charge that they ignored

25. Her talk was titled "Religion: Its Errors and Its Dangers" (Police reports to prefect, August 3–9, 1903, M6 3291, AD/BR).

26. J. Charpenel, *Le Progrès de Salon*, January 8, 1902. Eight years later the author served as a poll watcher, representing the Salon Comité Pelletan (Police report, 1910, IKF 7/10, Archives Municipales, Salon-de-Provence).

27. Loubère, *Radicalism in Mediterranean France*, 168.

the interests of their constituents to further their own careers. Perhaps the most telling indication of the considerable importance which local ties and local politics retained for the deputies was the decision to eliminate public parliamentary sessions on Saturday and Monday to enable deputies to visit their districts.[28]

Although Pelletan's biography does not conform to that of the typical Midi politician, the candidacy of this Parisian political personality in a southern district during the elections of 1881 was by no means a novelty. Although lacking any national organization or any uniform strategy, republicans had been pursuing similar methods to achieve electoral success since the 1870s. During the inhospitable climate of the 1860s and 1870s, victories had been secured in working-class and petit bourgeois neighborhoods of large cities, especially Paris. Radicals branched out to provincial districts in the 1880s. Multiple candidacies were permitted until 1889 so these forays into the provinces could be pursued with little risk. In the ideal situation, the candidate won in both urban and provincial constituencies; he could then influence the election of a like-minded colleague in the second-round election following his own withdrawal. Several important Radicals followed this strategy in the election of 1881 as they loudly proclaimed their opposition to the governing moderate republicans. Radicals criticized the government for calling early elections that did not permit them enough time to prepare or find candidates.[29] One explanation for the several multiple candidacies may be simply that there were not enough Radicals to go around.[30] Edouard Lockroy, Georges Clemenceau, and Camille Pelletan all became candidates in both Parisian and southern districts.

Edouard Lockroy's campaigns in Paris and Aix-en-Provence typified Radical electoral strategy and its shortcomings. His career was closely inter-

28. Guiral and Thuillier, *Vie quotidienne*, 197.

29. Radicals confronted the well-orchestrated efforts of the republican minister of the interior, Ernest Constans, to control the elections. Constans was a member the Ferry government and had a reputation for energetic, some would say authoritarian, administration. He would fill the same post in a later moderate republican government of 1889, pursuing similar tactics to block the Boulangist movement (Gordon Wright, *Notable or Notorious? A Gallery of Parisians* [Cambridge, Mass., 1991], 100, and Chapter III).

30. *La Justice*, no. 552, July 21, 1881; no. 573, August 10, 1881.

twined with Pelletan's, as a colleague on the editorial board of *Le Rappel*, an intimate member of the Hugo circle, a Radical deputy, and finally as a bitter political enemy in the first decade of the twentieth century.[31] In the 1880s Lockroy, only a few years older than Pelletan, had already established his parliamentary career. For the 1881 elections he chose to stand both in the eleventh Paris arrondissement and for Aix-en-Provence, where he was the incumbent. A native of Paris and well-known boulevardier, he presented himself as a genuine man of the people and defended workers' right to unionize. During a Marseilles speech to a large audience just a year before the elections, Lockroy extolled the republican victory over the Right and called for the continuation of reforms, especially the separation of church and state, the progressive income tax, and old age pensions, but he warned against revolutionary violence as a means to resolve the "social question."[32]

Because of his cautious stance, the departmental police spy listed Lockroy among the Opportunist candidates. Lockroy also failed to receive the endorsement of the departmental Comité Central Radical. In effect, his Aix campaign in 1881 pitted him against the representative of local Radical militants. In this instance the well-known outsider won against several local candidates.[33] In the Paris eleventh arrondissement, with a more substantial turnout, Lockroy also won by a similarly large margin.[34] Lockroy opted for the Paris seat, which he would continue to represent until his retirement in 1910. He explained to his *comité* in Aix that the North was in greater need of Radicals than the South, where radicalism was much stronger. In the November by-election, which this withdrawal necessitated, Lockroy's former rival was again defeated. This time the victor was a local businessman and member of the municipal and departmental councils who was Lockroy's close protégé. Some reports to the subprefect claimed that all these

31. See Chapter VIII.

32. Edgar Monteil, *Célébrités contemporaines. Edouard Lockroy* (Paris, 1886). There were actually two meetings, one in the afternoon attended by thirty-five hundred and one in the evening, where there were ten thousand (Police report to prefect, August 1, 1880, M6 3305, AD/BR).

33. Lockroy's opponent was Alphonse Pautrier. Of 15,974 eligible voters, 8,067 voted, 5,285 for Lockroy, and 2,614 for Pautrier (Elections 1881, Bouches-du-Rhône, C 3985, AN).

34. There were 19,654 eligible voters, 15,080 voted, and Lockroy received 8,501 (Elections 1881, Seine, C 4057, AN).

189

men had identical politics but were separated by personal differences.[35] On one hand, Lockroy's electoral victories marked an expansion of radicalism, which Lockroy represented through his Paris association with *Le Rappel* and his affiliation with the far Left in the Chamber. On the other hand, this particular election demonstrated persistent problems facing Radicals: their inability to impose programmatic and electoral discipline over either individual deputies or local committees and the permanent tension between more militant and more cautionary politicians, both of whom considered themselves loyal Radicals. These difficulties led a Marseilles police spy to observe: "I can assure you . . . that there have never been more disgusting scenes, in a word the Radical party has never been so divided as it will be in the next elections."[36] Although he exaggerated, he was certainly not wrong. Despite these continuing divisions, politicians adopting the label *Radical* continued to make electoral gains.

The undisputed leader of radicalism in the 1880s, Georges Clemenceau, also chose to run in both Paris and Provence. Like Lockroy, Clemenceau already had established his legislative career. He too had been elected to represent the Seine in 1871 and resigned to protest the peace treaty. In 1876 he became deputy for the eighteenth Paris arrondissement, Montmartre, where he had been mayor during the Prussian siege and the Commune. In 1881 he presented himself for reelection in Paris and also in Arles, one of the three major cities of the Bouches-du-Rhône. Largely because of *La Justice* and his role as leader of the parliamentary extreme Left, Clemenceau was already a well-known personality in the South. In the fall of 1880 he had made a successful speaking tour to Marseilles, where a crowd of five hundred greeted him at the station together with the subprefect of Aix, members of the Marseilles municipal council, and trade union representatives. He appealed to large audiences of both Radicals and socialists. On this occasion Clemenceau delivered his first clear challenge to the moderate republicans.[37] The intrepid police spy identified his principal opponent

35. Letter of August 12, 1881, Report, December 2, 1881, II M3 30, AD/BR.

36. Police report to prefect, May 19, 1881, M6 3305, AD/BR.

37. He attacked them for having achieved only "la République conservatrice" (Police reports, October 28, 1880, M6 3376 and M6 3305, AD/BR). The full speech is cited in Barral, ed., *Fondateurs de la Troisième République*, 125–28.

in Arles, Félix Granet, as an "official candidate." The informant predicted a close contest.[38]

During the closing days of August, Clemenceau actively campaigned in Arles, holding a series of meetings with an average attendance of two thousand. At the same time he continued his campaign in Paris.[39] In both districts he insisted on his Radical platform of constitutional revision, separation of church and state, electoral reform, reduction of military service, progressive income tax, and labor reforms, including the ten-hour day.[40] The contest in the South was extremely close, 5,735 for Clemenceau, 5,667 for Granet, requiring a runoff election.[41] Ultimately, Clemenceau opted for his Paris district. Amazingly, in the election required by his withdrawal, Clemenceau threw his support behind Granet, who now pledged to adhere to the Radical platform which he had denounced only weeks earlier. Granet faced a new republican candidate who had been defeated in a first-round campaign in neighboring Marseilles. This election aroused considerable attention when Granet accused his opponent, a Protestant minister, of collaboration with the Prussians in Alsace during the Franco-Prussian War. The minister denied these claims but withdrew his candidacy, leaving Granet deputy for Arles.[42] Even more dramatically than the Lockroy election, the Clemenceau 1881 campaign demonstrated the persistent characteristic of Radical politicians to alternate between strong ideological programs and subsequent practical negotiations to meet the requirements of electoral success. Four years later Clemenceau stood for the Seine and the southern department of the Var; this time he opted for the southern constituents.

Clemenceau's campaign in Arles permitted him to introduce and promote the candidacy of his then close collaborator Camille Pelletan. The

38. Granet had held a post in the Ministry of the Interior under the energetic Ernest Constans (Police report to prefect, July 7, August 10, 1881, M6 3305, AD/BR).

39. *La Justice*, no. 581, August 18, 1881; no. 577, August 14, 1881.

40. Clemenceau, "Profession de foi," XVIIIᵉ arrondissement Paris, 1881, in Derfler, *Third French Republic*, 121–23.

41. *La Justice*, no. 588, August 25, 1881.

42. Elections 1881, Arles, II M3 30, AD/BR. Minister Dide was the director of a scholarly journal on the French Revolution whose editorial board included Eugène Pelletan; there were many protests about the shoddy conduct of the election, but the result was not overturned.

1881 elections were Pelletan's initiation into the electoral process.[43] During the first round his campaign centered almost exclusively on the second district of the Paris tenth arrondissement for which he had declared his candidacy on August 6. *La Justice* published his platform, one very similar to Clemenceau's, which had appeared only a few days earlier in the paper.[44] Possibly they had drawn up their programs together. According to the southern police spy, however, Pelletan's name began to appear on Radical lists of candidates in the Bouches-du-Rhône as early as May. Camille had an independent reputation as a journalist through his articles in the Hugos' *Le Rappel*. But in the South he was principally known as Clemenceau's protégé on *La Justice*, especially after he had accompanied Clemenceau during his 1880 visit to Marseilles.[45] Camille's father had been wrong when he had predicted that this connection would be a political liability for his son. Before the first round of voting on August 21, there was little evidence of an active campaign on Pelletan's part in the second district of Aix, where he faced a moderate republican incumbent.[46] His entire southern campaign appeared to be a somewhat rushed, last-minute affair, possibly encouraged by Clemenceau. Most likely it was a response to the acute shortage of Radical candidates with recognizable names.[47]

In the tenth Paris arrondissement Pelletan won overwhelmingly against two other republican candidates. In the second district of Aix the vote was much closer and required a runoff.[48] In preparation for that second round Pelletan became much more visible among his potential southern constituents. On August 26 he addressed a letter to the electors of Aix, stressing his commitment to the district and the larger Radical cause: "I am proud to have been adopted by the valiant democracy of the Bouches-du-

43. In 1879 his name had appeared as a candidate in the colony of Guinea, where the Communards were interned. It is not clear how serious that candidacy was.

44. *La Justice*, no. 581, August 18, 1881; no. 583, August 20, 1881.

45. Police report to prefect, May 29, 1881, M6 3305, AD/BR.

46. There were reports of Radical committees insisting that Clemenceau and Pelletan visit the Bouches-du-Rhône (Police reports to prefect, July 7, 1881, *ibid.*).

47. *La Justice*, no. 573, August 10, 1881.

48. In the Paris election 15,587 voters were eligible; 11,196 voted; Pelletan received 5,918, Hattat 2,207, and Hamel 1,238 (Elections 1881, Seine, C 4057, AN). In Aix 16,659 voters were eligible; 8,536 voted; Pelletan received 2,983, Fournier 2,893, and Labadié 2,656 (Elections 1881, Bouches-du-Rhône, C 3503, AN).

Rhône which has always been in the avant-garde of the republican party. You have designated my combat station; you can count on me." One cannot avoid noting a trace of reluctance at the possibility of abandoning an enthusiastic constituency in his native metropolis, which he loved dearly, for the essentially unfamiliar small towns of the far South. In a Paris speech immediately after the first round of elections Pelletan had spoken of his eagerness to become a member of the "family of the tenth arrondissement."[49] Instead, he would have to create a new electoral "family" in Provence.

The constituents Camille Pelletan now addressed were located in the western half of the region, in the southwestern corner of the department of the Bouches-du-Rhône. This second electoral district of Aix-en-Provence stretched north from the Mediterranean coast for about twenty miles, bordered the Rhône River on the east, and surrounded the inland waters of the Etang de Berre.[50] Small towns and villages in close proximity to one another made up the district, whose economic, social, cultural, and political existence was dominated by Aix and especially by the great port of Marseilles. Political life was based on sociability similar to that of an earlier period. In café meeting rooms of Aix and Marseilles militants formed republican organizations, honed their rhetoric, and established networks which then spread to nearby smaller communities. Police reports recorded the rich and varied structures of sociability that flourished in Aix after the establishment of the Third Republic. During the 1870s there was a significant expansion of *cercles d'amitié*. Despite the repressive atmosphere of this decade, provincial republicans felt secure enough to organize publicly.[51] They formed *cercles* with names such as Indépendance, Liberté, and Progrès. Politics was an important activity, but most of these organizations devoted considerable time to leisure and sociability.

Republicans also created the explicitly political Cercle républicain d'Aix in October, 1871. The conservative subprefect carefully weighed the pros and cons of dissolving this group, whose influence he viewed as "unfortunate and . . . in general hostile to authority." He finally concluded that it would

49. *Le Petit Provençal*, August 26, December 5, 1881.

50. The Etang is thirteen miles long and three to eight miles wide.

51. Associations in Aix, Police reports: Cercle républicaine, Aix, M4 634, AD/BR. Government efforts to control organizations and especially the republican press in the 1870s are documented in departmental police files, Z1 32 and 28, AD/BR.

be difficult to refuse their application and that it might be more valuable to observe their activities; suppression might only increase their prestige. The Cercle républicain was open to any man sponsored by two members; monthly dues were a not insignificant one franc. The membership lists of this *cercle* for 1872, 1881, 1882, and 1898 reveal important characteristics and changes among the republicans of Aix. They indicate the decline of a united republican organization and the probable emergence of contending republican groups. Membership fell steadily and finally precipitously, from 102 members in 1872 to 24 in 1898. Although some members remained involved from 1872 to 1882, none of the members at the end of the century had appeared on earlier lists.[52] Their social backgrounds changed as well. In the early 1870s men practicing distinct urban trades overwhelmingly dominated this republican circle: a large number of hat makers, many in the construction industry (masons, carpenters), and a broad representation of essential urban skills (such as bakers, locksmiths, and tailors). In all likelihood, many of these men were small owner-producers, perhaps even employing other workers. In 1872 these tradesmen made up more than half of the members of the Cercle républicain. The two other largest occupational categories were businessmen (manufacturer, merchant, and shopkeeper) and professionals (lawyer, pharmacist, and physician). The much smaller later lists show a clear decline in the percentage of tradespeople. By 1898 businessmen constituted nearly a third of the *cercle's* small membership. Civil servants were entirely absent in 1872; their numbers slowly increased in the 1880s.[53] This change may have reflected the increasing republican influence in local government and republican ability to secure state employment for supporters. By the end of the century the earlier, more "popular" social base of republicanism had given way to a more homogeneously affluent group.

52. Associations in Aix, M4 634, AD/BR. Nineteen members continued between 1872 and 1881, sixteen between 1881 and 1882. Of the latter, six had also appeared in 1872.

53. In 1872 tradespeople made up 65 percent of the members, businessmen 15 percent, and professionals 14 percent. In 1882 tradespeople stood at 44 percent; the following year they constituted 33 percent of the total. By 1898 they were only 25 percent of the total (six out of twenty-four). During the 1880s the membership of businessmen fluctuated between 12 and 15 percent. *Fonctionnaires* represented 7 and then 12 percent of members in 1881 and 1882. There were five *fonctionnaires* in 1881 and again in 1882 but only one in 1898 (*ibid.*).

In the major metropolis of Marseilles, the reports of an energetic police spy during the early 1880s provide an interesting portrait of local, specifically Radical militants. The material from this source must be used with some circumspection because, paradoxically, the informant clearly identified with intransigent revolutionary socialists and despised the Radicals for their lack of militancy. He reported on the local Radical committee, describing men lacking real convictions, passionately involved in municipal politics, avid to gain government positions. In January, 1881, he submitted the following character analysis of the Marseilles Radicals' nominee for mayor: "Politically, Brochier is one of those men who, in order to gain recognition, in order to become popular, will push radicalism to the extreme. He is puffed up with pride. Personally, he's not worth much, a great egoist, loving only himself and incapable of loosening his purse to help out some unfortunate. . . . Where others give five francs, Brochier will give two sous. His business is not flourishing; he has applied for bankruptcy, his payments have been suspended and actually he's in very bad shape."[54] Clearly the subject was a petty entrepreneur at the very margins of bourgeois respectability, seeking political office for personal gain.

The 1881 municipal program of these same Marseilles Radicals recorded by the police informant suggested a more generous political perspective. As expected, the Marseilles Radicals were strongly committed to anticlerical policies, calling for the replacement of all religious personnel in municipally financed hospitals and charitable institutions with nonclerical staff. They pledged to remove all religious symbols from city schools and change street names from those of saints to those of patriots. Cultural policies had an important place in this program, including projects for monuments to the Republic and to the victims of the local 1871 rising. They demanded that the Grand Theater offer two performances weekly at half price and that municipal subsidies to the aristocratic hunting and horse racing clubs be ended. The most significant portion of the program was devoted to issues of employment carrying both political and economic implications. The Radicals called for "a formal commitment to dismiss immediately all city employees designated as not devoted to the Republic, and to replace

54. Police report to prefect, January 22, 1881, M6 3305, AD/BR. This Marseilles police informant for 1880 and 1881 was a member of the socialist Cercle des travailleurs and on April 8, 1880, stated that he would present himself as a socialist candidate for the municipal council.

them by capable citizens whose republicanism could not be doubted." Such an unambiguous endorsement of a political purge was unusual in its clear insistence on jobs for republican loyalists, but all Radicals shared such concerns and objectives, from those in the smallest village to national leaders in Paris. They were part of one of the most serious issues for Radicals: how to gain thorough control of the state at all levels and in all its jurisdictions; how to republicanize the Republic. As important, such a purge promised material advantages often associated with social advancement and security for republican supporters.

The Radicals of Marseilles and elsewhere were not simply interested in plundering public resources. In 1881, when they called for a salary increase for the lowest paid municipal workers, to a minimum of 1,200 francs annually, they also intended to reduce the highest paid salaries to a maximum of 3,000 francs. Thus they would create a relatively narrow pay scale, appropriate to their egalitarian social ideal. In addition to municipal employment, the Radicals pledged to create jobs through a series of public works programs. Construction of port and market facilities would be a high priority. The structure of such work would encourage a particular form of social organization. The working day would be limited to ten hours, and the minimum daily wage would be four francs. Access to these jobs would be restricted; not only would applicants have to be devoted republicans, but they would also have to be French citizens. The Radicals' public works projects were intended both to create jobs and to improve the life and economy of the city with new sewers, sidewalks, schools, and less expensive railroad transportation.[55] This municipal program conveys the aspirations of local Radical activists: a commitment to republican principles in support of a secular, more egalitarian, and more nationalistic society and culture, coupled with an ambitious search for individual advancement and an eagerness to promote economic and social progress requiring state intervention.

Pelletan's district, the "deuxième circonscription d'Aix-en-Provence," was a world of small towns caught between the divergent economies of inland stagnation and coastal development.[56] The district consisted of five can-

55. Police report to prefect on Comité central républicain, Programme communal, January 30, 1881, M6 3305, AD/BR.

56. Gras, "Les Disparités économiques régionales," 342.

tons. Residents depended on a mixed economy of maritime, agricultural, and industrial activities. The largest canton was Martigues, where a significant population of sailors was engaged in commercial fishing. The commune of Port de Bouc in this canton was the site of a small naval arsenal. Salon, a city of six thousand in 1851, served as the administrative, political, and commercial center of the district. It was surrounded by ancient olive groves whose harvests were transformed into soap and oil in the city and adjacent villages. In addition, there were three smaller cantons of Berre, Istres, and Lambesc, each with clusters of subsidiary villages. As early as the 1840s, food industries had appeared all around the Etang de Berre processing fish, durum wheat, and especially the local olives. In addition, proximity to salt beds favored the development of a chemical industry, which in turn stimulated small cement and metallurgy plants. Although the economy was diverse, it experienced hard times in the 1880s, and the key sectors of fishing, chemicals, and olives had difficulties in adjusting to new conditions.[57]

These small towns shared with the larger urban centers an active associational and political life. In 1881 the eligible voters in the entire district numbered 16,620. Like most of Provence, they had already sent a republican deputy to Paris. La Société du progrès, Le Cercle républicain de la fraternité, Les Amis de l'ecole laique, La Société de la jeunesse républicaine, and a variety of Comités républicains flourished in the district.[58] Salon had a small Masonic Lodge of the Grand Orient rite, L'Unité, whose membership fluctuated around thirty-five between the 1880s and the 1910s. It played a permanent role in the district's social and political life and was increasingly affiliated with Radical politics. Most of its members were men

---

57. Edouard Baratier *et al.*, *Atlas Historique: Provence, Comtat venaissin, principauté d'Orange, Comté de Nice, principauté de Monaco* (Paris, 1969), 76, 79, 251. This was especially true of Martigues, where the fishing industry failed to adapt to larger steam-powered boats and the inadequate port facilities inhibited the development of naval construction. Between 1851 and 1896 the population of Martigues declined by approximately one-third. Only after 1900 did economic conditions begin to improve (A. Tramonia, "Martigues de 1848 à 1914" [Diplôme d'études supérieures préparé sous la direction de M. Le prof. Guiral]). Creating further difficulties, inland olive producers long resisted adjusting to the northern markets that favored peaches, apples, and pears.

58. Evidence of these committees can be found in congratulatory addresses sent to the Combes government, Adresses de sympathie et félicitations à Combes, Carton 3, Bouches-du-Rhône, AP 73, Archives personnelles et familiales, AN.

of some property who became increasingly more active in the municipal government.[59] Of the major issues Radicals addressed, anticlericalism and lay education seemed especially popular with activists in the region, as evidenced by the number of associations of freethinkers. The residents of coastal Martigues were deeply committed to anticlericalism. In 1885 the prefect rejected its citizens' effort to institute an anticlerical circle. By the turn of the century, the anticlericals controlled the municipal council and endorsed an extreme measure calling for the abolition of priests' skullcaps because they were an affront to "rational men." Three years later two hundred residents of Martigues attended a meeting at which a woman gave a speech titled "Religion, Its Errors and Its Dangers." The police informant described the talk as atheistic and revolutionary.[60]

Like their counterparts in Marseilles, these small town citizens were also interested in specific reforms. A local paper, *Le Reveil salonais. Journal républicain organe des intérêts du commerce et de l'agriculture,* on February 5, 1887, called for "significant reforms . . . useful improvements," and fewer political promises. The article emphasized the need for large public works projects. Local Radicals were particularly interested in an extended canal system along the Rhône to aid transport and irrigation. Although issues of general economic development were clearly a high priority in the district, the sailors of Martigues raised specific working-class concerns. In the spring of 1893 they went on strike demanding a reorganization of their work.[61] They introduced a militant edge to the politics of the region; many would eventually declare themselves socialists.

Some of these politically active citizens must have participated in the preelection discussions in 1881 in which Camille Pelletan was proposed as the Radical candidate for the second district of Aix. Pelletan's association with Clemenceau and *La Justice* provided him with a reputation, but that association was still very recent. As important were his ten years with *Le Rappel.* The distribution and discussion of the Parisian political press was a significant function of local republican social circles.[62] Journalism

---

59. By the end of the century, however, an agricultural day laborer and a postal employee appeared on the membership list of the lodge (Fonds maçonnique, Loge de l'Unité, Salon, Rés FM 2 115, Bibliothèque Nationale, Paris).

60. Tramonia, "Martigues," 1–2; Police report, August 3–9, 1903, M6 3291, AD/BR.

61. *La Justice,* no. 4895, March 11, 1893.

62. In 1887 the short-lived Société de la jeunesse républicaine of Salon subscribed to

served as one of the best means to achieve a national political following. In addition to his own reputation, his father's career in the department must have been a positive factor in Camille's candidacy. Eugène Pelletan had been elected in 1871 to represent the Bouches-du-Rhône; in 1876 he became the department's senator. He was one of the well-respected elder statesmen of the Republic in the Senate when his son ran for election in Aix. Although he was no Radical, Eugène Pelletan's departmental contacts must have been an asset to Camille.

In the second district of Aix, the younger Pelletan faced two opponents: the republican incumbent, a local businessman, and Alfred Fournier, a lawyer and member of the departmental council. Gambetta's paper *La République française* supported Fournier, who was rumored to have given thousands of francs to the regional paper, *Le Petit Provençal*, for its endorsement.[63] The results of the first round on August 21 did not produce a clear majority; Pelletan and Fournier were almost tied. The runoff election held in early September was more heated. In a Martigues election rally, which both Pelletan and Clemenceau attended, the candidate confronted the principal criticism brought against him: he was an "exotique," who knew nothing of the region and would ignore its interests if elected. Pelletan claimed that on the contrary, his national standing would enable him to do much more for his constituents. He "commanded a newspaper and he had advantages through his friendship with Clemenceau and his ties to his father, one of democracy's patriarchs, which no one else could match."[64] In this first election some voters viewed Pelletan as the workers' ally, others as the harbinger of revolution. He won the runoff by an extraordinarily slim margin of less than one hundred votes.[65] Inevitably there was considerable discontent, petition signing, and grumbling about the legiti-

L'Intransigeant, La Justice, Le Rappel, La France, La République française, and *La République illustrée* (I 33 235, Archives Municipales, Salon-de-Provence).

63. Police report to prefect, August 10, 1881, M6 3305, AD/BR.

64. *Le Démocrate,* September 3, 1881.

65. Such views appeared on the invalid ballots. One from Istres supported Pelletan, calling him a "man whose heart is with the workers"; another from Salon denounced him, declaring, "We don't want to have a revolution. Long live the republic of Labadié" (Elections 1881, Bouches-du-Rhône, C 3503, AN). Neither of the other candidates withdrew; the total number voting increased by 953, and Pelletan gained only 534 more ballots than in the first round; 9,489 voted; Pelletan received 3,517, Fournier 3,456, Labadié 2,484 (*ibid.*).

macy of the election.[66] But the Chamber confirmed Camille Pelletan, and he began an uninterrupted thirty-year career as deputy from the second district of Aix.

Pelletan's political style corresponded well with the conventional characterization of the voluble, outgoing southerner. He must have appeared as a larger, more noteworthy, or more notorious version of those local "morally marginal bourgeois" who were so influential in southern republicanism. A parliamentary colleague described the pleasure Pelletan had while campaigning: "After the meeting . . . round after round of beer. I was dead tired. . . . But Pelletan, who enjoyed mingling with the residents of a popular neighborhood where he was well known and well liked, didn't want to go home. He drank pint after pint, reviving his thirst with hard boiled eggs which he peeled with fingernails so black they would make you shudder."[67] Pelletan's easy conversation, loaded with historical and literary references, his drinking and gourmandism, his perpetual "pipe prolétarienne," and perhaps even his purported dirty fingernails all made him more accessible to at least some of his constituents.

In the elections of 1889, which nationally put an end to the Boulangist movement, Pelletan decisively established himself as the district's representative.[68] Although a two-term incumbent, he still had to face the charge of being an outsider. Boulangists challenged his candidacy, joining local grievances to the national movement of discontent. Pelletan's eventual victory demonstrated that the majority of voters accepted his priority of national over local issues. Police reports indicated that among his constituents, especially among the sailors of Martigues, there was little support for General Boulanger.[69] Nonetheless, Pelletan faced two local Boulangists.

66. Elections 1881, 2ᵉ Circonscription d'Aix, II M3 30, AD/BR.

67. General Messimy, *Mes Souvenirs*, 21, quoted in Guiral and Thuillier, *Vie quotidienne*, 48–49.

68. The preceding 1885 elections were department-wide following the new *scrutin de liste* procedure. In the second-round runoff the Radical list won with Pelletan in third place receiving 55,278 of the 93,426 votes cast; 139,346 citizens were registered (Elections 1885, Bouches-du-Rhône, C 5301, AN).

69. A year and a half before these legislative elections, a Radical, Félix Pyat, had badly defeated the general himself in a special department-wide by-election. Pyat was a former Communard who campaigned on a strong Radical platform. There were 138,524 citizens eligible to vote; 77,995 voted, a 56 percent turnout. Boulanger received 1,071 votes, 1 percent of the votes (Elections, March 25, 1888, II M3 33, AD/BR).

Pelletan succeeded in convincing his constituents that he shared their disappointment with the existing Chamber but that despite their reservations the vulnerable Republic merited their loyalty. These sometimes conflicting sentiments were expressed in the local press. One short-lived republican paper in Salon had originally applauded General Boulanger as a much needed republican minister of war. By 1888 this same *Reveil salonais* was critical of the general, who mixed politics and the military.[70] This Sunday paper, which was consistently suspicious of the Paris parliament, demanded practical reforms and called for republican unity and patriotic commitment. On January 29, 1888, *Le Reveil salonais* reminded all deputies that they had one sovereign, "their electors." Though it was critical of the Chamber, there were no harsh words for the local deputy, Camille Pelletan. In fact, the local paper borrowed freely from Pelletan's *La Justice* articles to condemn the Boulangists.[71] By the end of 1888 this small sheet ceased publication; it was soon replaced by another local paper.

Le Petit salonais described itself as "a republican organ of the political, commercial, agricultural and industrial interests in the central region of the Bouches-du-Rhône." It constantly reiterated its political independence and insisted that its position was "republican without further adjectives." Despite such disclaimers, it should probably be counted as one of several papers created or funded to support local Boulangist candidates in the 1889 elections. In August, 1889, *Le Petit salonais* reported somewhat favorably on Pelletan's visit to the district, but by September, immediately before the elections, it vigorously endorsed a local Boulangist, Nicolas Hornbostel, against "exotiques" candidates. Hornbostel was a lawyer from Marseilles, and his "Commission Executive" was a heterogeneous group of property owners, artisans, and professionals, similar to the membership of local republican and Radical associations.[72]

Particularly during the first round of this 1889 election the Boulangist movement succeeded in creating confusion among republicans and Rad-

---

70. *Le Reveil salonais*, January 30, 1887, March 18, 25, April 22, 1888. The paper was published between 1885 and 1888; its original title was *Le Ralliement de Salon*, becoming *Le Reveil salonais* in January, 1887.

71. See especially *Le Reveil salonais*, November 27, 1887, February 5, April 8, 22, 1888.

72. *Le Petit salonais*, no. 1, July 7, 1889; no. 12, September 22, 1889; Irvine, *Boulanger Affair*, 125–37. There were perhaps more property owners and fewer professionals than in other republican associations (*Le Petit salonais*, no. 12, September 22, 1889).

icals as it had elsewhere. Six candidates presented themselves: two Boulangists, two republicans, Pelletan the incumbent Radical, and one independent "worker." Four were serious contestants. The more important Boulangist, Hornbostel, although affiliated with the national revisionist committee, made few references to Boulanger. Instead, he unrelentingly emphasized the need to respond to local concerns. Pelletan, in contrast, insisted on national issues and the threat the Boulangists posed to the Republic by having organized a "syndicate of every malcontent." He acknowledged that there was legitimate discontent caused by the failure of the moderate-dominated legislature to enact sufficient social and economic reforms, but he urged his constituents to respond by electing a strong reformist, republican majority, not by undermining the state. He reminded voters of the Boulangists' reputed relations with royalists and their less than militant position on the Catholic church. At the end of his official program Pelletan almost disdainfully asked: "Is it necessary for me to add that . . . I will consider it my strict duty to pursue with the greatest diligence regional interests whose designated defender I will be?"[73] This was his only concession to local issues during the campaign.

In the inevitable second round Pelletan faced Hornbostel directly. The result was a clear victory for Pelletan with 71 percent of the vote. This local defeat of Boulangism certainly encouraged Pelletan and his supporters, although there were some negative factors in this election. Abstentions, which followed the national trend, remained exceedingly high.[74] It may have been obvious from the beginning that Pelletan would be victorious and therefore both supporters and opponents stayed home. Or perhaps neither the defense of the Republic nor the defense of the local interests with which Hornbostel identified had much appeal to voters. The 1889 election did, nonetheless, demonstrate that increasing numbers of citizens

73. *Le Petit salonais*, no. 12, September 22, 1889; no. 7, August 18, 1889; Annales de l'Assemblée nationale, Chambre des députés, *Programmes et professions de foi et engagements électoraux des députés* (Paris, 1903), 125.

74. In the first round 16,237 were registered and 9,252 voted. Pelletan received 4,558, Hornbostel 2,281; the two republicans 1,160 and 1,031 respectively (Elections 1889, 2ᵉ Circonscription d'Aix, II M3 33, AD/BR). In the second round 8,581 voted; Pelletan received 6,096, Hornbostel 2,358 (*ibid.*). Only 56 percent of the eligible voters participated in the first round and even fewer in the second, when it must have been clear that Pelletan would win.

were being drawn into the political process. They accepted universal male suffrage as the norm of political behavior. At the same time, however, a significant group of citizens existed for whom the all-important right to vote was not a significant political act.

By 1901 circumstances had changed somewhat in this southern electoral district. Pelletan was now a solidly entrenched six-term deputy, the Radicals were an organized political party on the national and local levels, and voting participation had increased considerably.[75] Pelletan had long ago ceased to be someone else's protégé and was himself a powerful patron within the newly organized Radical party. As one of the undisputed leaders of left-wing politics in the Midi, he promoted Radical and even socialist politicians throughout France. Since the early 1890s one of the local electoral committees in his district had adopted the name Comité Pelletan. It included municipal counselors and mayors who frequently organized successful preelectoral regional banquets to honor their deputy. Pelletan himself maintained regular contact with his constituents and was involved in local issues and disputes. He frequently addressed rallies, banquets, and meetings throughout the district, often using the Salon municipal theater, which could accommodate two thousand people.[76] His influence extended to neighboring Arles, where Pelletan actively and successfully endorsed a Radical deputy in the election of 1898.

In addition to this important direct contact, by the 1890s Pelletan had become an important and regular contributor to the Marseilles daily paper *Le Petit Provençal*, founded in 1880 to compete with the existing more moderate daily. Ardently republican, initially stridently nationalist, it represented Radical and socialist sentiments. It was almost exclusively devoted to politics. Although much of the coverage focused on the often internecine conflicts of the Marseilles Left, it also addressed regional issues and national debates. The paper proudly advertised its exclusive telegraph

75. Pelletan had won both the elections of 1893 and 1898 on the first round with relatively high rates of participation (Elections 1893, Bouches-du-Rhône, C 5334, AN, and Elections 1898, Bouches-du-Rhône, C 5116, AN).

76. At one such banquet more than eight hundred guests were invited (Police report, June 13, 1893, Dossier Pelletan, MI 25359, AN). For other examples see Police reports, meetings, Martigues, Fos-sur-mer, and Port-de-Bouc, October 13, 1894, Salon, théâtre municipal, April 27, 1898, May 5, 1900, and May 4, 1901, *ibid.*

connection with Paris, which permitted the publication of exact transcripts of parliamentary debates. In January, 1902, *Le Petit Provençal* announced a new attraction, the regular publication of articles by well-known Radical and socialist deputies: Maurice Allard, socialist of the Var; Gaston Doumergue, Radical-socialist of the Gard; Clovis Hugues, southern native, former Communard, and socialist of Paris; Henri Michel, Radical-socialist of Arles; and, of course, Camille Pelletan. Together with *La Dépêche* of Toulouse, another important left-wing southern paper, *Le Petit Provençal* provided Camille with his most significant public platform, as well as additional regular income. As small town weeklies declined in number, *Le Petit Provençal* was a major source of political information for Pelletan's district.[77] In 1902 *Le Petit Provençal* staunchly supported Pelletan. In a lead article, Maurice Allard described Pelletan in the following terms: "The moral virtue of his political life, the consistency of his opinions and the energy and talent with which he defends them, all command respect. . . . He remains independent."[78]

The 1902 election, the first in the new political environment created by the end of the Dreyfus Affair, was viewed as a victory for the Radical party and a personal triumph for Camille Pelletan. Radical-socialist and Radical deputies increased their number of seats in the Chamber from 178 to 233. Nationally the 1902 election was a contest between the Left and the Right, supporters of the Republic and secularism in opposition to clericals and militarists, if not avowed antirepublicans.[79] During the campaign Pelletan frequently shared platforms with the independent socialist leader Jean Jaurès. Both urged their constituents to unite against what Pelletan denounced as the "collectivism of high finance . . . [and] the clerical menace." Pelletan insisted that in this election, "there are no longer so-

77. Throughout most of the 1890s there was no regularly appearing republican journal published within Pelletan's district. In 1899 a new bimonthly and then weekly, *Le Progrès de Salon*, was established. It continued publishing until 1912.

78. Maurice Allard, "Suspects," *Le Petit Provençal*, March 29, 1902. Tony Judt identifies Allard, deputy since 1898, as the leader of the more rigorous socialism of rural Var, *Socialism in Provence*, 76–78.

79. Participation was very high, and most contests were decided on the first round. Voting results, especially after that first round, indicated an electorate separated into two opposing camps by a margin of only two hundred thousand votes (Rebérioux, *La République radicale?*, 56–58).

cialists, Radicals or moderates; there is only the republican flag on one side and on the other that of counterrevolution." In the Bouches-du-Rhône he was called on to support Radical candidates in the city of Aix and to intervene in the endemic internal conflicts of Marseilles, which pitted factions of Radicals against one another, as well as against similarly divided socialists.[80]

In his own district Pelletan was the man of the hour. The Salon electoral organization aligned itself more closely with the new Radical party, changing its name from Comité pour la défense republicaine to the Comité radical-socialiste and energetically endorsing Pelletan. Its eighty members pledged to bring out both Radicals and socialists in support of the incumbent.[81] The election of 1902 was the first and only one in which Pelletan faced no officially declared opponent. The local *Progrès de Salon* spoke glowingly of the candidate who had "so valiantly defended democratic principles and regional interests in the Chamber." Despite the absence of a contest, the paper urged republicans "to vote for Pelletan, thus bearing witness to their complete confidence in him and giving him even greater authority."[82]

Pelletan spent a week of hard campaigning in the district, traveling from banquet to rally to meeting. Most speeches ended with the usual rousing "Vive la République démocratique et sociale!"[83] In a relatively short political program he underscored that his relation with his constituents had become a personal, family affair. What in 1881 had been a hasty, Paris-arranged relation of political expedience had by 1902 become a durable and emotional tie. Pelletan again declared himself the adopted "child of that Provence which marches in the democratic avant-garde." As in other elections, he emphasized that his political program had not changed. He also included the usual and often repeated reforms: greater equality in the tax structure, the enactment of workers' pensions, the promotion of popular

80. Police report, Atmosphère politique, Elections 1902, Dijon, May 7, 1902, F7 12541, AN; *ibid.*, Bouches-du-Rhône. Pelletan supported Flaissières, an independent socialist.

81. Police report, March 14, 1902, Dossier Pelletan, MI 25359, AN. The report is not clear if this was a joint committee of Radicals and local socialists or if it was a committee of Radical-socialists who had gained the adherence of local socialists.

82. *Le Progrès de Salon*, April 6, 1902.

83. *Ibid.*, April 13, 1902.

interests over those of the privileged, the disarming of clericalism, and the liberation of democracy from the shameful power of wealth. Although the outcome of the election was absolutely certain, almost half of the eligible voters in the district turned out. The rate of abstention for this uncontested election was comparable to those for the closely contested campaigns of the 1880s. Of the 49 percent of the eligible voters who chose to participate, 87 percent voted for Pelletan.[84]

Despite this overwhelming support for Pelletan in his district, there were small but persistent pockets of passionate opposition. A write-in campaign for a local socialist worker accumulated a 12 percent protest vote. As in previous elections, the greatest opposition was concentrated in the town of Salon. Some of Pelletan's constituents had intense feelings toward their deputy. A few went so far as to invalidate their vote by writing comments across the ballot to express their animosity toward the Radical deputy. Some simply crossed out his name; others substituted another local or national politician; some vented their rage. About five expressed revolutionary socialist sentiments. Most wrote in a local name and criticized Pelletan's failure to represent his district. A handful of these protests were written in Provençal. Several expressed personal grievances. "Pelletan represents his own interests, not those of the people. Send some delegates to Pelletan in Paris and you'll see how they're treated. Martigues won't forget." Some linked their anger at Pelletan's failure to represent the district to their support for nationalists such as Déroulède. Others denounced Camille as a "friend of the Jews."[85] These invalidated ballots reflected the views of less than a hundred voters, although some who abstained undoubtedly shared these sentiments. The bitter frustration of this limited opposition highlighted the amplitude of Pelletan's victory. The summer of 1902 must be counted as the apogee of Pelletan's popularity in his own district and a moment when his brand of radicalism had the greatest resonance throughout the country.

84. Dossier Pelletan, Profession de foi, 1902, MI 25359, AN. There were 17,181 eligible voters, and 8,450 voted. Pelletan received 7,381 votes or 42 percent of the eligible voters (Elections 1902, Bouches-du-Rhône, C 6037, AN).

85. Elections 1902, Bouches-du-Rhône, C 6037, AN. The protest in Provençal read: "Pour la bouillabaise degolit qu'el vengoun moun bon surtout, leil chivalt; Vivo ley lapin des monies poussion" (ibid.).

The election of 1906 was more complex. It followed the fall of the Radical government in which Pelletan had been a prominent member and the dissolution of the parliamentary coalition between Radicals and socialists, the Bloc des gauches, which had been committed to long-promised political, social, and economic reforms. The failure of the Radical-dominated Chamber of 1902–1906 to realize any substantial reform other than the separation of church and state was one factor that led to the formation of the unified Socialist party (SFIO) in 1905. The Socialists pledged to present their own candidates in as many districts as possible. Nonetheless, on a national level in the election of 1906 Pelletan's left-wing radicalism once again was endorsed. Twenty-eight more deputies campaigned as Radical-socialists than had in 1902. Two hundred and forty-seven Radicals and Radical-socialists were returned to the Chamber, an increase of seventeen over the previous legislature. In the southwestern corner of the Bouches-du-Rhône Camille Pelletan faced two opponents. Socialists for the first time officially supported a local mason, trade union leader, and member of the newly created SFIO, Louis Shoë, against their longtime ally. Auguste Bouge, a lawyer and former deputy from Marseilles, who declared himself an independent Radical and was endorsed by several powerful parliamentary figures, also challenged Pelletan.[86]

It would be inaccurate, however, to portray Pelletan's position in the district as entirely defensive. The fall of the Bloc des gauches government in early 1905 and particularly the bitter controversy over Pelletan's Ministry of the Navy, which had preceded it, had evoked considerable support for the local deputy, who was simultaneously regarded as a powerful national figure of the leading political party *and* a victim of dangerous reactionary forces. The strength of Radical politics in the district was reflected in local organizations' decisions to send letters and telegrams praising the Bloc des gauches government and usually, although not always, with special wishes for Camille Pelletan. Many of these endorsements came in the spring and summer of 1904, arriving soon after Pelletan had survived the attacks of several enemies. They also followed the May municipal elections in which the number of Radicals on local councils throughout France increased. In the small towns and villages of Pelletan's southern district

---

86. Elections 1906, Bouches-du-Rhône, C 6289, AN.

at least a dozen municipal councils sent support to the embattled Radical government, stressing their loyalty to their deputy. Following their annual banquet on January 20, 1904, the assembled mayors of the canton of Salon reaffirmed their commitment to Pelletan and the Bloc des gauches. The commune of Salon, the second largest town in the district, was especially concerned to communicate its endorsement, sending several messages. In most cases these letters of congratulation required a vote by the municipal council, often arrived at unanimously. All noted their commitment to anticlericalism, their devotion to the Republic, and the need for further reforms. The municipal council of Miramas, *chef-lieu* for the canton of Salon, was most explicit in its call for "democratic and social reforms so impatiently awaited by the nation . . . needed to affirm the Republic in the people's spirit: workers' pensions . . . separation of Church and state . . . the improvement of the workers' conditions."[87]

In addition to these indications of Radical strength in local government, the even larger number of fraternal associations sending messages attested to the continuing vitality of social-political life in this southern district. Almost twenty local organizations sent letters of support to the Bloc des gauches government. As might be expected, they included the explicitly political committees of the Radical party now located in Istres, Salon, Martigues, and Port-du-Bouc, several of which had adopted the name Comité Pelletan. Others were more general republican associations continuing older traditions of sociability. In addition, there were several groups of freethinkers and supporters of secular education. Naturally the Masonic Lodge of Salon, L'Unité, and the more recently established lodge in Saint Chamas added their good wishes.[88] Such endorsements made clear that local Radicals identified strongly with their deputy, Camille Pelletan. These expressions of support in 1904 reflected the extent to which radicalism had become an essential element of political and cultural life for the men of the second district of Aix.

87. Félicitations à Combes, 73 AP, Bouches-du-Rhône, AN. The national political significance of these congratulations has been analyzed in an insightful article by Gérard Baal, "Combes et la 'République des comités,'" *Revue d'histoire moderne et contemporaine*, XXIV (April–June, 1977), 260–85. I am indebted to Gérard Baal for his suggestions on this source.

88. *Ibid.*

Pelletan's 1906 campaign statement, published in *Le Petit Provençal* on the first of May, amplified themes that had already appeared in his earlier electoral literature: his incumbency, the critical importance of republican unity against the forces of reaction, and the unchanging nature of his program. He stressed his proven ideological consistency over time and guaranteed that with Pelletan the Provençal voters knew what they were getting. He proudly proclaimed that he and his electors had shared a commitment to the same principles and program for twenty-five years. "I have neither changed, nor retreated. Neither have you." In his view, he had successfully undergone the most challenging test for a deputy. "As a government minister I remained what I had been in the opposition." Pelletan must have realized that there was an element of irony in the claim that he had never changed in twenty-five years. He replied directly to the charge from both Right and Left that the Radicals had neglected their social program. Not true, he insisted. Real legislative gains had occurred: military service had been reduced to two years, public assistance had been established for the elderly, and the Chamber had passed workers' pensions. With the separation now accomplished, he promised that the next legislature would enact economic and social reforms, including the long-awaited progressive income tax, pensions, expanded union rights, and nationalization of the railroads. The list was substantial and, although nothing was new, it was more specific than in the past. For the first time it addressed issues of immediate interest to local constituents. Not only would an income tax be instituted, but the taxes on personal property—doors, windows, and land—would be abolished, especially benefiting rural small property owners. Disabled sailors would receive increased pensions, and railroad workers would finally be granted a pension plan. State workers, *fonctionnaires*, should be awarded the right to unionize. To end "la féodalité financière," railroads and mines should be nationalized. And railroad rates should be set according to the "needs of the nation." A national credit system must be established so that farmers, retailers, and workers might have easy access to capital.[89]

89. "For our sailors an increase in the pension contributions made by the Disability Fund; for the railroad workers the Berteaux law, too long delayed" (*Le Petit Provençal*, May 1, 1906).

Le Petit Provençal labeled his opponent to the Right, Auguste Bouge, a "traitor and renegade" to radicalism for his support of Méline's conservative republican, anti-Dreyfusard government of the late 1890s. Moderate republicans at both the local and national levels endorsed Bouge in the hopes of defeating Pelletan.[90] The local committee for Bouge, which significantly took the label "independent Radical-socialist," simply stated that its candidate's program was "to do what Pelletan had not done and not to do what he had." The Bouge supporters were centered mostly in the smaller cantons of Berre and Lambesc. Pelletan had also lost support in Salon, where the local republican paper, *Le Progrès de Salon,* had been denouncing the Bloc des gauches government and the alliance with the socialists since 1904.[91] His opponent portrayed Pelletan as "a traveling salesman of disorder and hatred . . . the collectivists' accomplice," who had ignored local concerns for twenty-five years. Bouge's campaign statement first excoriated the incumbent as "a man who has placed our national independence in danger" and then called his defeat a "task of political purification and social pacification." Bouge elaborated a program that went beyond mere opposition to Pelletan. Though emphasizing some of the same social and economic problems as Pelletan had, Bouge proposed different solutions. He called for greater equity in the fiscal system, but he did not endorse the income tax. He presented himself as a defender of agricultural interests, and he spoke more directly of the crisis caused by wine overproduction. The immediate solutions he offered were increased state support for "bouilleurs de cru" (property owners who distilled their own alcohol), further subsidies for the raising of silkworms, and subsidies to encourage the cultivation of olive trees and the production of olive oil. For the maritime population Bouge offered improvements for the Etang de Berre and the port of Martigues that he charged Pelletan had neglected for so long. He also subscribed to a pension program for sailors. Although Bouge made few broad ideological appeals, other than opposition to Pelletan and the Bloc des gauches, he

90. *Le Petit Provençal,* April 25, 1906. These forces now included dissident Radicals who had broken with the Combes government, especially over Pelletan's presence in the Ministry of the Navy. See *ibid.* and Chapter VII.

91. *Le Progrès de Salon,* see especially January 20, April 3, 6, 20, 13, 1904, and January 1, 1905.

presented himself as a candidate who understood immediate local problems and had a specific set of solutions.[92]

The SFIO candidate, Shoë, also criticized Pelletan's neglect of local concerns, especially those of workers and small peasants. But like Pelletan, his perspective was national. He presented his candidacy as part of the larger Socialist decision to distinguish itself from all "bourgeois" parties, particularly the Radicals. The Socialists intended to demonstrate that only a party with a clear working-class, anticapitalist perspective could benefit workers and peasants. Here, too, national politics—the dissolution of the Bloc, socialist unification, and the more militant position of the newly organized SFIO—all shaped this local election. On the district and departmental levels, however, socialists had been bitterly divided in their attitudes toward Pelletan since the late 1890s. Some were deeply dissatisfied with his record; others were extremely reluctant to present a working-class candidate in opposition to their Radical-socialist deputy. The departmental congress of the Fédération socialiste, meeting in November, 1897, agreed to support Pelletan's candidacy, but with reservations. A few months later a meeting of collectivist socialists from Pelletan's district seconded this decision with enthusiasm. They echoed the views of most parliamentary socialists and observed that "it is useless to oppose a man who is a socialist, not by his declarations, but by his acts." The meeting also promised to oppose vigorously any dissident socialist who might challenge Pelletan. This motion passed unanimously at the district level, but six communities boycotted the meeting.[93] In the 1890s socialists critical of Pelletan were still in the minority, but they had already organized and were willing to defy the local socialist mainstream.

In 1906 these differences among socialists reemerged. Departmental police reports in the fall of 1905 commented on the growing tension among socialists regarding their relations with the Radicals. On one hand, elected Socialists and SFIO leaders hoped to maintain some form of their alliance with the Radicals. On the other hand, the decisions of the first national

92. Manifeste du Comité Bouge and Déclaration du Candidat, Elections 1906, II M3 45, AD/BR. Interestingly, Bouge's calls for state intervention in the agricultural economy were largely directed at declining sectors such as raw silk and olives.

93. Police report, February 1, 1898, Dossier Pelletan, MI 25359, AN.

SFIO party congress and, most important, pressure from local activists called for Socialist candidates in every district, including those where Socialists would oppose Radicals. In the second arrondissement of Aix demands for a Socialist candidate came initially from groups in Salon. During the departmental congress held in the beginning of 1906, the decision to select a Socialist candidate to oppose Pelletan was endorsed. Now the impetus came from the Socialist group of Saint Chamas, which had met earlier to promote this action. This new socialist independence corresponded both with the national direction of the SFIO and with at least some local sentiments, but Socialist party discipline was not fully effective. In March, l'Avant-Garde socialiste, the largest SFIO group in Salon, voted to support Camille Pelletan in the upcoming election.[94] Le Petit Provençal, which had strong socialist sympathies, never wavered in its ardent support of the Radical deputy.

Pelletan had a variety of reactions to this opposition from the Left. Several contradictory political demands determined his responses: the need to criticize a challenger, the importance of maintaining his support among Socialist voters, the desire to demonstrate his continued commitment to a parliamentary alliance of Socialists and Radicals, and the ideological need to repudiate the class politics of the SFIO. Police reports in 1905 predicted "a hotly contested election" requiring a second round. Perhaps because of the complexity of the political situation, Pelletan chose to ignore or belittle the significance of the Socialist candidate. In a Petit Provençal article only a few days before the election, Pelletan reminded readers that "a certain Shoë . . . wasn't even born while we were already struggling against the Empire." This may have been the most astute immediate strategy because in the end, Shoë received hardly more votes than the socialist candidate of 1898. But there can be no doubt that the appearance of an official candidate of the unified Socialist party, led by important parliamentarians, seriously disturbed Pelletan. He genuinely feared the further erosion of the electoral and parliamentary alliance of the Bloc des gauches. From his perspective, Socialist class politics undermined the various alliances of democratic forces. Pelletan argued that such an erosion would, in the long run, prove

94. Elections 1906, September 21, 1905, February 5, 1906, March 26, 1906, II M3 45, AD/BR.

unfavorable to the development of socialism. In addition to these political considerations, Pelletan appeared to have been personally wounded that anyone would think to call him "an exploiter who had deceived his constituents for a quarter of a century." Even worse, the SFIO leadership, which included some of his closest parliamentary collaborators, men whom he continued to call "my friends," implicitly endorsed these attacks.[95]

Pelletan accurately gauged the political forces in the 1906 elections and reserved his principal attacks for his moderate republican opponent. A coalition of socialist and Radical voters gave Pelletan a somewhat unexpected first-round victory. The 75 percent voter turnout was the highest for all of Pelletan's campaigns.[96] He won 7,450 votes, over half of those voting and 43 percent of those eligible to vote. These were the highest percentages he had ever gained in an election. His moderate opponent won 33 percent of the votes cast and 25 percent of the eligible voters. The SFIO candidate, Shoë, made a weak showing, winning 8 percent of the votes and 6 percent of those eligible. One police report identified Pelletan's greatest support as located in Istres, Martigues, and the city of Salon.[97] In his postelection message to his constituents, Pelletan could not resist a last bitter swipe at "a strange revolutionary socialist who never attacked the common enemy." This 1906 victory reflected Pelletan's powerful personal standing within his district. Paradoxically, his embattled position within the Combes government and the fall of that Radical government had enhanced his prestige. The electoral victory also suggested that despite the newly independent stance of the SFIO, the promises of a parliamentary reform coalition of Socialists and Radicals still carried considerable appeal to both sets of voters in the far South. An October, 1906, banquet held in

95. *Ibid.*, September 26, 1905; *Le Petit Provençal*, May 2, 1906; "Les Nouvelles Impressions de Voyage," *ibid*.

96. Of 17,149 eligible voters, 12,919 voted (Elections 1906, Bouches-du-Rhône, C 6289, AN).

97. In 1898 a socialist candidate, Tressaud, gained a small 6 percent of the 11,889 voting and 4 percent of all eligible voters, who numbered 16,895; he won 733 votes (Elections 1898, Bouches-du-Rhône, C 5116 and C 5350, AN). Comparing the Socialist votes of 1906 to those of 1898 it seems that, especially in the maritime town of Martigues and in its outlying communes, Socialists chose to vote for Pelletan rather than the SFIO candidate. In Saint Chamas, where there had been long-standing criticism of Pelletan, the Socialist candidate did extremely well (Elections 1906, Bouches-du-Rhône, C 6289, AN).

Salon in honor of Pelletan's twenty-five years as deputy exemplified this support. National and local supporters of the Bloc des gauches, many of them government officials, attended.[98] Several independent socialists were present, but significantly no member of the SFIO was included.

The year 1906 was the last time Pelletan could easily present himself as the leader of a party committed to fundamental social and economic reforms. After 1906 it became steadily more apparent that his brand of radicalism was losing its force. Criticisms of Pelletan's left-wing radicalism were heard more frequently from within the Radical party itself. This difficulty was compounded by the newly independent position of the SFIO, the failure to reconstitute the Bloc after 1906, the Radicals' division over support for the Clemenceau government, and, most important, the inability and unwillingness of the Radical party to deliver on most of its promised reforms. The reorientation and restructuring of radicalism after 1906 marked an end to the leading role Pelletan had previously played. In this context, several local observers predicted his political demise. In September, 1907, one anonymous police source from Salon announced, somewhat prematurely but with great enthusiasm, "the end of M. Pelletan's reign in the Bouches-du-Rhône." This same source reported that "in most communes M. Pelletan can't open his mouth and two or three times he's been shouted down. . . . In addition . . . there are some solid Radicals who cannot forgive him for attacking the Clemenceau government and his shifting attitude toward the socialists." Despite exaggeration and obvious wishful thinking, the informant did not misrepresent the situation. The first congress of southeastern Radicals, held in the spring of 1907, expressed serious discontent with the party's failure to deliver on promised reforms and mounting hostility toward the SFIO with its principle of class politics. The regional congress called for greater party discipline, more legislative results, and, above all, a critical scrutiny of the alliance with the Socialist party. Several conflicting attitudes on the part of Radicals toward the Clemenceau government exacerbated this pervasive dissatisfaction. In the South these issues were all

98. *Le Petit Provençal*, May 8, 1906. The guests included General André; Siméon Flaissières, mayor of Marseilles and senator of the Bouches-du-Rhône; the departmental prefect and subprefect; Bouches-du-Rhône deputies Bonfer and Baron; and Deputy Henri Michel from Arles. Camille and his wife were presented with commemorative gifts (Police report, October 14, 1906, Dossier Pelletan, MI 25359, AN).

the more acute because of the 1906–1908 crisis among winegrowers and the government's failure to resolve the situation.[99]

This simmering discontent with the practice of Radical politics was the backdrop for Camille's final campaign for the Chamber of Deputies in 1910. While disagreements among Radicals resulted in criticism of Pelletan from within the party, this same controversy galvanized his dedicated supporters, eager to defend traditional beliefs and standards. The *Progrès de Salon* had changed hands once again and now substituted lavish praise for its 1904–1905 criticism of Pelletan. He was presented as one of the few Radical politicians with genuine values and integrity. Unlike previous elections, that of 1910 was an unambiguous contest between Pelletan and a member of the Socialist party, P. Marius-André, thus definitively breaking the pattern of socialists and Radicals joining to support Pelletan. The twenty-nine-year veteran narrowly won the election on the first round against this outsider, a railroad employee, union activist, and Socialist party militant. Voter participation remained high with an almost 70 percent turnout, but Pelletan's percentage of votes cast declined from the previous election. The trend was obvious. The combination of socialist independence and the SFIO's commitment to present viable candidates, coupled with discord among local Radicals, strongly suggested that 1910 should be Pelletan's last campaign.[100]

Camille Pelletan was sixty-six years old in 1912, when a Senate seat for the Bouches-du-Rhône became vacant. He must have had several second thoughts about standing for a ninth reelection campaign to the Chamber in 1914, facing at best a demanding contest and at worst the very real possibility of a humiliating defeat at the hands of a Socialist opponent. Therefore, he presented his name for the Senate, the institution he had denounced for so many years, demanding its abolition or thorough reform. His friends

99. *Ibid.*, September 25, 26, 1907. For a fuller discussion of the wine crisis and Radicals, see Chapter VIII.

100. *Le Progrès de Salon*, June 24, 28, 1908. In 1910 12,255 citizens voted, of whom 6,197 cast their ballots for Pelletan. He received 50.5 percent of the vote to Marius' 42 percent or 5,149 votes (Elections 1910, Bouches-du-Rhône, C 6556, AN). In 1906 Pelletan had received 57.6 percent of votes cast. In local municipal elections republican critics of Pelletan joined with "reactionaries" to break the deputy's influence (Police report, Port-de-Bouc, December 21, 1911, M6 3404, AD/BR).

explained that only the urgent need to increase support for the progressive income income tax among resistant senators had convinced Pelletan to serve in this conservative institution.[101] Without doubt some local Radicals were relieved that they would no longer have to defend Pelletan's unwavering support for the Bloc des gauches alliance. The moderate wing of the Radical party must certainly have hoped that this new position would signal the retirement of the aged leader and his brand of radicalism. His contacts throughout the Bouches-du-Rhône with Radical and Socialist departmental and municipal councilors, who decided senatorial elections, ought to have assured him an easy victory. Of course, it had been precisely such political connections and the indirect election procedure which Pelletan had so bitterly decried in the 1880s as an assault on the principle of "universal suffrage."[102] But even in this environment of local political insiders Pelletan could no longer count on automatic support. He was elected to the Senate only on the second round of balloting and then with 230 opposed and 439 in favor.[103]

Universal male suffrage in the second district of Aix over several decades favored the Radical-socialists. The electoral results demonstrated that although Pelletan retained this seat for thirty years, it was not simply his personal fief. Only in 1902 did he run uncontested. In the early campaigns there were two rounds (1881, 1889), and even in those in which Pelletan won on the first round it was usually following a strenuous campaign, and his majorities were narrow (1898, 1906, 1910). By the early twentieth century, Pelletan was appealing to a heterogeneous electorate composed of distinct Radical and socialist groups. According to his close collaborator, Tony Révillon, these faithful constituents included "peasants, shepherds, sailors . . . workers, artisans and small businessmen," all of whom addressed their deputy as Camille.[104] Unlike the socially homogeneous agricultural villages of the neighboring Var, which Tony Judt has so profitably studied, Pelletan's district remained much closer to the hetero-

101. Pelletan funeral, Le Radical, June 9, 1915; Pelletan obituary, Le Petit Provençal, June 6, 1915.

102. See long quote from Pelletan in Laisant, Anarchie bourgeoise, 201–206.

103. Police report, Elections senatoriales, November 27, 1911, II M2 10, AD/BR.

104. Révillon, Camille Pelletan, 195.

geneous urban villages characteristic of mid-nineteenth-century Provence. In addition, the proximity of Marseilles powerfully affected the area. In the political and cultural spheres the role of *Le Petit Provençal* was only one indication of this influence. The agricultural economic crises of the 1880s and the early twentieth century were less acute in this region than in the monoculture villages of either the Var or Languedoc, but here too older agricultural and industrial activities were giving way to those more compatible with new markets. Judging from various membership lists, local bourgeois retained their importance and continued to dominate Radical associations. As in the Var, an independent Socialist organization emerged, but as late as 1906 Socialists remained divided about their position in relation to Pelletan and his form of radicalism. The image of Radical politics in Provence which emerges from these elections differs somewhat from the usual stereotype. In most elections Pelletan did face a challenger, usually from the Right and in the final campaigns also from the Left. He took them seriously and campaigned effectively. From 1881 to 1906 he was able to double his support among voters. (In the 1881 election 18 percent of eligible voters voted in the first round and 21 percent in the second; in 1906 43 percent of eligible voters voted in the first round.) His opponents usually accused him of neglecting his constituency and failing to defend their interests, especially those of agriculture. Pelletan, particularly in the final campaigns, stressed his support for specific social and economic reforms and insisted that the well-being of his electors was linked to the larger national issues of creating an authentic social republic. These charges of neglect had some validity, however. For example, inadequate port facilities at Martigues were never improved, seriously impeding economic development in the district. By the 1910 election Pelletan himself must have felt his support slipping when he was unable to deliver the promised reforms and the very meaning of radicalism was drifting away from him.[105]

105. The district did remain in the Radical-socialist camp. Pelletan's protégé, Auguste Girard, won the special by-election in 1912 in a hotly contested race. The second round pitted him against the Socialist André Marius; Girard clearly won. Of 12,026 voting, Girard had 7,332 and Marius 4,485. By 1914 Girard was able to win on the first round against another serious Socialist candidate (Special Election 1912, Bouches-du-Rhône, C 7225, AN, and Elections 1914, Bouches-du-Rhône, C 6862, AN).

In addition to the implantation of radicalism in the South, these elections also revealed increasing participation in the political process. By the early twentieth century a clear majority of the male population regarded voting as a meaningful act. Abstention rates fell from 43 percent in the second round of the 1881 election (48 percent in the first round) to 25 percent in the election of 1906 and remained at that level until 1914. Not surprisingly, this commitment to the electoral process, the essence of republicanism, was especially high among Pelletan's supporters, whether Radicals or socialists. This was clear from the turnout for the 1902 election when he ran unopposed. Forty-nine percent of the electorate chose to voice their opinion, overwhelmingly for Pelletan (87 percent). The vote was both a vehicle for political choice and a means of affirming commitment to the regime. Without doubt this group of citizens had internalized the Radicals' view of suffrage. They would readily endorse the sentiments of a 1902 Radical electoral pamphlet that proclaimed: "Citizens: There is one great and noble act in life. It is the vote. Your vote is free; it belongs to you and only to you."[106] These southern voters would also have agreed with the Radical Parisian deputy Ferdinand Buisson that "universal suffrage is the soul of the democratic system."[107] Yet neither politicians nor electors viewed the vote as an end in itself; the political choice was intended to implement certain programs. That implementation required parliamentary activity, and it is to that Parisian arena we now turn.

106. Comité républicain radical-socialiste, Pamphlet, Montpellier, April, 1902, Atmosphère politique, Elections 1902, F7 12542, AN.

107. Buisson, *Politique radicale*, 307.

VI The Parliamentary World

François Furet characterizes the Third Republic as "a parliamentary regime based on the sovereignty of the people."[1] He also suggests that this dual foundation was fraught with both ideological and practical tensions. The Radicals of the early Republic would have essentially agreed with this basic definition and would certainly have concurred that there was tension between the parliamentary process and the expression of popular sovereignty. Radicals began their political careers with an unwavering commitment to popular sovereignty expressed through universal male suffrage. They never abandoned this faith, although the Boulanger Affair had shaken it. From their origins, however, Radicals were much less committed to the legitimacy of parliamentary institutions. Yet by the first decade of the twentieth century they formed the largest political group in the Chamber of Deputies and dominated much of the debate in the Senate. Their emphasis on electoral success makes their increasing presence in the parliamentary chambers hardly surprising. By 1900, three hundred parliamentarians in the Chamber and in the Senate adhered to the label *Radical*.[2] This chapter explores the changing attitudes of left Radicals, such as Pelletan, to parliamentary institutions and processes. It also examines how parliamentary responsibilities and careers affected these politicians. Radicals, who first became a force in the Chamber in the 1880s, led the way in the transformation of an elected position into a lifelong career, *un métier*, with implicit rules and sought-after rewards. Radicals were recognized and often decried as the quintessential politicians of the Third Republic. By the twentieth century these professionals had become important members of a new republican political elite. It was an elite still uncertain of its status and prestige but

1. Furet, ed., *Jules Ferry*, 10.
2. Berstein, *Histoire du parti radical*, I, 35.

committed to directing national politics. Like most new elites, it was vulnerable to criticisms of vulgarity and greed.

Until the late 1880s the Radicals regarded parliamentary institutions and procedures with suspicion. They viewed the Senate as illegitimate and questioned whether the Chamber of Deputies could authentically represent the "will of the people." In the spring of 1871, filled with the euphoria of creating a new regime, extreme leftists like Camille Pelletan declared "that imperial France and *parliamentary* France are dead."[3] In the early 1880s, Pelletan was still denouncing "those rotting Assemblies of the July Monarchy, those Assemblies hostile to the most minimal reform, discredited by venality and intrigue."[4] The Third Republic must be something different. Outspoken antiparliamentarianism was a major issue among those Radicals of the 1880s who were instrumental in the creation of the Boulangist movement. This antiparliamentary tradition was part of the ideological legacy these disenchanted Radicals contributed to the development of right-wing nationalism. By the late 1880s, although Radical leaders Clemenceau and Pelletan had dropped such strident antiparliamentarianism, they never entirely eliminated it from their discourse. It remained a muted strain in their political outlook and one that made left Radicals, like Pelletan, comfortable with oppositional attitudes.

Following the Boulangist episode, the Radical mainstream clearly identified itself with the parliamentary system. Their essential commitment to legality and political stability, despite their criticism of parliamentary institutions, brought them to repudiate former colleagues who came to lead the Boulangist movement. Most Radicals, like other republicans, much preferred the role of defending rights and laws against usurpers. Celebrating the first official July Fourteenth in 1881, Pelletan suggested that the real meaning of the storming of the Bastille was the people's *defense* of their natural rights, which the monarchy threatened. During the Boulangist episode he directly criticized antiparliamentarianism, while still noting the problems of the institution. "It's become a fashion to attack the representative system which safeguards the country. We bear the brunt of early errors." Yet even at the very end of his life, after amassing an impeccable record

3. *Le Rappel*, no. 94, May 8, 1871, emphasis added.
4. *La Justice*, no. 490, May 19, 1881.

as a parliamentary defender, Pelletan still expressed a lingering uneasiness with his lifelong profession. Writing his memoirs in 1913, he described his attitude as a young man of twenty-one: "Despite our very passionate republican convictions, we had little taste for a political career."[5] Pelletan certainly was one of the consummate politicians of the early Third Republic. He contributed significantly to defining what a republican political career meant, but he himself never quite silenced those youthful criticisms of parliament and those who filled its chambers.

In his 1880s denunciation of parliament Charles Laisant, the future Boulangist leader, identified two constraints which even the best intentioned new deputy could never escape. The first was the intricate rules of parliamentary organization and the second the informal force of the deputies' collective experiences. These institutional and social pressures imposed conformity to the status quo, strengthened the existing parliamentary regime, and, in Laisant's view, made it impossible to carry out a democratic mandate.[6] In the decades between 1880 and 1910, the Radicals moved fairly quickly from the periphery of this parliamentary world to its center. By the first decade of the twentieth century they were often the arbitrators of "parliamentary rules." They succeeded so well because they had come to dominate the principal institution of French parliamentary life, the Chamber of Deputies, the only national governing body elected by universal male suffrage.

By the 1880s the Chamber unquestionably had attained greater importance than either the office of president or the Senate. The Chamber's legislative term lasted four years. Each year was divided into a *session ordinaire*, beginning in January and usually ending in May or June, and a *session extraordinaire* held in the fall when necessary. The dominant political position of the Chamber was in part a result of the complex politics of the 1870s and 1880s, when the existence of the regime had been in question. In part it also reflected the strength of republican, and specifically Radical, ideology, which recognized election by "universal suffrage" as the only legitimate source of political power. Some commentators have compared this primacy of the Chamber to monarchical authority, a "divine

5. *Ibid.*, no. 548, July 16, 1881; no. 3210, October 26, 1888; Pelletan, "Mémoires (inédites)," in Baquiast, "Pelletan," 341.

6. Laisant, *Anarchie bourgeoise*, 221.

221

right" of the legislature.[7] Moderate republican deputies, such as Raymond Poincaré, often denounced the absence of what they considered appropriate parliamentary limitations on the lower house. In 1896 Poincaré spoke out against "the Chamber [which] has little by little appropriated most government prerogatives. . . . The deputies govern, administer, appoint. . . . Under the appearance of parliamentarianism we have, at certain times, in reality the Convention."[8]

The numerous critics of the Radicals have often focused on what they perceived as the Radicals' near total control of the Chamber, which arguably gave them tantamount control over the French state.[9] This view distorts both the Radicals' position within the Chamber of Deputies and the Chamber's role within the state structure. Of the approximately 600 members of the lower house, the Radicals, at their prewar height between 1902 and 1910, held 250 seats. Only the governments of Bourgeois, 1895–1896, Combes, 1902–1905, Ernest Monis, 1911, and Joseph Caillaux, 1911–1912 can be labeled as genuinely Radical.[10] In addition, though the Chamber was the most powerful legislative body of the state, it was emphatically not the entire state. Even in the realm of legislation, the Senate retained considerable power. All histories of reform legislation indicate the regularity with which the Senate blocked, delayed, and drastically amended reforms central to the Radical platform, from workers' old age pensions to the long-promised progressive income tax.[11] Furthermore, the Senate retained the ability to overthrow governments by refusing to act on vital legislation. Although used only once in the mid-1890s against the Bourgeois Radi-

7. R. K. Gooch, *The French Parliamentary Committee System* (Charlottesville, Va., 1935), 229; for a very strong statement of the Chamber's power see also Jean Pierre Rioux, "Le Palais Bourbon," in *La Nation* (Paris, 1986), 502, Vol. II of *Les Lieux de mémoire*, ed. Nora, 2 vols.

8. Quoted in Guiral and Thuillier, *Vie quotidienne*, 246.

9. For one example see Halévy, *La République des comités*, 107–108 and *passim*. A similar portrait, although without the rancor and condemnation, can be found in Rioux, "Palais Bourbon," 502–503.

10. There is, of course, room for debate about this list. I exclude the Clemenceau government of 1906–1909, which was often perceived as Radical and had Radical members. Its policies departed from the Radical party program, and the party leadership officially criticized the government, although a significant portion of Radical deputies supported Clemenceau. See Chapter VIII.

11. Stone, *Search for Social Peace*, 104, 111, 119.

cal government and its proposed income tax, the threat of such action reflected real power. In the next chapter we will examine the complex relation among Radicals in the Chamber, the government, and the Senate.

At least as powerful as the Senate and often more resistant to the influence of the Chamber was the highly centralized administration of the state, many of whose institutions had been established during the First Empire. Especially in the ministries of the army, navy, foreign affairs, and, to a lesser extent, finance and justice, a significant number of important staff positions remained filled with men whose allegiance to the Republic was at best lukewarm. Pelletan frequently considered the most important of all reforms "that of the organization of the State and the significant reduction of government administrative costs." Throughout his parliamentary career he pitted himself against the state bureaucracy, which he characterized as archaic and inappropriate for a democratic regime. "We live in one of the nations of the world . . . where there have been the least reforms for the last eighty years . . . [the least] administrative and budgetary reforms. . . . We have gone through revolutions and coups d'état, but we have maintained the entire structure of the Consulate. The France of 1888 is suffocating in clothes tailored for the France of 1800." [12]

By the 1890s Camille Pelletan had become a key protagonist in this struggle between the Chamber and the administration. He was able to assume this role not simply because of conviction but also because of his membership in the most powerful body in the Chamber, the Budget Committee. Major debates and particularly the interpellations of government ministers were public events that at times approached high drama, but the various committees in their closed-door hearings carried on the actual legislative work of the Chamber. They had the responsibility to screen all legislative initiatives, deciding whether to recommend them to the Chamber. If sent to the Chamber, which normally gave them two readings, the committee's detailed report would accompany the legislation. Originally, selection for these critical committees combined the official policy of random selection with unofficial political influence. From its beginning and following precedents established in 1848, the Chamber was divided into eleven offices (*bureaux*) whose members were selected by lot. These *bureaux*

---

12. *La Justice*, no. 2936, January 28, 1888; no. 2939, January 31, 1888.

then appointed two or three of their members to serve on each of the committees; the committees traditionally (at least until 1910) had thirty-three members.[13] A deputy's political allegiance and less frequently his expertise largely determined appointments. The power of the committees increased steadily. During the 1870s no permanent committee existed; every piece of legislation required the creation of a special body to review it. Such an ad-hoc system soon proved impractical. Slowly, in the face of much resistance from individual deputies and especially from government ministers, a certain degree of continuity was established. Key committees (*les grandes commissions*) were appointed to sit for one year. The first such committee, established in 1876, reviewed the budget, and the Army Committee followed in 1882. By 1898, eleven annual committees had been created. Of course, ad-hoc committees continued to be created to examine special legislation and, most important, to conduct special investigations.[14]

In November, 1902, the permanent committees gained even greater influence when their terms were extended to equal the four years of the legislative session and their number was increased to sixteen. The Chamber's *bureaux* continued to make the official appointments to the committees, but the various political groups informally agreed on proportional representation and individual appointments. Most Radicals in the new Chamber and the new Radical government of Emile Combes supported the reform to extend the length of the committees. Although a strong majority of the Chamber endorsed this change (351 deputies voted for it), a significant minority opposed the new power of the committees (179 deputies against). Following this reform, committees often had a longer existence than governments. The reform, intended to make legislative action more efficient, reinforced a dual system of authority in which committees and government ministries competed for control over legislation.[15]

13. Absences were a permanent problem as they were for many public sessions.

14. In 1898 there were 184 ad-hoc committees (Guiral and Thuillier, *Vie quotidienne*, 227). These special committees investigated diverse issues such as general social and economic conditions, parliamentarians' involvement in the bankruptcy of the Panama Canal company, and the political implications of the Humbert family fraud. Committees could also create investigative subcommittees such as the budget subcommittee that investigated Pelletan's handling of the Ministry of the Navy in 1904.

15. *Ibid.*, 226–28; Gooch, *French Parliamentary Committee System*, 88.

The key Budget Committee reviewed not only the minister of finance's budget proposal but all legislation that included any appropriation.[16] One of the original tasks of the committee had been to expedite the annual public debates on the government's proposed budgets. These debates were extremely lengthy because individual deputies attempted to increase allocations beneficial to their constituents. Efforts to limit such amendments were viewed as infringements on the deputies' prerogatives. The final passage of the budget rarely occurred in time to meet fiscal deadlines; government activities were then conducted through a variety of provisional measures. Most sensitive were military allocations, which increased regularly every year. Significantly, the president of the Budget Committee in 1905–1907 requested that certain military expenses be accounted for outside the regular budget. Paradoxically, the Budget Committee, which had been created to accelerate the budget debate, itself came to be viewed as a major obstacle. Outside the committee, its members were seen as powerful figures attempting to rewrite the minister's priorities and introduce their own fiscal proposals. An 1888 article in La Revue administrative expressed the exasperation of high-level civil servants: "The official wreckers who are members of the Budget Committee . . . think of themselves as great politicians, powerful statesmen, because they have carried out, without care or moderation, some cuts in government credits granted to ensure the proper functioning of public services. . . . All or almost all of them knew not the least thing about administration before they entered parliament, and all of a sudden . . . they become masters of the budget."[17] The tension between state administrators and deputies could hardly be better expressed.

Membership on the Budget Committee was one of Camille Pelletan's principal activities during his parliamentary career. Critics of the committee

16. Gooch, French Parliamentary Committee System, 184–85. For a general discussion of state budgets in this period, see François Caron, "Les Politiques économiques de l'état," in L'Ere industrielle et la société d'aujourd'hui (siècle 1880–1980) (Paris, 1979), 244–56, Vol. IV of Histoire économique et sociale de la France, ed. Braudel and Labrousse, 4 vols.

17. 1900 Berthelot resolution, in Guiral and Thuillier, Vie quotidienne, 239–40. The years 1905–1907 are especially significant because they follow immediately after the Combes government. See Chapter VIII. Similar "quasi-clandestine" procedures occurred in 1914 for rearmament. The quote from La Revue administrative is from ibid., 238. Both sides of this struggle well understood the political importance of the budget.

often selected him as their favorite target. Following his second electoral victory in 1885, Pelletan joined this powerful and prestigious committee headed by moderate republican Maurice Rouvier. As early as 1887, Pelletan was selected to present the committee's general report to the Chamber. It was on the Budget Committee in 1888 that he began his long-term interest in the navy. In 1897 he was given responsibility for reporting on the naval budget, a position he held several times and a subject on which he was already considered expert. He prepared the committee's report on the railroad conventions in 1889. A year later he served as the committee's vice-president and once again in 1898–1899 as its general reporter.[18]

All accounts of Pelletan's activity on this committee belied the usual stereotypes, which described him as a disheveled, slightly drunk, unwashed, disorganized, and bombastic Radical.[19] Even unsympathetic commentators had to acknowledge his diligence and expertise. Paul Bosq, a journalist, was one such critic who condemned radicalism as having "returned France to the Wars of Religion." Nonetheless, Pelletan came off rather well in Bosq's 1899 collection of witty, illustrated mini-biographies of leading deputies. (This collective biography might more accurately be called a series of political caricatures.) Despite his own inclinations, Bosq not only acknowledged Pelletan's positive contributions in specific committees but also recognized what must have been a major reform of parliamentary life—Pelletan's insistence on clarity and directness in committee reports: "[Pelletan] . . . goes off to war against abuses. He surprises his Radical companions by his laborious activity. . . . It seems one can do nothing without him. He is very visible, he stands out. His reports on Tonkin and on the budget are almost events. In any case they initiate a daring reaction against classical parliamentary language. It is perhaps the first time that a reporter dares to replace the atrocious jargon of the Chambers with a style in which the

18. After 1906 Pelletan also served as vice-president of the special committee for electoral reform, La Commission du suffrage universel, which Ferdinand Buisson headed. This committee examined the proportional representation question and women's suffrage.

19. In a very sympathetic obituary Pelletan's "intense hard work" in parliamentary committees was underscored (*Le Petit Provençal*, June 6, 1915). See also Revillon, *Camille Pelletan*, and Jean Joly, *Dictionnaire des parlementaires français; notices biographiques sur les parlementaires français, 1889–1940* (8 vols.; Paris, 1960–77), VII, 2637–38, for a full list of his committee responsibilities.

nuance of the insights takes nothing away from the force of the thought, and ponderous conclusions are superseded by lively themes." Bosq concluded what remained a mixed portrait of Pelletan by placing him at the very center of parliamentary life. "One finds him everywhere and in everything." From this vantage post, Pelletan attacked what Bosq identified as his "two personal enemies": the large railroad companies and the state administration.[20]

Pelletan's long membership on the Budget Committee provided an effective position from which to carry out this campaign. By 1890 his record of hard work and his knowledge of financial issues won him election as committee vice-president. He gained this post in a committee whose majority was weighted toward republican moderates and whose president, Jean Casimir-Périer, was one of France's wealthiest and most powerful industrialists. The report on the country's financial situation, which Pelletan prepared and the committee finally endorsed, combined the author's own Radical views with accommodations necessary to gain the entire committee's approval. This general report was issued in November, 1890, less than six months after a majority of the full committee had rejected Pelletan's subcommittee report on state-owned railroads. His calls for further state intervention and his attacks on the six major rail companies dismayed several moderates. When the first draft of the more general report appeared, similar criticisms were raised. Pelletan agreed to tone down some of his proposals but not to modify the essential thrust of the report.[21] This compromise apparently worked, and the report was issued November 22, 1890.

Pelletan began this fiscal analysis with proposals for procedural changes that were as significant as specific policies. He demanded that state budgets cease to be a mystery, accessible only to a very restricted circle of political and financial initiates. Clarity and simplicity in financial matters were the appropriate characteristics of a democratic state. He then turned his attention to the major problem of French finances: the debt, "the largest

20. Bosq, *Nos Chers Souverains*, 43–46, 73–74. The title of Bosq's collection, *Nos Chers Souverains*, revealed the author's attitude toward parliamentarians. The only deputy who received an unequivocally positive description and portrait was the Comte du Mun, the conservative Catholic leader (194–95).

21. *Procès verbaux, Commission du budget*, July 24, 1890, p. 897, C 5441, AN; *ibid.*, November 12, 1890, p. 1049.

in Europe relative to national populations." In 1890 the debt constituted one-third of a steadily growing budget. Although mounting state obligations on loans were the principal cause of increased costs, other important expenses were the military, education, and public works, especially road and port construction. The latter two Pelletan labeled as "new and fruitful expenses." Education was a "sacred duty . . . strengthening the worker, the soldier." After a comparative study, he claimed that French military costs were proportionally the highest in Europe. His recommendations, however, were surprisingly moderate, perhaps reflecting the composition of the entire committee. He cautioned that "the very high cost of these sacrifices renders absolutely necessary the most scrupulous attention in order to spend nothing beyond the resolution."[22]

Here in carefully worded dispassionate language he raised his lifelong concern about the power of large capital and whether it was compatible with an authentically democratic state and democratic politics. Significantly, the term "la féodalité financière" with its politically charged references never appeared in this text, but the report examined the same issues that phrase evoked. Pelletan asked for a review of the terms governing the loan extended by the Morgan Bank of New York at the time of the Franco-Prussian War. Even more seriously, he then questioned what had become one of the cornerstones of moderate republican government finance: the state guarantee of a 3 percent minimum interest on the bonds of the six major railroad companies. In this text written for the entire Budget Committee, Pelletan could not raise the standard Radical demand of state repurchase of the private railroad lines. Perhaps, too, Pelletan, the careful financial researcher, may have even questioned the feasibility of that demand. Instead, Pelletan did note the large portion of the state debt spent on securing these private bonds and called for their replacement with direct state loans to the companies. Such a change could be viewed as a first step toward nationalization.[23]

22. "Rapport fait au nom de la Commission du budget sur la situation financière de la France par M. C. Pelletan, Député," Annales de l'Assemblée nationale, Chambre des députés, Annexes, November 22, 1890, no. 1031, pp. 8, 82, 62, 54.

23. Ibid., 133–48. Pelletan's position assumed that in the continuing recessionary climate of the 1880s government dividend guarantees would continue to be a serious drain on the budget. Beginning in the early 1890s and until the war, however, some, but not all, companies actually

Pelletan's persistent concern with the relations between the railroad companies and the state cannot be dismissed as a cranky obsession. Long after the 1878 Freycinet Plan and the 1883 Railroad Convention between the companies and the state, Pelletan insisted on returning to these questions, which he clearly considered to be among the most vital financial and economic issues of the day. Not a few political and economic historians of the Third Republic have agreed on the central role of railroad development and the special importance of the state's involvement in that enterprise.[24] Sanford Elwitt in his key study *The Making of the Third Republic* astutely identifies the centrality of the railroad issue in the political debates of the late 1870s and early 1880s. The pivotal Freycinet Plan essentially continued the imperial tradition of low-cost, state-subsidized credit for the large companies, which the major banks largely controlled. Elwitt plausibly argues that this plan fundamentally shaped the economic and social direction of the new Republic. He also proposes that this debate was for all practical purposes concluded by the early 1880s with an outcome that favored large capital and encountered little serious political opposition. Elwitt insists that the Freycinet Plan, which marked the Republic's abandonment of the economic interests of small producers, definitively defeated what he calls radical democracy or radical populism.[25] Although most of the parliamentary struggles over economic policy and especially social legislation were ultimately concluded in favor of large capital and large finance, these struggles certainly did not end in the early 1880s. Serious conflicts among politicians, often reflecting permanent intraclass tensions within the bourgeoisie, dominated the first half of the Third Republic. Pelletan's activity on the Budget Committee demonstrated that these economic policy questions were not

---

reimbursed the treasury in the more buoyant economy of the early twentieth century. See François Caron, *An Economic History of Modern France*, trans. Barbara Bray (New York, 1989), 70–74; Roger Price, *An Economic History of Modern France, 1730–1914* (London, 1981), 25; Michael Smith, "Railroads," in *Historical Dictionary of the Third French Republic, 1870–1940*, ed. Patrick H. Hutton (2 vols.; Westport, Conn., 1986), 830–31.

24. François Caron, *Histoire de l'exploitation d'un grand réseau. La Compagnie du chemin de fer du Nord, 1846–1937* (Paris, 1973); Caron, "L'Extension des infrastructures et des équipements et l'intensification des échanges de marchandises," in *L'Ere industrielle et la société d'aujourd'hui (siècle 1880–1980)* (Paris, 1979), 143–53, Vol. IV of *Histoire économique et sociale de la France*, ed. Braudel and Labrousse, 4 vols.

25. Elwitt, *Making of the Third Republic*, 109, 114, chaps. III and IV, 129–30, 146, 165, 168.

merely electoral rhetoric. Their persistent appearance on Radical candidates' campaign platforms in 1902 and 1906 attested to a continuing effort to explore what constituted a democratic state and society. This left Radical position may not have triumphed, but it certainly merits examination.

Considering the left Radicals' economic concerns, those issues that were not addressed in Pelletan's 1890 Budget Committee report were as noteworthy as those that were examined. The report did not hint at problems of inadequate revenues or the inequities of the tax structure, which remained essentially unchanged since the beginning of the century. Certainly one of the leading demands of the Radicals had been and would continue to be tax reform, particularly the introduction of a progressive income tax. Yet in 1890 the Budget Committee, as constructed by parliamentary rules, would not seriously entertain such a proposal. Within the structure of this powerful committee, a multiterm, hardworking Radical like Pelletan succeeded in introducing some of his concerns into the document that would direct serious legislative debate. At the same time, however, very clear limits existed as to how far such concerns could deviate from the ultimate and necessary consensus among committee members. These inevitable limitations certainly must account for Pelletan's noticeable circumspection in his comments on military spending in this 1890 report.

The military together with the debt, large banks, and the railroads were among his principal interests. In the 1895 committee, whose president was fellow Radical Edouard Lockroy, Camille Pelletan headed the subcommittee on the navy. In October he presented a special report whose main points summed up what would be Pelletan's criticisms of the navy throughout his political career. They would serve as the basis for his actions while minister of the navy from 1902 to 1905. Pelletan's central objective was to establish parliamentary control over an organization which in his view functioned without appropriate democratic constraints. No government had adequately supervised this service because "ministers were dominated by the committees and councils of the ministry which were directed by the admirals. . . . [Parliamentary] responsibility did not exist." After comparing the French navy to other European fleets, he argued for significant reductions in personnel attached to the general staff in France and in the administrative staffs of the naval arsenals. He demanded greater accountability over the purchase of material. His investigations had led to the conclusion that the arsenals were in a state of "the most grievous disorder . . . [and that] abuses . . . even frauds" were being perpetrated. He criticized the navy's purchasing policy of setting "official prices." Items such as knives and forks cost the government five times their current market price. He attacked naval traditionalism and urged that the construction of eight wooden battleships be abandoned. Finally, he questioned the effectiveness and usefulness of the East Asian fleet sailing off Indochina.[26]

Not surprisingly, the minister of the navy, Admiral Gustave Besnard, objected strenuously to Pelletan's proposed cuts. The moderate republican premier, Alexandre Ribot, supported his minister in testimony before the committee. An astute conservative republican on the committee, Maurice Lebon, promised to vote against the entire Pelletan report, calling it an attempt "to modify constitutional laws through the budget." In the end, however, the entire Budget Committee unanimously approved Pelletan's version of the report on the naval budget. Pelletan then reported on this portion of the budget to the Chamber. By the time that debate occurred, Pelletan's report also had the support of the newly formed Radical government of Léon Bourgeois in which Lockroy served as minister of the navy.[27]

In 1900 Pelletan was again called on to prepare a report for the Budget Committee examining an army request for additional funds.[28] The minister of war had requested special appropriations outside the existing budget for the improvement of ordnance and installations. The proposal also included a funding project that depended on the sale of short-term bonds, which the

26. "Camille Pelletan Rapport du Budget de la marine," Commission du budget, October 11, 1895, pp. 365, 369, C 5548, AN.

27. Procès verbaux, Commission du budget, October 19, 1895, p. 500, October 11–12, 1895, p. 375, December 4, 1895, November 8, 1895, p. 571, ibid. Although Lockroy as president of the Budget Committee had been a staunch supporter of Pelletan and many of his actions as naval minister were influenced by Pelletan's committee reports, his new position as minister of the navy marked the beginning of a growing antagonism between these former colleagues. Lockroy increasingly identified with the concerns of the admirals, especially after his second and third appointments as minister of the navy in short governments of 1898 and 1899. The consequences of this antagonism will be explored in Chapter VIII.

28. Gustave Mesureur, a fellow left Radical, presided over this committee. He had defeated the moderate Rouvier for this position as committee president. This election demonstrated the increasing numbers and influence of the Radicals in the central workings of the Chamber. See Commission du budget, 1899, C 5624, AN.

sale of army-owned land on the outskirts of Paris would eventually support. Perhaps because of the controversial atmosphere of the Dreyfus Affair, the committee majority welcomed Pelletan's report, knowing that it would be highly critical of the military's request. At the same time, the majority may also have recognized that Pelletan, who by now was a veteran of both the Chamber and the Budget Committee, would be able to criticize the army without closing off all its funding options. It was precisely such a report that Pelletan presented in April with the endorsement of the committee.

The report condemned the accepted methods of military financing, particularly the regular recourse to such special appropriations. These out-of-budget requests lacked itemized costs and were infinitely more difficult for the Chamber to supervise. Pelletan reminded the committee that in 1899 alone the minister of war had already requested 66,705,000 francs. In addition, the current proposal included a mechanism of finance which Pelletan found both inadequate and inappropriate. He was sure that the sale of army property would not generate adequate funds to reimburse the sums borrowed to purchase the equipment and therefore funding would inevitably increase state debt. Pelletan predicted that the actual cost to cover interest on short-term bonds would reach 100 million francs. Pelletan saw this as a maneuver by the Ministry of War to circumvent the express decision of the Chamber to eliminate military budgets funded by loans. He pointed out three major faults of the proposed legislation: it was a budget based on loans; the guarantee for those loans was insufficient; and there was every indication that the costs would continue to rise. Following these sharp criticisms, the final recommendation of Pelletan's report was surprisingly moderate. He recognized that some funds must be appropriated for these "highly necessary" expenses. This was not the moment to discontinue the unfortunate practice of special budgets. The Pelletan report recommended a special appropriation of 55 million francs for the improvement of ordnance and installations. Of this amount almost 4.5 million were to be designated for interest payments.[29] This particular report

29. "Rapport fait au nom de la Commission du budget chargée d'examiner le projet de loi portant ouverture de credits au titre du compte special 'Perfectionnement du materiel d'armement et reinstallation de services militaires' pour l'année 1900 par Camille Pelletan député," Chambre des députés, *Annexes*, no. 1590, April 6, 1900, pp. 797–98.

underscores the restraints the committee system placed even on influential Radical politicians. The process, largely one of consensus, encouraged recommendations that might marshal evidence and arguments for reform but at the same time hesitated to endorse specific measures for fundamental change.

Committees, especially the permanent ones, could become a political force in themselves. Their reports expressed a carefully constructed consensus that often corresponded more to a general parliamentary viewpoint than to a partisan one. There can be no question, for example, that regardless of the political composition of the Budget Committee it inevitably arrived at positions critical of excess expenditures and jealous of parliamentary prerogatives over the budgetary process. At the same time, however, though consensus might occur, committee members did engage in serious political debate. (Camille Pelletan and Casimir-Périer never agreed on specific questions.) The committees oscillated between a unity imposed by their involvement in shared projects and the inevitable divisions resulting from their composition. The political makeup of the committees roughly corresponded to the weight of the various political groups in the Chamber. Until 1910 these groups worked informally and often inefficiently through the randomly created *bureaux* to ensure their representation on the committees. Following the organizational reform of 1910, the power of the *bureaux* and to some degree that of the individual deputy was reduced. The *bureaux* were not dismantled, but political groups were now officially recognized. Working through the *bureaux*, the political groups directly determined how many and which of their deputies would sit on particular committees.[30] The committees were also expanded to forty-four members. This reform institutionalized what was already a reality, the importance and influence of the political groups within the Chamber.[31]

The political groups whose power would increase over time had always been an element in parliamentary functioning. The appearance of

30. The more organized political groups had already been attempting to impose this system, first the socialists since the early 1890s and the Radicals soon thereafter. Even the Center and Right eventually followed suit. See Rioux, "Palais Bourbon," 508.

31. Guiral and Thuillier, *Vie quotidienne*, 230.

organized political parties outside the Chamber in the twentieth century further complicated their role. The parliamentary groups were not political parties, and even on the eve of World War I the Radical groups remained distinct from the Radical party. The relations among the deputies, their parliamentary political groups, and their political parties were complex and highly individualistic.[32] Originally the political groups were formed as much to enable individual deputies to maneuver and succeed in the Chamber as to express a specific political persuasion. Nonetheless, it would be a serious distortion to assume that ideology was entirely absent from these groups. Shared principles and political objectives, as well as shared social backgrounds in many cases, brought deputies together in efforts of mutual promotion, protection, and endorsement. One historian of the Radicals has succinctly identified the parliamentary functions of these political groups: to "ensure members' input into bills and membership on Committees. . . . The groups were part of the functioning of the Chamber of Deputies and not parallel to political positions outside."[33]

In the 1880s under Clemenceau's leadership Radicals (who had only begun to use that label in the Chamber during this decade) made an effort to forge much stronger links between electoral programs, adherence to parliamentary groups, and the legislative actions of individual deputies. This early and tentative attempt at party formation collapsed during the conflict surrounding the Boulangist movement. Attempting to recoup from a series of losses—Radical disarray after Boulanger, the damage of the Panama scandal, and Clemenceau's electoral defeat—Camille Pelletan formed a new political group in the 1893 Chamber, the Left Radical-socialists (La Gauche Radicale-socialiste). Although it united the most intransigent Radicals, this group was never the only Radical political group in the Chamber. A second affiliation, the Left Radicals (La Gauche Radicale), represented more moderate Radical deputies such as Léon Bourgeois and Henri Brisson. These two groups grew considerably after Radical electoral victories

32. Only those Socialist deputies who adhered to the SFIO could be said in the prewar era to represent a genuine political party within the Chamber. After 1919 there was a trend, not accepted by all, to view the SFIO organization as an appropriate model for relations between deputies and their parties.

33. Peter Morris, "The French Radical Party and the First Ministry of Georges Clemenceau" (Ph.D dissertation, Cambridge University, 1973), 131A.

in 1902, 1906, and 1910. In the 1906 Chamber the Radical-socialists constituted the largest group. Electoral success, however, did not necessarily lead to greater organizational coherence. In fact, for the Radicals their very expansion in the early twentieth century led not to their consolidation within the Chamber but to further fragmentation. During the years 1904–1906, the two Radical groups became three.[34] Factions proliferated within each of these groups. As a further complication, most deputies belonged to more than one group. Membership in the two Radical-socialist groups overlapped considerably, and even more disturbingly, many deputies of the Gauche Radicale also participated in one of the more centrist republican groups. Nor was there any obligation that a member of one or the other Radical parliamentary groups had to be a member of the Radical party. Although some political designation identified most groups, particular interests also organized pressure groups within the Chamber, some of which wielded enormous influence. Individual Radical deputies frequently belonged to one of these, depending on their constituents' concerns.[35] Consequently, a dense and complex affiliation of overlapping committees and groups governed political life in the Chamber.

During the Third Republic and since, there has been considerable commentary on the impact of this parliamentary structure. For nationalist antiparliamentarians of the period such as Maurice Barrès and Robert de Jouvenel, this organization of fluid groups and committees maintained a system in which personal advantage became the exclusive and only possible goal. In their view, the need to negotiate compromises in corridors and back rooms constantly eroded commitment to larger objectives such as the nation.[36] Significantly, the socialist Left had similar criticisms, although its larger objectives obviously differed from those of the nationalists. The requirements of party discipline placed on Socialist deputies after 1905

34. La Gauche radicale, Extreme Gauche radicale-socialiste, and Gauche radicale-socialiste. See Liste des groupes parlementaires avant 1914, Police générale, F7 12714, AN; Morris, "French Radical Party," 130.

35. Two of the most powerful were the Groupe agricole with 218 members in 1900 and the Groupe coloniale headed by the moderate Eugène Etienne with 109 members in 1900 (Guiral and Thuillier, Vie quotidienne, 253).

36. This was the essential theme of Maurice Barrès' Dans la cloaque and Robert de Jouvenel's La République des camarades, both quoted ibid., 187–90.

reflected an effort to break those parliamentary traditions decried by the Right and the Left. The Radicals, as always, were more equivocal, especially after 1900, when they came to dominate the Chamber. One of the most serious unresolved dilemmas to plague the Radical party was relations between deputies and the party.

Undoubtedly this structure of committees and groups impeded the efficient implementation of any comprehensive political program. Even the enactment of specific, long-promised, electorally endorsed reforms was difficult to accomplish. The very fluidity and multiplicity of the groups inevitably undercut their power. Lacking clearly organized and disciplined parties, the committees functioned to assign and rank parliamentary work. Occasionally they established minimal agreements on bills; more often they delayed, revised, and buried proposals. But they facilitated the necessary day-to-day preparation of legislation and provided expert information to deputies not directly involved with or interested in a growing number of increasingly complex and technical questions. Committee reports offered persuasive direction for eventual voting decisions. The committee structure offered all this without constraining the decisions of individual deputies and especially without distracting them from the often dramatic confrontations during the public sessions of the Chamber. The public sessions provided those deputies who were seriously pursuing their political careers one of the most important forums in which to display their political program and their rhetorical prowess.

Much of the work and the negotiations of parliamentary life took place in committee rooms, political groups, and, of course, the corridors of the Palais Bourbon. Nonetheless, the public sessions held in the Chamber's well-appointed auditorium, *l'hémicycle*, retained critical importance. Political success required that a deputy demonstrate his abilities in that arena as well. The complete session was transcribed and then published within forty-eight hours in the *Journal Officiel*, a widely consulted publication. Speeches that were acclaimed by large majorities often received the Chamber's endorsement to be printed and posted outside every city hall in France, a procedure called *affichage*. Even if a deputy's argument might be lost in the fine print, at least their names would be known to a national audience. Coverage of Chamber debates was a regular feature on the front pages of all major Paris and provincial dailies. If the speech was deemed important enough, some newspapers might reproduce the text verbatim or at least the key excerpts.[37]

Although an informed public closely followed parliamentary activity, public sessions were not frequent. In 1900 they totaled approximately only 450 hours. Until 1911 no formal agenda existed, nor were any time limits imposed on speakers. Critics considered sessions shockingly chaotic, filled with interminable orations and punctuated by countless interpellations. These questions could be posed at any moment and required a government response, which might lead to a vote of confidence. Between April, 1896, and June, 1898, the Méline government faced 218 interpellations; between 1906 and 1909, there were 294 interpellations. In the second decade of the twentieth century some efforts were made to control this extraordinary explosion of words which filled the Chamber's sessions. After 1909 written questions could be submitted to the government, and the answers were published in the *Journal Officiel*. In 1911 a grand committee consisting of the presidents of the legislative committees and the heads of the political groups attempted, not always successfully, to impose a parliamentary agenda. Not until 1927 were interpellations restricted to Fridays.[38]

Within this tumultuous setting, the Chamber did enact significant legislation during the first half of the Third Republic. Nonetheless, it is difficult not to conclude that the principal function of these general sessions was grand theater and the display of rhetorical talent. In a recent essay on parliamentary traditions and culture Jean Pierre Rioux appropriately selected "Les Mots" as a subtitle. Successful verbal performances in a society that so valued the individual's ability to manipulate words had significant political and cultural meaning. A comparison of the texts of the general budget debate in the full Chamber with the preliminary discussions and reports of the Budget Committee shows that these two bodies had dramatically different rhetorics, styles, audiences, and functions. Although not without disagreements, committee work was precise, statistical, coolly presented, and contained a minimum of obvious political discord. The committee or

---

37. To give only some examples, Clemenceau's addresses appeared regularly in *La Justice* during the 1880s; *Le Petit Provençal* carefully covered the Chamber; *L'Éclair* reprinted Pelletan's address December 15, 1896.

38. Guiral and Thuillier, *Vie quotidienne*, 244–45; Rioux, "Palais Bourbon," 504, 511.

the subcommittee collaborated to arrive at agreement on a specific problem. Jean-Pierre Rioux suggests that a certain tone was appropriate to committees, especially after 1910, in which there was "a more intimate oratory; [one] discusses the documents and controls one's voice."[39] The public debates on the budget, in contrast, were often flamboyant displays of erudition supporting passionate assertions of political allegiances, sometimes lasting several hours. An important debate among leading deputies was expected to be high drama. It was common to admire or criticize certain politicians because of their oratorical styles. Frequent speakers were associated with a particular declamatory pose. Gambetta was expected to "gesticulate and be passionate; Clemenceau to be dry, staccato and sharp."[40]

Camille Pelletan once defined political eloquence as "passion within reasoning, the gift to evoke the larger side of things and to present direct objections vigorously to an adversary, the talent to amplify arguments with thunderclaps." He and most of his colleagues hoped to follow what he called an "art of oratory." In Pelletan's view what distinguished oratory from other means of communication was that "the ideologue directly and bodily faces his audience." He experienced such contact as a "physical communication."[41] Pelletan's longtime opponent, the moderate leader Joseph Reinach, essentially agreed with this view of oratory. In an introduction to a text on rhetoric intended for first-year lycée students, Reinach stressed that a successful speech required words that were "acts." The speaker had to function as if engaged in a physical encounter. "Modern political eloquence. . . . that action. . . . almost physical of a man grasping another man; those are the stakes of the parliamentary regime."[42]

Although a successful speech in the Chamber might be transmitted to political circles in the capital, to one's constituency, and occasionally to

39. Rioux, "Palais Bourbon," 508.
40. Barral, ed., *Fondateurs de la Troisième République*, 18–19.
41. Camille Pelletan, *Victor Hugo*, 154–55, 165.
42. Reinach, Introduction, *"Conciones" français*, iii. The collection offers an interesting commentary on the importance given to oral performance by the key educational institution of the Third Republic. It also indicates that oratory was assumed to have a political function. Almost two-thirds of the historic examples given to the students were selected from political speeches.

the entire nation, the most immediate and tangible audience was one's parliamentary colleagues. They were rarely a docile public. Speakers felt compelled to dominate them; deputies frequently left and returned to their seats; attendance might be sparse; interruptions were accepted and frequent. Tradition absolutely forbade the reading of a prepared text.[43] To address the Chamber of Deputies was truly to discourse. Their shared lycée and university education amply prepared the men who did so. There was a preponderance of those who had prepared for law and teaching, professions in which words and oral presentations held a privileged position. After 1871 one-third of all deputies were lawyers, and during the entire first half of the Third Republic 45 percent of all government ministers were trained in the legal profession. Between 1898 and 1940, 34 percent of all deputies were either lawyers, professors, or teachers. Between those same dates among Radical deputies, 68 percent followed these three professions. Jean Estèbe in his study of Third Republic ministers stresses that even more influential than professional training was the experience almost all deputies shared of a classical lycée education. Higher education only reinforced the hierarchical, competitive, and literary system of secondary education, where oral performance was critical to advancement. The importance of both secondary and university education in the formation of the parliamentary elite leads Estèbe to portray the Chamber as dominated by a "bourgeoisie diplomée."[44]

Issues examined with careful circumspection in committee deliberations exploded into heated and dramatic rhetoric in the general session. In the Budget Committee, Camille Pelletan's questioning of military spending, though often probing, had been cautious and largely restrained. In general sessions, either from his seat or from the tribune, his style was markedly different. Joseph Reinach claimed that such impassioned rhetoric was largely restricted to the Radicals and socialists of the opposition who had not

43. According to Pelletan, this style had started during the 1830s in the July Monarchy as a reaction to the prepared, polished speeches of the Revolution and the early Restoration. Perhaps it also marked the influence of romanticism. See Camille Pelletan, *Victor Hugo*, 166–67. See also Reinach, *"Conciones" français*, xix–xx, and Rioux, "Palais Bourbon," in *La Nation*, 491, Vol. II of *Les Lieux de mémoire*, ed. Nora.

44. Estèbe, *Ministres de la République*, 102–106, 224. For the significance of classical education see Barral, ed., *Fondateurs de la Troisième République*, 16.

yet adopted the more up-to-date, practical, and businesslike style of the moderates.[45] Yet Pelletan gained considerable prestige from his heated public performances. Even his most bitter opponents had to admit that Pelletan was an "orator," if a rather sentimental one relying on "interminable phrases."[46] These were qualities one might expect from a speaker who hoped to emulate Victor Hugo. A less than sympathetic police reporter conceded that "he is a remarkable orator."[47] His supporters called him a "powerful orator, the glory of the rostrum, and one of the most heard speakers."[48] But parliamentary oratory was not merely words, it was also the physical presentation of the discourse. In this, whether despised or applauded, Pelletan made a striking impression. His disheveled dress and unruly hair had become a signature by the 1890s. Paul Bosq's ambivalent portrait of Pelletan included a description of his demeanor at the rostrum: "One sees appear at the tribune this tall body, leaning like the Tower of Pisa about which clothing flutters in strange wrinkles, a head sparkling with malice, eyes always on guard and the lively impudence of his turned-up nose. His telegraph pole arms pelt ministers with ironic arguments and bombard the majority with sarcasm, falling like a shower of coconuts. This humorist has amusing fallacies and droll paradoxes, and one laughs at the witty flashes of this bizarre independent."[49]

In December, 1893, when the moderate Casimir-Périer government requested supplemental credits for the army, a fiery Pelletan rose to attack the minister of finance. He hammered away at his favorite theme: the need for the Chamber to control administrative, especially military, expenses. Without such constant parliamentary vigilance, the hard-earned money of French citizens would be wasted. He reminded the Chamber that voters viewed government spending with extreme suspicion and were appalled by the continuing deficit. "You know the deep and legitimate aversion harbored by our democracy of labor and savings for this gaping hole in the

45. Reinach, "Conciones" français, xxii–xxv.

46. Ernest Charles, "Portraits politique. Camille Pelletan," La Revue politique et parlementaire, XXIV (April–June, 1900), 625–54. Even Le Figaro, which had long hounded him, had to admit his "eloquence as an orator and his broad culture" (Obituary, June 6, 1915).

47. Police report, June 12–14, 1902, Situation politique, 1899–1905, F7 12553, AN.

48. Pelletan obituaries, Le Radical, June 6, 1915, and Le Petit Provençal, June 6, 1915.

49. Bosq, Nos Chers Souverains, 72–73.

budget which reveals the improvidence of the government." Stressing his patriotic commitment, he offered a rousing call for genuine defense spending. "It is the honor of the Republic, the honor of France that all parties agree not to refuse one centime for the necessary defense of the country and for its dignity in the world, however heavy the national expenses may be. . . . But the more this country and its representatives are resolved . . . to give everything necessary for the flag, the more governments . . . have the duty to view these millions . . . as sacred, that they belong exclusively to the needs of defense." He urged his colleagues to adopt a genuine "financial patriotism" whose first obligation would be to put an end to "the squandering of public revenues." Pelletan then presented a motion to return the request for supplemental funds to the Budget Committee. The motion was defeated, 128 to 358. In the final vote for the military credits Pelletan joined the new group of socialist deputies in the Chamber and abstained.[50]

Three years later, during the annual debate on the budget, Pelletan joined with the socialists to criticize the failure of the conservative Méline government to monitor the legal restriction of railroad rates. Pelletan was especially hostile to the new moderate republican ministry of Jules Méline, who was committed to breaking all ties with the Radicals, abandoning anticlericalism, and governing with a center-right majority. Pelletan revealed that the railroads had been flouting the law. Their fraudulent rates had benefited foreign companies, enabling their goods to circumvent government duties which Méline's protectionist government had been eager to increase. Sardonically Pelletan referred to the government's support for increased tariffs but ignored the Compagnie du Nord's systematic evasion of custom duties. Seconding Jaurès, he reiterated the theme of the government's inability to control either the public administration or powerful industrial firms. The combined Left of Radicals and socialists did extract a special investigation of the Compagnie du Nord and the state inspectors, but Pelletan's proposition that this information be directly communicated to the Chamber was overwhelmingly defeated.[51]

* * *

50. Annales de l'Assemblée nationale, Chambre des députés, Débats, December 19, 1893, pp. 430–32, 439.

51. Ibid., December 5, 1896, pp. 873–79.

A few weeks later Pelletan dominated the discussion on the naval budget for 1897. The popular Paris daily *L'Eclair* gave front-page coverage to his speech, which, according to the reporter, lasted an amazing five hours, forty-three minutes, and twenty-three seconds. Even more impressive in the paper's sympathetic account of Pelletan's oratorical "talent" was that his "friends and opponents listened until the very end, without tiring, to the remarkable indictment which he delivered against the naval administration."[52] In this lengthy oration Pelletan again argued vehemently and repeatedly about the need for parliamentary control. In December, 1896, facing the Méline government, Pelletan excoriated a naval establishment that had "more clerks than Herodotus' Persian army" and had not changed since "Louis XVI and the War of American Independence." He denounced the navy for creating a bureaucracy that made any rational planning or control impossible. The admirals themselves had no idea of actual conditions within the fleets because their offices were so choked with bureaucratic forms and red tape. The admiralty consistently had resisted technological innovation. Of all the major European navies, only the French still had ten active wooden battleships and had spent 5.4 million francs to stockpile a twenty- to thirty-year supply of timber for future ship construction. Furthermore, everything about the navy was alien to a democratic state. He especially stressed inequities and nepotism in advancement, which undermined democratic assumptions of social mobility through merit. "What is it if not a piece of the *Ancien Régime* preserved in the middle of modern France. It doesn't seem to belong to our democratic institutions. . . . The navy is not subject to our democratic law. It is an oligarchy . . . of the admirals . . . a government unto itself."[53]

In 1896 Pelletan's delivery took on a sharper, more impassioned rhetoric appropriate to the general session and the new, more polarized political climate. The message, however, repeated themes expressed the year before in committee meetings. In reality the Chamber had little control over the

52. *L'Eclair*, December 15, 1896. *L'Eclair* had a readership of about fifty thousand, which included both Radicals and nationalists. Pelletan was a regular contributor. The paper had a special interest in financial issues, expressed a definite anti-Semitic stance, and would take a strong anti-Dreyfusard position. *L'Eclair* is listed with other right-wing papers by Bellanger *et al.*, *Histoire générale de la presse française*, III, 345.

53. Chambre des députés, *Débats*, December 4, 1896, pp. 1129–39, 1141, 1145.

navy and none over its expenditures; its highest positions were fiefdoms for men whose loyalty to the Republic was questionable. Pelletan demanded that the Chamber be fully informed about naval projects. He was willing to support expenditures for needed repairs and maintenance, but he refused "to give one cent for who knows what plans of the admiralty, presented with the pretext of replying to sacrifices made abroad." Echoing his position on army expenditures in 1893, Pelletan insisted that his criticisms reflected only his highest devotion to the nation, "his heart of a patriot." He ended this long speech with a resounding patriotic address: "Do your duty toward the French nation by demanding that the vices of the navy be corrected." Méline personally rebuked him for introducing "political" objectives into budgetary and military issues. The premier also observed that no genuine patriot would reveal the "pessimism" Pelletan had expressed about the condition of the French navy. The Radicals became totally isolated in their effort to shift priorities in the naval budget.[54]

It was not surprising that budget debates were delayed even more than usual at the height of the Dreyfus Affair in 1898–1899. Pelletan was once again the general reporter for the Budget Committee, now dominated by Radicals. His position had shifted; not only did he explain the decisions of the committee, but he was also called on to justify the Radicals' position on the committee. His new tone combined pleas for reasonableness in the area of administrative reform and a staunch defense of his Radical colleagues' integrity. The socialists proposed to slash five million francs from the costs of departmental administration by reducing the number of civil servants who worked for the subprefect. The proposal was in keeping with Pelletan's earlier concerns to limit administrative expense. Yet on this occasion he spoke in opposition, explaining, "It is not acceptable that one should thus all of a sudden fire the staff . . . all the low level staff of the sous-préfecture." Such an action would "completely disrupt our system of administration," and in any case these positions were "established by law." Any reform proposal would have to be addressed to the "committee on administrative reform." The continuing transformation of local government must have influenced Pelletan's resistance to this administrative and financial reform.

54. Ibid., 1177, 1146. An amendment proposed by Lockroy gained only 73 votes and was opposed by 335 deputies. The socialists abstained, adhering to their principle of rejecting any military expenditures (Chambre des députés, Débats, December 4, 1896, p. 1182).

More and more of those "petit personnel" on the departmental and mu-nicipal levels were devoted small town Radicals some of whom owed their positions to their Radical deputy. The socialist motion was easily defeated, but the extreme Right gleefully joined the socialists to expose the Radicals as defenders of their own costly sinecures.[55] Although speaking against the motion, Pelletan could not bring himself to vote against a money-saving reform. Perhaps he could not bear to be accused of hypocrisy, and he too voted for the losing socialist proposition.

A few days later, Maurice Allard, socialist deputy from the Provençal department of the Var, called for the elimination of the budget to support religious institutions, which in effect would separate church and state. The socialists knew such a motion had no hope of success, but they were forcing the Radicals to vote against their own dearly held anticlericalism. Pelletan recognized that the larger issue was the socialist criticism of Radical inac-tion on reform issues. He turned to the socialists with a tone that combined warm collegiality and a chiding, almost patronizing, rebuke. It was a tone Pelletan frequently adopted in the next decade toward the socialists. "A certain number of my friends, sitting on the far left of this Chamber, seem to make it a habit . . . to assert that the Radicals . . . are abandoning their life-long convictions." His response denied this accusation, and he pointed to his own voting record. He reminded the socialists that the committee had to present a budget that would pass the Chamber and did not neces-sarily reflect the views of either the reporter or the president. But following this short lesson on the realities of parliamentary politics, Pelletan grandly acknowledged that nothing should be allowed "to disturb the union now established between the most ardent servants of democracy." Being con-sistent, Pelletan voted to eliminate the budget for religious institutions, which was defeated by a wide margin.[56]

Perhaps the most interesting aspect of this budget report was Pelletan's discomfort with his new position of speaking for the majority. Also clear was the new alliance between socialists and Radicals, as well as the considerable tension between them as socialists persistently questioned the Radicals' reform commitment.

55. *Ibid.*, January 25, 1899, pp. 197–98, 202.
56. *Ibid.*, January 30, 1899, pp. 286–89.

During the public debates on the budget and the more technical discussions in the committees, Radicals were concerned with defending and extending their increasingly prominent position in parliament. Complex conflicts were waged: the government, the highest level of permanent civil servants, and the deputies disputed control and distribution of resources. In the case of the deputies, the permanent committees often set their priorities. At times government ministers and high civil servants might collaborate; they could also be bitter opponents. This three-sided structural conflict sometimes duplicated and at other times countered the overtly ideological disputes concerning the appropriate functioning of a democratic state. In the Chamber a variety of parliamentary political groups with some connections to emerging national political parties defined public political differences. Much of the substance of these shifting conflicts was over disputed jurisdictions and access to power.

Charles Laisant had predicted in the early 1880s that the rules of parliamentary life would create a common perspective in which differences of political ideology, regional origin, and class background would, after two or three legislative sessions, become at best secondary. The committees, in particular, with their shared work experience and their institutional importance, provided deputies with a unifying experience, irrespective of individual political affiliations. The *bureaux* and participation in the theatrical setting of the general sessions reinforced one's primary identity as a deputy. Although explicit institutional rules were extremely powerful and created some of the unique marks of the deputy's profession, Laisant had also observed that the daily experience of the parliamentarian's life distinguished him from others. "Second—and this is the more serious—the shared life in this environment of sterile agitation has the effect of creating a sort of barrier between the nation and [the deputy]. One breathes a special atmosphere, one loses sight of the aspirations and needs of the democracy which elected you."[57]

Despite Laisant's insights, however, his own political career demonstrated that the institutional and social forces of parliamentary life did not simply forge an indistinguishable mass of deputies all grasping for personal

---

57. Laisant, *Anarchie bourgeoise*, 221.

power. Without question, politics was becoming more professionalized in the late nineteenth century, and the Radicals, perhaps more than any other political group, led that trend. For the professional politician, his political office provided support for himself and his family, as well as the possibility of upward social mobility associated with increased prestige and perhaps even power. But the Radical who was a professional politician was distinctly different from those professional politicians who declared themselves nationalists, moderate republicans, or socialists. The status of professional politician was yet another facet in the complex identity of a multiterm Radical deputy.

In their study of the daily life of Third Republic deputies, Pierre Guiral and Guy Thuillier draw a sharp distinction between those who had independent sources of income, power, and prestige and the increasing number of "petit bourgeois physicians, journalists who wanted to make a career of politics. . . . Those deputies who supported themselves by politics [vivent de la politique]."[58] Not every Radical deputy fitted into the second category, but after 1900 a majority did. Leading Radicals with independent social and economic positions outside the political world were exceptions, such as the elegant, well-to-do Joseph Caillaux or the successful stockbroker Maurice Berteaux. Most Radicals continued their careers in law, journalism, and medicine as necessary auxiliaries, supporting their political ambitions both for self-promotion and much needed additional income. Reflecting changing social origins, there was a sharp decline in deputies' fortunes between the beginning of the Republic and the years 1900–1914. This reduction of wealth affected both the most successful politicians of the Republic, namely government ministers, and the deputies in general.[59] Increasingly, parliamentarians were being drawn from lower strata of the bourgeoisie, which could not rely on accumulated family fortunes.

58. Guiral and Thuillier, Vie quotidienne, 150–51.

59. Estèbe calculates the median fortune for ministers at the time of their death during the years 1871–1877 to be 520,000 francs. If this sum becomes the base of 100, then the median fortune for the years 1900–1914 is 26 (Ministres de la République, 160–61). For information on doctors, who constituted approximately 10 percent of the deputies during the first half of the Third Republic, see Jack Ellis, The Physician-Legislators of France: Medicine and Politics in the Early Third Republic (New York, 1990), 4, 51, 113–14.

Perhaps one of the most important social realities shared by all deputies that in most cases physically separated them from their electors was life in Paris. For the provincial bourgeois embarking on a political career, this move must have been a cultural shock, although even among this group few were complete strangers to the capital. Born and raised Parisians such as Pelletan, Lockroy, and Bourgeois still faced the financial difficulties of living in Paris and supporting a family. Like most bourgeois families who were comfortable but not inordinately wealthy, money was a persistent, if not overwhelming, concern. Radical deputies had to maintain the essential material comforts that designated a bourgeois existence. Their annual salary of 9,000 francs, which had been established during the Second Republic, hardly supported a bourgeois lifestyle in Belle Epoque Paris; it remained unchanged until 1907.[60] Deputies complained incessantly that they were inadequately compensated. By the late 1890s an average deputy's expenses were almost twice his parliamentary salary. The largest items on this average deputy's budget were food, housing, and costs for electoral campaigns. If one was above average, expenses could mount quickly over the years. The 9,000-franc salary was especially galling when compared to the equivalent of 25,000 francs paid annually to representatives in the other major republic, the United States.[61]

Camille Pelletan, of course, never intended to be an average politician. He began his parliamentary career proclaiming himself politically unorthodox and continued his bohemian lifestyle. In the 1880s he and his companion lived in the Latin Quarter on the Avenue de l'Observatoire. The rent may not have been extravagant, but the apartment did have the requisite bourgeois piano, and the household had a reputation for elaborate and frequent soirées.[62] By 1900 the couple had moved to the newer, more decidedly bourgeois fourteenth arrondissement, living in "a small residence on the rue d'Alésia."[63] The increased costs of the better address and the

---

60. In the 1890s a skilled male cabinetmaker, among the highest paid workers, earned approximately 2,100 francs annually; a male chemical worker 1,400 francs (Hause, *Hubertine Auclert*, 15). The average Paris reporter at the end of the nineteenth century earned between 4,000 and 6,000 francs annually (Bellanger, *et al.*, *Histoire générale de la presse française*, 285).

61. Guiral and Thuillier, *Vie quotidienne*, 108–109.

62. Geffroy, *Clemenceau*, 57.

63. Guiral and Thuillier, *Vie quotidienne*, 86.

continuing tradition of generous entertaining placed Pelletan in constant debt.[64] After the death of his longtime companion in 1902, Pelletan increased his bourgeois respectability. The year following his appointment as minister of the navy, 1903, he married a schoolteacher, Joséphine Dénise, a younger woman from a solidly bourgeois family. The couple set up a new household in the fashionable seventh arrondissement on the rue de l'Université, just a short walk from the Chamber of Deputies and around the corner from the newly completed Gare d'Orsay. As minister of the navy Pelletan had received a significant salary increase for two and half years, but his expenses had mounted as well.[65]

Unlike the pattern followed by most bourgeois families and many deputies, his marriage in 1903 did not seem to have provided the windfall of a large dowry. Nonetheless, in good bourgeois fashion Pelletan's marriage began with a story about money. Camille met his future wife through her brother Paul, who had saved Pelletan from a foreclosure. In the course of his work in the Paris courts as a bailiff, colleagues had informed Paul Dénise that Pelletan's possessions were about to be seized. As a dedicated Radical and admirer of Pelletan, he personally paid off these debts and proudly brought Camille Pelletan home to meet his mother and sister, Joséphine.[66] For deputies less idiosyncratic than Pelletan, marriage was often of critical economic importance. Almost all the ministers of the Third Republic, most of whom were married, significantly improved their financial standing through their marriages. On an average, the wife's resources when marrying were at least twice those of her husband. Certainly many provincial politicians depended on their wives' dowries to launch parliamentary careers and maintain their Parisian lifestyle.[67]

Another way deputies of the Left augmented their parliamentary income was through journalism, as director of one's own paper, as a member of an editorial board, or as a free-lance writer contributing regularly to the Parisian and provincial press. After his editorial position with Clemenceau's

64. Mme Bréchet, Interview by Paul Baquiast, in "Pelletan," 373.

65. Ministers earned 60,000 francs (Estèbe, *Ministres de la République*, 152).

66. Mme Bréchet, Interview by Baquiast in "Pelletan," 374.

67. Estèbe, *Ministres de la République*, 86–89, 143, 161; Guiral and Thuillier, *Vie quotidienne*, 99. For a discussion of Jules Ferry's marriage to Mlle Risler see Barral, ed., *Fondateurs de la Troisième République*, 13.

La Justice came to an end in 1893, Pelletan maintained a steady and often voluminous output of articles which appeared in *Le Radical*, *L'Eclair*, *Le Petit Provençal*, *La Lanterne*, *Le Matin*, *Le Petit Républicain*, *Le Petit Méridional*, *Le Bonnet Rouge*, and *La Dépêche* of Toulouse. It was entirely fitting that when he died in 1915 he was in the midst of completing an article for *Le Radical*. Once a deputy was elected, regular newspaper columns permitted him to maintain his reputation, advance a political agenda, and cover his expenses. Again Pelletan serves as an excellent example. This constant interaction between the worlds of journalism and politics brought many deputies perilously close to large sums of money, which an astounding range of diverse financial and political interests circulated throughout the press, seeking to influence reporters, editors, and politicians.[68] The financial pressures on deputies dependent on the income from their political careers made them all the more vulnerable to such enticements. The Panama scandal was only one spectacular instance of this semiclandestine intermingling of finance, journalism, and politics.

Radical deputies shared with many of their constituents a bourgeois lifestyle based on property and security, although the deputy with more resources and prestige usually occupied a higher rung of the complex bourgeois social hierarchy. The deputy and his constituent also shared similar anxieties about maintaining and improving a middle-class status that was easily threatened by financial uncertainties. Both representative and elector tended to come from families that had only recently joined the expanding middle class. They were committed to the principle of upward social mobility and to the proposition that access to such improvement should be as broad as possible. Both were also dedicated to the defense of their own social position and to ensuring that their own mobility was neither threatened nor obstructed. An important means for deputies to enhance their positions was to ensure the advancement of colleagues, supporters, and constituents at all levels of the growing state bureaucracy. Such patronage was quickly identified as one of the major defects of the republican system, much as it was during the same period in the United States. The moderate

---

68. Among left-wing politicians Clemenceau was probably one of the most successful in establishing and directing journals. *La Justice* and *L'Aurore* are examples from his early career. See Bellanger *et al.*, *Histoire générale de la presse française*, III, 367, 258–61.

politician André Tardieu denounced this practice as one of the most serious vices of French political life: "Everyone in France is recommended and spends their time getting recommendations. Everyone solicits something and looks for . . . help. This spawns from the lowest to the highest a shady association of favor seekers. . . . France is an immense network of small committees of patronage which create two categories of citizens—those to whom one says yes, even when they are wrong; those to whom one says no, even when they are right."[69] Tardieu's disdain for this system perhaps reflected the views of someone who had already arrived, not of someone painfully climbing his way up through an intricate hierarchy, welcoming any support he could find.

Access to the networks of patronage could be found in the various Parisian political salons. As in the eighteenth century, the salon was a social, semiprivate space in which a small number of women could become visible in the exclusively male world of politics. The political salons of the Third Republic never attained anything like the political, intellectual, and cultural significance of the aristocratically dominated salons of the previous century. Because political discourse in the Republic could take place in many formal and informal settings that were exclusively male, the need for the salon with its inevitably disturbing presence of women was much less pressing. But they did not entirely disappear, and they remained useful for those exploratory conversations in which private and public interests overlapped and which were best conducted in the semiprivate context of an affluent woman's entertaining.[70] Even before 1871, republicans created their own version of this Parisian tradition that had been so important to earlier political elites. Among the republican *salonnières* only a few influenced larger political agendas. During the first decade of the Republic, the salon and activities of Juliette Lamber Adam, wife of a republican senator, were critical in the defense of the Republic and the career of Léon Gambetta.[71] In the 1880s, Marguerite Durand, then married to the Radical

69. Quoted in Guiral and Thuillier, *Vie quotidienne*, 216.

70. Estèbe notes the declining influence of women in informal political settings during the Third Republic. Provincial wives of newly arrived ministers did not always have the requisite social skills for Parisian entertaining (*Ministres de la République*, 93–95).

71. For an interesting introduction to her life and the inevitable contradictions that emerged when women engaged in republican politics see Wright, *Notable or Notorious?*, 59–71.

deputy Georges Laguerre, entertained all the leaders of radicalism and by the end of the decade had turned her salon into the informal headquarters of the Boulangist movement.[72] An aristocrat with republican convictions, the Marquise Marie Arconati-Visconti, organized an important gathering place for Dreyfusards in the beginning of the twentieth century.[73] The Hugo family during the late 1870s and until the writer's death in 1885 established a very different kind of republican salon. "Le Maître" dominated the weekly Sunday gatherings at which eager young and middle-aged artists, journalists, and politicians mingled; his daughter-in-law, Alice Hugo-Lockroy, supervised the refreshments.

A more typical republican salon was Thérèse Humbert's, which began in the early 1880s and became an important social gathering place until its dramatic end in 1902. Thérèse Humbert's husband, Frédéric, was the Radical deputy for the Seine-et-Marne for just one legislative session, 1885–1889. In the Chamber he sat with the less militant Gauche radicale group, although he subscribed to *La Justice* in the 1880s. Most important, he was the son of Gustave Humbert, one of the "founding fathers" of the Republic. In the 1870s, as a dedicated republican lawyer from Toulouse, the older Humbert had represented the Haute Garonne in the Senate, defending the new regime together with his friend and colleague Eugène Pelletan.[74] Gustave Humbert then conscientiously pursued an extremely successful political career in the new Republic, serving as minister of justice in 1882 and vice-president of the Senate from 1889 to 1890. He also filled positions at the Cour des Comptes, the court supervising government audits, first as prosecutor and then as presiding judge in 1890. In 1880 he was decorated with the Legion of Honor.

Gustave had advanced a good distance from his origins as a wine merchant's son and provincial lawyer. He provided his son Frédéric not only with a legal education but also with relative affluence and leisure. Some-

72. After divorcing Laguerre, Marguerite Durand became a journalist, feminist leader, and important Dreyfusard.

73. Gérard Baal, "Un Salon dreyfusard, dès lendemains de l'Affaire à la Grande Guerre: La Marquise Arconati-Visconti et ses amis," *Revue d'histoire moderne et contemporaine*, XXVIII (July–September, 1981), 433–63.

74. Gustave Humbert delivered one of the eulogies at Eugène Pelletan's funeral in 1884 (Petit, *Eugène Pelletan*, 245).

what surprisingly, in 1878 Frédéric married the daughter of his father's local Toulouse wine supplier, Thérèse Daurignac.[75] The young couple was eager to continue the family's upward social ascent, and the elder Humbert readily aided them with contacts in Paris, where they moved immediately after the wedding. In 1882 Gustave appointed his son his administrative aide, *chef de cabinet*, while he served as minister of justice in Freycinet's government. The young Humberts, now comfortably settled in the fourteenth arrondissement, initiated a salon.[76] Historians have access to details about this salon because of its spectacular collapse. In December, 1902, Thérèse and Frédéric Humbert were arrested and then tried and convicted for having orchestrated a twenty-year fraud of Balzacian proportions. Beginning in the early 1880s, the Humbert couple created a fiction of a soon-to-be-settled American inheritance, which they offered as collateral for loans amounting to hundreds of thousands of francs. Trading on Gustave Humbert's prominence and their skill in fabricating legal procedures around this bogus inheritance, they were able to live as if they were fabulously wealthy. Their complex system of deceptions and loans financed a move from the solidly bourgeois fourteenth arrondissement in 1886 to a luxurious *hôtel* on the Avenue de la Grande Armée, off the Place de l'Etoile. In addition, they purchased several country properties and entertained extravagantly in Paris and in the country.[77]

Through Gustave Humbert's connections and through political colleagues whom Frédéric cultivated, the Humberts had an exceedingly long list of contacts with the republican political world, including the most prestigious and powerful. They made little obvious effort to cultivate any one particular strand of republicanism. The Radicals, in fact, were relatively

75. Benjamin F. Martin, *The Hypocrisy of Justice in the Belle Epoque* (Baton Rouge, 1984), 84. Martin is perhaps too willing to accept all the negative evidence against the couple, including the speculation that Thérèse tricked Frédéric into the marriage by fabricating tales of a large dowry. Nonetheless, it was a surprising marriage, unlike the bourgeois norm in which the groom profited from the bride.

76. The address was rue Fortuny, near the "chic Parc Monceau" (*ibid.*, 85).

77. When arrest warrants were issued in May, 1902, the Humberts fled and left behind an empty safe which they had claimed contained the evidence of their inheritance. This decades-long swindle was abetted by Thérèse's two brothers, who posed as American relatives contesting her supposed inheritance. The family fled to Spain where they were finally seized in December, 1902 (*ibid.*, 89).

rare in this salon, where moderates such as Paul Deschanel, Jules Siegfried, Jean Casimir-Périer, and even Jules Méline were welcome. Those Radicals who did frequent the Humberts were less likely to be Radical-socialists and more often were closer to the Gauche radicale group, men such as Henri Brisson and Paul Doumer. Possibly the most prominent Radical figure seen at the Humberts was General Boulanger, a regular visitor in 1886. Georges Clemenceau was also a guest that year, but despite his well-known enthusiasm for hunting he declined a second invitation to join a weekend shoot at the Humberts' country house. The Humbert salon was most definitely not a place for the discussion of doctrinaire Radical politics. Members of Les Oeuvres Catholiques assumed (correctly it turned out) that they could approach Mme Humbert for a donation to their overseas missions. Not surprisingly, Camille Pelletan does not appear on the lists of those invited to the Humbert salon.[78]

Rather than a meeting place to pursue the strategies of electoral or parliamentary politics, this salon provided the possibility of contacts for loans, recommendations to civil service positions, and perhaps even connections for lucrative marriages.[79] In the early 1890s, Paul Doumer approached Frédéric several times hoping he would finance a new republican journal aimed at a more solidly bourgeois audience. Nothing seemed to have come of this request. In March, 1901, just a year before the collapse of their fabulous fraud, Mme Marguerite Pringué, the wife of an examining magistrate (juge d'instruction) attached to the tribunal of the department of the Seine, earnestly solicited Thérèse Humbert. The Pringués were among the lesser lights who attended the Humbert salon. Mme Pringué hoped that the recent death of an associate justice on the Paris appeals court would create a series of vacancies in the judicial system which would enable her husband to move into the position of assistant attorney general in that same court. Thérèse passed the request on to Frédéric, who, with considerable dispatch, wrote to a contact close to fellow Radical Ernest Monis, then minister of justice in the Waldeck-Rousseau government. Frédéric highly recommended M. Pringué for the position of assistant attorney general and hoped that his friend would pass this request on to the minister, reminding

78. Enquête parlementaire, Humberts, Correspondance saisie, C 7313, AN.

79. Paul Deschanel, the moderate leader, was a very frequent visitor and rumored to be interested in arranging a marriage with Thérèse's sister Adèle (ibid.).

him that M. Pringué had been a favorite of his esteemed late father, Gustave Humbert. The patronage system must have functioned smoothly in this case. Three months after Mme Pringué's initial letter, she wrote once again to Mme Humbert to thank her for "the great goodness which you have done for us."[80]

The Humberts seemed both to have enjoyed the role of grand patrons and to have recognized its usefulness. The Pringué example reached into fairly high government and social circles. The Humberts also received much more modest requests for aid in the precarious ascent into middle-class respectability and security. Among Frédéric's seized correspondence was an 1892 letter from a fellow Freemason seeking a recommendation for a position with a business firm. The young man was a former pharmacy student who had been forced to give up his studies because his savings were exhausted and who now, according to his letter, was the sole support of two aged and infirm parents.[81]

With impressive resourcefulness and energy, Thérèse and Frédéric Humbert had exploited to the absolute maximum, and well beyond the limits of legality, their family and social connections with the new republican elite. In turn, others attempted to profit from their association with the Humberts. When the Humberts' vast fraud was revealed in 1902, a portion of that elite was publicly exposed as hypocrites, lacking any commitment to the public good and interested only in their own personal advancement.[82] The critics of the Republic delighted in this latest scandal and eagerly expected it to blossom into a political crisis of proportions equal to the Panama affair. As we shall see in greater detail in Chapter IX, the potential crisis died before fully ripening, partly for lack of evidence and partly because the ever more powerful republican elite was able to squelch the investigations. Nonetheless, the Humberts' rapacious venality and the lesser, entirely legal, social climbing of those surrounding them confirmed well-established negative assumptions about corrupt parliamentarians, assumptions the Radicals themselves had once helped to promote.

80. *Ibid.*, Scelle 33 ter #16-21, C 7314, AN.

81. *Ibid.*, C 7316, AN.

82. Demands to investigate the Humberts had been circulating in the right-wing press since 1895, especially in Edouard Drumont's *Libre Parole*.

The connection between politicians, especially republican politicians, and money was full of dangers and contradictions. It led to corruption—the use of public office for personal gain—and it transformed independent citizens into dependent clients anxiously scurrying about intricate circles of patronage. In addition, the very fact that politicians were paid to pursue their careers, and that they were increasingly becoming professionals raised questions for many about their ability to fulfill their mandate. No issue more clearly expressed these apprehensions about the contamination of republican politicians by money than the question of the deputies' salaries. On November 11, 1907, legislation was enacted to increase the deputies' salaries from 9,000 to 15,000 francs annually. The national response was a widespread and vociferous outcry. Since 1899 there had been efforts to raise the deputies' salaries. The frequent claim that the cost of living in Paris had doubled since the original amount of 9,000 francs had been set in 1849 was certainly no exaggeration. The political elite recognized that deputies without additional income had extraordinary difficulties maintaining the required bourgeois lifestyle. To this concern about standard of living, republican politicians and their supporters added the more principled consideration that an adequate parliamentary salary would permit citizens who were not independently wealthy to pursue political careers. During the debate following the salary increase, one deputy claimed that "in a democracy such as ours . . . no one should find themselves excluded from parliament for financial reasons."[83] Even the 15,000-franc salary did not eliminate all economic barriers. Throughout the first half of the Third Republic, with few exceptions, deputies were overwhelmingly recruited from the middle class, although an increasing portion of them began their parliamentary careers without great wealth or independent means of income. Many of the lawyers, professors, teachers, doctors, and journalists who were elected to the Chamber had origins close to, if not on, the lowest rungs of the middle class. Certainly the new republican political elite and most voters agreed that deputies should be paid. Only a year before the salary increase, the left-wing Marseilles paper Le Petit Provençal pointed out with pride that French deputies were the best paid parliamentarians in

83. Etienne Pugliesi-Conti, Chamber budget debate, November 30, 1906, quoted in Guiral and Thuillier, Vie quotidienne, 106.

Europe. The article contrasted republican France with imperial Germany, where Reichstag members received no compensation. But the article went on to note that the 9,000 francs paid to French deputies was a paltry sum when compared to the generous salaries of members of the United States Congress.[84]

Although it was clear that a republican state must pay the people's representatives, the question still remained how much. In 1907 there was considerable feeling that a 66 percent pay increase was too much. The deputies must have anticipated this outcry because they had hesitated for eight years before voting themselves an increase. In 1906 they had hoped to pass the increase with very little publicity. The original vote taken in November, 1906, followed a procedure in which deputies could be absent from the roll call and not publicly register their vote. General outrage about this tactic forced a new vote the following year, when the increase passed with 318 supporters and 189 opponents. The 15,000-franc yearly salary did not make deputies fabulously wealthy, but it placed them securely within the bourgeoisie. It certainly gave them an income far above that of even the most skilled male worker and considerably above the majority of civil servants. Not surprisingly, the new and growing Socialist party was extremely uncomfortable with the increase. One of its deputies asked, "Why should we, us deputies, live better than the majority of our electors?" During their 1907 Congress the SFIO passed a motion that each Socialist deputy must contribute one-half of the increase, 3,000 francs, to the party's treasury.[85]

The Radicals had been among the strongest supporters of the increase. They had long urged that all representatives of the republican state receive adequate salaries to guarantee "careers open to all."[86] In their 1907 Congress they devoted considerable time to discussing the implications of the imminent salary raise for deputies. Several speakers reminded party members that this increase was vital for the preservation of democracy, "to ensure the independence of the representatives of the people." It would enable

84. "Les Indemnités parlementaires," *Le Petit Provençal*, May 12, 1906.

85. Charles Mouchel, Socialist mayor of Elbeuf, quoted in Guiral and Thuillier, *Vie quotidienne*, 111. There were problems with enforcing this resolution; some deputies resisted (*ibid.*).

86. During the 1905 Radical Congress such a motion was passed regarding judicial positions, which at the lower ranks had almost no compensation (Le Parti républicain radical et radical-socialiste, *5ᵉ Congrès*, tenu à Paris, October, 1905, p. 199).

deputies "to live *honorably* supported by their own resources . . . protected from all *temptations.*" According to this perspective, economic pressures had driven some deputies to improprieties that justifiably scandalized the public and created political instability. The Radical Congress unanimously passed a motion endorsing the increase as a welcome step further to democratize the political system. They explained that it was "a matter of the dignity and in the interest of universal suffrage to award its representatives a sufficient indemnity which permits their exclusive devotion to legislative functions . . . [and] permits the people's representatives to live with integrity, independence and honor."[87] The public concerns were the protection of "universal suffrage" and the creation of a democratic society in which moral virtues could flourish.

This fine-sounding rhetoric did not satisfy all constituents. The press denunciations continued largely from the right wing and the nationalists. Until the war, deputies were denigrated with the label "quinze-millistes," applied in the same negative way that the epithet "Panamistes" had been used in the 1890s.[88] The criticism was so common that simply to add the abbreviation "Q.M." after a deputy's name automatically linked the politician to money and ill-defined malfeasance. This issue contributed to Camille Pelletan's waning popularity among his constituents. Pelletan had been a strong supporter of the increase, hardly surprising considering his personal finances and his ideology. He visited his district shortly before the final vote on the increase was taken. According to one police report, the Radical committee of Salon was especially concerned about the repercussions of the "quinze-milles." The report claimed that Pelletan grandly dismissed their worries. He would simply tell the voters that "the increase was necessary and that will be enough." At least according to this informant, that did not suffice, and Pelletan "in most of the small towns couldn't open his mouth, and two or three times he was booed."[89] Despite this issue, which certainly widened the social gulf between most electors and long-time Radical incumbents, Pelletan retained his seat in the next legislative

---

87. Député Chapuis, Le Parti radical, 7e *Congrès*, tenu à Nancy, October, 1907, pp. 21–22, 77, 75, 79, emphasis added.

88. Guiral and Thuillier, *Vie quotidienne*, 110.

89. Police report, September 26, 1907, Dossier Pelletan, MI 25359, AN.

election. Earlier in 1907 a police report on general conditions in the central department of the Saone-et-Loire noted that "public opinion is actually uncertain and disoriented. . . . No one had imagined the persistent dissatisfaction caused by the increase in parliamentary salaries. This increase has dealt the most serious damage to parliament's prestige. It is being used daily to incite the jealousy of the agricultural and working populations."[90] Although the criticism of increased salaries never coalesced into any organized campaign, it contributed to a permanent rancor toward politicians and particularly toward Radicals, who increasingly were identified as the quintessential politicians of the Third Republic.

By the beginning of the twentieth century, Radical deputies were one clearly identifiable group within a new republican political elite that had been developing over the last four decades. This elite gained control of at least one of the most powerful institutions of the state, the National Assembly, and particularly the Chamber of Deputies. Most Radicals in 1900 would still claim that the authentic republic had yet to be created, but they were convinced that their growing numbers in the Chamber would enable them to accomplish that end. They had largely, though not entirely, abandoned their misgivings about a parliamentary system inherited from aristocratic regimes. Their confidence in parliamentarianism expanded as they occupied more and more benches in the Chamber. The Radicals now applied their mystique about "universal suffrage" to the role of the deputy, whom they identified as the only authentic representative of the popular will. Thus the position of deputy became the most important, the most sought after, and the most honorable political office. Nonetheless, the tension between the "voice of the people" and parliamentary structures continued to perplex left Radicals.

By 1900 being a deputy had also become a career, *un métier*, of considerable prestige and influence with a comfortable bourgeois income.[91] As

90. Rapport d'ensemble, Viticulteurs du Midi, June 17, 1907, Police générale, F7 12794, AN. The report was prepared because of fears that the discontent of southern winegrowers might spread to other wine-producing regions. The informant found no evidence of local concern with the wine market but did find hostility to the deputies.

91. The term *politicien* entered the French vocabulary in the 1870s at the same time that the Third Republic was created. It was borrowed from the English (Estèbe, *Ministres de la République*, 97).

Charles Laisant had predicted, success in this profession followed a path through the various committees, political groups, and offices of the Chamber. Increasing recognition and responsibility marked a deputy's rise. The greater number of Radicals in the Chamber was matched by their growing influence in public debate and, as important, in the powerful committees and informal interactions of the corridors. Success within this republican political elite also depended on a deputy's ability to maneuver in the social world surrounding the Chamber. For Radicals, that was a world of newly arrived men and women connected by ties of education, law courts, Masonic lodges, editorial boards, republican salons, friendships, marriages, and loans. The intersection of parliamentary power and this social world frequently tempted deputies to use their position to enhance their own sometimes precarious financial situation. To some, the attraction of the political career was its prestige connected to a bourgeois Parisian existence.

A symbol of the conflicting political and social aspirations of the new republican elite was the Gare d'Orsay, inaugurated on July 14, 1900, in time for the latest Paris World's Fair. This was a very different structure from the Eiffel Tower of 1889, whose function had been to display the feats of modern technology and where much was made of the solidarity between workers and engineers. The ornate Gare d'Orsay, like many of the projects associated with the 1900 World's Fair, sought to drape its modern structural elements with design motifs recalling an earlier, more aristocratic age. The new station was intended to accommodate affluent visitors, bringing them directly to the opulent commercial city center. In particular, it would service the nearby Palais Bourbon, site of the Chamber of Deputies, making train travel more convenient and more exclusive for the politicians.[92]

In 1907, when the Radical party Congress endorsed the salary increase for deputies, they projected an image of an ideal representative: one who was "exclusively dedicated to his legislative tasks . . . and who lived honorably in probity and independence."[93] But hard work was not always automatically rewarded with honors, and scrupulous honesty did not always guarantee financial and political independence. The Radical deputy was to be a representative of the "people," yet he also had to be a success-

92. Henri Mercillon et al., Orsay, Connaissance des Arts, numéro spéciale (Paris, 1987), 14–15; Silverman, Art Nouveau in Fin-de-Siècle France, 133, 159, 160–69.
93. Le Parti radical, 7ᵉ Congrès, tenu à Nancy, October, 1907, p. 79.

ful member of an upwardly mobile, middle-class profession that promised power and affluence. Caught within these tensions, it is not surprising that many Radicals fell considerably short of the projected ideal. This disparity between the ideal representative in a democratic state and the realities of parliamentary life fueled the frequent scandals of the Third Republic. The public could still be outraged that men who spoke of egalitarian political principles would be avidly pursuing the advantages of their positions within the political elite.

In response to such fundamental tensions, left-wing Radicals such as Pelletan often insisted that they were not members of the political elite. Pelletan was among those who repeatedly evoked his plight as an outsider. From the beginning to the end of his career he portrayed himself and his politics as being on the defensive, fighting the good fight and never achieving real victory. In all likelihood, this consummate politician, who for decades stood at the center of legislative maneuvers, actually believed that he was this imagined permanent outsider. His 1895 obituary for Auguste Vacquerie, editor of *Le Rappel,* elaborated this stance. Pelletan's laments for the past, for the "good old days, the days of heroic struggle," had become fixtures in his rhetoric by the early 1880s and would persist into the 1910s. The past was contrasted to the deeply disappointing present; bitter questions followed about "what have we come to." Then the hard reality was acknowledged: we thought we had won, but the genuine republic still eludes us. "We have always been the conquerors—and we are defeated." This refrain of regret and sense of defeat permeated all Pelletan's addresses. But the closing line always attempted to transform the bitterness of disappointment into the energy necessary for one last final, definitive victory. "Democracy has triumphed, but its victory has been stolen. She will recapture it."[94] Pelletan, the veteran insider, had difficulty imagining himself anything other than an outsider. This successful manipulator of the parliamentary world constantly decried his defeats. These paradoxes profoundly shaped Pelletan's left-wing radicalism and dominated his term as minister of the navy in the Radical government of Emile Combes.

94. Pelletan, "Souvenirs," *Le Rappel,* no. 9119, February 27, 1895.

VII Dilemmas of the Republican State

As the new century began, the Radicals were well positioned to wield power in the republican state. Their political support as measured by election results had grown steadily. The creation of a national party in 1901 further strengthened their electoral showing, and by the end of the first decade of the twentieth century they were the largest group in the Chamber. Since the 1880s individual Radicals had established themselves as leading personalities within the Chamber's committees and had secured important positions of power in its governance structure. Even in the Senate, which Radicals had long denounced, by 1900 they held a dominant position, reflecting the deep support for radicalism in provincial France. More and more frequently their oppositional stance and rhetoric contrasted sharply with the realities of their daily political practice. Radical parliamentarians had indisputably joined the republican political elite. The Dreyfus Affair demonstrated, however, that the republican political elite did not have a monopoly on power. Whatever their ambivalence about Dreyfus's innocence or the instances of anti-Semitism within their own tradition, the Radicals came to view the Dreyfus Affair as proof that the Republic did not fully control all state institutions. Committed to republicanizing these institutions, the Radicals finally rallied to the Dreyfusard cause. In particular, they rededicated themselves to bringing the army under parliamentary control and to curbing the privileges of the Catholic church.[1] With these goals as their priority, the Radicals were prepared to govern in the first years of the twentieth century.

But were they? The central theme of the Radical attack during the 1880s against moderate republicans from Gambetta to Ferry had been the failure

---

1. In accordance with the 1801 Concordat governing relations between the church and the state, the Third Republic had, in theory, considerable control over the church. See Maurice Larkin, *Church and State After the Dreyfus Affair: The Separation Issue in France* (London, 1974), 47–62.

of these politicians to implement their original program once they had attained political power. It was for this reason that the Radicals labeled and denounced them as Opportunists. Such opportunism seemed at times not to be connected to a particular politician or even to a particular political ideology; the betrayal of principles was often presented as inherent in the pursuit of governing power. Corruption and deception may not always have been the inevitable consequences of political success, but Opportunist politicians had so besmirched government offices that it was increasingly difficult to view government as credible. In 1888, writing in *La Justice*, Camille Pelletan decried the degree to which politics and all politicians had become suspect. "Nothing has done more to reinforce the dangerous political skepticism in this country, than the spectacle of men coming to power and doing the opposite of what they demanded the day before . . . this prolonged deplorable spectacle has propagated the idea in the majority of the public . . . that no politician should be trusted; that there is no one who, coming to power, would not be willing to exchange his program with that of his adversaries. . . . This has ruined the reputation of representative government."[2] As early as 1883, preparing for the next legislative elections, Pelletan had recognized the dangers of political success for a party promising change and improvement. "It is a terrible test for a party of progress and liberty to join the government." As Radicals achieved the position of a governing party, these same anxieties were expressed with even greater frequency at a variety of meetings and congresses.[3]

In addition to this long-standing uneasiness about the consequences of governing and political power, the Radicals had developed a well-established critique of the institutions of the French state. They had long suspected that parliament was an Orléanist inheritance, replete with aristocratic pretensions; they had always insisted that the administrative and ministerial organs of the state were the legacy of authoritarian imperial regimes. In the 1880s the militant Radical Charles Laisant, shortly before joining the Boulangist movement, denounced the state apparatus as Napoleonic despotism, "serving the bourgeoisie as an instrument of

2. *La Justice*, no. 3261, December 18, 1888.
3. Camille Pelletan, *Georges Clemenceau*, 27. For only one example of such anxiety, see Le Parti radical et radical-socialiste du sud-est, *1er Congrès*, tenu à Nice, April, 1907, p. 30.

oppression."[4] Though somewhat less extreme, Pelletan endorsed similar sentiments. His persistent objection to administrative expenses, partly motivated by a deep fiscal conservatism, was also inspired by an even stronger suspicion of state institutions not directly controlled by universal male suffrage. He called for a thoroughgoing reform of the hierarchical and outmoded bureaucracy and the creation of an administrative structure appropriate to a genuinely republican state.[5]

Such rhetoric conveyed the serious ambivalence toward state power shared by many leading Radicals. Their moderate and conservative opponents viewed this language as clear evidence that the Radicals were incapable of governing. The historian Daniel Halévy said of them that their "raison d'être was to defend not to govern."[6] Critics on the Right questioned whether the Radicals were capable of exercising state power and of functioning within the hierarchical discipline of bureaucratic institutions. A few Radicals themselves were uncertain about their governing role. Left Radicals in particular remained highly ambivalent about the legitimacy of bureaucratic authority. A clear question was whether Radicals could govern in the way governing had traditionally been understood. And if they could not or would not govern through the established hierarchical system, were they capable of developing and introducing alternative democratic methods? Both Radicals and their opponents recognized the possibility of serious dilemmas should the principle of republican egalitarianism be applied to the authority of the state.

Following the elections of 1902 there was no question that a new government must include a significant Radical presence.[7] Almost all candidates

4. Laisant, *Anarchie bourgeoise*, 30–31.

5. *La Justice*, no. 2939, January 31, 1888; see Chapter VI.

6. Halévy, *République des comités*, 95.

7. Radicals had not been entirely absent from the governments of the 1880s and 1890s. Individual Radicals were in the short-lived ministries of republican concentration headed by Freycinet, Goblet, and Floquet. The Freycinet government of 1886 included Lockroy and Boulanger. The first Radical-led government, that of Léon Bourgeois, 1895–1896, was forced to resign after a few months as a result of the Senate's opposition to tax reform. Waldeck-Rousseau's government of republican defense depended on Radical support and had three Radical ministers, but it was not led by Radicals.

approached the 1902 legislative elections as a critical confrontation between broad coalitions of Right and Left. The Left associated itself with
republican defense and the Right with the protection of the army and especially the church. Radical campaign promises delineated a broad reform
platform, which included both anticlerical and labor issues. In the Midi
several Radical-socialist candidates even endorsed the working-class demand for an eight-hour working day.[8] For months, violent, confrontational
rhetoric filled the campaign. As early as January, Pelletan, speaking at a
rally in the South, laid out the great themes of the electoral conflict and
stressed the necessary union between Radicals and socialists, between the
republican middle class and workers. He identified "two enemies, the one
of yesterday, clericalism, and the enemy of tomorrow, . . . the new *féodalité financière* . . . industries . . . factories . . . large transportation companies . . . organizing the slavery of workers and employees."[9]

Both the coalitions of the Right and the Left succeeded in mobilizing the
voters, as demonstrated by the dramatically low abstention rate.[10] The large
number of seats won in the first round also suggested that the electorate
had recognized the ideological confrontation even though few candidates
offered precise programs.[11] These clear victories also indicated that in most
areas electoral alliances had been effective, particularly those between socialists and Radicals. In one such instance the Radical committee of the
northern industrial city Lille had called on Camille Pelletan to campaign
for a socialist candidate. He acceded to the request without hesitation.[12]
The May victory went to the left coalition which Pelletan promoted, but by

8. Mayeur, Vie politique, 185–86. Mayeur stresses the importance of the 1901 Law on
Associations that severely limited, if it did not abolish, unauthorized religious associations. For
an example of such promises see Gaston Doumergue's campaign statement for Nîmes, Annales de
l'Assemblée nationale, Chambre des députés, Programmes et professions de foi, Annexe au procès
verbaux de la séance du July 3, 1903, p. 302; on the eight-hour day, ibid., 121.

9. Police report, Bezier, January 14, 1902, Dossier Pelletan, MI 25359, AN.

10. The national abstention rate stood at 20.8 percent; it had continued its decline from
the already low national rate of 23.9 percent in the 1898 elections (Mayeur, Vie politique, 185).

11. There were first-round victories in 415 districts out of 589 (Rebérioux, La République
radicale?, 57).

12. Gustave Delory, Guesdist, won the election, but joined with the other Guesdists in the
Chamber refusing to support officially the left coalition. When the time came to vote on actual
issues, however, even the most militant Guesdists usually voted with the majority.

a modest margin.[13] Within the Left the recently formed Radical republican and Radical-socialist party made the largest gains.[14] This electoral success was regarded as a strong mandate for the implementation of a Radical program, and a wave of popular enthusiasm greeted the success of the Left. Toasts, parades, demonstrations, and occasional brawls with the defeated Right accompanied the announcement of Radical triumphs.[15] Two years later, the elections for municipal councils repeated this Radical victory. At the most local political level, Radicals associated with the left coalition withstood the attack of nationalists, republican moderates, and even disgruntled members of their own party.

The 1902 election resulted in a Radical-dominated Chamber that supported the government of Emile Combes. Radicals and Radical-socialists controlled 233 of the 589 seats. The informal parliamentary alliance that had sustained the Waldeck-Rousseau government of republican defense and had consolidated its alliance in electoral cooperation now became a more formal parliamentary majority, the Bloc des gauches. It included a group of thirty-six socialists who followed Jaurès's reformist strategy, a large contingent of Radicals whose internal divisions would in time become more pronounced, and a small but critical number of moderate republicans. Initially, the Bloc des gauches could count on a majority of between eighty and ninety deputies. Departing from the tradition of highly fluid, extremely individualistic parliamentary coalitions, the Bloc des gauches in July created a twenty-six-member Délégation des gauches which maintained and directed the left-wing majority.[16] The Délégation, in which Jaurès had a leading position, further accentuated the leftward direction of the parliamentary majority. It also provided unprecedented coherence and stability for the Combes government, which it supported. For the first time in French parliamentary practice, a mechanism existed to main-

13. After the first round only two hundred thousand votes separated Left and Right. Candidates of the Left increased their support at the second round (Rebérioux, *La République radicale?*, 58).

14. Rebérioux claims that it was the moderate elements among both Radicals and socialists that had the greatest success in this election (*ibid.*, 59).

15. Police report, Atmosphère politique, Élections 1902, May, 1902, F7 12541, AN.

16. Rebérioux, *La République radicale?*, 58. Rebérioux notes that the Délégation first emerged in late 1900 to study the question of the religious congregations (*ibid.*, 64).

tain constant communication between the parliamentary majority and the government.[17]

There were obvious tensions within the Délégation and the majority it led. The dramatically opposed philosophies, political programs, and constituents of the Jaurèsian socialists and the moderate republicans pulled the Bloc des gauches in different directions. Also significant for both socialists and moderates were their divided loyalties—adherence to the Bloc and republican defense on one hand, and commitment to older, more traditional allies either to their left or right on the other. Most participants and commentators at the time, as well as historians since, have attributed the eventual collapse of the formal Bloc in early 1905 to the departure of the socialists under pressure from their more orthodox comrades. But the most destabilizing elements in this potentially powerful parliamentary reform coalition were located within its largest component, the Radicals.[18] As we shall see, these tensions were complex, intertwining personal feuds and political disagreements. At their heart was an often vague, sometimes confusing debate among Radicals as to whether they could actually govern and, if they could, how they ought to direct the state. These developments among the Radicals in the parliamentary majority, in the Délégation des gauches, and in the Combes government will be the focus of this and the following chapter.

The Bloc des gauches and the Combes government have been appropriately associated with the final victories of the republicans' long anticlerical campaign. The 1902–1906 legislature endorsed the vigorous implementation of the new Law on Associations, passed in 1901, essentially carrying through the disbanding of unauthorized religious orders.[19] Even more dra-

17. R. A. Winnacker, "The Délégation des gauches: A Successful Attempt at Managing a Parliamentary Coalition," *Journal of Modern History*, IX (December, 1937), 449, 451, 454.

18. In his memoirs Combes takes the conventional view. He identifies the departure of the socialists as much more damaging to the Bloc des gauches than the pointed criticisms of the dissident Radicals (Emile Combes, *Mon Ministère. Mémoires, 1902–1905* [Paris, 1956], 226). For the socialist and especially Jaurèsian view see Goldberg, *Life of Jaurès*, 330–42.

19. While enthusiastically demanded by Radical supporters, in regions of greater religious devotion this disbanding met serious resistance. For the strength and complexity of the opposition see Caroline Ford, "Religion and the Politics of Cultural Change in Provincial France: The Resistance of 1902 in Lower Brittany," *Journal of Modern History*, LXII (March, 1990), 1–33.

matically, this legislature finally fulfilled the long-standing Radical promise to separate church and state.[20] Such anticlerical enthusiasm has frequently been presented somewhat disparagingly as a demonstration of the Radicals' inability to deliver on anything but this particular issue. Anticlericalism is often portrayed as the only policy that held the tenuous coalition of the Bloc together. It has also been identified as the fulfillment of the vindictive fanaticism of Radical anticlericals under the leadership of the single-minded former seminarian Emile Combes. These judgments can be found among contemporary critics of the Radicals, as well as later historians.[21] A case can be made for each of these portraits, but they all distort the specific political, social, and cultural contexts in which the anticlerical issue occurred and the Radical government functioned.

Historians sometimes underestimate the seriousness with which the entire French Left and especially the Radicals addressed the clerical issue. The Combes government unquestionably advanced secularization as an essential element of republican culture and polity. Both inside and outside the Chamber of Deputies most supporters, and as many opponents, of the Bloc des gauches assumed that the anticlerical issue was the first and most pressing of a series of reforms.[22] For the Radicals the purpose of such legislation was first to republicanize the state and second to promote a more egalitarian society that would further extend and support democratic practices. Left Radicals such as Pelletan had long argued that the republican state had inherited policies in which public authority and public resources were being handed over to what Pelletan called "private interests." Such "interests" might be the major railroad companies, large banks, mining firms, or the Catholic church. These interests benefited tremendously from privileges extended by the state and rarely fulfilled the legal agreements under which

20. See Jean-Marie Mayeur, *La Séparation des églises et de l'état* (Paris, 1991), and Larkin, *Church and State After the Dreyfus Affair*. The actual law was not voted on until December, 1905, after the Combes government had resigned.

21. For examples see Watson's excellent biography, *Clemenceau*, 161–62; Theodore Zeldin's well-mannered but biting portrait of Combes in *France, 1848–1945: Politics and Anger* (Oxford, 1979), 319–24.

22. Rebérioux, *La République radicale?*, 65. For an assessment of the popular support for Combes's anticlericalism see Baal, "Combes et 'La République des Comités,'" 276.

such privileges had originally been conceded.[23] In his view, this was blatantly the case with the 1801 Concordat governing relations between the Catholic church and the state. To Radicals these legally constituted, specially privileged, quasi-private institutions smacked of the *Ancien Régime* and benefited only their own narrow interests rather than the public good and the nation.

In addition to the necessity for the state to reappropriate the authority it had ceded to these private institutions, there was also the question of the republican character of all state institutions. Throughout the existence of the Third Republic, Radicals were convinced that high-level, powerful civil servants hostile to the Republic controlled entire government ministries and influenced advancement in many others.[24] The ministries in which this antirepublican sentiment was assumed to be most pervasive were the two in charge of the military services. In 1880 Stephen Pichon, writing in *La Justice*, characterized the navy as "a refuge of clericalism and the enemies of the Republic . . . [where] the Jesuits played a considerable role in recruitment." The solution he offered to "ending these abuses" was "a republican minister, concerned with the needs of civil society."[25]

Throughout the nineteenth century various regimes had followed an unacknowledged agreement that the armed forces were not to interfere in political issues and the state would permit the armed forces considerable autonomy.[26] During the early decades of the Third Republic, republicans attempted to alter this agreement and to extend effective parliamentary control over both the navy and the army. Camille Pelletan, of course, had led this struggle in the Budget Committee in regard to the navy. Especially during the Dreyfus Affair the army high command had dramatically

---

23. Pelletan elaborated this view in a long parliamentary speech of 1886, arguing for the repurchase of the railroad lines (Annales de la Chambre des députés, *Débats*, March 6, 1886, reprinted in *La Justice*, no. 2254, March 17, 1886).

24. After Combes's resignation this view was expressed in Le Parti radical, Comité executif, Rapport, 5ᵉ *Congrès*, tenu à Paris, October, 1905, p. 25.

25. *La Justice*, no. 102, April 26, 1880.

26. For the independence of military ministries see Estèbe, *Ministres de la République*, 127–31.

demonstrated the degree to which it was dedicated to protecting its independence from serious parliamentary control and its bitter resistance to any attempt to alter its traditional power. The Dreyfus Affair had brought to public attention a number of military officers who were outspoken in their hostility to the Republic. It also had most explosively linked the army and the church. The decision of some prelates and some religious orders, the Assumptionists in particular, to defend vociferously the army's condemnation of Dreyfus led to a polarization between those who identified with army and church and those who identified with the Republic. Especially in the aftermath of the Dreyfus Affair, fervent Catholicism among army or naval officers was universally read as a sign of a critical attitude toward the Republic. During the 1902 elections, reform of the military figured prominently in the programs of many left-wing candidates. As a consequence, the Bloc des gauches reduced military service to two years.[27] Significantly, the first public outcry over Pelletan's presence in the new Combes government occurred in response to a speech the new minister of the navy delivered about the army. Addressing an annual republican banquet commemorating the birth of the revolutionary general Lazare Hoche, Pelletan called for military reforms: the creation of a people's army, the disciplining of officers, and an exclusively defensive strategy. While left-wing Radicals and socialists applauded him, Bonapartists and nationalists bitterly denounced this assault on the army.[28]

The subsequent furor over Pelletan would, of course, concern his direction of the navy, but in addition to all the other reasons opponents had for criticizing Pelletan, there was always the fear that his naval reforms would set a pattern for the army. Among critics of the Bloc and among moderates in the original coalition there was mounting concern that the combination of army scandals from Boulanger to Dreyfus *and* the new reform efforts would dangerously undermine the prestige of the French military. Radicals themselves, even those most committed to military reform, recognized

27. Although prepared by the Combes government, that law passed in March, 1905, after Combes had resigned. The law reduced the universal military service from the existing three years to two years. In July, 1913, the legislature returned to the three years of military service. The Three Year Law became a key issue in the last prewar election.

28. Police report, June 30–July 1, 1902, Dossier Pelletan, MI 25359, AN.

that when dealing with this question they were involved in "extremely delicate matters."[29] Of the two military services, the army was by far the larger, the center of all French strategy, and the one dependent on citizen conscripts. These concerns occurred in the first decade of the twentieth century, when military preparedness had become a key political issue as international tensions and the European arms race intensified.

This first decade of the twentieth century was also a time of intensifying working-class militancy, which raised questions about the army's role as an internal police force, maintaining what previous governments had called "order" during confrontational strikes. Socialists and Radicals had long criticized this domestic police function. In the very beginning of his political career, when analyzing the Commune, Pelletan had bitterly denounced the use of the French army against French citizens. "One must choose between a national army, established against foreign dangers, and a political army, directed against the nation."[30] He had consistently condemned the use of troops in the strikes of the 1880s and 1890s. In addition, much anxious speculation existed in government circles about the reliability of the army when called on to intervene between labor and capital.[31] The Bloc des gauches government was faced with the question of whether to use the army as an internal police. November, 1902, saw the first, albeit not very successful, general strike by miners. That same year the government failed in its attempt to arbitrate the bitter Marseilles dock strike. During 1904 four million working days were lost in strikes, a number that continued to mount.[32] On several of these occasions, in spite of earlier opposition to such

29. Le Parti radical, Massimy Rapport de réformes militaires, 3e Congrès, tenu à Marseille, March, 1903, p. 124.

30. Camille Pelletan, Semaine de mai, 408.

31. Police report, Situation politique, 1899–1905, Police générale, November 10, 1903, F7 12553, AN.

32. Worker militancy, largely in the form of more and longer strikes, had intensified since 1899–1900 and continued at least until 1907. It was in 1902 that strikes attained their longest duration, an average of twenty-two days. The number of strikes rose steadily from 1899–1900 to 1902, slowed in 1903, and then rose sharply from 1904 to 1907. The number of strikes in 1904 was double that for 1903. Demands were principally for wage increases, union recognition, and reduction in work hours. See Rebérioux, La République radicale?, 88–89, and Jean Bron, La Contestation du capitalisme par les travailleurs organisés, 1884–1950 (Paris, 1970), 89–92, Vol. II of Bron, Histoire du mouvement ouvrier français, 3 vols.

action, this most Radical of governments mobilized the army to protect the "right to work."

The republicanization of the state was not only a matter of parliamentary or government control over ministries and the military forces but also an issue of ensuring that republicans staffed the ever-increasing number of positions in the state administration. On the most immediate level, the Radicals as new members of the political elite had to deliver to their supporters what every French political elite had provided. positions, protection, and advancement. In the early twentieth century, this patronage had to be carried out in far greater numbers for an emerging middle class and within the context of democratic politics. The Radicals insisted that their efforts to fill as many state positions as possible with those whom they considered loyal Radicals served their publicly proclaimed aim to republicanize the state and bring it fully under parliamentary control. Patronage and the republicanization of resistant state institutions were viewed as entirely interdependent and as entirely legitimate. Emile Combes in one of his first communications to all prefects explicitly stated that his government's intention was to create a republican and "sympathetic administration."[33] Days after issuing this circular, which demanded that civil servants be loyal to the state, Combes publicly defended his position and responded to the controversy it had aroused. He wrote in a provincial republican journal, "We have a deep aversion against anything which would tend to investigate . . . the personal convictions of loyal servants of the State; but we will never tolerate systematic malevolence to hide in the shadow of our republican government."[34] The consequences of such a policy clearly raised the issue, could Radicals exercise the double prerogatives of employer and the state? Could Radicals discipline state employees who constituted a significant segment of their electorate and who were often recipients of Radical politicians' patronage?

The Radicals' intentions appalled conservative and moderate opponents. One can still sense Daniel Halévy's revulsion and terror thirty years after the Bloc as he contemplated the reality that in "taking over the army

---

33. Police report, Situation politique, 1899–1905, June 26, 1902, F7 12553, AN.

34. L'Indépendant of Pau cited in Police report, Situation politique, June 24, 1902, F7 12553, AN.

the Radicals have control of 30,000 positions."[35] The Radical party enthusiastically promoted a policy of republicanizing the state through the
appointment of reliable republicans. The 1903 Radical Congress clearly
endorsed the general principle that the government should reward republicans by placing them in civil service positions. The Congress even formally
protested to the Combes government that it had permitted its minister
of foreign affairs, Théophile Delcassé, to designate a former Boulangist as
French consul in New Orleans.[36] At the 1905 Congress, which followed the
fall of the Combes government, there was much debate on the need for the
party's Executive Committee to establish a subcommittee for "republican
defense and vigilance . . . to review openly and publicly the nominations
and promotions of all civil servants and to defend republican civil servants."
Ultimately, the proposal was rejected because of the recent furor over the
former minister of the army's methods of surveillance. The delegates also
concluded that the Executive Committee would be better able to accomplish this task without a special committee. All agreed, however, that such
protection of republican civil servants was a vital necessity.[37]

This practice of patronage was not an innovation, although it was more
extensive and systematic during the Combes government than before.[38]
The insistence on republican loyalty was somewhat of a departure, particularly when applied to the armed services. In response to that effort, nationalists, defeated anti-Dreyfusards, and conservatives began a campaign
to demonstrate that parliamentary control and republican patronage were
undermining the essential organization of the French army and navy. They
insisted that Radical commitment to egalitarianism would erode the necessary discipline, authority, and, in their terms, "manliness" of the military.
Ultimately, republican moderates and, most significantly, moderates within

35. Halévy, *République des comités*, 60.

36. Le Parti radical, 3e *Congrès*, tenu à Marseille, March, 1903, pp. 107–108. For even earlier Radical demands to purge antirepublican civil servants see discussion of Marseilles Radicals,
Chapter III. For general popular support for such policies see Baal, "Combes et 'La République
des comités,' " 278.

37. Le Parti radical, 5e *Congrès*, tenu à Paris, October, 1905, pp. 199–202. At the same
Congress the Executive Committee expressed concern that with the collapse of the Combes
government reprisals would be taken against republican *fonctionnaires* and that already they had
received an increasing number of requests for protection (*ibid.*, 30).

38. Mayeur, *Vie politique*, 188.

the Radical party became convinced that to pursue the full republicanization of the state would indeed endanger the French nation. These diverse groups were convinced that national defense could not be entrusted to Radicals, who claimed to adhere to republican egalitarian principles. Central to these arguments was the assumption that the most dedicated Radicals were incapable of governing. They were unable to wield the authority of the state, and their very policies jeopardized that essential authority. To evaluate this charge requires a closer examination of the Radical-dominated government of 1902–1905.

The political negotiations surrounding the formation of a new government after the elections of 1902 seemed to confirm the right-wing characterization of the Radicals' inadequacies. Police reports following Waldeck-Rousseau's resignation portrayed the Radicals as being in a "panic." Although many had been only lukewarm supporters of Waldeck, they were momentarily at a loss when it became clear that a Radical government would have to be formed. Particularly the more militant Radical-socialists feared that their presence in a government would coalesce a conservative and right-wing opposition. Léon Bourgeois flatly refused to head a new government.[39] Finally, the senator from the Charente-Inférieure, Emile Combes, agreed to form a government. Radicals, as the leading force within the parliamentary majority and its steering committee, the Délégation des gauches, were instrumental in supporting and influencing the new government. Party congresses were enthusiastic in their support for the new government. Adulatory telegrams were exchanged between party congresses and government ministers Combes and Pelletan in 1903 and 1904. Nonetheless, no formal ties existed between the Radical party and the ministry. Both government and party were content with this arrangement. Neither Combes nor Pelletan attended party congresses, and there was some consternation when Pelletan's administrative aid, Louis Tissier, played too active a role during the 1904 Congress.[40]

The new government was not made up exclusively of Radicals. In fact, the Combes government was less homogeneously Radical than the Bour-

---

39. Police report, Situation politique, 1899–1905, May 22, 1902, F7 12553, AN.
40. Le Parti radical, 4ᵉ Congrès, tenu à Toulouse, October, 1904, pp. 20, 168–69.

geois government of 1895–1896. Its most unique characteristic was its close cooperation with the parliamentary majority through the mechanism of the Délégation des gauches. Few governments of the Third Republic have been so closely tied to a parliamentary majority or so aware of the electoral coalition that stood behind the deputies. This majority, whatever its internal tensions, enabled the Combes government to be among the longest-lasting governments of the first half of the Third Republic. The composition of the government reflected the strength of the various groups in the Bloc des gauches with the exception of the socialists. In all likelihood, both Combes and the socialists were relieved not to renew the controversy that had surrounded the participation of socialist Alexandre Millerand in the previous government. Only three members of the Waldeck-Rousseau government continued in the Combes ministry. The most important was Théophile Delcassé in foreign affairs at the specific request of the president of the Republic. This discontinuity soon became a source of bitterness within the republican majority. The government included four moderate republicans, the most significant of whom, after Delcassé, was Maurice Rouvier as minister of finance. There were four Radicals and two Radical-socialists, the most prominent being Camille Pelletan in the Ministry of the Navy.[41]

Immediately after its formation, tensions emerged within the government, particularly between Rouvier and Pelletan. Rouvier had been the most important Opportunist deputy accused of financial improprieties during the Panama scandal. Although never charged, he had resigned from the Chamber in 1892. Even more damaging from Pelletan's perspective were Rouvier's successful career in banking and his financial policies while holding government positions. Rouvier adamantly opposed the major Radical fiscal reform, the progressive income tax. For Pelletan, Rouvier was *"la féodalité financière"* personified. Combes had selected Rouvier precisely for his financial conservatism, to calm panicked bankers, whereas he had called on Pelletan, in part, to mollify Radical protests against

---

41. Combes, *Mon Ministère*, 228; Rebérioux, *La République radicale?*, 64–65; Mayeur, *Vie politique*, 186–87. The Combes government lasted from June, 1902, to January, 1905. Two longer governments were those of Waldeck-Rousseau, June, 1899, to June, 1902, and Clemenceau, October, 1906, to July, 1909.

Rouvier.[42] Pelletan joined the government, but he barely tempered his long-standing criticism of Rouvier.[43] At the end of June, Pelletan questioned Rouvier's financial program; it was unheard-of for members of the same government to be publicly at odds. The right-wing press enjoyed itself immensely, publishing articles describing the government as "Anarchy" and "The Harem in Revolt."[44] Republicans and moderate Radicals were extremely uneasy. The feud between Rouvier and Pelletan never ended. In the fall of 1904, Louis Tissier, Pelletan's *chef du cabinet* persuaded the Radical Congress to modify a proposed endorsement of Rouvier's policies.[45] In addition to the permanent tension between the ministers of finance and the navy, little sympathy existed between Pelletan and his counterpart in the army, General Louis André, who was one of the three holdovers from the Waldeck-Rousseau government.[46]

Until the last months of the Combes ministry it was Pelletan who drew the most criticism. At the time of its formation, the moderates in the Bloc des gauches expressed their unhappiness about his selection.[47] Through June, 1902, police reports to the minister of the interior corroborated the negative stereotypes of this deputy, although they also grudgingly admitted his talents. "Camille Pelletan . . . a strange character for a minister. . . . He knows neither combs nor brushes and his manners are too democratic. But he is a remarkable orator." Two days later, a second report was even more specific in its negative assessment: "Pelletan more a critic of governments than a member. He is not at all liked and will have much difficulty winning the sympathy of his subordinates. The caricaturists will appreciate his position. For the rest, he is an assiduous and intelligent worker." In

42. Combes, *Mon Ministère*, 25. Waldeck-Rousseau had maneuvered a similar balancing of political allegiances when he appointed General Galliffet and then called on the socialist Alexandre Millerand.

43. Police report, Situation politique, 1899–1905, June 14, 1902, F7 12553, AN.

44. "L'Anarchie" appeared in the Bonapartist *L'Autorité*, July 1, 1902, and "La Révolte au Serail" in Rochefort's *L'Intransigeant*, July 1, 1902.

45. See "La Politique. Ministre d'opposition," *La République*, July 1, 1902; Le Parti radical, 4ᵉ Congrès, tenu à Toulouse, October, 1904, p. 143.

46. Police report, no. 1907, September 19, 1902, Dossier Pelletan, MI 25359, AN. Pelletan lobbied to oust André and replace him with a friend, probably a civilian.

47. Winnacker, "Délégation des gauches," 453.

contrast to these assessments, Radical party militants and many who had voted for Bloc des gauches candidates in the 1902 elections regarded Pelletan as the incarnation of the left Radical. Both supporters and detractors predicted that he would not behave according to the traditions of ministerial decorum. In the first four weeks of his new position, Pelletan fulfilled those expectations. He publicly denounced a government colleague and delivered what were perceived to be inflammatory criticisms of the army.[48]

Pelletan's refusal to conform to the conventional standards of ministerial behavior was calculated. Throughout his two and a half years as head of the French navy, his actions and pronouncements made it clear that he intended to preserve his already well-known positions on the armed services, military expenditures, and the relations between ministries and the parliament. In the Chamber the conservative republican deputy the Baron Amédée Reille, a major critic of the Bloc as well as a Catholic and reserve naval officer, quipped to Pelletan, "Your being Minister of the Navy is a bit as if one of us found themselves Minister of the Interior and had to enforce the Law on Associations."[49] Pelletan had major personal, political, and ideological stakes in demonstrating that having arrived at power he would not revise his policies, unlike so many other republican members of previous governments. To a large extent, although not completely, Pelletan accomplished this goal, and therefore his ministry could be considered a political success. Unlike those he had been denouncing for decades, Pelletan remained an outsider within his own ministry, often locked in a bitter struggle with longtime administrators and naval officers. Even as a government member, his principal identity remained that of a left-wing Radical, not the chief of a military service.

That his relations with the government bureaucracy he was appointed to direct should be uniformly antagonistic could hardly have surprised anyone. Pelletan had established a reputation as a major critic of the admirals. In one of his earliest articles in *La Justice* he derided the government for permitting the navy to celebrate Easter officially. In 1880 he had been inspired

48. Police report, Situation politique, 1899–1905, June 12–14, 1902, F7 12553, AN; Police report, June 23, 1902, Dossier Pelletan, MI 25359, AN.

49. Assemblée nationale, Chambre des députés, Débats, *Journal Officiel*, November 24, 1902, p. 2734. Reille represented the Tarn, having been elected to the family seat in 1898 which his father had held for decades.

Caricature of Camille Pelletan. Cover illustration
from *Guignol*, XXXIV, No. 2 (1904).
(Phot. Bibl. Nat., Paris)

by a palpable anticlerical fury at the thought of the Mediterranean fleet
draped in black to commemorate Good Friday. The intervening decades
had diminished neither the naval officer corps' Catholicism nor Pelletan's
anticlericalism. Also well established by the 1880s was his highly critical
attitude toward military spending. His activity in the Chamber's Budget
Committee, his frequent assignment to report on naval appropriations, and
his interventions in general budgetary debate had led him time and time
again to demand cuts in the naval budget. In an 1888 article he called for
patriotic vigilance in regard to military spending, especially naval spending. Four years later, he wrote a searing condemnation of the officers who
staffed the naval ministry. He labeled them "chauvinist admirals," whose
"patriotism consists . . . of getting as many millions as possible from the
taxpayers to give to the navy." During the 1896 budgetary hearing on the
navy, Pelletan reiterated with damning evidence his already established
criticisms: the navy had been incapable of change for the last fifty years;

money spent had been wasted; parliamentary control did not exist; the much overburdened taxpayers of France, the working people, could not be expected to support this "absurd waste."[50]

All of these themes would be further amplified while he was minister of this same navy. Pelletan did make some minor concessions and attempted to temper his rhetoric in public. He sought to convince admirals, officers, and the parliamentary naval lobby that his proposed reforms would create a better, more efficient navy. Nonetheless, it remained clear to supporters and opponents that his view of the navy officer corps had altered little since the 1880s. Certainly little had changed within the service to transform the new minister's opinions. Pelletan never became what the French call "*ministra-ble,*" a politician easily accommodating to the needs of various governing coalitions and the demands of entrenched bureaucrats. He proudly and somewhat defiantly proclaimed that he was what he had always been. The nationalist Right and conservative politicians denounced him for precisely that reason. Pelletan, in their view, had completely misunderstood the function of government ministers, who had to shift their focus from electors to the institutions of the state for which they must now speak. The Bonapartist press lampooned him as "bohemian Pelletan [who] thinks he's still in the opposition and permitted to be a lone *cavalier.*" More important, some in the republican press echoed similar views. They too were shocked that a member of the government would speak out against its military leaders.[51]

Although his insistence on maintaining his earlier critical stance earned Pelletan much criticism from moderates, conservatives, and the Right, it also gained him respect from the Left of his own party and its socialist allies. The 1903 Radical Congress sent warm congratulations to the minister of the navy, who "with rare democratic courage applies to the ministry the doctrines and theories which he espoused as a deputy." The following year, the Congress again officially praised both Combes and Pelletan. The delegates singled out Pelletan's success in being "a man who in power remained what he was while in the opposition."[52] Not surprisingly, the socialist Fran-

50. *La Justice,* no. 75, March 30, 1880; no. 3107, July 17, 1888; no. 4556, July 5, 1892; Annales de la Chambre des députés, *Débats,* December 14, 1896, pp. 1129–35.

51. Paul de Cassagnac in *Autorité,* July 1, 1902; *La République,* July 1, 1902.

52. Le Parti radical, *3e Congrès,* tenu à Marseille, March, 1903, p. 20; Le Parti radical, *4e Congrès,* tenu à Toulouse, October, 1904, p. 15.

cis de Pressensé cheered the minister of the navy, seeing his presence in the government as a guarantee that the broader reform program—separation of church and state, the progressive income tax, a two-year military service, and workers' pensions—would be enacted. Pressensé hoped that Pelletan would be an authentically republican minister.[53] The enthusiasm of these greetings suggests how novel an occurrence this was and how welcome such a show of political integrity was among both Radical party militants and socialists. Pelletan had demonstrated that Radicals could resist the temptations of power and the lure of opportunistic accommodations.

Pelletan's policies and behavior as naval minister were compared not only to the previous positions he had espoused as a deputy but also to the records of two earlier Radical naval ministers, Edouard Lockroy and Jean de Lanessan. Lockroy, an old colleague from the editorial board of *Le Rappel* and the Hugo circle of the 1870s, had in the 1890s become the first Radical to be appointed minister of the navy. He served in this position in three short-lived governments—Bourgeois' all Radical cabinet of November, 1895 to April, 1896; the republican concentration governments of Henri Brisson, June to November, 1898; and that of Charles Dupuy, November, 1898 to June, 1899. Lockroy clearly intended to modernize the navy, and he partly supported the new strategic viewpoints which some officers, known as the Jeune Ecole, were developing. In the 1880s Admiral Hyacinthe-Laurent Aube had championed new deployment theories; he had argued for a shift away from large battleships and to a new emphasis on smaller torpedo boats for both rapid coastal defense and cruiser warfare. Lockroy's most important innovation as minister of the navy was the establishment of the Ecole supérieure de la marine to provide naval officers with advanced technical training.[54]

At the first announcement of Pelletan's appointment, there had been speculation that Lockroy would be a strong supporter because they seemed

---

53. *L'Aurore*, July 1, 1902.

54. Admiral Hyacinthe-Laurent Aube was minister of the navy in the republican govern-ment of René Goblet, 1886–1887. Lockroy had established a reputation as a modernizer and supporter of technological innovation when he promoted the construction of the Eiffel Tower while minister of commerce in Freycinet's 1886 government. For the influence of the Jeune Ecole see Paul Baquiast, "La Jeune Ecole de la marine française, la presse et l'opinion publique" (Unpublished paper, Université de Paris IV, 1987).

to share similar views on strategic reforms.[55] Lockroy, however, had always been careful not to interfere with the authority or prestige of the traditional naval hierarchy. On the contrary, he established close and amicable relations with the admirals.[56] Lockroy's attitude toward the navy was well characterized years later in one of the eulogies delivered at his funeral. "When the ship, leaving French shores, gains the high sea, the divisions in the distance are effaced; one sees only one France and one Republic. [Lockroy] understood this; he spoke for the navy as a leader, a patriot, a statesman."[57] Even at the time of Pelletan's appointment and immediately after, there were indications of tension between the two men. Rumors circulated that Lockroy was furious at the failure of a Radical government to appoint him once again to a highly valued ministerial position.[58]

Lockroy played a critical role in delegitimating Pelletan's ministry; contemporaries and historians, however, have too easily dismissed his motives as merely personal interest. To categorize Lockroy's actions in such a way misses one of the crucial functions of republican and especially Radical governments—to find places for their supporters. This securing of positions ran the gamut from the poorly paid provincial postal clerk to the minister of the navy. The clashing of Pelletan's and Lockroy's personal ambitions for political advancement was the consequence of the democratic promise that had been held out both to electors and to professional politicians. Their conflict further represented important divisions within the Radical party. Lockroy had been willing to follow the traditional pattern of behavior for ministers to defend and identify with their service. Pelletan refused to relinquish his earlier criticisms of the navy. Lockroy and Pelletan embodied opposing responses to the responsibility of governing; Radicals as a group were called on to endorse one or the other.

Pelletan's ministry was also compared to that of Jean de Lanessan, who had been minister of the navy in Waldeck-Rousseau's government of republican defense, immediately preceding the Combes government. At the time

55. Police report, August 16, 1902, Dossier Pelletan, MI 25359, AN.

56. Lockroy Papers, Don 24601, Bibliothèque Nationale, Paris. His funeral in 1913 was attended by several admirals, including Bienaimé, former chief of the Mediterranean fleet and one of the most outspoken of Pelletan's critics.

57. Eulogy delivered by Paul Deschanel, a moderate republican, *ibid*.

58. Police report, February 27, 1904, Dossier Pelletan, MI 25359, AN.

of the Waldeck ministry, rumors were rife that Pelletan had expected this position and was bitterly disappointed at having been passed over.[59] During the formation of the Combes ministry, de Lanessan was among those ignored and therefore one of the discontented former ministers. Here, too, the important issue of position and success was intertwined with programmatic political differences.[60] De Lanessan even more than Lockroy had proved to be an eminently "ministrable" Radical. Trained as a physician, he had served in the French Health Corps while a naval officer. In 1891 he was appointed governor general of Indochina; he was recalled from the Asian colony in early 1895 amid rumors of corruption. From 1898 to 1906 he served as Radical deputy from Lyons. As minister of the navy from 1899 to 1902 not only did he respect the traditional hierarchies of the admiralty and establish good relations with the officer corps, but he succeeded in gaining parliamentary endorsement for an extended program of naval construction. Abandoning Lockroy's interest in the innovations of the Jeune Ecole, de Lanessan urged the French government to pursue the international arms race centered on battleship construction. Over the bitter denunciations of Pelletan, he succeeded in securing a naval construction budget in 1900 which mandated specific additions to the French fleet by 1906. The most expensive items were eleven new armored and unarmored battleships. De Lanessan promised to maintain France's position as the second largest European naval power.[61] After Pelletan was appointed minister of the navy, he did everything he could to impede or reverse this construction program, which continued to be legally mandated. Lockroy and de Lanessan as members of the Radical party and as part of the government majority would become instrumental participants in the opposition to Pelletan. They served as dramatic alternatives of how Radical ministers ought to behave.

Pelletan did not behave. Even worse was his *chef du cabinet*, Louis Tissier, a Radical militant in his late thirties who had taught industrial chemistry. Parliamentary supporters of the navy especially resented this supposedly ill-mannered native of Lyons. He was reported to have literally thrown one of

59. Police report, October 21, 1901, *ibid*.

60. Alexandre Millerand initiated the criticism of the Combes government by interpellating it on the failure to enact social reforms (Stone, *Search for Social Peace*, 82–83).

61. For de Lanessan's defense of his program while he was a deputy see Chambre des députés, Débats, *Journal Officiel*, November 13, 1902, p. 2587.

the admirals out of the naval ministry. Tissier was seen as the embodiment of the devastating effect the direction of lower-middle-class civilians was having on the navy. Shocking rumors circulated of "women being brought to the ministry." As late as 1909 these stories would surface once again, elaborated by a disgruntled chauffeur who provided sordid details of "picnics . . . pleasure rides . . . and soiled car seats." Deputies denounced Tissier in the Chamber and, as important, *Le Figaro* launched a campaign against him in the press.[62] Ultimately, Pelletan conceded and dismissed his aide. For the naval hierarchy and its political supporters, the very person and demeanor of Pelletan and his immediate associates must have seemed an invasion of barbarians prepared to vandalize a centuries-old and venerated military institution.

If his comportment and style infuriated the admirals, Pelletan's actual program drove them to a frenzy. This program was not a hastily improvised set of antimilitarist denunciations. Rather, it was the culmination of Pelletan's decades of experience as recognized parliamentary naval expert and as a member of the Chamber's Budget Committee, frequently reporting on naval appropriations. It is important to remember that Pelletan had been appointed to his ministerial post not only to satisfy left-wing Radicals and to "épater" the admirals but also because he had obvious qualifications. Following interpellations in the fall of 1902 and during the February, 1903, debate on the proposed naval budget, Pelletan laid out the broad outlines of his program. It contained three essential elements: the defense of the taxpayers' interests, which in his view were identical with national as opposed to particular interests; the democratization of the military services, thus genuinely integrating the navy into the French state; and finally, a much needed reassessment of France's international naval position.

Pelletan reiterated that his primary responsibility was to the electors and to parliament, which represented them, rather than to the navy. Explaining why he refused to request additional funds to complete construction of

62. Police report, May 29, 1909, Dossier Pelletan, MI 25359, AN; Police report, Situation politique, 1899–1905, November 14, 1902, F7 12553, AN; Police report, December 17, 1902, Dossier Pelletan, MI 25359, AN. Tissier continued to be active in the Radical party and in 1912 became deputy for the Vaucluse in a by-election. He occupied the seat held by the former Boulangist Georges Laguerre, who died soon after he had defeated Tissier in the 1910 elections.

three contracted battleships, he stated his fervent "budgetary patriotism": "I consider that the natural role of those in whose care is temporarily entrusted a great state service is *not* to gain as much as possible of the national resources, ignoring the total needs of the nation." He was convinced that this construction was not in the national interest but benefited only particular interests. His duty was to uphold the larger good and especially to defend the taxpayers. Pelletan explained that his naval budgets would be based on the "interests of the taxpayers and the real needs of the navy."[63]

Second, he was very clear that the public attitudes of the navy must be transformed. The navy like the army must be brought under parliamentary control, and its officers could no longer overtly express sentiments hostile to the Republic. He pursued a "political administration" that was, in his view, intended to end the separation of this armed service from the nation. From Pelletan's perspective, the naval hierarchy was entangled in a "special sphere, a state of habits, ideas, attachments, loyalties" untouched by modern developments. His reforms would "attempt to . . . restore a stronger unity between modern France and each of its armed services." The "spirit of particularism" he saw in the navy was "the worst enemy of true patriotism." Although his aim was to reduce this separation, he would not require naval officers to "conform to the convictions of the majority of France." What he would demand as minister was no "public expression . . . no open opposition to the law" by naval officers and within the "naval general staff," which was largely hostile to republican opinion, no "republican, however insignificant he may be, could be suspended or in any way persecuted because of his loyalty to the Republic." In this way Pelletan intended to maintain and in some cases restore appropriate discipline, the discipline of the parliament over its military services.[64]

Finally, a thorough reevaluation of naval strategy was required. Pelletan was seeking a major departure from the traditional assumptions governing the function of the navy. His interpretation of the Jeune Ecole innovations and his own political and cultural traditions led him to call for the abandonment of all offensive policies. He hoped to take France out of the intensifying European arms race, which demanded increased expenditures

63. Chambre des députés, Débats, *Journal Officiel*, November 13, 1902, pp. 2577, 2582, emphasis added; *ibid.*, November 24, 1902, p. 2739.

64. *Ibid.*, February 6, 1903, pp. 500–502.

and the construction of larger battleships, modeled after the British plans for naval expansion. He called on the Chamber to recognize France's actual position in Europe. It must accept the impossibility of simultaneously maintaining a fleet equal to that of the British, matching the German naval budget, and supporting a large conscript army comparable to the German one.[65] If modern rapid torpedo ships and submarines could be substituted for massive battleships, France would have a technologically advanced and highly efficient naval defense force. Pelletan was even willing to see this defensive navy extended to the colonies, whose acquisition he had always opposed but which he now viewed as "a part of the territory and honor of France." With endless patriotic references he argued that he had "dedicated all the energies that I have to find the best means to defend the honor and integrity of France." His emphasis, however, was decidedly on defense, which would permit the material and financial reduction of the navy.[66]

The Radical Congress of 1903 enthusiastically endorsed this program. Two lengthy reports on military reforms were presented to the militants assembled in Marseilles. The army report called for a "profound and rational transformation based on the actual evolution of our forces." It specifically endorsed the much debated reduction of conscription from three to two years. The naval portion of the report insisted on the creation of a defensive navy guaranteed by two principles: "the renunciation of naval conquests . . . [and] the limitation of [naval expenses] to financial resources." It also stressed that the navy, like all other republican institutions, could not be permitted to "remain foreign to democratic reason." The report further called for the abandonment of policies that dated to the time of Louis XIV and asked Radicals to recognize that France did not have the resources to maintain both a conscript army and a fleet equal to the British.[67] The Congress unanimously endorsed both military reports.

The three elements of this ambitious reformist program—reduction of expenditures, democratization, and emphasis on defensive strategy—

65. This interest in transforming naval policy was shared by Georges Clemenceau, who also was influenced by the concepts of the Jeune Ecole and who in the Senate supported Pelletan's proposed modifications. See Duroselle, *Clemenceau*, 462.

66. Chambre des députés, Débats, *Journal Officiel*, February 6, 1903, pp. 503–507.

67. Le Parti radical, Messimy report, *3ᵉ Congrès*, tenu à Marseille, March, 1903, p. 125; Aubertin report, *ibid.*, 132–33.

affected all Pelletan's actions as minister. His ultimate goal was to transform the navy into a model republican state service. Almost immediately upon assuming office, Pelletan halted construction on three battleships. In the fall of that same year the government was interpellated on the naval minister's decision. Pelletan defended his refusal to request additional funds necessary for the completion of construction: "Before my conscience as an honest man and a Frenchman I do not believe that given the general interests of France the premature construction of these ships has as much importance as many projects you would sacrifice." He claimed to be protecting the national interest against the particular interests of the navy, the banks, and the large steel industry. Everyone understood that Pelletan was using budgetary considerations to scuttle de Lanessan's program. That former naval minister, though not yet willing to criticize his Radical colleague directly, made it clear that any halt in construction would jeopardize the entire program and certainly the 1906 deadline the Chamber had voted. De Lanessan also pointed out that if there were no funds for battleships, there also could be no funds for submarines of which Pelletan was so fond.[68]

At the end of the 1902 debate the government and Pelletan received a strong vote of confidence. With 485 voting, 331 supported the government, only 154 opposed. This vote only five months after the formation of the new government demonstrated the strength of the Bloc des gauches majority. Even members of the majority who were clearly critical of Pelletan, such as Paul Doumer, Alexandre Millerand, and, surprisingly, de Lanessan himself, voted for him in this instance. The motion was a peculiar one, however, sidestepping the complex web of issues Pelletan's action presented. It neither endorsed nor rejected the de Lanessan building program. It did not address Pelletan's use of budgetary limitations to renege on previous legislation. Rather, it expressed the Chamber's confidence that the government could reconcile "national defense with the implementation of the program delineated by parliament with the financial needs and the right of budgetary control." Further examination of these questions was referred to the Budget Committee. The government and Pelletan had easily obtained the Chamber's endorsement, but it was not clear that the reform policies of the naval minister had.

68. Chambre des députés, Débats, *Journal Officiel*, November 13, 1902, pp. 2582, 2587.

On October 20, 1902, Pelletan issued a decree reducing the Mediterranean fleet by 1,750 men. The outrage of the naval establishment soon reached the Chamber when Baron Reille interpellated the government the following month. Reille expressed the views of much of the officer corps. In addition, as one of the representatives of the powerful southern Solages-Reille clan the baron was an important spokesman for conservative, large industry.[69] Like his family, business associates, and other conservative republicans, now called Progressistes, he viewed the Bloc des gauches as an extremely serious threat to traditional institutions, especially those protecting the prerogatives of industrialists. In 1902 Reille launched a powerful attack on Pelletan in which he questioned the minister's patriotism. He accused Pelletan of endangering the national defense and destroying France's naval grandeur. The rhetoric was becoming less polite. Pelletan replied in kind, claiming that the large French Mediterranean fleet had spent most of the year anchored at Toulon enjoying the amenities of the Côte d'Azur and wasting limited resources. His decree reduced costs and simply brought the southern fleet in line with the number of men in the northern fleet. Furthermore, he rejected the assumptions that justified a large Mediterranean fleet: that war was inevitable and that it would necessarily lead to a maritime confrontation between France and Great Britain. He again praised the Jeune Ecole strategies. The government and Pelletan once again won this vote of confidence but with a smaller margin. In a vote on Reille's motion to maintain the Mediterranean fleet as it had existed before 1902, of the 524 deputies voting, 231 supported the motion and 293 opposed it. In the actual confidence vote only 492 deputies voted, 288 supporting the government and 204 opposed. Some important Radicals, such as Lockroy and de Lanessan, abstained, and some were conveniently absent attending committee meetings, among them Paul Doumer.[70]

69. The family had interests in mining, metallurgy, and glass production. They were founders of the Comité des forges and members of the Comité houiller. The closely aligned Solages branch had battled the socialist leader Jaurès in nearby Carmaux for decades (Goldberg, *Life of Jaurès*, 59–60, 101–102, 228–29). The father of the current Baron Reille had sat in the Chamber from 1876 to 1898 and had ardently defended management during the highly charged Carmaux miners strike of 1892. The 1898 occupant of the seat retained it until 1914, when it passed to his nephew.

70. Chambre des députés, Débats, *Journal Officiel*, November 24, 1902, pp. 2733, 2736, 2739, 2744.

In addition to these major policies that led to lengthy parliamentary debates, Pelletan instituted a variety of administrative innovations intended to promote his goals of reduced costs, democratization, and a defensive naval posture. During his two and one-half years as minister he practically ignored the admiralty's Conseils supérieurs, advisory bodies that had been powerful in previous administrations. By shifting authority within the ministry from military bodies to his own civilian office, Pelletan considered that he was recovering power for the principle of "universal suffrage." New programs were instituted to reduce the unassailable authority and privileged position of officers. The introduction of small crews on the new submarines and torpedo boats was welcomed as leading to closer bonds between sailors and officers. In addition, sailors could now appeal their officers' decisions to the civilian minister, and the recruitment of officers from the ranks was to be encouraged. The navy's official employment of religious personnel and the use of religious ceremonies, a clear sign that it stood outside the secular Republic, were terminated. Catholic nursing orders were banished from naval hospitals, and even the traditional ritual of baptizing new ships was abandoned. All these new policies were intended to imprint the navy with a republican stamp, and all increased the outrage of the navy hierarchy and its supporters.

Among Pelletan's innovations few were more controversial than his attempts to improve conditions for the twenty to twenty-five thousand workers in the state-run naval shipyards. Many viewed his modifications of established labor relations as an attack on military hierarchy and discipline. In addition, Pelletan's reforms were seen as encouraging syndicalists, who had vowed to resist the state and its preparations for war. He insisted that as naval minister he would act on his sympathy for workers. "I have always . . . considered as one of the Republic's duties making the necessary efforts to continue the improvement of the little guys' [les petits] condition, which is one of the principal justifications of a democratic regime."[71] In the case of the navy, the "petits" were shipyard workers located in five principal ports: Brest, Cherbourg, Lorient, Rochefort, and Toulon. Although these employees were technically civilians, naval personnel had traditionally supervised the organization of their work, imposing military discipline. Shipyard workers did have the advantages of job security and a pension after

71. Chambre des députés, Débats, *Journal Officiel*, February 6, 1903, p. 499.

twenty-five years, but rigid, hierarchical control constrained their working day.[72] Ultimate responsibility for the arsenals rested with the naval prefect in each port city. Labor relations in the shipyards had become increasingly tense since the 1890s as workers organized and demanded some say over their conditions. Pelletan's response was to offer cooperation between the workers and the state. He even imagined that the state as employer might set a pattern which the state as lawmaker could later impose more widely.

Through a series of ministerial decrees in late 1902 he officially recognized the workers' union, the Fédération nationale des travailleurs de la Marine de l'Etat, improved working conditions, and relaxed military control. Pelletan hoped that the union, which had become a national organization in May, 1900, and was affiliated with the syndicalist Confédération générale du travail (CGT), would provide a vehicle to avoid labor unrest. He called for regular meetings between the local *syndicats* and the maritime prefects. Continuing an already established policy, he met with the national federation following each of its annual congresses. But Pelletan's recognition of and cooperation with the union emphatically did not include the right to strike. His most important reform of labor conditions in the naval arsenals was to decree an eight-hour day with no reduction in pay. A ministerial circular of January 6, 1903, implemented this new regime; thus state shipyard workers gained the most sought-after labor reform of the era sixteen years before it became a universal law. Paul Guieyesse, Radical deputy from Brittany and spokesman for the shipyard workers, praised Pelletan's action. He also hoped that it would satisfy the workers inasmuch as their demand for further pay increases could not be met.[73] Another circular six months later permitted naval arsenal workers the freedom to leave the work site during the workday, thus reducing the military atmosphere of the docks.[74]

---

72. Donald Reid, "The Third Republic as Manager: Labor Policy in the Naval Shipyards, 1892–1920," *International Review of Social History*, XXX (1985), 184, 186. The benefits of this system went only to full-time workers, who received security and pension. There was a slow but steady increase in the number of temporary workers who received no benefits.

73. Chambre des députés, Débats, *Journal Officiel*, February 6, 1903, p. 495.

74. Rapport, "La Propagande anti-militariste et révolutionnaire dans les Arsenaux de la Marine de 1899 à 1911," Ouvriers d'arsenaux, Police générale, 2, F7 13637, AN; Reid, "Third Republic as Manager," 193–94.

Pelletan sought to influence conditions not only for the state workers but for the even larger number of commercial sailors, fishermen, and private sector shipyard workers. Although they were civilians working for private employers, many were former naval seamen, and all were classified as part of a permanent naval reserve. The navy governed their pensions, and many of their work activities were under the jurisdiction of maritime law, which the navy administered. During the 1903 budget debate he identified the naval reservists, *inscrits maritimes*, as the most exploited because they were still governed by regulations of the Ancien Régime and the most deserving of improvement. A board of naval officers, a *commissaire maritime*, in each of the major French ports regulated the reservists' conditions. Pelletan issued yet another decree in October, 1902, replacing these military commissions with civilian administrators, *administrateurs de l'inscription maritime*. Again Pelletan had sought to expand civilian control and to dismantle what he viewed as ancient, unnecessary military regulations. Heated protests were mounted in the Chamber. Pelletan explained that he had sought to eliminate the possibility that past or future officers might determine nonmilitary issues affecting sailors. In addition, the new structure represented a financial saving for the state. Finally, he was convinced that four or five regional Chambers of Commerce, in which employers were lobbying to retain military discipline over their workers, had orchestrated this protest.[75] The vote on a motion to override the minister's decree was close. Of 523 voting, 273 supported Pelletan's change to a civilian administration of the reservists and 250 defended the older, military *commissaires maritime*.[76] Issues of military discipline and tradition undermined the Bloc des gauches majority.

Pelletan's efforts to democratize and modernize the navy revealed the dilemmas and contradictions of the Radicals' attempt to republicanize the state, especially their uncertainty as to whether workers were citizens or members of an exploited class or both. Even Pelletan's relatively limited

75. Chambre des députés, Débats, *Journal Officiel*, February 6, 1903, pp. 503, 512. Pelletan also spoke on this issue before the Chamber's Navy Committee on November 11, 1903, and February 3, 1904 (Commission de la marine, Procès verbaux, C 7258, AN).

76. Chambre des députés, Débats, *Journal Officiel*, February 6, 1903, p. 517. For more on the "statut de l'inscription" and sailors' support of it, see Pierre Barral, "Regards sur les transformations de la pêche," in *L'Ere industrielle et la société d'aujourd'hui (siècle 1880–1980)* (Paris, 1979), 392, Vol. IV of *Histoire économique et sociale de la France*, ed. Braudel and Labrousse, 4 vols.

efforts to reduce hierarchical discipline in the military service and to increase civilian control created a furor. The full extent and consequence of this protest will be analyzed in subsequent chapters; for now I will only identify those who opposed and those who supported Pelletan. The naval minister's policies alienated an influential group of moderates within the Radical party and members of the Bloc des gauches majority, who were to become his most powerful opponents. Affiliated with them were moderate republicans, some inside and some outside the government majority, who represented colonial and naval interests. They also often spoke as supporters of the Franco-Russian alliance.[77] In the Chamber of Deputies Baron Reille quoted Russian newspapers to demonstrate the extent to which Pelletan's ministry endangered French national interests.[78] Admirals, officers, and members of the permanent staff at the naval ministry were outraged by Pelletan's actions.[79] Reportedly, some officers obliged by convention to shake the minister's hand "threw their tainted gloves into the ocean." Pelletan had also angered certain industrialists.[80] Police reports cited rumors of a campaign against Pelletan organized and financed by companies that were in danger of losing their naval contracts because of his proposed technical changes. Those shipyards whose state contracts for battleship construction were no longer being honored brought civil suit against the navy.[81] All these opposition groups shared an aversion to his labor policies for the naval arsenals and for sailors attached to the naval reserve. They were especially incensed that state workers, whom they viewed as privileged and protected civil servants, should be permitted to organize and assume an adversarial relation with their employer, the state. Such concessions had

77. Little effort was made to mask the Russian foreign office's distrust of Pelletan and its press campaign to discredit him. See Police report on foreign press, March 22, 1904, Dossier Pelletan, MI 25359, AN.

78. Chambre des députés, Débats, *Journal Officiel*, November 24, 1903, p. 2734.

79. Ouvriers d'arsenaux, 1911 Report, 2–3, F7 13637, AN.

80. Ronald Chalmers Hood III, *Royal Republicans: The French Naval Dynasties* (Baton Rouge, 1985), 12. Industrialists located in the Atlantic seaboard department of the Gironde were particularly incensed. See Situation politique, 1899–1905, Police report, March 1, 1904, F7 12553, AN.

81. Companies producing "boilers with small machine pipes" felt especially endangered. See Police reports, March 14, 1904, November 15, 1902, Dossier Pelletan, MI 25359, AN.

fostered a dangerous atmosphere in the naval shipyards, one "of anarchy and lacking all discipline," which could be contagious.[82]

Not surprisingly, the arsenal workers and their unions were among Pelletan's warmest supporters. The minister actively cultivated this support, visiting work sites and holding public meetings with union leaders. A 1911 report prepared for the "Direction de la Sureté générale commissaire" on "La Propagande anti-militariste et révolutionnaire dans les Arsenaux de la Marine" identified the period of Pelletan's ministry as having been an important stimulus to union growth and militancy. In December, 1902, he first visited Cherbourg, one of the smaller shipyards, where the union was relatively weak. He appeared again in August, 1903, for the launching of the *Jules Ferry*. On both occasions he made a point of attending banquets hosted by the union. Such official recognition increased the union's stature. Also in the spring of 1903 he visited the largest shipyard at Toulon, and the workers gave him a triumphal welcome. When he made a second visit in August, 1904, the well-organized union offered the minister an "impressive demonstration" of five thousand workers, the playing of the "International," and a grand banquet. Pelletan's speech was loudly and warmly acclaimed as one worthy of a "reformist minister."[83] He also visited the large shipyard at Brest, where once again the "International" greeted him and red flags waved.[84] The institution of the eight-hour day brought Pelletan enormous praise from the union.[85] In the summer of 1904 in a state foundry located at Indret on the Atlantic coast, workers applauded Pelletan as a politician who kept his promises even while a minister. This meeting ended with cheers of "Long live the union, long live Pelletan and long live the social republic."[86] Although enthusiasm generally characterized the state arsenal workers' attitude toward Pelletan, it was not universal. These

82.   Ouvriers d'arsenaux, Report, 1911, 2–3, F7 13637, AN.

83.   *Ibid.*, 2–3, 5; Police report, August 29, 1904, Dossier Pelletan, MI 25359, AN; *L'Emancipateur*, September 15, 1904.

84.   Police report, Ouvriers d'arsenaux, Fédération nationale des travailleurs de la Marine de l'Etat, Congrès, July 7, 1904, F7 13638, AN.

85.   Police report, Ouvriers d'arsenaux, Fédération nationale des travailleurs de la Marine de l'Etat, 8, F7 13637, AN.

86.   Police report, Ouvriers d'arsenaux, Ouvriers de la Marine, Congrès, Indret, July 7, 1904, F7 13638, AN.

workers, like those in all sectors of the economy, had neither uniform circumstances nor uniform responses to their conditions. Tensions had always existed within the shipyard workers' union between moderates attracted to the political strategies of the various socialist parties and more militant syndicalists promoting direct action and affiliation with the Confédération générale du travail.[87]

Donald Reid, in an important article on Third Republic labor policies in the naval shipyards, has placed Pelletan's ministry in the larger context of restructuring labor relations in both the public and private sectors during the twentieth century. He has identified broad developments that have transformed labor relations from being dependent on "military styles of management" to those that "recognized the workers as citizens of the Republic." Ultimately this transformation was accomplished through an "institutional framework for incorporating labor into the industrial enterprise without fundamentally challenging managerial authority."[88] This trend certainly characterizes the *longue durée* of twentieth-century labor relations; however, when examining Pelletan's efforts in greater detail and the specific reactions they elicited we can see that this transformation was far from smooth. On one hand, in the first decade of the twentieth century a significant minority of workers refused to compromise with managerial authority or to accept integration. On the other hand, the naval establishment, with the support of a broad coalition of centrist and moderate politicians, insisted that any reduction of the state's managerial authority was a threat to the fundamental authority of the state itself. This dual intransigence reminds us that Pelletan's policies were intended to go beyond the introduction of more efficient labor relations and higher productivity in the naval shipyards. They were part of a larger vision of a republican state in which workers, as citizens, would operate and flourish within networks of patriotic duties and guarantees of democratic rights.

The immediate interests of the shipyard workers were usually more concrete; they concerned pay and the structure of managerial authority. After 1900 shipyard workers were a highly organized, vociferous, and contentious

87. For shifting syndicalist commitments and strategies, see Gérard Baal, "Victor Pengam et l'évolution du syndicalisme révolutionnaire à Brest, 1904–1914," *Mouvement social*, LXXXII (January–March, 1973), 55–82.

88. Reid, "Third Republic as Manager," 206.

group. They had special political leverage because the deputies from the five ports where naval arsenals were located had formed a parliamentary group actively pursuing their interests led by Radical reformer Paul Guieyesse from Lorient in Brittany. Since the Waldeck-Rousseau government, delegates from the shipyard workers' union had met with the minister of the navy and—as significant—with members of the Chamber's Budget Committee. Although workers enthusiastically endorsed Pelletan's appointment as minister of the navy and his policies concerning the shipyards, militant union activity did not diminish; on the contrary, it intensified. In Toulon, the largest and best-organized shipyard, brief strikes over pay issues and the implementation of the eight-hour day, as well as demonstrations in support of workers fired for political activity, occurred in 1903 and 1904. Authoritarian foremen and the maritime prefect himself, Admiral Bienaimé, were ridiculed and caricatured in charivaris and posters.[89] Fellow workers at other shipyards demonstrated their solidarity with a call for one-day strikes. The height of this worker militancy in public sector naval construction coincided with the most concerted and ultimately successful attacks of moderates and the Right against the Combes government.

Some workers may have viewed themselves as enforcing the implementation of Pelletan's directives. A minority of unionists, however, began to express a lack of confidence in the minister. Union representatives from the Rochefort shipyard who had attended the annual congress and met with the minister reported back to a large meeting of fifteen hundred local unionists in the summer of 1904. They were clearly dissatisfied with Pelletan's failure to secure a promised pay increase and his explanation that budget deficits made the raise impossible. These militant syndicalists complained of the manner in which Tissier and Pelletan himself had received them. After ironic references to "Comrade Camille" and the denunciation of all politicians as a "bunch of phonies," the meeting endorsed a future general strike.[90] Throughout the fall and winter of 1904 discontent and short walkouts among shipyard workers increased when Pelletan failed to secure the promised pay increase. Demonstrations of four to five thousand workers,

89. Ouvriers d'arsenaux, Report, 1911, 4–5, F7 13637, AN; Police report, Ouvriers d'arsenaux, Fédération nationale des travailleurs de la Marine de l'Etat, 8, F7 13637, AN.

90. Police report, Ouvriers d'arsenaux, Ouvriers de la Marine, Congrès, Rochefort, July 7, 1904, F7 13638, AN.

reportedly led by anarchists, took place in Brest in September specifically directed against the maritime prefect, Admiral Mallarmé. Similar incidents occurred in Rochefort. In early December, Pelletan suspended relations between the navy and the Rochefort union. The Lorient workers went out on a brief solidarity strike on November 24.[91]

The Combes government was then in a precarious situation; four weeks later it would fall. In late November, Pelletan issued a circular stating that "any workers' strike in the arsenals is a crime and threatens the most sacred interests of the country."[92] A year later, when no longer minister, Pelletan would continue to defend his opposition to strikes of state workers. At a banquet in Nancy, which included republicans, Radicals, and socialists, Pelletan explained that he "had granted the workers all that they asked, but he had always denied them the right to strike in order [that we do] not become weaker than the always menacing Germany." To defend national interests was to defend the principles of the Revolution.[93] The popular, democratic minister had clearly marked the limits of what he considered legitimate working-class demands. National interests, which Pelletan defined, had to supersede those of the arsenal workers.

Pelletan's motives, loyalties, and actions in the case of the arsenal workers would be easy to analyze if they could be portrayed simply as the expression of mounting exasperation at syndicalist resistance and the adoption of a more intransigent defense of state authority, legitimated with the rhetoric of national interest. But a similar repudiation of all working-class militancy did not accompany his rejection of strikes by state workers. His obvious concern for stability at the arsenals remained tied to his notion of state authority as the embodiment of the Republic. The protection of social hierarchy and traditional social relations was not his principal concern. Only two months before his decree declaring the strikes of state arsenal workers illegal, he wrote to Combes concerning a strike of shipyard workers in the private sector who were also naval reservists. In this instance, Pelletan

---

91. *L'Emancipateur*, December 1–15, 1904.

92. Police report, Ouvriers d'arsenaux, Fédération nationale des travailleurs de la Marine de l'Etat, 11, F7 13637, AN.

93. Police report, Nancy, November 27, 1905, Dossier Pelletan, MI 25359, AN. This same position was reaffirmed by Le Parti radical du sud-est, *1er Congrès*, 143.

was highly critical of the shipyard owners, whom he believed were sabotaging efforts to settle the strike and whose aim was "the pure and simple abolition of the reservists' legally guaranteed rights." In effect, he accused the employers of attempting to abrogate the workers' right to unionize, a right the Republic confirmed and protected. Such actions were, in Pelletan's view, "monstrous and inadmissible for any *republican government; those who acted thus ought not to be* employers associated with the state and receiving state contracts."[94] The defense of the right to organize was strong and clear, and within this context Pelletan seemed to accept the legitimacy of these workers' strike. A second letter of October 3, 1904, criticized the employers' efforts to bring the issue of the sailors' right to strike before the Conseil d'Etat. He viewed that judicial body as biased, with "a scandalous partiality," against workers and the right to strike.[95]

In the cases of the arsenal workers and the Marseilles sailors, Pelletan applied what he understood to be the same criterion to judge their actions: their relation to the republican state. The strike of the state-employed shipyard workers threatened national defense. That of the privately employed naval reservists was in defense of the right to unionize guaranteed to them by law. The employers' resistance flaunted an important right which had the force of the Republic behind it. Pelletan consistently employed the standard of republican defense to workers' actions. It was impossible for him to concede that syndicalists, socialists, and rank-and-file unionists might have different criteria of workers' interests. These working-class representatives questioned the Republic's vaunted commitment to egalitarianism when only workers were expected to subordinate class interests to larger national concerns. Pelletan as government minister was in difficult straits here because he too had expressed doubts about the authentic republicanism of the state.

In this most explosive area of the state's relations with its employees, and particularly those in the defense sector, Pelletan's policies at least in the short term can be counted as a failure. Whatever his sympathies toward the

94. Camille Pelletan to Emile Combes, n.d., Emile Combes Archives Personelles, Archives Départmentales de le Charente-Maritime, emphasis added. Gérard Baal kindly brought the Pelletan-Combes letters to my attention.

95. Pelletan to Combes, n.d., *ibid.*

shipyard workers, certainly one of his aims had been to establish better labor relations to benefit the state and ultimately enhance naval construction. In this he failed. In contradiction to the conclusions of most of Pelletan's contemporaries, however, there is no evidence to assume that Pelletan's policies caused or intensified workers' militancy. Union organizing and affiliation with the CGT had preceded his tenure as minister. His successors who pursued different policies were no more successful than he had been. Demonstrations and strikes continued up to the eve of World War I. In 1911 the naval shipyard workers were among the most strongly unionized of French workers, and ardent syndicalists continued to influence the union.[96] Taking a longer view, Donald Reid has argued that Pelletan's policies of labor conciliation complemented subsequent state initiatives, all of which led to an eventual restructuring of labor relations not only in the state shipyards but ultimately throughout French industry. Clearly, some of the consequences of this restructuring were already in effect by the summer of 1914, when syndicalist commitment to an antiwar general strike evaporated once war was declared. From this longer perspective, one could argue that Pelletan's efforts to transform labor relations had contributed to this outcome.

Pelletan's relations with the state shipyard workers were extraordinarily complex. His support for working-class demands was congruent with the declared goals and composition of the Bloc des gauches parliamentary majority. That support sustained the image of defending "les petits" which Pelletan's left-wing radicalism had always promoted. But it presented the Radicals with the acute dilemma of the potential conflict between the identities of citizen and member of a social class. This dilemma was further accentuated when Radicals occupied positions of state authority responsible for a military service that also functioned as an employer. Within this complex situation of several opposing forces—employer and worker, state and citizen, military hierarchy and subordinate, state as employer and civil servant—Pelletan attempted to develop a republican resolution that would enhance the legitimacy of the state, the loyalty of citizens, and the

96. In the Toulon yard over half the workers were members of the union, a figure unheard-of in most of French industry. In Brest, where unionization was lower—23 percent or fifteen hundred were union members—no less than sixty-four union members were placed on the government's list of most dangerous antimilitarist revolutionaries, le Carnet B, to be immediately arrested at time of war (Ouvriers d'arsenaux, Report, 1911, 3, F7 13637, AN).

conditions of public sector employees. During his much applauded banquet speech for the Toulon union in August, 1904, he explained: "Our relations are not those of an ordinary employer and his workers. The boss must have his profit, his dividend, just as the workers must defend their piece of bread. As for me, what I would ask of you, if I have to demand more from you than you already give, would not be a dividend; it would be the very survival of our national defense whose servant I am as you are." The essential mechanism of establishing this unity between the state-employer and the citizen-worker was a shared commitment to the nation and a shared belief that the state legitimately represented all interests. He called on the arsenal workers to accept a discipline superior to that of the military or industry, to accept the discipline of "duty to the French fatherland."[97] Pelletan certainly failed to convince all arsenal workers of these assumptions, and one doubts if he entirely believed them himself. The contradictions between egalitarianism and authority which surrounded relations between the republican state and its employees would persist and become particularly intransigent soon after the fall of the Combes government.

How to respond to state shipyard workers' dissatisfaction was only one of many dilemmas that emerged during Pelletan's tenure in the Ministry of the Navy and dramatized the still unresolved questions surrounding Radicals and the republican state. Would Radicals be able and willing to exert the authority of the state over resistant workers who sometimes defended themselves by claiming their rights as citizens? Could Radicals exercise the double prerogatives of employer and the state? Could Radicals discipline state employees who constituted a significant segment of their electorate and who were often recipients of Radical politicians' patronage? Could national defense be entrusted to Radicals who claimed to adhere to republican egalitarian principles? In sum, could Radicals govern as governing had traditionally been understood? And if they could not or would not govern through the established hierarchical, authoritarian system, were they capable of developing and introducing alternative democratic methods? Increasingly committed Radicals, such as Pelletan, found it more and more difficult to maneuver within the confines of these fundamental contradictions.

97. *L'Emancipateur*, September 1–15, 1904.

Throughout the spring of 1904 both critics and supporters of the Radicals viewed Pelletan and his ministry as being at the very center of this dispute on the Radicals' ability to govern. As the number of his opponents grew, police reports were ever more certain that an impending vote of confidence on the naval minister's policies would lead to the collapse of the Combes government.[98] Nonetheless, the much announced interpellation of Pelletan did not occur; the government majority held, largely because socialist support did not waver. The Chamber passed Pelletan's naval budget in the spring of 1904, but the essential contradictions of Radicals in control of the state were not resolved; in less than a year the Bloc government fell. Although the issue that eventually ended the Combes ministry was not related directly to Pelletan, the persistent campaigns against him prepared the way for the eventual unraveling of the Bloc des gauches and the declining influence of left-wing radicalism.

98. Police reports, March 1–25, 1904, Dossier Pelletan, MI 25359, AN.

The Combes government brought the left Radicals as close to exercising state power as they ever would in the prewar period. And even during that episode they represented neither the entire government nor even the views of all the Radicals in that government. The strength of the left Radicals, and particularly that of Pelletan as minister, lay in popular electoral support outside the Chamber, in the leftward tilt of the parliamentary majority (as much influenced by the socialists as by the Radicals), and in the enthusiasm within the Radical party for its left wing. The Combes ministry and its fall stimulated a period of internal debate and self-examination among Radicals that would ultimately marginalize the tradition Pelletan represented. That conclusion, however, was by no means obvious to any of the participants at the time. This chapter and the next will examine the criticisms launched against the left Radicals and their responses. First, we look at the emerging division among Radicals and how moderates within the party hoped to wrest the control and identity of radicalism from the left wing. Three areas of conflict among Radicals will be examined: attitudes toward state power voiced by Pelletan's critics; conflicting perceptions of the Radicals' important constituency, the petite bourgeoisie; and differing attitudes among the Radicals toward women's suffrage. The following chapter will turn to the external critics of the Radicals, the Socialists and the nationalist Right.

Pelletan's ambitious program to upgrade and democratize the French fleet coalesced a powerful array of opponents. His efforts to implement policies that would make the nation's military services compatible with the republican state and its democratic values raised serious objections to the egalitarian program of advanced radicalism. The attacks on Pelletan as minister of the navy revealed deep concerns throughout the political elite about the reliability of left-wing Radicals in positions of state power. Growing divisions emerged within the Radical party about Pelletan's ministry, the advisability of the Bloc des gauches reformist coalition, and more generally about the consequences of the democratic policies applauded at party congresses. Initially, a group of dissident Radicals led the most powerful opposition to Pelletan's naval program. Their opposition then broadened into a debate within the Radical party about who ought to be its appropriate constituents and what should be its program. Ultimately this opposition and the inadequate response of the Radical Left contributed significantly to the decline of left-wing radicalism.

Moderates within the Radical party focused their complaints on Pelletan's inability to wield governing authority. They decried his inefficiencies as an administrator and his pursuit of policies which they believed weakened national defense. These politicians had considerable power within parliamentary commissions and influence within the government majority.[1] They intended to protect their associates in the naval hierarchy and industry from the minister's reforms. They also feared for themselves and the Radical party, which they regarded as more vulnerable to the criticisms of the nationalist Right since the formation of the Bloc des gauches government. More generally, they experienced a deep uneasiness about the security of the Republic and the nation should Pelletan's radicalism succeed.

Paul Doumer, Jean de Lanessan, and Edouard Lockroy led this group who opposed both Pelletan and the left-wing majority of the Bloc des gauches. In the early 1890s Paul Doumer (1857–1932), also a Radical expert on finance, had collaborated closely with Pelletan. He then served as minister of finance in Léon Bourgeois' brief Radical ministry of 1895–1896. It was Doumer who had presented the controversial government bill for a progressive income tax. Only months later, in a surprising shift of political associations, he accepted Méline's appointment as the governor general of Indochina. There he quickly became an ardent advocate of colonialism. Beginning in 1900, Doumer held the position of vice-president of the Union des industries minières et métallurgiques, the political lobbying organization for the major steel and iron manufacturers. A longtime deputy from the northern department of Aisne, he replaced Pelletan in 1902 as the president of the powerful parliamentary Budget Committee. From that position Doumer reviewed Pelletan's naval budgets of 1903 and 1904 with increasing alarm.[2]

1. Rebérioux, *La République radicale?*, 106–107.
2. Doumer set out to "modernize" the colony through a program of railroad construction,

Jean de Lanessan (1843–1919) had preceded Doumer as the first gover-nor general of Indochina in 1891. Already in the 1880s he had broken with more doctrinaire Radicals like Pelletan and had supported French imperial expansion in Asia. During his tenure in the Ministry of the Navy (1899–1902) de Lanessan developed the building program which Pelletan fought so hard to dismantle. The personal and political rivalry between these two Radicals had reached such intensity that, according to police reports, Pel-letan encouraged candidates to stand against de Lanessan in Lyons in the 1902 elections. De Lanessan was also active in academic and journalistic circles. Trained as a biologist, he held a professorship at the Sorbonne in natural history. He energetically supported and popularized Lamarckian evolutionary theories.[3] In 1902 he purchased the established republican daily, *Le Siècle*, which he intended to use to influence the direction of the Radical party.

Edouard Lockroy (1840–1913), another former naval minister, joined this opposition despite his own sympathy with some of the strategic changes Pelletan contemplated. Rivalry for government appointments seems to have been at least one motive in Lockroy's early and bitter criticism of Pelletan. Just two weeks after the formation of the Combes ministry, police reports identified Lockroy as the leader of those Radicals opposing Pelletan. Like his colleagues, Lockroy was convinced of France's imperial mission. At his funeral in 1913 he would be eulogized as having strengthened the union between the navy and France's "hegemony in the Mediterranean and North Africa."[4]

---

new and more efficient tax collection, and greater centralization of the French administration. The principal costs were born by the Vietnamese people, and anti-French sentiment grew apace (J. K. Munholland, "Doumer," in *Historical Dictionary of the Third French Republic*, ed. Hutton, 294). Rumors had it that Doumer organized opposition to Pelletan within this critical Budget Committee (Police report, December 28, 1902, Dossier Pelletan, MI 25359, AN).

3. Police report, October 21, 1901, Dossier Pelletan, MI 25359, AN; Stuart M. Persell, "Jean de Lanessan and the French Positivist School of Criminal Reform, 1880–1914," *Criminal Justice Review*, XII (Fall, 1987), 1–6.

4. Police report, June 19, 1902, Dossier Pelletan, MI 25359, AN. According to police reports this rivalry dated back at least to early 1900; see Police reports, March, 1900, Dossier Pelletan, MI 25359, AN. For the eulogy see Discours aux obsèques de Edouard Lockroy, Lockroy Papers, Don 24601, Bibliothèque Nationale. For more on de Lanessan and Lockroy, see Chapter VII.

The various associations of Doumer, de Lanessan, and Lockroy with the previous government put them in contact with its disgruntled leader, Waldeck-Rousseau, who was often rumored to be the ultimate source of republican antipathy to Pelletan. That Waldeck, longtime architect of a conservative, solidly haute bourgeois republicanism, should detest everything about Pelletan was hardly surprising. Pelletan had not been a warm supporter of Waldeck's ministry of republican defense, and one of the earliest reports of discord in which Pelletan faced de Lanessan and Lockroy occurred in March, 1900, during the Waldeck government. The recorded cause of friction among these Radicals seems almost farcical. De Lanessan, then minister of the navy, reportedly refused one of Pelletan's protégés a position as inspector of fishing grounds. This apparently minor cause of political discord should not be dismissed too lightly, keeping in mind the important interconnections of patronage, politics, and personal standing.[5]

Eventually, Doumer, de Lanessan, and Lockroy agreed with the most moderate members of the Bloc des gauches that the Combes government had gone too far, especially its most intransigent and popular member, Camille Pelletan.[6] Their close connections to the navy, including personal ties to individual admirals, and their commitment to an imperial France linked the three Radical dissidents. The naval prefect of Toulon and head of the Mediterranean fleet, Admiral Bienaimé, complained directly to Lockroy of "chaos" in the service under Pelletan.[7] They believed that Pelletan's ministry posed serious dangers to close associates, national interests, and the ability of the republican state to govern. Most immediately, Pelletan's efforts to block or reduce the naval building program of 1900 placed signed contracts in jeopardy. Even the submarine construction, which Pelletan promoted, upset established relations between the ministry and major suppliers because it shifted production to more recent models. His critics accused him of endangering the essential "moral" principles of contractual

5. Police reports, December 16, 1902, May 29, 1903, June 5, 1903, Dossier Pelletan, MI 25359, AN; Police report, Situation politique, 1899–1905, March 6, 1900, F7 12553, AN.

6. Other important members of this growing dissident circle were Jean Chaumet, Eugène Etienne, and Emile Chautemps. See also Police report, February 29, 1904, Dossier Pelletan, MI 25359, AN; Police report, Situation politique, 1899–1905, February 26, 1904, F7 12553, AN; Rebérioux, La République radicale?, 64; Mayeur, Vie politique, 189.

7. Police report, August 20, 1903, Dossier Pelletan, MI 25359, AN.

obligations.[8] Still more disturbing to parliamentary friends of the navy, Pelletan circumvented the power of the admiralty to control or even influence decisions in naval construction and strategy. Pelletan openly expressed his deep suspicions of the naval hierarchy, which he believed was staffed with clerical and royalist enemies of the Republic and therefore of the nation. His program clearly threatened the interests of at least some established naval contractors and the entire admiralty.

For committed colonialists such as Doumer, de Lanessan, and Lockroy there was no question that Pelletan also endangered the existence of France's colonies, particularly in southeast Asia. The politically powerful Eugène Etienne, a moderate republican, who headed the colonial lobby and presided over the Chamber's Committee on Foreign Relations, Protectorates, and Colonies, shared the fears of the dissidents. Pelletan, unlike the Radicals who now criticized him, had never renounced his anticolonialism of the 1870s and 1880s. In addition, his support for the Jeune Ecole naval strategy, with its emphasis on the mobile defense of the French coasts, relegated the protection of distant Asian territories to a low priority.[9] The deterioration of international relations further exacerbated the colonialists' fears. The most concerted parliamentary attack against Pelletan, in the spring of 1904, took place immediately following the outbreak of the Russo-Japanese War, which reordered power relations in the Far East and dramatically revealed the naval weakness of France's major ally. In early February, 1904, moderate republicans met with the president of the Republic to point out the danger "which Pelletan's presence posed in case of an international conflagration."[10] Still another disturbing international development was the escalating British and German arms race in heavy battleships at the very time that Pelletan was attempting to limit French large ship construction.

Of all his critics' concerns, no issue was more important than that of the maintenance of authority and discipline within the navy. During parliamentary debate on the naval budget in 1903, a Radical, Emile Chautemps, sounded the alarm. He accused the minister of "disorganizing one of our

8. Both Charles Chaumet and Jules Siegfried raised this issue (Chambre des députés, Débats, *Journal Officiel*, November 13, 1902, pp. 2576, 2586).

9. Baquiast, "La Jeune Ecole de la marine française."

10. Police report, February 11, 1904, Dossier Pelletan, MI 25359, AN.

most important naval services." Reaching a rhetorical climax, Chautemps asserted that "Pelletan is destroying the impressive and admirable work of Colbert." Police reports of late 1903 and early 1904 again and again identified "disorganization and negligence" within the naval administration as the principal cause for antigovernment sentiment among members and former members of the republican majority.[11] "Disorganization and anarchy" became the refrain in all the criticism directed against Pelletan's ministry. In the winter of 1903–1904 not a few Radicals were coming to regard the traditional Radical critique, which had regarded the military hierarchy as undemocratic, as decidedly old-fashioned and inappropriate. From their perspective, Radicals, as a governing party, could ill afford to question the loyalty of the French officer corps, especially in a world of rapidly escalating tension and, as important, in a society of intensifying class conflict. A Radical minister who called for a more democratic navy was viewed as a dangerous liability to the party, the state, and the nation.

The daily large circulation press, such as *Figaro*, and more restrained, serious journals cultivated this negative view. In the summer of 1903 the prestigious *Revue politique et parlementaire* published a long article titled "Quatre Ans de Marine." Pelletan's ministry of thirteen months was sharply condemned in this conservative republican journal: "A dangerously peaceable spirit has reigned in the councils . . . [and] the confusion was complete." Most damaging, the morale, "the duty and the discipline" of the navy were being undermined by "introducing politics into the arsenals . . . permitting intrigues . . . [and] rewarding . . . the appearance of loyalty to government institutions . . . or rather to the minister." In less than a year a special commission on the navy, dominated by dissident Radicals, would confirm these allegations. Both in the moderate press and among some Radical parliamentary insiders the refrain was the same: Pelletan was carrying out a "war without mercy against the spirit of discipline and duty."[12]

The major Radical-led parliamentary attack on Camille Pelletan came during the early spring of 1904 and was sharpest in the less public committee rooms of the Chamber. The press, seconded by important naval committee members Lockroy and de Lanessan, had been demanding an

11. Chambre des députés, Débats, *Journal Officiel*, February 6, 1903, pp. 512–13; Police reports, December 17, 1902, January 5, 13, August 20, 1903, Dossier Pelletan, MI 25359, AN.

12. "Quatre Ans de la Marine," *La Revue politique et parlementaire* (July 1903), 5–20.

investigation of the naval minister's policies. President of the Naval Committee Gaston Gerville-Réache, a Radical supporter of the Bloc des gauches and sympathetic to Pelletan, finally agreed to hold hearings in February, 1904. Issues pertaining to the defense of the Indochina colony, the 1900 building program, conditions in the arsenals, and the state of reserve forces were pursued. Although Lockroy in particular expressed his criticisms, the final report of the Naval Committee issued in April supported Pelletan. The committee president reported to the Chamber that "considering the documents and the statistics furnished by the Minister, the [committee] generally had a favorable impression." Gerville-Réache also implied that Pelletan was the victim of a well-orchestrated rumor campaign in the press and the corridors of the Chamber. Although the criticisms of dissident Radicals had been heard, the Bloc des gauches majority, at least within the Naval Committee, remained loyal to the government's minister. Gerville-Réache was explicit in his positive view of Pelletan's leadership. During the February hearings he stated, "Our navy is today what it was yesterday," and again in his April report he reiterated, "[The] navy . . . is not in the deplorable condition that has been stated."[13] Nonetheless, responding to the crisis of the Russo-Japanese War, Gerville-Réache and other members of the Bloc agreed that continued investigations might be required. They raised no explicit objection to the special inquiry that had been carried on almost simultaneously in the Budget Committee.

The Combes government could not resist the pressure to form a special commission on the navy. It also conceded that Pelletan's most vociferous opponents, de Lanessan and Lockroy, would serve on the commission, which the Budget Committee's president, Paul Doumer, would chair.[14] This parliamentary inquiry developed serious and damaging condemnations of Pelletan's ministry and his conception of republican national interest. The most important testimony was taken in March, 1904, in a tone of great gravity. The committee members' concerns were the essentials of military power such as cruisers, port construction, coal, naval reserves, boilers, and colonies. Referring to testimony from French colonists and admirals, Lockroy accused Pelletan of not spending enough on ships and development (a

13.   Commission de la marine, Procès verbaux, February 24, April 16, 1904, C 7258, AN.
14.   Police report, April 7, 1904, Dossier Pelletan, MI 25359, AN.

complaint rarely heard during the parsimonious Third Republic). In addition, evidence was presented of insufficient troops and insufficient coal to support a French naval presence internationally and particularly in the South China Sea. The expertise and experience of the admiralty were being ignored. In one stormy session, when Pelletan attempted to defend his policies on naval reserves, Lockroy sternly rebuked him, reminding him that he was faced with deputies experienced in naval matters. "Truly one hears things here that are extraordinary. . . . Whom do you take us for? Do you think that we don't understand what reserves are? What you have done has never been done. The entire navy protests and I protest as well. . . . And please don't tell us any stories."[15] This was far from the usual tone in which deputies addressed ministers in committee hearings and certainly surprising for men of the same party.

The most persistent issues during the hearings concerned general naval morale, discontent within the admiralty, labor conditions at the arsenals, and the organization of the ministerial staff. Throughout his interrogation, Pelletan maintained that though differences of policy might exist (submarines rather than cruisers), his procedures differed little from those of his predecessors and he was as committed as they had been to build a strong navy and national defense. He implied that technical questions of construction and deployment were mere smoke screens for the real issue, which was his efforts to introduce greater democracy. Responding to what he correctly perceived as the essential question, Pelletan declared: "I have upset certain officers of the old school, but I have not encouraged insubordination. On the contrary, I have done everything to maintain the most strict discipline by giving the humble the right to air their grievances."[16] *République et patrie* were indissolubly linked for Pelletan. A navy more responsive to the needs of rank-and-file sailors and arsenal workers would be a more effective military force. Only a genuinely republican navy could defend the republican state and nation.

The moment had not yet arrived for Pelletan to make peace with the military hierarchy. His suspicions of their loyalty had only been reinforced since becoming minister. He was not the one undermining principles of

15. Commission du Budget, Enquête sur la Marine, March 16–18, 1904, pp. 3, 18, 17, 66, 149, C 7283, AN.

16. *Ibid.*, March 15, 1904, p. 154.

discipline and devotion to the nation; it was his opponents who were threatening a vital institution of the Republic and undermining the authority of one of the highest representatives of the state. Pelletan described the conditions under which he worked:

> You see my situation. There has been a permanent inquest . . . into the activities of a man who right or wrong is nevertheless at the head of one of the most important armed services of the nation. . . . It has been conducted, let me not say by outright treason or revolt, but rather by the removal of documents, indiscretions, the leaking of all sorts of information, by a campaign of semi-insurrection which has unfortunately found men to foment, encourage and exploit it. . . . Letters of military chiefs, perhaps disappointed in their ambitions, and the correspondence of officers and subordinates, who perhaps expressed their anger in confidence, have been revealed. This is certainly a novel way to develop the habits of good order and discipline.

Pelletan insisted that he must protect ministerial authority and prerogatives. He refused to turn over documents that dealt with the internal administration of the naval ministry, claiming that to relinquish them would place him under the surveillance of his subordinates and compromise the authority of his position.[17] That same authority of the state legitimated his efforts to integrate the navy into the Republic, thus ensuring national strength.

The most vocal members of the commission adamantly rejected Pelletan's defense. In a concluding statement, Edouard Lockroy claimed that the minister's refusal to turn over all documents irrefutably demonstrated the "disorder and anarchy of his ministry." In Lockroy's opinion, Pelletan's testimony proved without doubt "the material and moral disorder of his administration, especially the lack of preparation for war, the failure to meet with the experts [i.e., the Conseils supérieurs]. . . . France now finds herself in a most difficult situation. We don't know what the European repercussions may be as a result of the events in the Far East; we don't know when we might find ourselves involved. We have a great colony there which

17. *Ibid.*, 65–68.

must be protected from the attacks of the enemy. . . . It is more vital than ever to prepare a battle plan, to place ourselves in a state of defense. . . . I don't want to say anything unfavorable about the honorable man who has appeared before us, but we do not have a chief of staff here whose authority and influence . . . could lead either colleagues or those above him."[18]

This damning evaluation of Pelletan's ministerial ability by a former minister of the navy and fellow Radical crippled his standing with the Chamber and his ability to carry out his government responsibilities. Jean de Lanessan, Paul Doumer, Eugène Etienne, and an expanding group of dissident Radicals and disaffected moderates all shared Lockroy's conclusions. Nonetheless, this powerful republican coalition failed to oust either Pelletan or the Combes government. The government survived the Chamber debate on the naval budget of March 29–30, 1904. An interpellation on the "administration of the navy" proposed by the moderate republican Jean Chaumet was defeated, 331 votes against and 231 for.[19] Strong support for the government and particularly for Pelletan outside the Chamber may have contributed to Lockroy's decision not to criticize the naval minister in a general session. The police reports, which in mid-March had predicted the imminent collapse of the government on the Pelletan issue, concluded by the end of the month that the Combes ministry and Pelletan had weathered a difficult period and the political waters were now calm.[20]

Still, serious damage had been inflicted on Pelletan's reputation, Combes's ministry, and the parliamentary majority. The government's success in March, 1904, was only temporary. By January, 1905, Combes resigned and the Bloc des gauches majority was in serious disarray. The immediate cause of the government's demise resulted once again from a bitter controversy concerning the disruption of traditional avenues of military

18. *Ibid.*, March 24, 1904, p. 5. Pelletan received a better hearing in the Senate inquiry of early 1905. The Combes government had already fallen, and Clemenceau headed the committee. Clemenceau often expressed his interest and support in the naval strategy of the Jeune Ecole, which Pelletan defended. Ironically, this sympathy for Pelletan and the Jeune Ecole was the immediate reason for the fall of the Clemenceau government in 1909, a government Pelletan bitterly opposed. See Watson, *Clemenceau,* 212–13; Duroselle, 542–43.

19. Chambre des députés, Débats, *Journal Officiel,* March 30, 1904, p. 1056.

20. Lockroy never interpellated the government on its naval policy. See Police reports, February 24, 27, 29, and March 1, 30, April 7, 1904, Dossier Pelletan, MI 25359, AN.

authority and discipline. The issue centered on the efforts of a minister in the Radical government to republicanize a military service. The earlier attacks against Pelletan and his naval reforms had well prepared the ground for the furor over army staffing which exploded in the fall of 1904. To identify and promote republican officers, the minister of war, General André, had asked Masonic lodges to supply information. The revelation of this practice elicited an extraordinarily powerful protest, bringing together deputies from the extreme Right, the center, Radical dissidents, and even former supporters of the government.[21] André resigned in November, and Combes followed two months later.

Underlying the intensifying divisions among Radicals was the issue of their relation to the state and the nation. Pelletan's policies had aimed to increase Radical control over a military service in which men far from enthusiastic about the Republic held numerous and prominent positions. Pelletan never doubted that his efforts to extend civilian, parliamentary control were in the best interest of the Republic and the nation. Simultaneously he was convinced that these policies would introduce greater democracy and equality in a service renowned for hierarchy and tradition. It was inconceivable to Pelletan that any of these objectives might conflict. He had frequently distinguished between "bad patriots and good ones" with complete assurance that he was a leader of the latter.[22] Two years after the fall of the Combes ministry, the Radical party officially adopted a programmatic statement on military issues which closely paralleled Pelletan's ministerial policies. The 1907 Radical Congress warmly endorsed what had long been the complex sentiments of its left wing on the military question. The party proclaimed itself "ardently patriotic and resolutely attached to peace. . . . It honors military duty, condemns militarism and supports the preparation of young Frenchmen for military service. . . . Military reforms [must include] the democratic recruitment of the officer corps and major economies."[23]

21. Clemenceau wrote a damning article in *L'Aurore* in January which badly damaged Combes's position. Clemenceau was both angry about the slow pace of the separation legislation and opposed to André's methods (Watson, *Clemenceau*, 161; Duroselle, *Clemenceau*, 482–83).

22. Camille Pelletan, Discours, Le Parti radical, 5ᵉ *Congrès*, tenu à Paris, October, 1905, pp. 180–81; Police report, Bézier, January 14, 1902, Dossier Pelletan, MI 25359, AN.

23. Le Parti radical, 1907 Program, nos. 23 and 26, cited in Buisson, *Politique radicale*, 256–57.

For those dissident Radicals who increasingly had become critical of the party's left wing and especially of Pelletan, such an association of apparent opposites was intolerable and chaotic. In the twentieth century they were convinced that patriotism and democratic officer recruitment, devotion to the military and condemnation of the military spirit, a prepared military force and reduced military spending could not coexist. These dissidents intended to modernize the Radicals' fervent nationalism, which was rooted in the nineteenth century. In the Chamber they applauded when the moderate Jean Chaumet spoke of the need to end "the incoherence of our [military which] weakens us materially and morally. . . . A people which does not seem to know exactly what it wants seems to me incapable of inspiring either respect or fear among its rivals, incapable even of maintaining complete faith in itself."[24] During the controversy surrounding Pelletan's ministry, the moderate press constantly extolled Lockroy's patriotism, contrasting it to Pelletan's dangerous experiments, which undermined the navy. One journal asked if it was necessary "to disorganize the navy in order to save the Republic?"[25] This same comparison between Lockroy, the genuine patriot who struggled for the unity of France, and the divisive sectarianism of Pelletan dominated even Lockroy's funeral eulogies and obituaries in 1913.[26] The dissidents intended to refashion Radical republicanism to accommodate and welcome a more assertive nationalism, consonant with traditional principles of order, authority, discipline, and manliness.

Paradoxically, these dissidents drew on the same republican tradition to which the left Radicals pledged their loyalty. Radicals of all varieties shared a conception of the state which ultimately recognized the importance of its authority. During the 1903 party Congress, when the Combes government and the Bloc des gauches were at the height of their power, one delegate delivered an especially ardent speech on the state. He was perhaps somewhat extreme, but many in the party accepted his assumptions. "The French,

24. Interpellation of Camille Pelletan, Chambre des députés, Débats, *Journal Officiel*, November 13, 1902, p. 2577.

25. Louis Latapie in *Liberté*, October 10, 1904.

26. "One could say that his final breath was spent in struggling every inch of the way against the serious mistakes of his successor, M. Pelletan. . . . M. Lockroy was a radical but of the heroic era . . . a great patriot" (*Le Nouvelliste*, December 26, 1913).

very Latin in this, basically love order. If the Republic doesn't supply it, they will look to a Caesar. [They need] republican authority, Jacobinism. Authoritarian-Jacobinism is necessary."[27] The dissident Radicals had no doubt that this republican tradition of a unitary and highly centralized state made the democratization of the military services impossible. At times, left Radicals such as Pelletan had viewed the nineteenth-century state as part of the illegitimate, despotic Napoleonic legacy and had attempted to reform it. These very reforms, however, often required extending the state's power and authority. Pelletan insisted that "[we] must end the absurd spectacle of a regime fought against or betrayed by a large number of its subordinates in the foreign service or the army."[28] In most instances, the Left of the Radical party aimed to promote both reforms toward greater democratization *and* the indivisible authority of the state. The dissidents, in contrast, preferred to emphasize the union of state and nation, disentangling them from the complex questions of democracy and equality.

Even more than the adulation of the republican state, all Radicals and all republicans accepted the glorification of *la patrie*. For politicians nurtured on Michelet and Hugo, the Republic and the fatherland were indissolubly joined. They identified the defense of the Republic with that of the nation, drawing on the tradition of 1792, the revolutionary nation in arms. Pelletan was among the most adept at articulating these sentiments. In an 1899 campaign speech Pelletan passionately defended the genuine—in other words republican—patriotism of Radicals and socialists against the false nationalism of the Republic's latest critics. His "blood boiled" to hear those who were the political heirs of the aristocratic émigrés criticize the loyalty of true patriots, sons of the Revolution. Not unlike the nationalist writer Maurice Barrès, he paid homage to "a material fatherland of native soil which has given us our life . . . and to which we owe the last drop of our blood." But the fatherland was not only a physical reality; there was also a *patrie* of ideals to which republicans were loyal and to which all humanity was attracted. "France is also . . . that glorious country which has given the

27. Speech by delegate Louis Lintilhac during a debate on the state education monopoly. Significantly, the Congress endorsed his support for such a monopoly (Le Parti radical, *3ᵉ Congrès*, tenu à Marseille, October, 1903, pp. 186–98).

28. Le Parti radical, Camille Pelletan, Discours, *6ᵉ Congrès*, tenu à Lille, October, 1906, p. 246.

world its men of genius. . . . great literary figures . . . those who struggled against theocracy. . . . It is the country of the eighteenth century. . . . It is the country which revealed itself to the world with the sublime explosion of the French Revolution. . . . and our magnificent motto: Liberté, Egalité . . . Fraternité."[29]

Such sonorous phrases and history-drenched associations began to grate on some Radicals by the early twentieth century. As radicalism shifted from a parliamentary left-wing opposition group to a party heading the parliamentary majority, a debate occurred over this republican tradition of patriotism. During the Combes government, questions of national defense and military preparedness seemed so urgent that dissident Radicals publicly questioned the ability of their political and parliamentary leaders to fashion a modern version of republican patriotism. The dissidents felt that their party would have to abandon some of the old slogans that indissolubly linked la république and la patrie. They argued for the primacy of the nation over all other considerations. Following the attack on Pelletan and the fall of the Bloc des gauches, it became much easier for a significant and growing element within the Radical party to endorse policies that gave priority to national defense and the protection of state authority. The corollary of this new formulation of republican patriotism was the endorsement of policies of social defense.

Immediately following the fall of the Combes government, however, this transformation of radicalism was not obvious. Paradoxically, the influence and prestige of the Pelletan wing of the party increased. To Radical militants and electors, the left wing appeared ever more as the authentic embodiment of the party. One can almost hear a collective sigh of relief as left Radicals resumed their more accustomed and more comfortable positions outside the government but still securely within the leadership of the parliamentary majority. During the 1905 party Congress those who had lost their ministerial positions, Combes, Pelletan, and André, were elected to the party Executive Committee by boisterous acclamation. The Congresses of 1904 through 1907 denounced and expelled dissident Radicals who had voted against the Combes government and broken with the Bloc

29. Camille Pelletan, speech reported in Le Progrès du Loiret. Organe démocrate et républicain, June 18, 1899.

des gauches majority. Lockroy was ousted while Combes was still in power in 1904. The principal charge brought against him was his role in calling for and then participating in the special commission that had condemned Pelletan's ministry.[30] Doumer was expelled in July, 1905, several months after he had successfully stood against Henri Brisson for the presidency of the Chamber of Deputies.

The mood in the 1905 Congress was understandably combative. The Combes government had fallen ten months earlier, and the party Executive Committee reported its fears "that the political situation would return to the worst days of the Dreyfus Affair. It had been a period of anguish for republicans." In the midst of discussions about party discipline and protests that such discipline should be based only on programs and ideas, not on personalities, Paul Doumer's expulsion was confirmed.[31] The furor against Doumer was especially intense. He had led the attacks against Pelletan, and his defeat of Brisson was viewed as the work of "reactionaries and clericals."[32] Many had read Doumer's election to the presidency of the Chamber as a sign of the majority's declining strength. In 1906 Pelletan led the Radical party in a strident campaign against Doumer's efforts to secure an even more prestigious position, the presidency of the Republic. He excoriated Doumer as a politician of the Right, corrupted by his colonial experience, dreaming of the conquest of China, and supported by colonial officers and defense industrialists.[33] The decision of the National Assembly to elect a

30. Le Parti radical, 5ᵉ Congrès, tenu à Paris, October, 1905, p. 203. There were twenty dissenting votes opposed to nine hundred for the expulsion of Lockroy (Louis Latapie, Liberté, October 10, 1904).

31. Rapport sur le Comité executif, 5ᵉ Congrès, tenu à Paris, October, 1905, pp. 22, 80, 125–26.

32. Georges Piermé, Compte rendu du 6ᵉ Congrès du Parti radical et radical-socialiste présenté à l'Association des inséparables du progrès (Aisne, 1906), 2. Brisson was defeated for the presidency of the Chamber by a vote of 265 against 240 (Rebérioux, La République radicale?, 107).

33. "Doumerisme," Le Petit Provençal, January 2, 1906. At the 1906 Congress Camille Pelletan supported a proposal to exclude all deputies who had supported Doumer's bid for the presidency; the proposal passed (Le Parti radical, 6ᵉ Congrès, tenu à Lille, October, 1906, pp. 160–61). Pelletan approvingly viewed the expulsion of Doumer as parallel to the Socialists' expulsion of Millerand, another "deserter" (Le Petit Provençal, March 13, 1906). Doumer was also expelled from his departmental Radical association as the reprehensible "ex-pro-consul d'Indo-Chine" and as a dangerous "tarentule" (Piermé, Compte rendu, 2, 6).

self-effacing republican, Armand Fallières, rather than Doumer, was greeted as a triumph for the Radical party and the Bloc des gauches.[34] After the legislative elections of May, 1906, Doumer withdrew his second bid for the presidency of the Chamber. Although Jean de Lanessan was not formally expelled from the party, his dramatic defeat in Lyons during the 1906 election was attributed to his identification with the dissident Radical group.[35]

The continuing optimism of the party's Left immediately after the fall of the Combes government was not only the result of their ability to label and punish their opponents. The sixth party Congress, held in the industrial city of Lille, jubilantly celebrated the 1906 legislative elections, which resulted in the largest Radical electoral victory ever.[36] Pelletan was enthusiastically elected president of the party. Ferdinand Buisson opened the Congress with ringing, patriotic praise for the voters' reaffirmation of the Radicals' central belief that "universal suffrage" supported the Radical vision of the republic. "The country surpassed our hopes; the country is more republican than we are; we didn't believe it. . . . The country took the responsibility upon itself to tell us that the Republic is established and it can no longer be undone— the secular, democratic and social Republic. . . . We are France; but we are also and will always be the French Revolution."[37] With renewed vigor and confidence Pelletan presented the official declaration of the party. The nation had demonstrated its support for the separation of church and state and now would insist on economic and social reforms.[38] The nation stood behind the Bloc, demanding a republican Republic and a government that would adhere to the Radical party program.

The success of 1906, which Buisson called "the apogee of the Radical party," created a strangely ambiguous situation.[39] An increasing number of Radi-

34. Armand Fallières was senator from the Lot-et-Garonne. He was elected by a vote of 449 to 371 (Mayeur, *Vie politique*, 211).

35. He received 1,657 votes as against his opponent's 9,065 (Joly, *Dictionnaires des parlementaires français*).

36. Radical deputies now numbered 115, Radical-socialists 132, for a total of 247, increasing their number from the 1902 total of 233.

37. Le Parti radical, 6ᵉ *Congrès*, tenu à Lille, October, 1906, pp. 4–10.

38. Le Parti radical, Déclaration du parti, 6ᵉ *Congrès*, tenu à Lille, October, 1906, pp. 243–52.

39. Buisson, *Politique Radicale*, 98.

cal deputies, some of whom had important and well-established positions within the republican political elite, were eagerly searching for ways to shift the direction of the Radical party. Certainly they wanted to disassociate it from the discourse and policies of a Pelletan. Minimally they sought to abandon the oppositional stance of radicalism and create a party fit for governing and exercising state authority. But the traditional Radical left-wing rhetoric continued to sway and attract much of the electorate. The 1906 electoral victory led the left Radicals to overestimate their strength, which rested largely with provincial petit bourgeois voters who themselves were experiencing social and political dislocations. It is to this important social stratum and the Radicals' debate about their relation to it that we now turn.

The 1906 victory reflected the popular support for the Combes government, despite all its limitations, and the Bloc des gauches, despite all its contradictions. There can be no question that the government, and Combes and Pelletan in particular, became objects of a republican enthusiasm outside the Chamber and beyond the circle of the national political elite. An examination of this support provides some insight into the most elusive aspect of French Radical democracy—its local, provincial proponents. Here too we find that during the early years of the twentieth century contradictions were intensified and transformations accelerated.

During the critical spring and fall of 1904, there was an outpouring of congratulatory messages to the Combes ministry from mayors, municipal councils, a broad range of political and fraternal organizations, trade unions, and Masonic lodges.[40] These expressions of support mentioned Combes and Pelletan most often and with the greatest praise. Dissident Radicals came in for frequent denunciations. In most instances these "felicitations" repeated fairly standard republican formulas. Combes and especially Camille Pelletan were addressed as "citoyens ministres"; most letters and telegrams concluded with a resounding "long live the social, democratic and secular republic." In Pelletan's department of the Bouches-du-Rhône, fifty-two municipal councils voted to send testimonials. Over a dozen were from Pelletan's own electoral district. These numbers reflected the political strength of the Radicals and the Bloc on the local level.[41]

40. Baal, "Combes et la 'République des Comités,'" 260–85. See also Chapter V.

41. Adresses de sympathie et félicitations à Combes, Carton 3, Bouches-du-Rhône, 73 AP, AN.

Even more interesting than the municipal councils were the 162 Bouches-du-Rhône organizations that sent greetings to what most perceived as a Radical government. When these congratulatory messages are read collectively, they reflect the strong petit bourgeois social base of Radical support. The ideology of republicanism played down class affiliation, and certainly the political associations sending messages gave no direct indication of their members' social position. Considering what we know of Radical militants in Pelletan's district, however, we can safely assume that petit bourgeois representation was high among these Radical political groups. A significant minority of groups, to which we will return in the next chapter, were socialist organizations of one stripe or another. There was also a sizable representation of fraternal groups, many of whom supported laicization either as *libre penseurs*, through *études sociales*, or by endorsing secular education. Fourteen Masonic lodges also sent greetings, but they were clearly overshadowed by the associations of freethinkers, which tended to attract less affluent members. These anticlerical groups included an especially militant one, La Groupe anti-religieuse de la Belle de mai. The group praised Combes during its annual banquet held on Good Friday and provocatively called "gras vendredi (dit saint)."[42] Some associations were entirely cultural or fraternal. Their members may have been drawn from both the petit bourgeois and the working class, with perhaps a sprinkling of more solidly bourgeois citizens. For example, the four hundred members of the Cercle philharmonique de Trets applauded Combes's anticlericalism as did the fire fighters of Casis. Among the most interesting and most difficult to identify socially were patriotic organizations. It is significant that in the midst of questions about Pelletan's commitment to national defense the Cercle nationalist de Tarascon-sur-Rhône voted to express its support for the government. The Association patriotique des Alsaciens-Lorrains en Provence et coloniaux sent no less than four greetings to the Combes government.[43] In March, 1904, they congratulated the naval minister on his victory and claimed it as one of which "all true patriots could be proud." Pelletan's republican nationalism still had devoted followers.

42. Félicitations à Combes, April 1, 1904, *ibid.*

43. Félicitations à Combes, January 23, 1905, September 11, November 16, March 15, April 1, July 14, December 31, 1904, *ibid.*

Some groups represented those who shared occupational or economic interests, and their petit bourgeois character is clear. Like the petite bourgeoisie throughout France in the early twentieth century, those of the Bouches-du-Rhône were far from being a homogeneous or static group. A scattering of small or medium property owners or small entrepreneurs could be found among Combes's well-wishers. On February 5, 1904, the newly created Marseilles section of the Comité républicain du commerce et de l'industrie notified the government of its support. It is not clear what ties, if any, existed between this association and its Paris namesake, which had served as a critical financial backer of Radical candidates since the Dreyfus Affair.[44] Of all the Bouches-du-Rhône felicitations the most idiosyncratic came from a group of "small property owners," sent in May, 1904. Although their meeting "of a large number" finally got around to denouncing clericalism, the main purpose of their communication was to condemn the Marseilles municipal council and to praise the Combes government. The national government had annulled a municipal decision on a local canal project. Combes was praised as a politician who "understood the expenses which weighed on small property owners and the working class." In this entire collection the only message from an individual came from a "humble citizen of Marseilles, Marius Bourre, who dealt in lead and was the vice-president of a union of plumbing contractors."[45]

Compared to this limited group of small businessmen, there was a larger collection of messages from employee associations. Many among these were civil servants such as the "employees of the customs service in the Marseilles district" and the "office inspectors of the customs service." Not surprisingly, the nonproduction employees and workers of the state-owned munitions factory in Pelletan's district joined them. Finally, the Cercle des instituteurs des Bouches-du-Rhône sent its support for the government's defense of secular institutions. Both male and female teachers voted to approve this endorsement of the Combes government.[46] Most of the messages, like

44. The Paris committee was formed in 1899 by Alfred Mascuraud, a successful manufacturer of costume jewelry and vice-president of the Syndicat général du commerce et de l'industrie. Its original aim had been to mobilize small business support behind Dreyfusard candidates. See Chapter IV and Nord, *Paris Shopkeepers*, 413.

45. Félicitations à Combes, May 1, November 5, 1904, Bouches-du-Rhône, 73 AP, AN.

46. *Ibid.*, May 28, 1904, December 6, 1903; *ibid.*, Saint-Chamas, November 8, January 28, 1904.

that of the teachers, indicated their general approval of the government's policies. The munitions employees specifically denounced the nationalist Right. The customs employees also added concerns about their pensions.

A few workers' political and union organizations also appeared among those who sent felicitations, such as the Société de retraite des travailleurs français and Le Syndicat des ouvriers du Port du Saint Louis du Rhône. Such working-class organizations existed in close ideological, social, and physical proximity to the more numerous petit bourgeois associations. The "petits propriétaires" of Marseilles applauded Combes for his sensitivity to the burdens of small property owners and the working class. Did these men consider those two categories synonymous or in some social continuum? Although nothing in the testimonials suggested that such social proximity created tension, there was a need to maintain distinctions among different social positions. The munitions employees, for example, specifically noted that they were not production workers. The testimonials obviously demonstrated a shared sense of republican loyalty, as well as in some cases a shared antipathy to "les gros." One municipal council of a small town near Aix explained that votes for the nationalist Right were the result of corruption and employer pressure.[47] This rich source, as Gérard Baal has cogently argued, demonstrates the depth of popular sentiment for the Combes government, for Pelletan in particular, and for the left radicalism they had come to embody.[48] This sample from the Bouches-du-Rhône suggests that this political identity was also linked to a social identity strongly colored by a petit bourgeois character. It was entirely appropriate that a "commercial salesman, a bookkeeper from a factory and a second bookkeeper from a cement works" should head a local southern Radical committee.[49]

Significantly, during those very years when dissident Radicals were questioning the left Radicals' ability to represent the state and the nation, they also raised questions about left Radicals' ability to speak for the petit bourgeois voter, that mainstay of radicalism. This debate among Radicals concerning their relation to the petite bourgeoisie was part of an important transformation of this politically critical social stratum. For convenience and consistency I have been using the term *petite bourgeoisie* to indicate a

47. *Ibid.*, September 1, 1903; *ibid.*, Eguilles, May 15, 1904.
48. Baal, "Combes et la 'République des comités,' " 282–85.
49. Police report, 8ᵉ canton of Marseilles, April 17, 1912, M6 3404, AD/BR.

social reality existing between the more readily identifiable manual wage worker and the secure, powerful, and wealthy bourgeoisie. In the final decades of the nineteenth century and the opening ones of the twentieth this social territory was not so easily demarcated.[50] A major social, cultural, economic, and political reorganization was affecting the petite bourgeoisie. The boundaries of this social category were being redrawn, and the relations of the petit bourgeois to both the affluent bourgeoisie and the working class were shifting. This protean condition affected the very language used to describe this social group. We find a large vocabulary, ranging from the very precise and functional to the most global and vague: small shopkeepers, small property owners, civil servants, employees, store clerks, the middle classes, new social strata, the people (*les petits commerçants, les petits propriétaires, les fonctionnaires, les employés, les calicots, les classes moyennes, les nouvelles couches sociales, le peuple*). Similarly, current historians who analyze this social phenomenon rarely employ a fixed and precise vocabulary. The terms *lower middle class*, *petite bourgeoisie*, and *middle classes* are frequently interchanged.[51]

In an insightful study of French impressionist painting, T. J. Clark has stated that "the emergence of the lower-middle class. . . . seems to me one of the main circumstances of modernist art." I would propose that the emergence of this same class was pivotal in the efforts to construct a democratic movement appropriate for the twentieth century. Clark further contends that at the end of the nineteenth century, "The world of leisure was thus a great symbolic field in which the battle for bourgeois identity was fought."[52] Related to this relatively new struggle was one within the apparently more traditional domain of politics. Just as leisure had been an exclusive privilege of the affluent, propertied bourgeoisie for most of the nineteenth century, so too had politics. Now both leisure and political activities had to accommodate new men and, in a very complex way, new women.

50. For general discussion on the petite bourgeoisie see Rebérioux, *La République radicale?*, 94–102; Nord, *Paris Shopkeepers*, introduction; Arno Mayer, "The Lower Middle Class as an Historical Problem," *Journal of Modern History*, XLVII (September, 1975), 409–36.

51. See Clark, *Painting of Modern Life*, 202, and Nord, *Paris Shopkeepers*, 3. Nord is more precise because he limits his study to shopkeepers.

52. Clark, *Painting of Modern Life*, 202, 203.

After 1900 this shifting social ground of the petite bourgeoisie became contested terrain among Radicals. Jean de Lanessan, in particular, championed efforts to redefine relations between Radicals and the petite bourgeoisie. He argued that Radicals must speak clearly to and for them. Opposed to this effort was the Left of the party, including Pelletan, which resisted the identification of radicalism with a particular social class and its interests. The Left also refuted de Lanessan's claim that the petite bourgeoisie consisted of socially conservative small property owners. Throughout the nineteenth century this ambiguous social position, somewhere between the working class and the securely propertied bourgeoisie, had been the home of French Radical democracy. At the same time, however, Radicals had also insisted that they were not a party of particular interests and that their support among men of small property enabled them to speak for all citizens and the entire nation. The democratic program was intended to forge interclass alliances and supraclass affiliations. At the end of the century, when the configuration of the petite bourgeoisie began to change, Radicals reexamined these traditions.

A leading spokesman of the party's Left, Ferdinand Buisson, addressed these issues with considerable passion at the second Radical Congress in Lyons. Like Camille Pelletan, Buisson (1841–1932) was a member of the generation that had reached maturity just as the Third Republic was established. He was a highly respected member of the liberal Protestant community and served as one of the major architects of republican educational reforms in the 1880s. From 1879 to 1896 he held the post of director of primary education in the Ministry of Education. A Sorbonne professor of pedagogy and an ardent Dreyfusard, he participated in the establishment of the Ligue des droits de l'homme.[53] In 1902 he stood for election and won, representing the Paris thirteenth arrondissement. He quickly became an important member of the Radical party and the parliamentary group of Radical-socialists.

At the Lyons party Congress following his election, Buisson proudly proclaimed the Radical party's allegiance to a particular version of the petite bourgeoisie. Paradoxically, he took up Gambetta's Opportunist slogan of

---

53. He succeeded Durkheim to this Sorbonne chair in 1896; in 1927 he was awarded the Nobel Prize for his work in education.

"les nouvelles couches sociales" but gave it a distinctly new meaning. For Buisson these *nouvelles couches* were less a stabilizing social phenomena than a source of political inspiration. "The new social strata are the deepest and most fundamental levels of democracy, being far from the bourgeoisie . . . and closer to the heart of [France]. The essential substance of that heart is the people. We, the Radical party, are that multitude, the masses of the nation." This Michelet-inspired rhetoric moved effortlessly from a relatively precise social location at some distance from the bourgeoisie, to an idealized concept "the heart of France," to come to rest with that traditional republican category, "le peuple." The people excluded no one, although it was more open to those below than those above. In Buisson's view, only the Radicals, the party of democracy, could authentically represent the people and "create a Republic for the present age."[54]

Then Buisson shifted his tone. He introduced the theme of the Radicals as political outsiders and sketched the derision that much of the established political elite and its affluent haut bourgeois supporters had directed toward Radicals and their supporters. Buisson accepted the derogatory comments. Yes, some might regard Radicals as vulgar, abrasive, materialist, and political newcomers. But these same attributes, Buisson claimed, were the signs of an emerging, energetic democratic regime. "We are insolently treated as incorrigible Homais. . . . But without all those Homais where would the Republic be? . . . Let them treat us as tiresome, troublesome, overzealous promoters . . . as neo-Jacobins, it doesn't matter to us. Very simply we are republicans who have too often been disappointed and no longer want to be. Common sense, ordinary citizens. . . . We who are not fashionable, whose manners are unpolished and whose exterior is a little plain, we believe that everyone must get used to this début of democracy . . . which is not elitist . . . [and] lays claim to being the nation."[55] Although his words resounded with populist fervor, Buisson offered the shifting petite bourgeoisie only a political identity and political victory as the somewhat vaguely defined heart of French democracy.

Four years later, in 1906, during preparations for the upcoming legislative elections, Jean de Lanessan had a very different message for the party

54. Le Parti radical, *2e Congrès*, tenu à Lyon, October, 1902, pp. 125, 127, 136.
55. *Ibid.*, 136–38.

and its relation to the petite bourgeoisie. Writing in his small-circulation but influential Radical journal *Le Siècle*, de Lanessan described what he saw as the plight of the petite bourgeoisie. He too viewed this social stratum as open to those below, who had "known the rigors of labor." But in this version, the petite bourgeoisie also included "the owners of small industries whose hands are as callused as those of their workers." Significantly, this social group was no longer amorphous and could be identified concretely with "small shopkeepers, small and medium farmers, small manufacturers, and employees in commerce, industry and the public sector." Most important, de Lanessan described the collective consciousness of this "hardworking, frugal, orderly, somewhat defensive" social class. A considerable amount of fear and timidity characterized them. Not eager to display their political opinions, they tended to refrain from protest against the wild statements of socialism. Nonetheless, de Lanessan was certain of their real anxieties. They had little sympathy for big business, but "revolutionary collectivism totally terrified [*ils tremblent de tous leurs membres*] the petit bourgeois who was ready to throw himself into the arms of anyone promising deliverance from the nightmare of socialism." Their principal concern was the protection of their "material interests." They wanted nothing to interfere with their continued ascent in the social hierarchy. De Lanessan urged the Radical party to take up the cause of this class and to deliver what they wanted: "social order . . . international peace . . . and conditions promoting upward social mobility."[56]

In 1908 Pelletan returned to Buisson's left Radical themes on the character of the petite bourgeoisie. The party Executive Committee reprinted Pelletan's parliamentary address defending the proposed progressive income tax and sold it as a pamphlet for five francs. This fiscal reform had been a key element of the Radical platform since the beginning of the Republic. It was one of the three essential reforms that left Radicals had pledged would be enacted during the 1906–1910 legislature following their electoral victories. Middle-class opinion, as well as politicians such as de Lanessan and Doumer, was wavering on this question. Even at the 1907 Congress questions about the income tax proposal and its impact on the

56. *Le Siècle*, no. 25773, July 15–16, 1906; Buisson viewed this article as an important statement of the party's right wing and included it in his study *La Politique radicale*, 110–12.

middle class had been raised from the floor.[57] The party executive hoped that the well-known voice of Camille Pelletan, currently presiding over the Chamber committee that was examining the fiscal proposal, would carry weight with the electorate. The last section of the speech was devoted to an analysis of the middle class and its politics. Pelletan acknowledged the political power of the middle class, stating that the key to social reforms was "the attitude of the great mass of the middle classes toward fulfilling the program." He had no doubt that "the interests of the majority of the middle classes supported democratic reforms against the financial aristocracy."[58]

Pelletan's essential message for middle-class voters, however, was not about their interests but about their traditions and responsibilities to the nation and the Republic. Pelletan concluded his discourse with a challenge, asking middle-class voters to choose between two contradictory traditions. One was middle-class unity with the people, as exemplified during the French Revolution and based on the popular origin of the middle class. The other was the tradition of the July Monarchy in which the bourgeoisie forgot and denied its popular origins and practiced a politics without ideals, without roots, and without principles. This second tradition was a self-defeating trap. It had already once led to revolution.[59] In this dramatic opposition of choices Pelletan, like so many other commentators, muddled the distinctions between middle classes and bourgeoisie. In his promotion of fiscal and other reforms, Pelletan urged his middle-class audience to make the choice of "good faith and goodwill which would lead to a peaceful and reasonable evolution." Pelletan's high-minded rhetoric did not abandon interest entirely. But unlike de Lanessan, who focused on immediate protection of what the middle class had accumulated, Pelletan promised future social peace and stability. According to Pelletan, moderates within the Radical party who were critical of the income tax and sought to define

57. Le Parti radical, Député Magniaude, 7ᵉ Congrès, tenu à Nancy, October, 1907, p. 226.

58. Camille Pelletan, L'Impôt sur le revenu, Discours prononcé à la Chambre des députés au cours de la session générale de l'impôt sur le revenu, séance du 3 février 1908 (Paris, 1908), 54, 52.

59. Ibid., 55–56. References to these two distinct forms of middle-class politics were standards of republican rhetoric from Michelet in the mid-nineteenth century through Victor Hugo to Georges Lefebvre and Marc Bloc in the early twentieth century. See, for example, Georges Lefebvre, 1789 (Paris, 1939), and Marc Bloch, Strange Defeat: A Statement of Evidence Written in 1940, trans. Gerard Hopkins (1949; rpr., New York, 1968).

the middle classes exclusively in terms of material interests were committing the grievous offense of engaging in "the worst kind of class politics." For himself he declaimed: "I am bourgeois. . . . I deny nothing of my origins. . . . I believe that a reduction of the middle classes' influence would be a great misfortune. . . . Opposed to the politics of class . . . I reject anything which would tend to divide . . . the nation's forces. . . . The day on which the struggle of ideas . . . would be replaced by a bitter conflict of antagonistic interests and rival egoisms would be one of real disgrace for French politics."[60]

Pelletan, Buisson, and the Left of the party continued to argue for a broader conception of private property, one that would be appropriate to their larger, more inclusive vision of democracy. They emphasized the extension, rather than the defense, of property ownership. Access to property could even include a minimum of security and human dignity guaranteed to all citizens by the state. They viewed de Lanessan's proposition as perpetuating and intensifying class hostilities, thus sharply restricting the democratic promise.[61] By the outbreak of the war, de Lanessan's vision in practice had largely come to dominate the party, although the left-wing rhetoric persisted for decades. But this ultimate outcome was in no way clear in the years following the fall of the Combes ministry. It would also be an error to conclude that the Right of the party had more accurately gauged the sentiments of the French petite bourgeoisie. In fact, both the Left and the Right of the Radical party misread this most difficult to comprehend social class. If the petite bourgeoisie could no longer simply be identified with the democratic aspirations of *le peuple*, neither could it be reduced exclusively to socially conservative small property owners.[62]

In the first decade of the twentieth century political and social militancy was not the monopoly of socialist and syndicalist factory workers. Key strata within the petite bourgeoisie—small winegrowers and civil servants—demanded that the republican state come to their assistance. These two groups in particular were important Radical supporters. As we have

60. Camille Pelletan, *L'Impôt sur le revenu*, 56–57.

61. Buisson, *Politique radicale*, 236.

62. Philip Nord cogently concludes his study of the Paris shopkeepers by arguing that their political trajectory was open-ended and not determined. This can certainly be extended to other sectors of the petite bourgeoisie (*Paris Shopkeepers*, 494).

seen, producers of *vin ordinaire* in the Midi, suffering a severe regional economic crisis, sought legislation that would guarantee their profits, property, and way of life.[63] They sought government intervention to maintain standards of production, protect markets, and limit output. A popular militant mass movement, which sometimes joined owners and workers, vowed not to pay taxes until the government came to their assistance. Especially in the southeastern departments of the Gard, the Aude, the Hérault, and the Pyrenées-Orientales, local Radical officials supported the movement. During the summer of 1907 in the Aude, a total of thirty-one municipal councils resigned in solidarity with the winegrowers' protest and their demand for government action. Half of these municipal councils were controlled by Radicals.[64]

This movement, largely composed of Radical electors and local officials, appealed to what was regarded as a Radical government, headed by Georges Clemenceau. This government had been formed after the elections of 1906. Clemenceau's long history as a spokesman in the press and in the Chamber for left-wing radicalism appeared to guarantee the implementation of the Radical party's reform program. His leading role in the Dreyfusard movement encouraged Radical partisans of active reform. Although they recognized that the parliamentary majority, since the formation of the unified Socialist party, was no longer as well organized or so clearly in control of the government, they hoped for major legislative breakthroughs. Initially left Radicals overlooked Clemenceau's recent repressive decisions as minister of the interior in the previous government and his aloofness from the formal Radical party.[65] Less than a year after the formation of the Clemenceau government, however, Pelletan had distanced himself. Addressing Radicals of the southeast in April, 1907, he expressed his regrets: "It was a sad moment when I saw him deviate from our path; I had counted on him to fulfill our ideal."[66] Only a few weeks later, Clemenceau was confronted with the southern winegrowers' refusal

63. Warner, *Winegrowers of France*, 22.

64. Police reports, Viticulteurs du Midi, October 12, 1907, F7 12794, AN. Where there were elections following the resignations, all those who had resigned were reelected.

65. He avoided all party gatherings and contributed nothing to the party's formation. His early Dreyfusard leadership had further estranged him from many leading Radicals.

66. Le Parti radical du sud-est, *1er Congrès*, tenu à Nice, April, 1907, p. 140.

to pay taxes and their escalating demonstrations. The premier had two responses: legislation to control fraud in wine production and use of the army to restore order. The legislation never satisfied the demands of the winegrowers, and they remained bitter about the display of military authority. The government's action appalled the left wing of the party. In the summer of 1907 in his regular lead column for *Le Petit Provençal*, Pelletan lamented the disaffection of winegrowers. "In the entire region of Languedoc which was one of the strongholds of the Radical-socialist party, [our friends who have been estranged from us] have delivered a possibly mortal blow to our party; because of legitimate resentment [they] have handed over the vote to the Socialist party and, what is worse, to reactionaries." [67] The Radicals failed to provide an economic policy for the southern crisis, and their support in the region declined. The rift between the Clemenceau government and the left-wing Radicals deepened. After 1907, Socialists replaced Radicals as the dominant political party in many southern towns and villages. [68]

Even more militant were the activities of at least some members of a growing sector of the petite bourgeoisie, civil servants, particularly postal workers and schoolteachers. In 1871 the Third Republic inherited a bureaucracy of 220,000; by 1901 the number stood near 800,000. Those who inhabited that significant but always porous boundary between the working class and the petite bourgeoisie accounted for much of this increase. Full-time state employees, whatever their particular occupation, possessed what the great mass of workers lacked, job security. Despite this advantage, members of the expanding government bureaucracy had numerous grievances related to pay, job discipline, and advancement. Since 1901 association had been the right of every French citizen, and growing numbers of low-level civil servants eagerly formed professional groups. Within a few years a minority was demanding the right to create unions, participate

---

67. "Les Malheurs," *Le Petit Provençal*, June 25, 1907.

68. Loubère, *Radicalism in Mediterranean France*, 232. For a contrasting analysis, but one that also stresses the decline of the Radicals but for different reasons, see Judt, *Socialism in Provence*, 138–53. Loubère suggests, as did Pelletan, that voters actually switched allegiance; Judt argues that different, new voters, especially small farmers from socially homogeneous villages, voted for the SFIO. Judt's study, however, focuses on the Var, which was much less affected by the wine crisis.

in strikes, and join the syndicalist-dominated Confédération générale du travail.[69] Since 1906 Clemenceau had followed a strategy of dramatic, often violent, confrontations with all revolutionary unionists. The premier aggressively applied this policy to state employees when they began to unionize, and in 1906 and 1907 the government dismissed union organizers among postal workers and teachers.

Searching for political supporters, the *fonctionnaires* appealed to the members of the Bloc des gauches. During the 1906 Radical party Congress the union leaders of the postal workers, the *sous-agents*, had written to Louis Tissier, Pelletan's protégé, requesting Radical support. The Congress adopted his motion, calling for the reinstatement of fired postal workers.[70] In 1907 the postal union's central committee now directly solicited the support of Camille Pelletan and the Radical party's Executive Committee. The Left on the committee criticized Clemenceau's repressive policies and supported the civil servants' unions. They pushed through a statement critical of the government, but even they refused to endorse civil service strikes.[71] One left Radical deputy, Théodore Steeg, proposed legislation that would reform the civil service and permit unions but still would not allow strikes. It was defeated by 309 votes to 152.[72] The Ligue des droits de l'homme, socialist led but closely connected with the Left of the Radical party, staunchly endorsed Steeg's position. It too disapproved of the government's action and called for a special statute unambiguously extending union rights to civil servants.[73] When a postal strike occurred in 1909, there were more dismissals, arrests, and police action; the Radicals were again divided and politically ineffectual. The Radical Executive Committee, by a vote of 78 to 47, condemned Clemenceau's actions and declared them "contrary to the traditions of the party." Despite such criticism, Clemenceau easily won the confidence of the Radical-dominated Chamber by a vote

69. Judith Wishnia, *The Proletarianizing of the Fonctionnaires: Civil Service Workers and the Labor Movement Under the Third Republic* (Baton Rouge, 1990), 2, 28–31, 41–45, *passim.*

70. Le Parti radical, 6ᵉ *Congrès*, tenu à Lille, October, 1906, p. 123.

71. Buisson interpellation, Chambre des députés, Débats, *Journal Officiel*, May 7, 1907, pp. 16, 22; Wishnia, *Proletarianizing of the Fonctionnaires*, 81–84.

72. Théodore Steeg interpellation, Chambre des députés, Débats, *Journal Officiel*, May 8, 1907, p. 137.

73. Wishnia, *Proletarianizing of the Fonctionnaires*, 80.

of 365 to 159.[74] The civil servants' demands for unionization had exposed the serious contradictions surrounding the Radical view of the republican state. Ultimately the left Radicals did not have a solution. Clemenceau's response, however, was clear: the police powers of the state preceded all its other attributes, even in a republican regime. Clemenceau reasserted the authority of the state as "premier flic" and as employer. With reluctance, regret, and calls for less brutality, most Radicals had no alternative but to accept the traditional view of the state as the guardian of public order.

Civil servants and winegrowers had demonstrated that the changing petite bourgeoisie was not exclusively committed to the defense of the status quo.[75] Winegrowers, although never precise in their demands, clearly sought a republican state that would intervene and protect them from the vicissitudes of the market. Organizing to defend their interests, *fonctionnaires* raised questions about the hierarchical authority of the state as employer. In the face of demands from postal workers and schoolteachers, Radical deputies found themselves confronting their own constituents and at times the very individuals their patronage had supported. On one hand, these civil servants, especially teachers, had often been selected to fill positions to further republicanize the state. In many instances their republican politics encouraged them now to call on the state to extend rights to them as both employees and citizens. On the other hand, the Radicals' very insistence on creating a fully loyal republican civil service, with more jobs for dedicated Radicals, carried with it a revulsion at the thought of *fonctionnaires* organizing strikes.[76] Some Radical deputies viewed such actions as yet another assault on the authority of the state. As in the case of Pelletan's attempts to transform the navy, Radicals were divided and hesitant

74. Comité executif du Parti radical républicain et radical-socialiste, *Bulletin du Parti*, May 12, 1909, cited in Bardonnet, *Evolution de la structure du parti radical*, 109. In 1909 Clemenceau was expelled from the Radical party.

75. Judith Wishnia's important and exhaustive study of French civil servant unionization differs somewhat from the interpretation presented here. She argues for their absorption into the working class. See esp. *Proletarianizing of the Fonctionnaires*, 8. I am suggesting that even low-level *fonctionnaires* continued to be distinct from the working class, although they frequently shared similar economic and democratic aspirations with socialist and syndicalist workers.

76. See comments on the republicanization of the civil service and civil servants' unions, Piermé, *Compte rendu*, 28; Le Parti radical du sud-est, *1er Congrès*, tenu à Nice, April, 1907, pp. 97–108.

about efforts to apply egalitarian principles to the state itself. No statute on civil servants' unions was enacted by the Radical-dominated Chamber before 1914. Radicals remained essentially unanimous in their opposition to strikes by state employees. Despite many good words and fine speeches, the Radical party, including its left wing, was unable to respond adequately to the new concerns of these particular petit bourgeois constituents, many of whom shifted their support to the Socialist party.

Among the organizing postal workers and schoolteachers were members of an even larger group that posed a special conundrum for Radicals and especially left Radicals with their democratic ideology. After 1900 neither the state nor the largest political party could any longer ignore French women. By the end of the century, women were increasingly represented in the new white-collar occupations. In primary education alone their numbers had quadrupled between 1876 and 1906, from fourteen thousand to fifty-seven thousand.[77] The organization of women for political action also accelerated. Since the beginning of the Third Republic, middle-class republican women had been demanding the extension of civil and political rights. They were deeply committed to the Republic and had assumed that its establishment would necessarily increase their participation in public and political life.[78] In reality, greater civil rights were won only slowly, over several decades, and suffrage remained a distant aspiration. Some gains were made: divorce became legal in 1884, although not by mutual consent; in 1893 single and separated women were accorded full legal status; women could be witnesses in law courts after 1897; and in 1907 married women gained control over their own wages. Education was extended to girls and young women. The Ferry laws of 1881 and 1882 mandated that free, secular, and compulsory

77. Hause and Kenney, *Women's Suffrage and Social Politics in the Third Republic*, 18. Throughout the nineteenth century French women had an especially high rate of participation in the labor force outside the home. It increased from 24 percent in 1866 to 38 percent in 1911. Although the majority of working women were employed in the large but slowly contracting agricultural sector, their presence in nonagricultural work doubled between 1856 and 1906. These women workers were concentrated in textiles, the garment trades, and the new white-collar occupations. See Karen Offen, "Women in the Labor Force," in *Historical Dictionary of the Third French Republic*, ed. Hutton, 1072–74.

78. Moses, *French Feminism*, 197–200.

primary education be available to boys and girls; public secondary education was established for girls in 1880. The republican politicians who promoted this expansion were very explicit: the goal of educating girls was to ensure a new generation of "republican mothers." In most towns educational institutions were segregated. The state-authorized primary curricula differed sharply for the two genders, and the girls' secondary schools did not prepare their students for the baccalaureate exam, required for university admission.[79] Although women remained subordinate in the republican educational structure, it did create new careers with the possibility of some upward social mobility.[80] With the new century, women's suffrage moved steadily to the foreground. Women teachers often led the call for the extension of the vote.[81] The moderate republican Conseil national des femmes françaises, founded in 1901 with a membership of twenty-one thousand, endorsed municipal suffrage for women. On the eve of the war its membership stood close to one hundred thousand with branches in almost every department.[82]

While this small but growing minority of women appealed specifically to republican ideology and the Radical party in their efforts to secure greater civic and political equality, conservative Catholic women were also organizing. Anti-Dreyfusards, nationalists, clericals, and the traditional monarchist Right mobilized bourgeois women into an antirepublican political force despite their disfranchisement.[83] Within the bourgeoisie the most

79. Linda Clark, *Schooling the Daughters of Marianne: Textbooks and the Socialization of Girls in the Modern French Primary Schools* (Albany, N.Y., 1984).

80. Jo Burr Margadant, *Madame le Professeur: Women Educators in the Third Republic* (Princeton, 1990); for limits encountered by women in education see Leslie Page Moch, "Government Policy and Women's Experience: The Case of Teachers in France," *Feminist Studies*, XIV (Summer, 1988), 301–24.

81. Among republican men endorsement of women's education had never inevitably led to support for women's suffrage. Eugène Pelletan, for example, had forcefully expressed his strong endorsement for rigorous women's education in 1878 at a special Masonic meeting, *la fête de famille*, but he refrained from endorsing women's suffrage (Police report, Eugène Pelletan, February, 1878, Ba 1216, APP).

82. Hause and Kenney, *Women's Suffrage and Social Politics in the Third Republic*, Table 5, 134–35.

83. The Right, like the Radicals, assumed that enfranchised women would be a conservative force. Despite their deep commitment to patriarchy, several individuals and organizations on the

common expression of alienation between men and women was sharply different attitudes toward the church. Most bourgeois women from Catholic families continued to practice their religion, some with increasing fervor as the century progressed. Bourgeois men, in contrast, were in many cases indifferent, or, among those who identified with the Republic and Freemasonry, actively anticlerical. This sharp difference in religious preference, which often reflected even more intimate barriers between many bourgeois men and women, became a bitterly debated public question. Catholic women's commitment to the church and a religiously dominated culture, coupled with their social and political isolation from republican politics, easily convinced some among them of the need actively to defend their beliefs and lifestyles against the attacks of the anticlericals.[84]

Joining together in national organizations such as the Ligue des femmes françaises and La Ligue patriotique des françaises, these mostly affluent women identified antirepublicanism as a woman's cause. For some this was a fervent personal crusade. In September, 1902, at the Marseilles train station three members of the Ligue des femmes françaises confronted Camille Pelletan. The Radical minister laughed at the women who had refused to shake his hand; some in his party shouted, "Long live the Republic" and "down with the priests," while the very vocal Catholic women hurled back "Long live liberty."[85] During the 1902 legislative elections La Ligue des femmes françaises engaged in a major national distribution of powerful campaign literature. In the Allier they appealed to "Jacques Bonhomme" not to be duped by wealthy Freemasons. In the Vendée they called on "Mothers, French women, Christians, and Vendéennes to pray, to fight and to influence your husbands and sons to defend the army and the lib-

---

Right endorsed women's suffrage. Drumont's *La Libre Parole* featured a column by one of the leading suffragists, Hubertine Auclert, for six months in 1894, and between 1906 and 1911 the anti-Semitic journal called for female suffrage (Hause, *Hubertine Auclert*, 157–60). In 1919 a significant portion of conservative and right-wing deputies would vote for women's suffrage (Hause and Kenney, *Women's Suffrage and Social Politics in the Third Republic*, 226).

84. Sociologists of religion have labeled this phenomenon "le dimorphisme sexuel." For a classic statement see Le Bras, *Etudes de sociologie religieuse*, I, 356–59. For a historical treatment of this phenomenon in the Nord, see Bonnie Smith, *Ladies of the Leisure Class: The Bourgeoises of Northern France in the Nineteenth Century* (Princeton, 1981), 94, 113, 116–17, 120.

85. Police report, September 23, 1902, Dossier Pelletan, MI 25359, AN.

erty of the church, all in the name of the blood of your ancestors. Long live God, freedom and France." In Lyons La Ligue des femmes françaises produced a striking color poster of Jeanne d'Arc accompanied by a song recounting the heroism of the virgin who had repelled the barbarians and saved Catholic France. Republican women did respond to this effort to equate antirepublicanism and women's interests. Trade union women in Marseilles—match makers, laundry workers, fish sellers, factory workers, and office employees—demonstrated to condemn Les Dames de la patrie française, denouncing them as "reactionary, clerical, aristocratic and capitalist." The female trade unionists urged "their men" to vote socialist. It is significant that socialists, not Radicals, organized this counterdemonstration and that the left-wing view of women's relation to civic life was the mirror image of that of the Right. Women should influence "their men" to do the right thing. Finally, this instance of left-wing women's activity was the only such incident in the police reports on the 1902 electoral campaign, although there were regular entries on the well-organized activities of the Ligue des femmes françaises.[86] By 1905 the membership of the Ligue patriotique des françaises stood at a very impressive 320,000.[87]

It is hardly surprising that women's political allegiances should become part of the debate surrounding women's suffrage. The Republican women's suffrage organizations appealed to the Radical party congresses, calling on them to make their commitment to universal suffrage a reality. But influential leaders, Emile Combes for example, as well as sections of the party's rank and file, remained adamant opponents of women's suffrage. The ostensible reason that most Radicals offered for postponing or denying them full political equality was defense of the Republic against the onslaught of clerically controlled women. This was hardly a logical argument for those dedicated to "the sovereignty of universal suffrage." Radicals had not inquired about the political allegiances of men when they demanded and then defended universal male suffrage. This purported republican defense was tied to some Radicals' fear that any change in the electoral system might threaten their recently established prominence. Many among them could admit no distinction between their own electoral victories and the

86. Police report, Atmosphère politique, 1902 elections, April–May, 1902, F7 12541, AN.

87. Hause and Kenny, *Women's Suffrage and Social Politics in the Third Republic*, 63. How active all these members were is another issue.

survival of the Republic. The reality of many women's continued commitment to the Catholic church and the prominent position of such women in
stridently clerical and antirepublican organizations supplied justifications
for the Radicals' hesitation and resistance.

Defense against the clerical danger also served as a rationalization for
the deeper misogyny of some Radicals, who could not conceive of women
acting in the public arena. During the first half of the Third Republic, these
politicians lived in a world in which most social intercourse occurred exclusively among men. For some this led to a bemused incomprehension and
reduced interest in the woman question, for others to a deep antipathy toward women. Even those Radicals who identified themselves as supporters
of women's "emancipation" through greater education continued to speak
of women as defective, alien creatures whose slightest engagement in political issues was both manipulated and extremely dangerous. In the fall
of 1906 a northern Radical described the very serious battle of the sexes:
"During the conflict surrounding the church inventories, women headed
the revolt, poor things influenced by the will of the priest and by religious
hysteria. During the elections, which coincided with Easter, carried away
by an increase in religious devotions, they brought home the voting ballots
given out by the priest in the confessional. . . . Woman brings war into
the family. . . . and refuses her husband conjugal rights unless he promises
to vote the right way."[88] Despite the apparently happy relations with companion and wife, another declared supporter of women's rights, Camille
Pelletan could not imagine women as genuine partners. Being excluded
from the world of politics, they remained outside the most important concerns of republican men. As late as 1910, Camille Pelletan identified the
real issue as being who had the right to control a woman, the priest or
her husband. This dedicated individualist told a large banquet of youthful
supporters of secularism in Nioret, "It is blasphemous to think that a wife
can have ideas opposed to her husband's."[89] For those even less sympathetic
to women, anticlericalism sometimes served as an expression of meanness
toward women. To take only one example, General André proposed to the
Radical Congress of 1907 that all orphanages for the daughters of veterans

88. Piermé, *Compte rendu*, 21.
89. Police report, February 6, 1910, Dossier Pelletan, MI 25359, AN.

run by the Legion of Honor be closed. The reason for this "reform" was that the girls were receiving religious instruction.[90] The fate of these girls, once liberated from the nuns, was never considered. Although republican ideology always claimed that women must be emancipated from the priests, it never imagined women as citizens.

At several Radical congresses, where women were barred from attendance as delegates or even as observers, motions to endorse women's suffrage were easily defeated with little or no debate. Not until 1907, when they promulgated an endless list of reforms as their party program, did the Radicals include a statement on women. The party program began by reasserting the Radicals' intention to "revise the constitution in the most democratic sense possible" and again proclaimed the party's dedication to "the sovereignty of universal suffrage."[91] Nonetheless, in that year, when Radicals had considerable political power, the party offered the disfranchised half of the population "the gradual extension of the rights of women who ought to be legally protected in all the circumstances of their lives. Communal, departmental and national assistance ought to be provided for pregnant and poor women; the legislated rest of six weeks before and after giving birth should include women in small workshops, stores and in offices."[92] Gender-specific protection for mothers was much easier to promise than the vote. With thunderous silence the Radicals ignored the question of votes for women.[93]

Strident antifeminists, however, did not constitute the entire party; it also included the leading parliamentary spokesmen for women's rights. Left radicals such as Camille Pelletan, perpetuating his father's support for women's rights, had been a member of the Groupe parlementaire de défense des droits de la femme since its founding in 1895. Originally the group had only thirty-six members and was largely inactive between 1895 and 1906. Bloc des gauches electoral victories revived it after 1906. Radicals such as Ferdinand Buisson, Joseph Caillaux, Justin Godart, and Adolphe Messimy were important members of the group, which in 1906 could count ninety-six

90. Le Parti radical, 7e Congrès, tenu à Nancy, October, 1907, p. 245.
91. Ibid., Party program, Articles 1 and 2; Hause and Kenney, Women's Suffrage and Social Politics in the Third Republic, 100.
92. Le Parti radical, 7e Congrès, tenu à Nancy, October, 1907, Party program.
93. Hause, Hubertine Auclert, 191–94.

members. Independent socialist René Viviani and moderates Jules Siegfried and Joseph Reinach were also adherents. By 1910 the group's membership stood at two hundred. But this parliamentary association did not unequivocally endorse women's suffrage and like many other parliamentary groups had a limited impact on legislation. Nonetheless, its existence and growth demonstrated the perception on the part of a growing number of republicans, and especially left Radicals, that they could not avoid the woman question.

Among the "friends of women's rights" in the Chamber the strongest and most sincere was Ferdinand Buisson. During the 1906–1910 legislature he was a prominent member of the important Committee on Universal Suffrage and a staunch supporter of women's struggle for political equality. In 1906 this committee received a bill calling for the municipal vote for all women. Finally, in 1909 Buisson reported favorably to the committee. The Radical party now promised the suffrage organizations its endorsement but cautioned that a full debate could only follow other major reforms of the electoral system.[94] By placing the discussion of women's suffrage *after* the resolution of the complex and controversial issue of proportional representation, the Radicals essentially guaranteed that they would engage in no serious debate. In 1911 Buisson published his report as *Le Vote des femmes*. Not surprisingly, the much awaited parliamentary discussion of women's suffrage did not take place before World War I.[95]

Buisson's widely disseminated argument in support of women's suffrage contained several contradictions as he struggled to promote the political emancipation of women with the democratic ideology of left radicalism. A staunch belief in progress, rationalism, and a Protestant-inspired morality sustained Buisson's republicanism. He discovered that there were difficul-

94. This was the third women's suffrage bill sent to committee. The first bill, proposed in 1890, recommended the vote for all unmarried women in national elections; the second, submitted in 1901, limited the vote to unmarried and divorced women. Yet another bill sponsored by René Viviani called for the vote for married women in municipal elections but was never formally sent to committee (Hause, *Hubertine Auclert*, 172–76, 193).

95. The bill was presented to the Chamber in June, 1914; the outbreak of war again postponed any debate. In 1919, 1925, 1932, and 1935 the Chamber passed bills for women's suffrage by overwhelming votes and the Senate, dominated by Radicals, blocked each bill. In April, 1944, General Charles De Gaulle decreed women's suffrage.

ties in adjusting the ideology of male equality, separate gender spheres, and gender hierarchy to the demands for women's political rights.[96] In *Le Vote des femmes* Buisson sought to present women's suffrage as another inevitable step in the march of human progress, fulfilling the rationalist vision of "the natural rights of all human beings." The actual political struggle for women's rights had begun with the French Revolution, according to Buisson. It seemed obvious to him that the Third Republic, heir of the Great Revolution, would inevitably extend political and legal equality to women. He proudly pointed out that steps in this direction had already been taken in the realm of republican educational reforms. "Elementary schools," he claimed, "have familiarized the nation with the idea of seeing children of the two sexes being treated with perfect equality. . . . In the lycée the female staff is subject to the same conditions, to the same manner of recruitment, the same exams and the same inspection as the male staff."[97] Buisson predicted that women's rights would continue to evolve naturally until they would eventually include the right to vote in municipal elections and even someday in national elections.

While he outlined this hoped-for progressive evolutionary development, Buisson was aware that it was at variance with historical facts and with contemporary French conditions. After surveying the advances of women's suffrage in other nations, he concluded with considerable dismay: "It is France that is backward. . . . We will soon be alone, or as good as alone, identified with Spain and Turkey." Buisson knew full well that the lycée curriculum for girls differed from that for boys and did not prepare young women to enter the university. Nor were female and male teachers or students treated the same. And no matter how energetically he sought to link women's rights and suffrage to the Revolution, he was too honest not to admit that in prerevolutionary France there had been "numerous, strange examples of the right to vote being given to women." Buisson's discomfort is palpable as he must concede that the Revolution deprived some women of rights they had had during the Ancien Régime. Further, he also had to grant that the Jacobin revolutionaries treated women who claimed their rights

96. Buisson's support for women's rights, his arguments, and the contradictions he encountered echoed the views expressed a generation earlier by Eugène Pelletan, whom Buisson admired. See Buisson's preface to Petit, *Eugène Pelletan.*

97. Buisson, *Vote des femmes,* 19, specifically referring to Condorcet; *ibid.,* 36.

with "extreme harshness and a most unjust disdain."[98] French republican-ism and women's claims for emancipation, though emerging in the same historical and ideological context, had from their origins been in conflict. Buisson's argument for evolutionary, inevitable progress lost much of its persuasiveness. Despite all his goodwill and commitment to women's suf-frage, Buisson could not simply incorporate the struggle for women's rights into the heritage of the Revolution and the nineteenth-century republican formulation of equality and progress.

Although few Radicals would acknowledge it, women's demand for the vote and the party's refusal to act struck at the very heart of republican legiti-macy. Universal suffrage was the most fundamental tenet of republicanism. Popular sovereignty had purportedly defeated the principles of monarchical rule and privilege. In the early twentieth century women, deprived of the vote, challenged the claim of the Third Republic to legitimacy based on universal suffrage.[99] The Radical party, despite prominent dissenters such as Buisson, rejected this demand. As they had in the late eighteenth cen-tury, republicans explicitly declared that half the population was, in their view, unfit to be citizens. Although some tried to alter the highly gendered republican ideology and practice, many more doggedly resisted any trans-formation. Women continued to be excluded from the essential republican categories of individual and citizen. The Radicals' inability to reform these critical categories revealed a deep immobility and rigidity. The question of votes for women exposed most dramatically that the Radicals' commitment to equality coexisted with a powerful allegiance to hierarchy.

The suffrage question underscored how deeply Radical republican ideol-ogy venerated patriarchal privilege. The profound impact of gender on the democratic movement enabled it to accept with greater ease other forms

---

98. *Ibid.*, 306–308, 15.

99. Simultaneously that legitimacy was also challenged by the Right and Left in their campaign to transform the electoral system and introduce proportional representation (David Sumler, "Domestic Influences on the Nationalist Revival in France," *French Historical Studies,* VI [Fall, 1970], 517–38). Ironically, the Radicals of the 1880s had made similar demands for electoral reform; see Chapter III. By 1906 Pelletan no longer wanted to alter the existing electoral system despite claims to the contrary (Le Parti radical, 6ᵉ *Congrès,* tenu à Lille, October, 1906, pp. 182–85).

of hierarchy, exclusion, and authority. Having achieved sustained electoral victories, the Radicals, as a dominant party, had to elaborate policies for institutions of authority in the state and society. An extended internal party debate took place, examining what precisely should be the consequences and content of democratic electoral victory. The conflict between their commitment to egalitarian reforms and a new responsibility to protect state power severely shook the Radical party in the early twentieth century. Left Radicals such as Pelletan and Buisson insisted that the Radicals' strength and enthusiasm were being squandered as they strayed from their popular democratic aspirations. Others such as de Lanessan called for a reevaluation of the party's constituents and programs and the elimination of what they viewed as outmoded Radical traditions.

In practice, most Radicals opted to maintain and defend the authority of the state, even against the demands of some of their constituents, such as vintners, teachers, and postal clerks. This practice increasingly contradicted their rhetoric, which fervently continued to defend the "Revolution as a bloc" and to call for the fulfillment of its egalitarian promises. The issue of their relation to authority and hierarchy was not only a subject for dispute among Radicals but also the subject of criticism directed at them from outside the party. Relations with the Socialists and revolutionary syndicalists constantly revolved around the question of the Radicals' commitment to state authority. In addition, the Socialists increasingly questioned the Radicals' ability and willingness to pass their own reform program. The nationalist Right denounced the Radicals as a party intrinsically incapable of maintaining and extending the discipline and authority which the French nation so desperately needed. As we shall see in the next chapter, these very different external critics also contributed to the unraveling of left-wing Radical democracy.

IX LEFT-WING RADICALISM AND ITS EXTERNAL CRITICS

The Radicals' uncertainties about how to respond to socialism and the organizing French working class have often been identified as the source of their dilemmas in the early twentieth century. The previous chapter demonstrated that serious differences existed among Radicals. These internal conflicts centered as much on competing visions of democracy and democratic governing as on proposals for alliance with the Socialists. This ongoing, often vituperative debate to define radicalism was central to its crisis in the early twentieth century. Nonetheless, voices outside radicalism further exacerbated this crisis; this chapter will explore those external criticisms and the Radicals' responses. Without question, Radicals, and especially left Radicals, were obsessed about their relations with the Socialists. As important, however, were the denunciations of the nationalist Right, which created a powerful negative image of radicalism.

Since the Commune, Radicals and socialists had had complex ties. The rapid growth and political consolidation of socialism in the early twentieth century made those relations even more problematic. The formation in 1905 of the unified Socialist party, affiliated with the Second International, the Section française de l'Internationale ouvrière (the SFIO), was a momentous development. Emile Combes was convinced that the creation of the SFIO and its commitment to oppose all bourgeois governments doomed the Bloc des gauches and his ministry.[1] Radicals were especially preoccupied with their electoral and parliamentary alliances with the SFIO; simultaneously, the members of the Left of the party were constantly examining how they could and ought to distinguish themselves from Socialists. The emergence of revolutionary syndicalists in the leadership of the Confédération générale du travail further complicated the connection between Radicals

---

1. Combes, *Mon Ministère*, 226.

and Socialists. Under syndicalist leadership the largest national trade union organization repudiated any links with parliamentary politics and promoted workers' direct action through strikes.

The Socialists challenged the Radicals as competitors for votes and contested their claim to be the inheritors of the Revolution. Socialists claimed to be the more legitimate "sons of the Revolution," fully dedicated to the egalitarian promise. They argued that their social and economic analysis, based on the "reality of class," was far superior to the Radicals' fuzzy talk of the "people." Perhaps the Socialists' greatest success and the Radicals' greatest weakness was the persuasiveness of this socialist class analysis. The Radicals did indeed have difficulty defining and defending their categories of the people and the citizen. Most Radicals, like much of the political elite of the early twentieth century, did view their world as one in which class dominated. The Right of the party, as we have seen in the previous chapter, hoped to transform the Radicals into the spokesmen for the economic and social interests of small property owners. Other Radicals, eager to remain men of the Left, reiterated their commitment to reform legislation essentially aimed at improving working-class conditions. At the same time, these left Radicals insisted that their party must represent all the "people." Socialists and Radicals competed not only for electoral support but also for the very categories that defined their world. In this latter competition, the Socialists clearly outdistanced the Radicals in the first decade of the twentieth century.

Although Socialists and Radicals viewed each other as competitors, they also needed each other as allies. Each group was indispensable to the other in the system of multiparty, runoff elections. Left-wing Radicals regarded the electoral and parliamentary alliance between Radicals and Socialists as the political means to establish a genuinely democratic republic able to implement programmatic reform policies, including not only the separation of church and state but also the progressive income tax, social insurance programs, and factory regulation. At the same time, then, that the organized working class was becoming a more assertive presence in the political and economic arenas, the electoral coalition between Radicals and Socialists continued. To be sure, there were local ruptures and a good deal of mutual denunciatory rhetoric at both the national and local levels, but in general the alliance worked. It secured second-round election victories for candidates of both parties.

Pelletan in particular was an important link in this association. His collaboration with the socialist leader Jean Jaurès dated back to the 1890s. They had shared innumerable platforms, speaking to audiences of workers, students, shopkeepers, and civil servants on issues ranging from the tyranny of the Senate to the need to liberate Crete. They also shared journalistic platforms. Pelletan and Jaurès were regular, featured contributors to the important provincial Radical daily, *La Dépêche* of Toulouse. The Socialist Francis de Pressensé, writing in the Radical *L'Aurore*, praised Pelletan as a Radical who on becoming minister had abandoned neither his program of reform nor his allies to the Left. As late as 1911, the conservative newspaper *Le Temps* identified Pelletan and Jaurès as "the Siamese twins of the extreme Left." Although not as reliable as the electoral alliance, the parliamentary coalition of Radicals and Socialists in the Chamber did elaborate and enact reform legislation.[2]

The growth of revolutionary syndicalism and its mounting militancy gave pause to many Radicals, even the most left-wing. In the first decade of the twentieth century there was much labor activism, and strike rates increased throughout the industrialized world.[3] In France, anarchists, leading the largest national trade union organization, formulated the praxis of revolutionary syndicalism. There has been considerable debate about the extent to which this leadership represented the working class or even the union rank and file, which itself was a small minority of all workers. What is clear is that syndicalists now dominated the rhetoric of labor relations.[4] Not only did the CGT call for militant direct action to forge class consciousness,

2. *L'Aurore*, July 1, 1902; *Le Temps* quoted in Goldberg, *Life of Jaurès*, 156; Stone, *Search for Social Peace*, chap. 4.

3. There were two dramatic peaks in the rising strike activity in France, Germany, and Great Britain: one in 1906 and the second in 1910–1912. See Peter J. Stearns, *Lives of Labor: Work in a Maturing Industrial Society* (New York, 1975), 314.

4. Peter J. Stearns, *Revolutionary Syndicalism and French Labor: A Cause Without Rebels* (New Brunswick, N.J., 1971), and F. Ridley, *Revolutionary Syndicalism in France: The Direct Action of Its Time* (Cambridge, Eng., 1970), take diametrically opposing views of the significance of syndicalism. Bernard Moss offers a longer view in *The Origins of the French Labor Movement, 1830–1914: The Socialism of Skilled Workers* (Berkeley, 1976). Michael J. Hanagan, *The Logic of Solidarity: Artisans and Industrial Workers in Three French Towns, 1871–1914* (Urbana, 1980), provides a useful analysis at the local shop-floor level.

culminating in the ultimate general strike, but its 1906 Amiens Congress repudiated all political parties and parliamentary institutions. Its members further declared themselves revolutionary internationalists, opposed to nationalism and militarism. They launched a passionate campaign against the use of the army during strikes and against military discipline. Parallel trends within the Socialist party supported and encouraged this antimilitarism. Gustave Hervé, socialist leader of the rural department of the Yonne, had already achieved notoriety for a 1901 article that called for planting the tricolor in a dung heap. By 1906 his weekly newspaper *La Guerre social* was widely read, and he was a force to be reckoned with in the SFIO.

In the fall of 1902 the Dreyfusard alliance was still savoring its electoral victory, the formation of a Radical government, and the Bloc des gauches parliamentary majority. The parliamentary Left felt certain of its ability to curb the power of the church and the army and perhaps even initiate social reform. It was also a time of growing confrontation between the new government and clerical supporters as the state began to implement the 1901 Law on Associations, which outlawed unauthorized religious congregations. In this climate the relatively new journal of the CGT, *La Voix du peuple*, printed an appeal to French soldiers. The final message of the manifesto, urging soldiers not to "murder your fathers! . . . not to kill your brothers! and . . . not to shoot down your comrades!" might have been read sympathetically by some Radicals. We know that Radicals of the Pelletan circle felt uneasy with the use of the army to maintain internal "order." But this manifesto began by praising a Catholic officer, Colonel de Saint-Remy, who had disobeyed orders and refused to close an unauthorized convent. "We consider that by refusing to act against 'the sisters' the CATHOLIC de Saint-Remy did well. We consider that by weighing the feeling which inspired this officer's act of insubordination and by delivering a decision which amounts to an acquittal the Conseil de guerre has done well. . . . SOLDIERS! Be sure to remember this decision and use it to your benefit." In a brilliant maneuver the syndicalists had inverted a whole series of traditional hierarchies and assumptions. They would support any form of opposition to the state and military discipline. Appeals to republican or anticlerical solidarity could in no way restrain their intransigent opposition to the state and the army.[5]

5. "Manifeste aux Soldats," *La Voix du peuple*, November 9, 1902; also Police report, antimilitarist meeting, Bourse du travail, November 9, 1902, M6 3328, AD/BR.

These issues of antiparliamentarianism, antipatriotism, and antimilitarism, much more than the question of class, drove Radicals to a frenzy. The 1907 official statement of the Radical party's Executive Committee was clear about what Radicals could and could not accept on the part of their working-class allies. "We do not want to exclude any element of advanced democracy; but those who . . . use criminal propaganda and attempt to give to the most evil instincts the appearance of a doctrine, they have already placed themselves outside the Bloc. They would repudiate the Fatherland and the Republic. The Radical and Radical-socialist Congress cannot divorce the fatherland from the Republic. . . . [The Congress] refuses its support to any candidate who would sanction the disorganization of the armed services of the Republic."[6] Three years earlier, dissident Radicals had accused their fellow Radical Camille Pelletan of "disorganizing" the navy. The entire party, including its left wing, feared that the syndicalists posed such a danger to the army. One of the staunchest leaders of left-wing radicalism, Ferdinand Buisson, repeated the same condemnation of antimilitarism. He identified revolutionary syndicalism as one of the principal causes for the increasing conservatism within the party. He was convinced that "there is no possibility of an understanding between revolutionary syndicalists and the Radicals, even those Radicals who are most socialistically inclined. Radicals may proclaim themselves and act like socialists and trade unionists; nothing could be more legitimate. But this can only be on condition that they remain Radicals, in other words radically republican . . . parliamentarians [and] the inheritors of democracy."[7] Buisson insisted that the revolutionaries in the CGT, with their rejection of parliamentary politics and their anarchist antipathy to any state, were fundamentally incompatible with Radical tradition and practice. In its very first electoral manifesto the Radical party Executive Committee had insisted on its patriotism: "We are greater patriots than anyone else."[8] The syndicalist stance was shockingly illegitimate to Radicals who identified so strongly with the republican nation-state.

6. Georges Gabius de Champville, *Le Comité executif du parti républicain radical et radical-socialiste de 1897 à 1907* (Paris, 1907), 41.

7. Buisson, *Politique radical*, 246.

8. Le Parti républicain radical et radical-socialiste, *Manifeste du Parti républicain radical et radical-socialiste* (Paris, 1902).

Buisson's statements also emphasized that there were some socialists and trade unionists with whom Radicals could and ought to be aligned. Buisson especially underscored the natural continuity between the Radical-socialist position and that of much of the Socialist party. The Radicals' patriotism included devotion to emancipatory principles. The same electoral manifesto also insisted, "We love France with all our mind and all our heart: it is the country where we were born, where we loved, suffered and hoped, but it is also the country of liberty."[9] This republican patriotism distinguished Radicals from their opponents on the Right. As patriots they considered themselves "irreconcilably antinationalists." The Executive Committee of the party declared: "In the army of democracy, each battalion maintains its own action and its own program, but all march as a tightly unified body in defense of the Republic. Nationalism is a mask concealing the reactionary forces. The union and discipline of all the republican forces will lead to our triumph. Long live the Republic."[10] At the beginning of the Bloc des gauches the Radicals recognized their differences with the socialists, but they also assumed considerable agreement in the struggle against their opponents, the "forces of reaction." And in political reality those bonds continued to hold for the entire pre–World War I period.

This socialist support was critical to the Combes government. It operated on both the national and local levels, reflecting a significant segment of working-class opinion. Socialist groups constituted a significant number of the testimonials sent to Combes and Pelletan from organizations of the Bouches-du-Rhône. From Marseilles they included L'Avant garde socialiste révolutionnaire, Les Etudiants socialistes, and La Jeunesse socialiste. These groups considered their support for the Radical government and the Bloc des gauches and their commitment to socialist aspirations as interdependent. In early 1904 they even generally agreed on the delicate issue of the military. The Groupe amical des Etudiants socialistes de Marseille et du Midi congratulated Combes and Pelletan and urged them to continue their struggle for the separation of church and state and for social reform. Most important, these students called for the passage of the two-

9. *Ibid.*

10. Comité executif du Parti républicain radical et radical-socialiste (Combes, Desmouns, Vallé, Bourgeois, Brisson, Faure, Mesureur, Pelletan) in Police report, Atmosphère politique, Gard, Elections 1902, April 23, 1902, F7 12542, AN.

year conscription law, "a democratic law . . . a step toward the abolition of standing armies and the creation of national militias." The prefect of the Bouches-du-Rhône reported to the minister of the interior that local political groups, "for the most part socialists," were organizing demonstrations in support of the Combes government.[11] Undoubtedly many of these groups were ephemeral, and in the years before the formation of a unified party the label *socialist* was adopted rather casually. Yet these socialist supporters of the Bloc did include even the Marxist Parti ouvrier français. From the coastal town of Ciotat the local section of the Parti ouvrier sent five messages to the Combes government between September, 1903, and November, 1904. Each endorsed government policies and members. The last message of November 7, 1904, was sent when the government was entering its final crisis. A family soirée held by the Parti ouvrier of Ciotat brought together six hundred "citoyennes et citoyens républicains socialistes" who sent their support to the government and urged its leaders to "maintain the course they have laid out."[12]

This broad left-wing sentiment did not evaporate with the fall of the Combes government. The 1905 Radical Congress stressed the party's confidence in the continuation of the Bloc. The Executive Committee was certain that the new SFIO would "proceed in alliance with the [Radical party] to liberate humanity from the slavery of religion and capitalism." Pelletan's address at the Congress promised, "What the last legislature has done against the power of clericalism, the next will do for the solution of economic problems." In preparation for the critical 1906 elections, Pelletan wrote a series of articles in the *Petit Provençal* criticizing the antimilitarism of Hervé, but he identified it with the antirepublicanism of the clericals. Pelletan equated the two "extremes" and described both as the "enemies of democracy, the nation and the real army." At the same time, he also clearly stressed that the majority of socialists were, like the Radicals, staunch opponents of reaction. In his electoral statement Pelletan spoke of "our socialist

11. Adresses de sympathie et félicitation à Combes, March 27, 1904, Carton 3, Bouches-du-Rhône, 73 AP, AN.

12. Messages were sent September 20 and November 15, 1903, January 25, March 19, and November 7, 1904 (Félicitations à Combes, Bouches-du-Rhône, 73 AP, AN). Ciotat was the site of a small naval arsenal with special ties to Pelletan. See also Parti ouvrier d'avant-garde Aix, May 19, 1904, *ibid.*

friends" and the critical need to maintain the Bloc des gauches to ensure further reform legislation. He pledged himself to the Bloc, to the extension of social reforms, and to continued opposition to "high finance, big business, [and] all financial privileges."[13]

The elections of 1906 attested to the continuing power of the Bloc des gauches. Radicals gained control of 46 percent of the Chamber's seats, and the number of Socialist seats increased as well.[14] Following the second round of voting in late May, Pelletan labeled the Left's victory a triumph in which "all those elements of the republican party which claimed the title socialist are those which won the most seats." In other words, his Radical-socialist group and the SFIO were the real winners. He praised the "admirable discipline . . . and solidarity of the Bloc." He was proud of his efforts in support of "the comrades, whether they might be Radicals, socialists or independents." Nonetheless, underlying this genuinely felt unity and triumph, Pelletan expressed a certain tension and disappointment. In the flush of victory Pelletan could afford to chide the SFIO for its orthodoxy. In a show of good spirits, he ironically questioned the Marxists, "As for the Radical-socialist party, you will grant that it hasn't yet become a fossil."[15] Differences had been less jovial before the election. In his own district Pelletan had faced challenges from both a moderate republican and a Socialist. In an article published immediately before the election Pelletan employed the biting sarcasm of his early journalism to criticize the SFIO for its policy of presenting Socialist candidates in every possible district, including his own.[16]

As we saw in Chapter V, Pelletan well understood his own local supporters, including the significant portion of socialists among them. Members of

13. Le Parti radical, Rapport du Comité executif, 5e Congrès, tenu à Paris, October, 1905, p. 29; Camille Pelletan, Déclaration, ibid., 179; "Révolte des officiers" and "Les Cléricaux et l'Armée," Le Petit Provençal, February 28, 1906, and March 20, 1906; ibid., May 1, 1906. For fuller discussion of Pelletan's attitude toward Socialists in 1906, see Chapter V.

14. The number of Socialists in the Chamber increased from forty-three to fifty-four. David Watson characterizes the 1906 election as one of the greatest victories of the Left during the Third Republic (Clemenceau, 177, 423).

15. "Le Vote du 20 mai," Le Petit Provençal, May 24, 1906.

16. Camille Pelletan, "Nouvelles impressions de Voyage," Le Petit Provençal, May 2, 1906. Similar criticism was voiced by other columnists; see Camille Freddy, "Pelletan et Brisson," ibid., May 4, 1906. For a fuller discussion, see Chapter V.

the Fédération socialiste des Bouches-du-Rhône were by no means unanimous in their support of a candidate to stand against Pelletan. Defying the departmental endorsement of Louis Shoë, an administrator of a local Bourse du travail, the largest group of Salon Socialists supported Camille Pelletan.[17] The issues of alliances between the Radicals and the SFIO and the maintenance of the Bloc created as much debate among Socialists as they did among Radicals. In 1906 the local SFIO candidate received only 8 percent of the vote and Pelletan won easily on the first round despite opponents from the Right and Left.

The election of 1906 did not put to rest the increasing doubts among Socialists about the Radicals' commitment to reform and the increasing fears among Radicals about the Socialists' commitment to revolution. These doubts and fears increased dramatically, partly reinforcing one another, partly sustained by the actions of Radicals, Socialists, and workers in the years 1906 to 1910. The Clemenceau government, formed in October, 1906, was a bitter disappointment to Socialists and even more so to left-wing Radicals. Initially, there seemed little doubt that Clemenceau as premier would be able to convince the Senate to approve the long-debated and long-promised old age pension which the Chamber had passed immediately before the spring elections. The creation of a Ministry of Labor and the appointment of an independent socialist to head it appeared to be an auspicious beginning. The presence of the Radical Joseph Caillaux as minister of finance seemed to ensure a serious commitment to the progressive income tax. Yet Clemenceau's ongoing war with the Confédération générale du travail preoccupied most of this ministry. The premier was committed to bringing the full force of the state against the revolutionary syndicalists. This conflict hardened Clemenceau's intransigence and made him willing to alienate traditional Radical constituencies such as southern winegrowers and civil servants rather than sacrifice any shred of state authority.[18] By the end of his ministry Clemenceau had earned the epithets "strikebreaker" and "head cop [le premier flic] of France."[19]

---

17. Police reports, Elections 1906, February 5, March 26, 1906, II M3 45, AD/BR.

18. See Chapter VIII.

19. Jacques Juillard, *Clemenceau, briseur des grèves. L'Affaire de Draveil Villeneuve-St Georges*, (1908) (Paris, 1965).

The majority of Radical deputies, ignoring their left leaders' condemnation of the premier, had endorsed Clemenceau's actions against the civil servants. With even greater enthusiasm, most Radical deputies supported Clemenceau in his campaign against revolutionary syndicalism, neglecting their party program. The Clemenceau government and the revolutionary stance of the CGT gave the left-wing Radicals little room to maneuver. In 1907 Le Petit Provençal, which had staunchly supported the Bloc, ran a series of confusing and contradictory articles. On April 16 Pelletan had condemned strikes: "Let us say very clearly that it is a bad business when one pushes workers into strikes." Ten days later, independent socialist Siméon Flaissières, several times mayor of Marseilles, denounced the syndicalists and Hervé. He asserted: "We will defend the government and at the same time we will improve it. . . . Its enemies are our enemies." True socialists in his view were patriots, and antimilitarism was a subversive German import. Yet by mid-May Pelletan was expressing greater concern about Clemenceau's actions. Pelletan criticized the Socialists for their unwillingness to repudiate "anarchism," but his principal attacks were reserved for his former collaborator. He was convinced that the premier was dividing the Bloc and that such disunity would destroy the Radical party. Radical deputies might support Clemenceau, but Pelletan did not think the entire rank and file would. They would shift their allegiance to the SFIO. Within the Radical party there were "old-timers who did not want to make a lie of their entire lives. . . . The party is committing suicide."[20]

For many Socialists, however, the actions of the Clemenceau government and its Radical supporters demonstrated the urgent need to follow a more rigorous politics of class and end all interclass electoral alliances. In the fall of 1909 Marcel Cachin, one of the founders of the Parti ouvrier français and an important leader in the unified Socialist party, visited the Bouches-du-Rhône, speaking at several workers' meetings. At a gathering of fifty Cachin urged workers to stop voting for Radicals: "The working class must not vote for the Radical-socialists, because this party for a long time has had the parliamentary majority, and has not had the courage up to

---

20. Camille Pelletan, "Grève manquée," Le Petit Provençal, April 16, 1907; Siméon Flaissières, "Vive la République," ibid., April 26, 1907; Pelletan, "Le Parti Radical et le Cabinet," ibid., May 14, 1907.

this moment to accomplish anything appreciable." A few days later, he addressed a much larger crowd of five hundred at Ciotat, whose socialists had in the past expressed their enthusiasm for the Combes ministry and the Bloc des gauches. Cachin warned workers against the Radicals' false promises and also appealed to civil servants: "The Clemenceau government, having violated the working class, murders and shoots down strikers, brutalizes low-level civil servants and creates disaffection in the Radical party."[21]

This visit of an important SFIO leader prepared the way the following year for a much more forceful challenge to Camille Pelletan by a Socialist candidate. A more unified local Socialist organization endorsed P. Marius-André, a railroad worker, trade unionist, party stalwart, and longtime follower of Jules Guesde. His campaign statement insisted that this was not a personal campaign against Pelletan but rather a repudiation of the Radical party. Pelletan would be confronted as *"the representative of a party, the party in power,* against whom, as the candidate of the *Socialist party,* I have the duty to fight; *the [Socialist] party [is] opposed to all fractions of the capitalist class.* " The Socialist condemnation of the Radicals was unremitting. Their politics were "powerless"; they had *"betrayed their promises";* they had outrageously voted to increase their own salaries by 6,000 francs. Even those Radicals who had voted against "the brutal blunders of the Clemenceau government" had no excuse as long as they remained attached to the Radical party. "They have no right to refuse the responsibilities of this party, in whose name they hope to be reelected." True (*sincères*) republicans would become Socialists.[22] The observation about "républicains sincères" was clearly directed at Pelletan and used the familiar Radical rhetoric of authenticity. Despite this challenge, Pelletan was able to win a first-round victory, although the percentage of votes cast for the veteran Radical deputy declined from the 58 percent in 1906 to 51 percent in the 1910 contest. More significant, the percentage of votes cast for the Socialist candidate increased dramatically, from 8 percent in 1906 to 42 percent in 1910.[23] Even in Pelletan's bastion the Radical hold was weakening. In addition to seniority and ill health, the very real possibility that he might lose

21. Police reports, November 30, December 1, 1909, M6 3404, AD/BR.

22. SFIO, "Aux Electeurs de la 2e Circonscription d'Aix," in Police report, Elections 1910, II M3 45, AD/BR.

23. Election results, 1910, Bouches-du-Rhône, 2e Circonscription d'Aix, C 6556, AN.

the 1914 legislative election motivated Pelletan to seek indirect election as senator from the Bouches-du-Rhône in 1912.

Throughout the department there were constant reports of declining support for the Radical party. In the spring of 1913 a meeting of Radicals in a Marseilles neighborhood (canton) attracted only twenty people. Much of their time was devoted to an analysis of why "their party has suffered a slowing down of its progress." Their answer: self-serving, false republicans had flooded the party. A few months later in Aix, a gathering of the Radical party was a complete failure. Most who attended were Socialists and trade unionists there to harass the Radicals.[24] In the years immediately preceding World War I there was no decline of electoral support for a broad democratic program of reform. There was, however, a shift away from the Radical party in the 1914 elections.[25] Some earlier Radical supporters voted for moderate republicans; some voted for the Socialist party. Many voters dedicated to democratic aspirations apparently believed that opposition deputies, rather than those entangled with the government, could better represent them.

Within the Radical party there was an ever-growing hostility to the Socialists and even more to revolutionary syndicalists. Although left Radicals continued to be revered publicly as the "grand old men" of the party, their influence waned. The very language of radicalism changed, and the most dramatic shifts occurred in the patriotic speeches of devotion to France. Pelletan's distinction between a republican patriotism, committed to the French revolutionary tradition of liberty, and an alien, bellicose nationalism was abandoned. Significantly, religious vocabulary was frequently adopted to describe the Radicals' loyalty to the nation. The emotionalism Radicals had condemned among clericals was now praised among patriots. A 1912 regional party pamphlet, Le Parti radical et le patriotisme, elaborated this new stance: "There certainly are reasons to love the fatherland . . . instinctively from the heart: memories of the most insignificant things . . . the power of filial love . . . our love of the French soil." The author went on to compare the "French soul" with that of the ancient Greeks. In a

24. Police reports, February 16, April 8, 1913, M6 3404, AD/BR.

25. Radical-Socialists, however, did retain Pelletan's seat in the second district of Aix. In the 1912 and 1914 elections the Radical candidate supported by Pelletan waged a stiff fight against an SFIO candidate. In both cases the Radical, Auguste Girard, was elected on the second round.

startling effort to identify France with all past heroes, he equated the soldiers of the medieval Crusades who fought for God with the soldiers of 1789 who fought for humanity. He pronounced the anarchists of the CGT anathema, having committed "sacrileges against reason." Even more reprehensible were the antimilitarists. The Republic, the nation, and the army all deserved the greatest respect. "The truth is that most officers . . . treat the soldiers parentally, fraternally."[26] Eliminated was the critique of the antidemocratic military hierarchy. Paternal authority and fraternal bonds easily coexisted in the view of the author of this Radical pamphlet. Barrès would have been comfortable with such sentiments. Similar rhetoric was heard from the podium of the Thirteenth Radical Congress in the far southern town of Pau. In the opening speech of the Congress, Radicals called on Socialists to restore the Bloc, but they also castigated the SFIO for having "blasphemed against patriotic duty." The Radicals presented themselves as "pious pilgrims proclaiming our love for France, immortal and sacred. Citizens, is not our party the ideal national party!"[27]

Yet even in the midst of this new nationalist fervor, the left Radicals continued to insist on the necessity of the Bloc alliance, and the party rank and file continued to applaud them. In 1910 Pelletan proudly explained his position to a provincial meeting of the Jeunesse laique. "I am neither a member of the SFIO nor a collectivist; I am a believer in individual property, but I fight side by side with the SFIO against the clericals and the financiers. . . . [We are] divided over principles . . . united in the battle. . . . All the children of the Revolution must be united in the face of the common enemy, the Church."[28] The rhetoric was a bit worn, and the Socialists would hardly concur that the church was their principal enemy. Nonetheless, Pelletan's urgency to maintain the alliance of the Bloc and to maintain the Radicals as a party of the Left was certainly genuine. Three years later, at the same Radical Congress inaugurated by the nationalist declaration cited above, Pelletan expanded on his position. He called for united action "among all those who want to lead the movement toward democracy and social progress whatever may be our doctrinal

26. J. Cinna, Le Parti radical et le patriotisme (Tarn-et-Garonne, 1912), 23–25, 31.

27. Le Parti radical, Ferron discours, 13ᵉ Congrès, tenu à Pau, October, 1913, pp. 7–8.

28. Police report, Pelletan address to La Jeunesse laique de Niort, February 6, 1910, Dossier Pelletan, MI 25359, AN.

differences. . . . We have no enemies on our Left. . . . We have changed neither our words nor our feelings." But they had changed. Even Pelletan, still committed to his left radicalism and the Bloc des gauches, was forced to add a caveat to his ringing call for unity of all "true sons of the Revolution." In a parenthesis he noted, "Of course, I exclude those who have declared their scorn for the French fatherland."[29]

Loyalty to *la patrie française* was an issue on which Radicals felt particularly vulnerable. Their adoption of an increasingly religious rhetoric when describing their patriotism and their frenzied attacks on antimilitarism attested to the Radicals' intense feelings and their insecurity on this issue. Questions about devotion to the "fatherland" had served as the dissident Radicals' principal and most pointed criticism of Pelletan as minister of the navy. It was the issue that most bitterly divided the party as a growing minority of Radicals doubted their own ability to exercise state authority. It was also the issue that most immediately dissolved the Bloc des gauches' parliamentary majority and its support for the Combes government. The majority could not hold when the government was exposed as having tampered with the army. Radicals who had always associated themselves with an ardent, Jacobin patriotism were not prepared to have their patriotism questioned. To some degree, this heightened sensitivity about "patriotic loyalty" was the result of serious internal inconsistencies within radicalism, its commitment to democratic egalitarianism, and its acceptance of the hierarchical state. As early as the 1880s, a new variety of nationalists persistently and vociferously attacked this inconsistency. This public, strident attack of right-wing nationalists paralleled the internal and more calmly argued criticism of dissident Radicals. Although there was no direct coordination between nationalists and dissident Radicals, their campaigns reinforced each other. Together they were much more damaging to left-wing radicalism than were its differences with the Socialists.

Even before they adopted the name, nationalists appeared during the Boulangist episode. Key members of the Boulangist leadership saw themselves as bitterly disappointed Radicals for whom the defective parliamentary system of the Third Republic was a travesty of popular sovereignty.

29. Le Parti radical, Pelletan discours, *13ᵉ Congrès*, tenu à Pau, October, 1913, p. 50.

They emphasized the strong nationalist traditions of the Revolution and identified with defeated Communards as republican revolutionaries defending the nation. As we saw earlier, several such Boulangists, Laguerre, Laisant, and to a lesser degree Rochefort, had been intimate associates of Clemenceau and Pelletan in the 1880s. The Boulangist episode brought these men into contact with forces they earlier would have abhorred—Catholics, monarchists, and militarists. No permanent alliances were established in the late 1880s, but a shared experience of defeat and persecution established a new common ground between disgruntled former Radicals, now former Boulangists, and some members of the antirepublican Right. During the Dreyfus Affair the nationalist presence, personnel, rhetoric, and organizations definitively emerged. The affair also unquestionably placed the nationalists on the Right as participants in an anti-republican crusade.

Anti-Semitism, as articulated by Edouard Drumont, was a critical factor enabling men such as Rochefort—who had vaunted his left-wing revolutionary credentials—to join with those who decried the Revolution and republicanism.[30] The left-wing tradition of merging anti-Semitism and anticapitalism, a tradition Pelletan shared with Rochefort, lent credence to Drumont's denunciation of "international Jewry." Having once accepted the central tenet of Drumont's ideology, former Boulangists found his Catholicism and antirepublicanism palatable as well. The Dreyfus Affair saw the flowering of the nationalist extraparliamentary leagues such as Charles Maurras' Action française. Yet after all the intense courtroom and street dramas of the affair were played out, most nationalist candidates were resoundingly defeated in the legislative elections of 1902 and 1906, as well as in the municipal elections of 1904. That the nationalists should be furious against the victors of those elections, the Radicals, was hardly surprising.

Through the entire prewar period the nationalists had relatively little strength in parliament and failed in their electoral efforts.[31] Despite such limits (or perhaps because of them), they succeeded in constructing an extremely persuasive negative image of radicalism that has persisted through

30. Edouard Drumont gained enormous recognition with his first anti-Semitic book, *La France juive* (Paris, 1886), and then sustained his influence as the editor of the widely read anti-Semitic *La Libre Parole*, which first appeared in 1892. See also Nord, *Paris Shopkeepers*, 407.

31. Eugen Weber, *The Nationalist Revival in France, 1905–1914* (Berkeley, 1968), 13.

the twentieth century. By 1914 the nationalists had achieved considerable influence in Parisian cultural circles, including those of high literature, elite style, journalism, and popular entertainment.[32] From such critical positions they successfully belittled the Radicals and their commitment to democratic egalitarianism. More than any other critics, the nationalists undermined the Radicals' self-confidence by demonstrating that the "people" of the "popular" Parisian neighborhoods were no longer automatic supporters of democratic republicanism. They could then assert that the Radicals did not represent the nation. The power of the nationalist attack rested on its ability to enlist and enlarge on evocative themes of authority, discipline, and gender roles. Dissident Radicals had also touched on such themes, but they never wanted or were able to exploit them fully. Many nationalists were newspaper editors and journalists; they relished going to extremes which their position outside the political elite facilitated; further, they possessed a sense of righteous outrage against the left Radicals. These qualities combined to make their anti-Radical campaign enormously powerful and successful.

In the 1880s Radical politicians had first sounded the call for an end to corruption and the need to clean up the government.[33] With the collapse of the Boulangist movement and the fragmentation of the original Radical group, some of those former Radicals, now moving quickly to the nationalist Right, redirected the charge of corruption against their former colleagues. The Panama affair was only one example of this political strategy. As we have already seen, vehement complaints about republican venality were constant. In September, 1895, Edouard Drumont's anti-Semitic Libre Parole, then at the height of its influence, accused Camille Pelletan of having accepted bribes from railroad interests a decade earlier.[34] This charge reversed Drumont's somewhat sympathetic attitude toward

32. For "high" culture of the period see Silverman, *Art Nouveau in Fin-de-Siècle France*. For popular culture see Eugen Weber, *France, Fin de Siècle* (Cambridge, Mass., 1986), and Rearick, *Pleasures of the Belle Epoque*.

33. See especially Camille Pelletan, "Les Scandales," *La Justice*, no. 2862, November 15, 1887, and "Il faut en finir," *ibid.*, no. 2865, November 18, 1887. See also Chapter III.

34. In the mid-1890s between the Panama and Dreyfus Affairs, the circulation of *La Libre Parole* stood around one hundred thousand (Bellanger *et al.*, *Histoire générale de la presse française*, III, 296).

Pelletan.[35] The *Libre Parole* article asserted, "When you wanted to close Pelletan's mouth . . . you used monetary arguments."[36] These accusations came to nothing, and Pelletan even won a defamation suit when they were repeated in a Toulouse paper.[37] Whether such allegations were proved was of little interest to the nationalists. They aimed to expose the existence of a particular Radical character—avaricious, disloyal, and hypocritical. The constant reiteration of rumors created a permanent atmosphere of scandal in which one set of rumors easily merged with the next.

The image the nationalists created of Radical politicians was especially memorable, not only because it focused on their lack of integrity and morality but even more important because it made the Radicals appear ludicrous. The nationalists assaulted the Radicals with the deadly weapon of ridicule. In 1888 Pelletan had predicted that the greatest danger to the representative regime was not violence but "being discredited, being laughed at."[38] The antirepublican Right, appropriating what had once been a Radical tradition of oppositional political satire, directed biting humor against republican politicians. This sarcastic, sometimes ribald wit appeared not only in nationalist journals but increasingly in Paris *café concerts*, cabarets, and music halls. We have already seen the importance of music hall promotion in Boulanger's 1880s campaign. The nationalist edge to this ostensibly popular entertainment continued and mounted as the new century opened. Benjamin Martin, in his study of the Humbert scandal, cites a 1902 music hall tune that made it very clear what was wrong with the Republic: "The big guys [*les Gros*] have all the freedom!"[39]

35.   In the early 1890s *Libre Parole* contained articles favorable to Pelletan's attack on the Haute Banque and especially his denunciations of Edmond Rothschild. See Jean Drault, "M. Pelletan et la Banque de France," *La Libre Parole*, January 17, 1893.

36.   *La Libre Parole*, September 9, 1895.

37.   Police reports, no. 427, June, 1895, no. 557, July 10, 1895, no. 738, September, 1895, no. 762, September 21, 1895, Dossier Pelletan, MI 25359, AN; *Le Télégramme*, Toulouse, February 14, 1896. The independent socialist René Viviani represented Pelletan in court in the late 1890s. The affair resurfaced when Pelletan was minister of the navy (Police report, no. 234, January 30, 1904, Dossier Pelletan, MI 25359, AN).

38.   *La Justice*, no. 3210, October 26, 1888.

39.   Martin, *Hypocrisy of Justice in the Belle Epoque*, 104. For a fuller discussion of Humbert, see Chapter VI.

The ludicrous vulgarity of the nouveaux riches was one side of the anti-republican farce; the other was the equally laughable left-wing deputy whose dress was a shambles, who affected an antiquated bohemianism, and whose personal hygiene was suspect. Such men had no style; they were pitifully out of touch with fashion and with politics. Pelletan was the favorite butt of such humor. After 1895 technological improvements permitted the much more regular appearance of political caricatures in daily large-circulation newspapers. The stereotyped Radical deputy was an easy target and became a favorite of the cartoonists.[40] Negligence about personal appearance, wrinkled suits with too many spots, and shiny elbows had been the props of the left-wing politician, the man of the people, the popular orator. By the end of the century and especially after 1900, the Right succeeded in making this style a comic device. The nationalists constructed a popular political farce in which the Radicals were exposed as fake democrats whose real aim was wealth and personal advancement and as phony social and cultural critics who had found a comfortable place for themselves within the bourgeoisie. In both images the recent political success of the Radicals connected them to money and the haute bourgeoisie, hopelessly corrupting their politics and revealing their essential lack of integrity.

Echoing and transforming the criticism of dissident Radicals, the nationalists organized an intense campaign against Pelletan after he joined the government of Emile Combes. Combining satire, character assassination, and political issues, they denounced him as a threat to national security and voiced grave concerns about the ability of such Radicals to govern and defend the nation. Nationalists asked, what would be the consequences if the Radicals were to act on their egalitarian ideals? How could a party so dependent on its electoral alliance with the socialists be trusted with real power, especially power over the military services? The nationalists had

40. Paul Bosq, with his condescending satirical biographical sketches of the deputies, *Nos Chers Souverains*, set the standard. These biting portraits were first published in *Le Figaro* in 1898. The tone and attitude were often imitated; see Ernest Charles, "Portraits politiques, Camille Pelletan," *La Revue politique et parlementaire*, XXIV (April–June, 1900), 625–54, and Georges Suarez' depiction of Pelletan in his biography of Aristide Briand, cited in Guiral and Thuiller, *Vie quotidienne*, 92. The cartoonists illustrated what had become a standard description. See "Doux Pays à la Marine," *Echo de Paris*, June 30, 1902, and many of Caran d'Ache's illustrations in *Le Figaro*.

correctly singled out Pelletan as the major spokesman for left radicalism and the Bloc.

The intensity and personal rancor of this attack went beyond political differences. It may be best explained by the fact that Pelletan and some of the nationalists shared the same political and cultural origins. The vitriolic condemnation of Pelletan's character can in part be attributed to the nationalists' perception of him as a renegade from their own camp. This was especially the case of the popular journalist Henri Rochefort. During the 1860s both Rochefort and Pelletan had joined the populist, bohemian, republican opposition to the Bonapartist Empire. They shared a sympathy and attachment to the Commune. Rochefort's paper of the 1880s, *L'Intransigeant*, competed successfully with the Pelletan-Clemenceau journal, *La Justice*, for the same Parisian artisanal, student, petit bourgeois, populist audience. Both newspapers denounced parliamentary moderates and called for an authentic Republic. Rochefort and Pelletan initially promoted General Boulanger. Each must have been surprised to find the other, by the late 1880s, on opposing sides of the Boulangist movement. In the 1890s Rochefort's anti-Dreyfus stance was to be expected. Pelletan's late affiliation with the Dreyfusard position required that he shed his anticapitalist anti-Semitism. Rochefort moved steadily toward total opposition to the Third Republic; Pelletan became an increasingly ardent supporter of the regime.

Not only did his youthful political attitudes link Pelletan to the nationalists, but they also shared the same culture as young men. Left bank, academic, journalistic, and literary Paris from the 1850s to the 1870s had shaped both future nationalists and future Radicals. They were products and defenders of "le vieux Paris," which had been disappearing since the 1860s under Haussmann's boulevards and the quickening, expanding commercialism of the city's center.[41] The preeminent spokesman and representative of this "old Paris" was Victor Hugo, whose influence set the tone for a whole generation of young men. With the establishment of the Third Republic the Hugo salon, which functioned until the poet's death in 1885, brought together a wide spectrum of republicans, artists, and writers. Camille Pelletan, Henri Rochefort, and Edouard Drumont were all visitors there. Rochefort

41. Nord, *Paris Shopkeepers*, 77–80.

was an intimate friend of the Hugo family, which had supported him during several periods of exile. As we know, Camille Pelletan viewed himself as a protégé of the great poet.

During these early years Pelletan had attempted to establish a life that combined both a lack of conformity to bourgeois norms and the pursuit of a respected, remunerative public career. Through the 1870s he seriously pursued poetry. His personal life was flagrantly unconventional; until the age of fifty-six he lived with a woman who was rumored to be outrageously eccentric and unfaithful. Pelletan and his companion held their own salon, entertaining politicians and artists.[42] By the 1890s Pelletan was a well-established member of the republican political elite. Nonetheless, he continued to cultivate the image of the bohemian outsider, with his trademark wild hair, neglected attire, and permanently lit cigar or pipe. His nationalist critics labored to present him as a dissembler, a false friend of the "people," a counterfeit bohemian, and a renegade from the Paris culture in which he and the nationalists had been raised.

In July, 1902, one month after the formation of the Combes government and Pelletan's appointment as minister of the navy, the nationalist Right initiated a strident attack against him. Rochefort led off as editor of the still popular L'Intransigeant. Rochefort lampooned the government and Pelletan, branding Pelletan a hypocrite who had betrayed his principles. "Besides it's a constant habit with the same Pelletan to berate at the rostrum and then to disavow his words with his votes." He was "a politician pretending to be the democrat in the working-class suburbs and backing down at the Quai d'Orsay." More damning, however, than the charge of deception was treating Pelletan as the punch line of a joke. With special malice Rochefort opened the article with a quote from Hugo's famous poetic attack on Napoleon III: "Suffering being my fate, laughter is my reward. [Souffrir étant mon lot, rire est ma recompense]." He promised his readers that this new government would afford them "some hilarious days."[43] Rochefort had

42. Mme Bréchet, Interview by Paul Baquiast in "Pelletan," 371–73.

43. Less popular than it had been in the 1880s, L'Intransigeant's 1905 circulation stood between fifty and seventy thousand (Bellanger et al., Histoire générale de la presse française, III, 296). See the issue of July 1, 1902. Rochefort and Pelletan seemed to be vying for the legacy of Hugo. In 1888, during the Boulangist episode, Pelletan had quoted Hugo to Rochefort (see Chapter III).

drawn the lines clearly. Pelletan had been expelled from the company of manly, honest rebels such as himself and Hugo. He was now a member of that ludicrous, deceptive, impotent, money-grubbing profession of republican politicians. Similar sentiments were found throughout the nationalist and right-wing press. Paul de Cassagnac, editor of the leading Bonapartist journal, seconded Rochefort's views. His article "L'Anarchie" disdainfully dismissed Pelletan, whose egalitarian programs really were of no concern because their author was a "practical joker and a liar," as well as a "huckster." Nonetheless, despite this absurdity, Pelletan did pose a major threat to the church and army; de Cassagnac assured his readers that this ludicrous figure would create anarchy.[44]

When he became minister of the navy, the nationalists accused Pelletan of scandals ranging from espionage to venality, to fraud, to drunkenness.[45] Although his critics were never able to prove these attacks, rumors circulated freely in the press and in the corridors of the Chamber and drifted into some of the capital's political salons. They convinced the already convinced that Pelletan was a menace to national security. More important, they suggested to the uncertain that the minister of the navy was possibly a hypocrite, often a fool, and perhaps even a drunken buffoon. Throughout 1903 Pelletan devoted considerable time to defending his past and his character. The refutation of scandals occupied him more than the direction of naval matters. The nationalist Right intended to reveal Pelletan as morally unfit to be associated with, let alone direct, an armed service such as the navy. In their view, his character, the product of radicalism and parliamentary experience, had made him incapable of shouldering the serious and "manly" responsibilities of the navy.

The purported inability of the Bloc des gauches government to defend the nation and to maintain France's military strength was the most effective criticism used against it. Their opponents portrayed the governing

44. Paul de Cassagnac, "L'Anarchie," L'Autorité, July 1, 1902.

45. In one instance Pelletan had employed a Swiss engineer to advise on the development of a new submarine. Not only was he Swiss, but he had been a Dreyfusard, which was clear evidence for the Right that Pelletan had introduced a German spy into the Ministry of the Navy (La Libre Parole, January 5, 1903). Rochefort's L'Intransigeant uncovered a story dating back to the 1890s when Pelletan's longtime companion pawned some jewelry and misrepresented herself as Mme Pelletan (ibid., October 29, 1902, and January 16, 1903).

Radicals as dismantling the armed forces both materially and spiritually. Nationalists, clericals, anti-Semites, conservatives, and moderate republicans all claimed that discipline—the essence of every military organization—was being undermined by the government, the very authority that must uphold it. Dissident Radicals subtly, perhaps even unconsciously, implied that Pelletan was not "man" enough to do the job. The Right much more clearly linked order, authority, discipline, and masculinity, denouncing the Radicals for their lack of those qualities.

Of the several scandals surrounding Pelletan, the most damning and damaging began May 28, 1903, when *Le Figaro* published a letter its editor claimed to have received anonymously. It had been sent to Pelletan at the Ministry of the Navy on September 25, 1902, and linked him to the most notorious and spectacular financial swindle of the moment, the Humbert Affair.[46] The letter identified Pelletan as the recipient of a political bribe in 1889 and named Frédéric Humbert as the source of that bribe. In the spring of 1903 the Humberts were in prison awaiting trial for fraud. Frédéric's private secretary, Armand Parayre, who was attempting to blackmail the minister, had signed the letter. Parayre wanted Pelletan to use his influence to secure his release through an *ordonnance de non-lieu* from complicity in the Humbert Affair. The letter claimed that Frédéric Humbert had paid Camille Pelletan for a political speech in which Pelletan sought to invalidate the election of Humbert's successful rival.[47] Many on the Right viewed this letter as the first clear sign that the Humbert Affair would assume the proportions of the Panama scandal. The nationalists intended to identify the republican elite with this astoundingly avaricious couple and their spectacular fraud. Now at last, corruption, fraud, and hypocrisy could be linked to the controversial Radical minister of the navy.[48]

The right-wing press, of course, pursued the story with jubilation for most of the spring of 1903. It is significant, however, that *Le Figaro*, ostensibly a politically moderate journal, but one bitterly opposed to Pelletan, first revealed this astounding information. Differing from the explicitly political journals of both the Right and the Left, *Le Figaro* was among the most im-

46. See Chapter VI.

47. Ironically, Pelletan's 1889 speech had accused Humbert's conservative opponent of bribing electors for their votes (*Le Figaro*, May 28, 1903).

48. *Le Soleil*, May 29, 1903.

portant representatives of the new journalism that had been capturing an ever greater portion of the reading public since the middle of the nineteenth century. This new journalism was essential to the success of the developing Parisian commercial culture and entertainment industry. Both notoriety and advertisement were vital to the life of boulevard enterprises, which in turn supported the new press. Its content and format emphasized diversion, scandal, advertisement, and large circulation. *Le Figaro* had pioneered this approach since its establishment in 1854. Using the press censorship of the Second Empire to its advantage, it had demonstrated the popularity of an ostensibly apolitical newspaper. In the first two decades of the Third Republic the management of *Le Figaro* expanded its circulation by introducing the first illustrated weekly supplement, the first want-ad section, *les petites annonces*, and then even more daring, the first personal columns, *les petites correspondences*. Moralists regularly accused these personals of promoting illicit affairs and adultery. Aiming to please everyone, *Le Figaro* also offered 50 percent discounts to all military officers and priests. Talented writers, regular correspondents, and short, lively articles reinforced these modern marketing techniques.[49]

By the 1880s, although not one of the largest Paris dailies, *Le Figaro* was considered among the most influential with a circulation of 105,000. Despite its avowed apolitical stance, it had, since its inception, supported conservative, if not reactionary, governments and policies. During the 1880s, however, it abandoned its antirepublicanism for a reluctant acceptance of the new status quo. With a new editorial board, politics began to figure more frequently in its columns. Following further editorial changes in the 1890s, two new editors took the surprising step of defending Alfred Dreyfus. They even went so far as to invite Emile Zola and Auguste Scheurer-Kestner to explain the Dreyfusard position to the paper's unsympathetic readers. The result was a disaster for *Le Figaro* and the editors. A barrage of readers' protests forced them to retract their stance, although they still refused to publish anti-Dreyfusard material. By 1901 circulation had plummeted to 20,000. The board of directors fired the editors, who refused to relinquish their positions; the ensuing legal battle dislocated the newspaper for another year. Finally, in 1902 the board appointed a new editor in chief, Gas-

49. Bellanger *et al.*, *Histoire générale de la presse française*, III, 349.

ton Calmette. He had been with the paper since 1883, and he was charged with rebuilding Le Figaro's circulation and reputation. Calmette's strategy was to introduce administrative reorganization, technological modernization, and an editorial position that combined conservative republicanism and exposés of sensational political scandals. This approach brought some rewards. By 1904 circulation stood at 32,000. The following year, the editor in chief could claim that Le Figaro had returned to its "natural" readers, "the aristocratic elite, the wealthy, big business, the army, and the most elegant members of the foreign community." [50]

Le Figaro's ambitious new editor had sharply criticized the parliamentary coalition of the Bloc des gauches, Combes's Radical ministry, and especially the minister of the navy, Camille Pelletan, since June, 1902. A daily column, "Dans la Marine," recounted with growing alarm the "Jacobin disorganization and anarchy" governing Pelletan's ministry. [51] One of Le Figaro's best journalists, using the pseudonyms Novi or Mermeix, carried on a two-and-a-half-year campaign against Pelletan. [52] The paper's immensely talented political cartoonist, Caran d'Ache, regularly made Pelletan the object of his devastating pen. [53] The May, 1903, publication of the shocking Parayre letter to Pelletan was only part of a well-orchestrated political and marketing strategy intended to reestablish the politically conservative but culturally fashionable reputation of Le Figaro after its brief but dangerous flirtation with the Dreyfusards.

Calmette's revelation of this letter became part of the scandal. Police reports recorded rumors that moderate republicans had encouraged Calmette to pursue this attack. [54] Evidence that Pelletan had been the victim of attempted blackmail became another indication of the disorganization

50.   Ibid., 349, 350.

51.   Le Figaro, July 17, 1903.

52.   Merimex was the pseudonym for Georges Thiebaut, a former Boulangist whose electoral ambitions had been squelched. Police reports suggested that his newspaper campaign against Pelletan was supported by defense contractors eager to see the new minister of navy resign (Police report, March 14, 1904, Dossier Pelletan, MI 25359, AN).

53.   For one example, see Le Figaro, September 22, 1902.

54.   Le Figaro had supported Waldeck-Rousseau's republican government. This led to speculation that the former premier had encouraged Calmette. See Pierre Sorlin, Waldeck-Rousseau (Paris, 1966), 459–60, and Police reports, May, 1903, Dossier Pelletan, MI 25359, AN, which named Waldeck-Rousseau and de Lanessan.

within the naval ministry. It raised the question of whether Pelletan had adequate control over his ministry. The letter had been sent to the rue Royale. Who, then, had had access to it and who had sent it to *Le Figaro?* Pelletan was faulted for not commanding the loyalty of all his subordinates at the Ministry of the Navy. Pelletan's programmatic efforts to modify traditional discipline and hierarchy were identified as the ultimate cause of this flaunting of discipline.

On May 28 an impassioned Pelletan addressed a tumultuous Chamber, denouncing these "monstrous calumnies." Though emotional, it was not one of his strongest speeches. Disdainfully he labeled the letter as "a puff of air blown in from the boulevard press." He insisted that he had never received one centime for his support of Frédéric Humbert, a fellow Radical. He promised to reveal the real identity of his attackers when "the time would come." Having personally searched the postal records, Pelletan claimed that the letter had never been received at the ministry and probably had never been sent. Later evidence disproved these assertions. Perhaps his most convincing oratorical strategy was to claim that his "words" were a sacred trust which he would never betray. "We freethinkers also have sacred objects . . . the words which we pronounce in what we consider the national interest." He concluded with a defense of his own character, reminding the republican majority of his ardent convictions, his modest personal resources, and the irreproachable legacy of his republican father. The official record noted that he left the podium "applauded and congratulated by many." He easily received the Chamber's vote of confidence; of the 524 voting, 343 voted for Pelletan.[55]

Nonetheless, by November of that year the unrelenting newspaper campaign and the constant innuendos of the Humbert lawyers created enough clamor in political circles that the Chamber supported the proposal of the Parisian nationalist deputy, Georges Berry, to create a special parliamentary commission of inquiry.[56] The commission received the charge "to throw

55. During the debate Combes broke parliamentary etiquette, left his seat on the government bench, and attempted to calm the deputies of the Center. The Center and the Right protested such unorthodox behavior. See Chambre des députés, Débats, *Journal Officiel*, May 28, 1903, pp. 1769–70, 1774.

56. Georges Berry had an interesting political career. He originally counted himself a Parnassian poet and royalist. In the 1880s he was elected to the Paris municipal council. He then

light on the involvement of politicians in the Humbert affair which had been a claim of the defendants' attorneys."[57] Berry, an astute representative of the strident nationalism in the capital, received the warm endorsement of the influential Libre Parole and its editor, Edouard Drumont.[58] He was joined on the commission by an even more militant nationalist, Gabriel Syveton of La Ligue de la patrie française. Despite such powerful spokesmen, the Right could not control the investigation. Berry had to withdraw his motion seeking to give the commission judicial powers, and he was defeated in his bid for commission president and reporter. The commission met fitfully from November, 1903, to February, 1904, exploring Frédéric Humbert's confiscated papers, taking depositions, and interrogating journalists. One member complained that colleagues viewed the commission as a joke, as did, perhaps more important, the press. Berry made certain that the Parayre letter blackmailing Pelletan, which had been public knowledge for seven months, was introduced into the commission's record. The right-wing deputy claimed that it had also been sent to him anonymously in the spring of 1903. He snidely noted that the minister of the navy's promised inquiry had yet to occur and that the parliamentary commission should take up that task.[59] Despite the great wealth of information (or perhaps because of it), the commission's majority held to its view that no evidence pointed to the collusion of politicians in the Humbert fraud.[60]

Strictly speaking, this seems to have been true; the commission was unable to locate direct evidence of politicians using their influence to aid the Humberts in their elaborate scheme to defraud their creditors. Early in 1904

---

became a Boulangist, a Catholic rallié, and a nationalist. In the 1890s he was elected deputy for the ninth arrondissement and championed a reform of the business tax, the patente. He always represented himself as the spokesman for "le petit commerce" (Nord, Paris Shopkeepers, 316; Stone, Search for Social Peace, 138).

57. Special report, Enquête parlementaire sur l'Affaire Humbert, November 20, 1903, C 7313, AN.

58. La Libre Parole, December 1, 1903.

59. Procès verbaux, Enquête parlementaire sur l'Affaire Humbert, November 20, 1904, C 7313, AN; ibid., December 23, 4, 1903, C 7314, AN.

60. These were the views of the two candidates for the position of committee reporter, Félix Marot, a moderate republican, and Armand Rouanet, an independent socialist (Report, ibid., November 8, 1904, C 7316, AN).

the imprisoned Thérèse Humbert, in a rambling and somewhat incoherent deposition to the parliamentary commission, corroborated Pelletan's assertion of innocence. As Armand Rouanet, independent socialist member of the commission, observed, "We have discovered . . . some more or less close connections, but all of them are of an absolutely private nature and there is nothing which might establish complicity." This same deputy did admit, however, that these "private" connections might lead to some very interesting conclusions but solely of a "social," not political, nature.[61] One such relation that was documented in Frédéric Humbert's account books and appointment calendars was his regular contact with Camille Pelletan from November, 1889, until January, 1902.

Although Pelletan did not appear to have frequented the salon organized by Thérèse, he certainly was one of Frédéric's close political colleagues. Humbert's personal papers clearly indicated that not only did Pelletan visit regularly, but that on many of these occasions Humbert paid Pelletan sums between 500 and 1,000 francs. Such payments began in January, 1894, and ended only a few months before the Humbert fraud was exposed in January, 1902. They amounted to a not extravagant total of 16,900 francs.[62] According to his own accounts, Humbert was repaying Camille Pelletan for a loan made in the summer of 1893. This was a curious activity for a man who, together with his wife, was, at this very time, defrauding major investors of much larger sums. Although this information does not necessarily refute Pelletan's claims of innocence, its revelation certainly would have made him much less credible and increased the precariousness of his political position. Amazingly, this financial arrangement was not made public or even widely disseminated among the political elite.

There can be little question that a broad republican majority succeeded in squelching the general investigation of the Humberts' political ties, including those with Pelletan. A large circle of republicans, well beyond the Radicals, had had financial or social dealings with the Humberts. Moderate republicans were well aware that the Right was most eager to demolish the reputation of Waldeck-Rousseau, who also was rumored to have received a

61. Mme Humbert deposition, *ibid.*, February 2, 1904, C 7314, AN; Procès verbaux, *ibid.*, November 8, 1904, C 7316, AN.

62. Pelletan's first visit noted in these agendas occurred immediately after the 1889 elections (Correspondance saisie, Frédéric Humbert agendas and livre de caisse, *ibid.*, C 7315–16, AN).

bribe from Humbert. With the exception of the extreme Right, the deputies agreed to end the search for corrupt politicians connected with the Humberts. No legal charges were brought against Pelletan, and he appeared to survive the moral accusations made against him; however, his political position and image had been injured.[63] The original *Figaro* article condemned Pelletan with a parody of his own republican rhetoric: "M. Camille Pelletan, do you intend to teach those authentic masses of voters . . . those hungry millions of humble unknown men such discouraging skepticism . . . and such a bitter aversion to all future political commitments?"[64] The right-wing and moderate press had been able to portray Pelletan as a fraud whose denunciations of "la féodalité financière" were mere posturing. They had linked him to the flashy world of the nouveaux riches and Parisian salons, an awkward place for a reputed man of the people. Although supporters of the Bloc dismissed these accusations as the continuing machinations of the "clerico-militarist-monarchist" clique, association with this scandal did reduce Pelletan's effectiveness as a member of the Combes government.[65]

In the winter of 1903–1904 the scandals surrounding Pelletan were multiplying at an alarming rate. During the parliamentary inquiry into the Humbert Affair, what came to be called the Scala incident surfaced and briefly occupied the Paris newspapers. Compared to Pelletan's other problems, this Scala incident was relatively minor, but it vividly illuminated the influential and shifting interconnections of politics, culture, and leisure in the early twentieth century. For the profitable Paris winter season the management of the La Scala music hall presented a risqué show titled *La Revue à poivre*. After some minor adjustments for "decency," the censor approved the first four scenes of the *Revue* in December; the fifth scene, however, even after revisions, was still considered "impossible."[66] None-

---

63. The Humberts received five years at hard labor (Martin, *Hypocrisy of Justice in the Belle Epoque*, 142–43).

64. *Le Figaro*, May 28, 1903, and Chambre des députés, Débats, *Journal Officiel*, May 28, 1903, p. 1769.

65. Francis de Pressensé, *L'Aurore*, July 1, 1902.

66. Ministère de l'Instruction publique, Direction des Beaux Arts, Inspection des théâtres, manuscript no. 5229, *La Revue à poivre*, F18 1499, AN. All subsequent references to dialogue and stage directions are taken from this manuscript. Theater scripts had to be submitted to the censor fifteen days before the performance.

theless, the *Revue* was performed at least fifty times without any substantial changes to the final scene. *La Revue à poivre* was fairly typical of the offerings to be found in the music halls on the grands boulevards. It mixed bawdy songs, double-entendre jokes, scantily clad actresses, patriotic assertions, and political satire directed at the Bloc des gauches government. As its name advertised, this particular *Revue* promised to be especially spicy. Government ministers and even the president of the Republic were the butts of jokes and innuendos. One of the funniest scenes centered on the recent reform of the divorce law. The abolition of article 298 now permitted divorced individuals to marry their former lovers. On the stage of La Scala this became a farcical disaster for a young bachelor who had seduced a long list of married women by agreeing to what he thought the law would always prohibit, a future marriage. Now his former lovers, accompanied by their former husbands and armed with the new legal reform, appeared, demanding the fulfillment of his promises.

It was the fifth scene, however, which most audiences viewed as uproarious. It portrayed a wedding party, identified as the servants, "la valetaille, of the republican aristocracy." The groom was considerably older than the bride; he had wildly unkempt hair, and his attire was disheveled and frayed. Both bride and groom were drunk, and they brought the wedding party into a "bar" to celebrate. Although the groom was introduced as the "barber" of the minister of the navy, every Parisian immediately recognized Camille Pelletan, who that August had married a women twenty-four years his junior. According to most newspaper accounts of the scene, the climax came when the inebriated bride danced the cakewalk or in some stories did the can-can.[67]

The *Revue* brought a steady audience to La Scala, but not everyone thought it was especially funny. On December 18, a group of at least twenty young men, students or recent graduates of the Faculties of Law and of Arts and Letters, organized an expedition to the music hall on the Boulevard Strasbourg. Two of this group were officers of the Alliance républicaine démocratique. When the fifth scene began, they met the parody of the drunken naval minister and his wife with boos, shouts, and demands that the curtain be lowered. Other members of the audience and the staff of

67. *L'Aurore*, December 20, 1903, and *La Lanterne*, December 21, 1903.

La Scala responded to this demonstration by trying to evict the republican students. Eventually the police were called and thirty-one arrests were made.[68] By December 20, this music hall brawl was dubbed "l'affaire Scala" and was reported on the front pages of all the major Paris dailies, led of course by Le Figaro.[69] Some supporters of the government demanded that the Revue be banned; nationalists and conservatives denounced republican attempts to censor the arts. Mme Marchand, the owner of La Scala, soon withdrew the controversial scene, and within a few days the furor faded. Fresher news replaced the Scala scandal.

This episode took place at the uniquely Parisian intersection of culture, entertainment, commerce, and politics. In advance of most other European capitals and many years ahead of the rest of France, Paris had experienced a rapid transformation of its physical environment, economy, social organization, and culture. By 1900 the reorganization of consumption and the commercialization of leisure and entertainment had increased dramatically. The impetus for much of this development had been Haussmann's redesign of the city during the Second Empire. The new physical space of the grands boulevards created the setting for new department stores, commercial displays, urban recreation, and tourism. This new Paris destroyed traditional working-class neighborhoods, long-established business districts, and the intangible atmosphere of le vieux Paris to which Radicals had been so attached.[70] Between 1880 and 1900 a new sensibility emerged from these transformations and fragmentations of urban culture. La Revue à poivre well expressed this new outlook, which was explicitly hostile to the Radicals.

68.   Cabinet de la Police, X^e arrondissement, December 20–28, 1903, Ba 1744, APP. Violent street confrontations were a regular activity among students of the faculties of Law, Arts and Letters, and Fine Arts. Brawls were frequent between student supporters of the nationalist antiparliamentary Right and those of the republican, anticlerical, socialist-leaning Left. Occasionally the hostile groups of students would unite to confront the police in bloody attacks, sometimes lasting several days. See Franz Jayot, "Les Etudiants parisiens de 1890 à 1906. Etude politique et sociale" (Mémoire de maîtrise, Université de Paris X, 1973), 58–60, 65–70; Rearick, Pleasures of the Belle Epoque, 43–46.

69.   Articles appeared in La Lanterne, Le Radical, La Petite République, L'Aurore, La Libre Parole, Le Gaulois, and La République française.

70.   Clark, Painting of Modern Life, 9–10, 37–46; for the economic impact of Haussmannization on traditional luxury trades see Nord, Paris Shopkeepers, 130–38.

Especially in the 1880s, artists, poets, writers, and journalists, as well as their less talented hangers-on, rejected the modernizing city. They adopted an oppositional, bohemian lifestyle facilitated by the cheap rents and the villagelike atmosphere of right bank Montmartre. There successful cabarets, such as Le Chat Noir, mixed contempt for their bourgeois customers with a sentimentalized populism and patriotism, as well as a growing disdain for the unheroic parliamentary regime. Montmartre symbolized a better, bucolic alternative to the modern, corrupt, financially dominated world that existed below the *butte*. Despite their oppositional stance, the cabaret owners and artists were interested in success. They had a keen sense for publicity, and several published their own broadsheets which combined advertising leaflets with poetry and literary discussions. In the late 1880s, following the lead of Rochefort's *L'Intransigeant*, many Montmartre bohemians were attracted to the Boulangist movement. A decade later, many supported the nationalist, anti-Semitic, anti-Dreyfusards.[71]

Paradoxically, this turbulent world of Montmartre bohemianism influenced the entertainment establishments of the grands boulevards which it had criticized. By the 1890s, Paris night life steadily abandoned Montmartre to increasing crime, working-class poverty, and the most daring practitioners of the postimpressionist avant-garde. The modern boulevards of the city's center, which the Montmartre bohemians had shunned, became the heart of a booming entertainment industry. There the outdoor *cafés concerts* that had flourished since the Second Empire became better lit and more elaborate. They successfully competed with the cabarets and dance halls of the *butte*.[72] In addition, popular entertainment was more and more concentrated in the newer music halls, which had fixed seats, entrance fees, and elaborate stage performances. All these enterprises were closely linked to the expanding commercial press, in which they advertised heavily, and depended on critics' reviews, as well as on coverage in the regular "About Paris" columns devoted to urbane gossip. Les Folies

71. Nord, *Paris Shopkeepers*, 330–45; Seigel, *Bohemian Paris*, 237–39; Oberthür, *Le Chat Noir*.

72. The popular dance hall or beer garden had already been immortalized and sentimentalized by Auguste Renoir in *Moulin de la Galette*, oil on canvas, 1876, Musée d'Orsay, Paris. Henri de Toulouse-Lautrec's representation of this same dance hall in the 1890s is strikingly different: *Moulin de la Galette*, oil on canvas, 1889, Art Institute of Chicago, Chicago.

Bergères, La Nouvelle Cirque, Le Petit Casino, L'Eldorado, L'Eden, and La Scala were all established in the 1890s and prospered in the first years of the new century. They all drew from the Montmartre repertoire but modified the acerbic antibourgeois comedy, emphasized sexual repartee and female flesh, vastly elaborated the special effects, and expanded the musical performance.[73] In 1894 the connection between the worlds of Montmartre and the grands boulevards was captured in an expensive album depicting the performances of the celebrated popular singer Yvette Guilbert. Henri de Toulouse-Lautrec composed the Art Nouveau illustrations and layout; Gustave Geffroy, art critic for La Justice and Clemenceau's close companion, provided the text. The social and political ambiguity of the crowds at the "café concerts" mesmerized and repelled Geffroy. Lautrec's acid green lithography underscored the artificiality, the gas and electric lighting, "the decay called fin-de-siècle. . . . the odor of beer and tobacco, the crowded rows of seats."[74]

The apparently safer neighborhoods and more luxurious interiors of the new music halls attracted an audience of mixed social composition dominated by the petite bourgeoisie. The art historian T. J. Clark has characterized this audience as largely composed of les nouvelles couches sociales, the petit bourgeoisie, the lower middle class. In the language of the day it was often labeled "populaire." The difficulty of finding a precise category to identify this social group underscores its ambiguity and indeterminacy, which, according to Clark, were its most significant characteristics. Attempting to describe the new petite bourgeoisie more concretely, Clark includes among them clerks, account brokers, petty bureaucrats, insurance agents, bank tellers, traveling salesmen, and especially the employees of the department stores, les calicots.[75] The contemporary observer of the café concert Gustave Geffroy suggested a similar composition: "[It was] a commercial

---

73. Clark, Painting of Modern Life, 211; Weber, France, Fin de Siècle, 159–76; and Rearick, Pleasures of the Belle Epoque, 74–78.

74. Gustave Geffroy and Henri de Toulouse-Lautrec, Yvette Guilbert, trans. Barbara Sessions (1894; repr. New York, 1968). The 1894 edition was sixteen pages, produced on a hand press with new techniques of graphic design. It was marketed as a deluxe edition, costing 50 francs, an unusual form and price for such a subject. The edition received only two positive reviews, one in Le Figaro and the other from Geffroy's colleagues at La Justice.

75. Clark, Painting of Modern Life, 154, 202, 205, 216.

and office workers' crowd at the Boulevard Strasbourg and the Faubourg St. Denis. They wanted music, lights and gaiety."[76] Adding further to the ambiguity and indeterminacy of the music hall audience was the presence of women in intimate proximity with men in a public setting. Jean Renoir's account of his first childhood visit to La Scala depicted a joyous family outing with his aunt and uncle, which his parents encouraged. Everyone laughed at the dirty jokes, and the only gender distinctions were that his uncle drank beer and his aunt a grenadine.[77] Other contemporary observers were less enthusiastic about the mixed audience. Most disturbing to conventional assumptions about gender roles was the inclusion in the same audience of women escorted by husbands, women accompanied by men to whom their relation might be termed "dubious," women alone, and women whose part-time or full-time profession was prostitution. When the music hall audience circulated in the theater foyers, it might often be difficult to distinguish the respectable women of any class from those who were not.[78]

Leisure and the ability to pay for entertainment were relatively new to this class and perhaps accounted for frequent awkwardness and uncertainty about how to use these new pleasures. The petit bourgeois were eager to enjoy this new leisure and to display it as a mark of their new mobility and somewhat tenuous membership within the bourgeoisie. On the surface, the established bourgeoisie seemed to dismiss these efforts as amusing signs of lower-middle-class vulgarity. Indeed, this was often a comic theme in music hall skits.[79] More fundamentally, this petit bourgeois search for cultural identity challenged the traditional exclusivity of bourgeoisie.[80] The *café concerts* and music halls were ideal sites to stake out new cultural terrain. They permitted bourgeois and petit bourgeois to occupy the same space but not to be confused with one another. White-collar workers could enjoy the same *chanteuse* as the bourgeois who was out "slumming," yet differently priced seats clearly separated the two.

76. Geffroy and Toulouse-Lautrec, *Yvette Guilbert*.

77. Jean Renoir, *Renoir My Father*, trans. Randolph Weaver and Dorothy Weaver (London, 1962), 362–63.

78. See Clark's discussion of Edouard Manet, *The Bar at the Folies Bergères*, in *Painting of Modern Life*, 251.

79. *La Revue à poivre* itself and see Clark on the Goncourts, *Painting of Modern Life*, 155.

80. Clark, *Painting of Modern Life*, 155, 202.

The entertainment itself, whose dominant themes were class and sex, further accentuated the class and gender ambiguities of the audience. The performances reworked the Montmartre repertoire, often presenting ostensibly working-class or at least antibourgeois sentiments.[81] The mixed-gender audience must have heightened the humor and titillation of the constant double entendres, of the incessant references to sex acts and organs. Geffroy observed, "There are positive fermentations within the bourgeoisie and within the people which unite and create a new world, where anything goes." The presence of women, tourists, and foreigners underscored this atmosphere of shared space and shared entertainment without eliminating distinctions.[82]

Gustave Geffroy, while celebrating a *café concert* singer, remained deeply ambivalent about this popular yet fashionable entertainment. He recognized that the culture emerging from the music halls and from the desires of its audiences posed a real dilemma for the older Radical traditions of "the people." At times he approached the music hall "crowd" with considerable sympathy. He asked what other alternatives for leisure "le populo" had: "Seriously, why don't you want this man to go to the *café concert*. It's the only door open to him, the only house to welcome him. . . . where he can go in and find his equals. After all, he has to do something with his free time. What other choice does he have for relaxation and pleasure?" But in the end Geffroy, like his fellow Radicals, rejected this new environment as artificial, vulgar, disorderly, and vaguely menacing. He reminded the reader: "The singer . . . when she's finished her song, she makes good her escape, her throat burning with the smoke she's inhaled, her entire being permeated with the overheated atmosphere; where does she go? She jumps in a train, leaves Paris, cools herself off in the fresh air of open spaces, and regains her country garden and river. Humanity, having fallen to the *café concert*, do as your singer does . . . get out of the big cities, and return to nature with what you have learned of history and civiliza-

81. *Ibid.*, 212, 229.
82. Geffroy and Toulouse-Lautrec, *Yvette Guilbert.* La Scala, for example, was located near the Gare du Nord and the Gare de l'Est, making it convenient to the increasing numbers of provincial visitors. Many of the largest music halls were close to stations in the ninth, tenth, and eleventh arrondissements.

tion."[83] Unlike the stars, however, the audience could not so easily escape the new urban environment, nor was it obvious what lessons of "history and civilization" had been learned.

It was in this burgeoning world of commercial entertainment and petit bourgeois leisure that a young, well-connected boulevardier, Paul Lafargue, convinced Mme Marchand, the owner of La Scala, to present his *Revue à poivre*.[84]

What exactly had been so funny to most and so outrageous to some Radicals in this musical hall farce? The portrayal of the inebriated barber of the minister of the navy incorporated all the negative political, cultural, and gender-related charges that had been hurled at Pelletan for the last two years. His reported slovenliness was associated with serious character defects that disqualified him from the responsible position of leading a military service. Already he had been denounced as someone "whose detestable political ideas . . . have seriously undermined the confidence which the head of the navy ought to inspire." *Le Figaro* singled out Pelletan's appointment as minister of the navy as the beginning of the "ultimate decadence of our poor country." In the nationalist press and in the *Revue* itself these failings were associated with an absence of appropriately masculine qualities, particularly martial instincts. *Le Figaro* had decried Pelletan's reforms as a "war without quarter against the spirit of discipline and duty made in the name of 'democracy.' . . . the ancient, Jacobin doctrine of disorganization [and] . . . anarchy." The article went on to hope that naval officers would have the strength to resist while waiting for better days.[85] This generalized fear of national decline associated with a loss of masculinity permeated the Scala *Revue*. An early scene portrayed an exchange between two young women and an army sergeant who had been entirely "civilized" by the reforms of General André and the Combes government. The young man has

---

83. *Ibid.* In his unpublished memoirs written in 1913 Camille Pelletan observed that he always remained "a foreigner to the boulevards" ("Mémoires [inédites]," in Baquiast, "Pelletan," 177).

84. *L'Aurore*, December 18, 1903. Lafargue came from an established bourgeois family. His father had been Jean Casimir-Périer's secretary while the latter was president of the Republic in the 1890s.

85. *Le Figaro*, May 25, 26, July 17, 1903.

lost his distinctive uniform, his rank, his authority, and by implication his sexual potency.[86]

But the *Revue* made clear that the absurdity of Pelletan was more than the absence of a "manly" character. He was ludicrous because he was old and out of date. The modern, stylish world of the boulevards had long replaced his particular brand of bohemianism. At the end of the scene, the members of the wedding party dance, not the fashionable cake-walk as reported in some of the press but an old-fashioned quadrille. Once they leave, the two women who had observed and commented on this absurd wedding party have a good laugh, and then, needing a change of pace, exit to see "real society . . . the chic crowd!" Denigrating the bohemian postures of the 1860s and 1870s affirmed the new polished, detached commercial culture of the boulevards. Pelletan's passionate romantic oratory was satirized as that of a "gladiator . . . in a black frock coat with worn-through elbows."[87]

La Revue à poivre also ridiculed specific Radical policies. Anticlericalism was bitingly parodied: the wedding party was off to visit the major Parisian churches to demonstrate that it was going to none. The expulsion of unauthorized religious orders was presented as a series of absurd actions. A member of the wedding party was the son of the president of the "Antiprotectionist League for Admirals," a double swipe, one against Pelletan's struggle with the admirals and the other a parody of the Ligue des droits de l'homme. The concluding dance sequence equated the intricacies of a quadrille with the convolutions of republican parliamentary alliances. Republican politics was so ridiculous that it had become a form of entertainment. Interestingly, the audience for this entertainment did not differ that much from that to which Radical politicians appealed. In Paris at least the petite bourgeoisie had difficulty taking its own democratic aspirations seriously. Perhaps some in the music hall audience were laughing at their own attempts to assert political influence.

Of course, the essence of the skit's humor was that it concerned a marriage, the most ancient of comic subjects. Some of the vitriol directed against this marriage may be attributed to disappointment that the actual

86. See Nye's analysis of the general anxiety about masculinity in this period, *Masculinity and Male Codes of Honor*, 71, 131, and *passim*.

87. This cultural revision meant that some older nationalists, such as Rochefort, had to distance themselves further from their own origins. See *Gils Blas*, May 29, 1903.

Pelletan wedding of August, 1903, had not afforded greater scandal. Before the ceremony there had been high hopes and many rumors in the right-wing press and political circles that Pelletan's fiancée, Joséphine Dénise, was a practicing Catholic and that the ceremony would be religious.[88] The anti-Bloc forces were disappointed. The bride was a committed republican schoolteacher, the ceremony civil, and Combes the witness.

In the *Revue* the audience was presented with an absurdly mismatched couple, each one playing a standard music hall comic role, the drunk. This marriage sequence must have reminded the audience of the earlier scene on divorce. Both spoofs permitted the audience to laugh at various comic, sexually charged predicaments of wives, husbands, and lovers, while at the same time decrying republican, anticlerical reforms, which were portrayed as ridiculous and creating chaos. Both skits implied that the Radicals' policies were dangerously undermining the institution of marriage. A groom of fifty-six, twenty-four years older than the bride, inevitably created opportunities for ribald humor. The *démodé* bohemian who had lived with another woman for thirty years and was now marrying for the first time provided the possibility for even more jokes. Pelletan could be made to look the fool for his earlier unconventional lifestyle, as well as for his present choice of respectable marriage. This right-wing farce lampooned Radicals as both vulgar social climbers and *démodé* bohemians who were inauthentic in either style. The ill-matched and disorderly couple reinforced the accusations that the Radicals were incapable of governing France. The traditional parallel between the governance of the family and the organization of the state underlay the comedy routine. How could a man incapable of controlling his bride control the navy? How could such men be permitted to govern France? At the same time, this skit also satirized the audience, who did not hesitate to laugh at themselves and their own claims to cultural independence and political sovereignty.

Since the formation of the Bloc des gauches and the Combes government, all critics of the Radicals had employed rhetoric colored with gender associations. *La Revue à poivre*, however, directed its derisive humor at a specific, respectable, married bourgeois woman. Being iconoclastic and outside the political elite, the nationalist Right relished such scandal, which mixed

88. Police report, June 6, 1903, Dossier Pelletan, MI 25359, AN.

the public and the private. It seemed that Pelletan's marriage was greeted as more of an outrage than his earlier, less conventional relationship.[89] In *La Revue à poivre* the central joke required that Mme Pelletan be portrayed as a drunken fool and that two other women whose propriety remained ambiguous discussed her behavior. Many thought the nationalists had gone too far.

Soon after the brawl at La Scala, irate Radicals demanded to know why the official condemnation of the offensive scene had not been enforced. Now the Scala incident became embroiled with an ongoing struggle over censorship of performances. Clemenceau's *L'Aurore* asked why "democratically inspired and socially committed plays, such as *Germinal*, are banned, while all the inept reactionary productions and all the filth . . . of the music halls and the Montmartre cabarets are permitted." The article continued to say that "we are all for theatrical freedom, but since we have the institution of the censor it should be used correctly."[90] Since at least the 1890s nationalists and anti-Semites had been producing plays which the Radicals, despite their theoretical commitment to free speech, wanted to have banned.[91] In the case of *La Revue à poivre* the Radicals demanded that their own minister of the interior enforce state censorship. It was a position that *Le Figaro* delighted in mocking. "Look here is M. Pelletan protected by the power of the state. Perhaps this situation doesn't thrill such a theoretical partisan of complete liberty. But state power is welcome when one needs it."[92]

89. Although during the winter of 1902–1903 Rochefort's *L'Intransigeant* had unsuccessfully attempted to create a scandal out of Pelletan's past, this was unusual. For thirty years no critic of Pelletan had thought to introduce his unusual household into the political debate. For an introduction to the issue of republican politicians and their marriages, see Estèbe, *Ministres de la République*, 81–82, 84–85.

90. *L'Aurore*, December 20, 1903.

91. Clemenceau's famous speech declaring the Revolution a "bloc" was part of an effort to ban a Sardou play critical of Robespierre (Chambre des députés, Débats, *Journal Officiel*, January 29, 1891). In 1901, the anti-Semitic play *Décadence* was banned. At the same time, the realist theater, whose plays stressed serious political and sexual problems, frequently encountered obstacles from the censor. In 1901 a realist play, *Les Avaries*, which dealt with venereal disease, was prohibited. In 1903 the anti-Semitic play *Le Retour au Jerusalem* was produced, but a production of Zola's *Germinal* was not permitted (Weber, *France, Fin de Siècle*, 161–62).

92. *Le Figaro*, December 20, 1903. The censorship of theatrical productions lapsed only three years later, when the Chamber neglected to vote a budget for the office, but censorship of the newest popular entertainment, the movies, continued up to World War I.

A general consensus emerged that the *Revue* had transgressed acceptable norms of behavior even within the permissive realm of commercial entertainment. Appropriate class and gender roles, as well as the rules of political discourse, had, in the opinion of most, been violated. The day after the incident, *La République française*, a moderate republican paper opposed to the Combes government, admonished: "Gentlemen let us remain French. . . . Yes we know that M. Pelletan is rarely that. . . . But we will never accept that women be introduced into *our* political quarrels."[93] The Radical journal *La Lanterne* was satisfied that the author of the *Revue* had "learned that one cannot with impunity rudely challenge good taste and French gallantry." The Left Bank republican students were portrayed as defenders of national standards of gentlemanly behavior. They had been assaulted by "street toughs, *les Apaches*," who frequented La Scala. The police were condemned for their failure to protect the students and for their brutality toward them.[94] Clemenceau's *L'Aurore* insisted that Lafargue's *Revue* had "overstepped the boundary of what is permissible when he put Mme Pelletan on the stage. . . . The students refused to accept this lack of respect toward a woman. M. Lafargue may ridicule government ministers, that's his business, but he must leave their wives alone."[95] In this version hired "*Apaches* from the Boulevard Sébastopol" and the agents of the Paris Police Prefect had attacked the students. Even the Bonapartist journal *Le Gaulois* admitted that "one never has the right to lack courtesy in regards to a woman." *Le Gaulois* added, however, that the Radicals had initiated the detestable practice of insulting women in political discourse. As early as the 1860s they had attacked the empress, and more recently Pelletan himself had lacked respect toward the "good nursing Sisters" of Toulon.[96]

The most intransigent on the Right dissented from this agreement on proper behavior. Edouard Drumont, whose *Libre Parole* constantly strained the boundaries of acceptable political discourse, escalated the degree of verbal violence and abuse and defended the author of the *Revue*. An article in *La Libre Parole* addressed Lafargue as "my colleague in spirit." It then claimed that the entire incident had been created by "five or six *Apaches*

93. *La République française*, December 20, 1903, emphasis added.
94. *La Lanterne*, December 21, 1903.
95. *L'Aurore*, December 18, 1903.
96. *Le Gaulois*, December 19, 1903.

who had come specifically to boo. . . . They had been thrown out on the sidewalk where they could express their affection for that filthy Protestant who disrupts and dishonors the French Navy."[97] Significantly, both Radicals and their most hostile critics claimed to defend the good "French" order which "barbarians, *les Apaches*" were assaulting.

In the end Mme Marchand bowed to pressure and removed the controversial scene. Almost all politicians and journalists agreed that the order of bourgeois households must be protected, including even that of a Radical minister. This masculine accord on proper gender roles permitted order to be restored and the Scala incident to be closed. Paul Lafargue wrote a public letter of apology to Mme Pelletan which was published on the front page of *La Libre Parole*. Lafargue insisted that he had never intended any insult and there had been no problem until "a dozen braggarts proclaimed themselves your knights and claimed that you had been injured. . . . I would be honored if the Minister himself might read this letter and recognize that no insult was ever intended to the minister's wife, but only some pinpricks to the Minister."[98] *Le Figaro* expressed the final assessment. Its article conceded that the Radicals had made their point on the impropriety of disturbing politicians' wives and thereby disrupting proper political discourse, but the front-page article also implied that there was something faintly ridiculous in the Radicals' outrage and demands for good manners. For *Le Figaro* and those further to the Right it was the Radicals who were irresponsibly upsetting the proper social and cultural order.[99]

La Revue à poivre and the controversy surrounding it touched off another round, albeit a minor one, in the continuing and intensifying battle among politicians—Radicals, republicans, conservatives, nationalists, and anti-Semites—as to what social order should be defended and who was most capable of defending it. Ordering and order were the underlying themes of the music hall skit. The Scala affair illustrated that the nationalists and the anti-Semitic Right had succeeded in constructing a powerful cultural critique of the Radicals. The transformations taking place within avant-garde,

97. *La Libre Parole*, December 20, 1903.
98. *Ibid.*, December 22, 1903.
99. *Le Figaro*, December 20, 1903.

elite, popular, and commercial cultures gave the nationalists an opportunity to identify themselves with a commercially created but nonetheless fashionable and popular culture. At the same time, the Radicals were forced to denounce the world of *café concerts* and music halls. They became the defenders of bourgeois "good taste." Further, they responded to the ridicule of the music halls by demanding that the police impose order and that the censor curb comic "excesses." Their right-wing critics countered that while Radicals wanted order on the music hall stage, they had created disorder in the army, the family, and among authentic patriots. All this only heightened the point of the joke, namely that these men of disorder should claim to exercise state authority. Especially through the powerful medium of the commercial press this cultural battle resonated far beyond the Paris boulevards.[100]

Neither Pelletan nor the Radicals in general seemed to realize how serious a battle they were losing when they failed to counter the nationalists' cultural attack. On the surface, it appeared that the Radicals emerged from the controversies surrounding the Combes ministry with their moral and cultural values intact. To many in the Paris political world the nationalists simply had gone too far, committing the offense of bad taste and behavior unbecoming Frenchmen. The supporters of the Bloc des gauches presented themselves and believed themselves to be the defenders of the Republic, the Revolution, and *la patrie* against its enemies. In May, 1903, a key spokesman for the Bloc, the socialist Francis de Pressensé, predicted that the scandals surrounding Pelletan would fail to topple either the naval minister or the government. He was correct. He characterized Pelletan's accusers as "the party of order, the church, the army, property, and public morality caught in the act of dirty tricks, up to their elbows in the muck, associating with crooks, black-mailers and swindlers!"[101] Pressensé was certain that to be slandered by such a party was an honor. The Right had succeeded, however, in moving the political debate onto the terrain of cultural modernity and

---

100. In the fall of 1903 the Marseilles police were concerned that a singer in the local music hall, the Alcazar, would insult the Radical government. The dangerous allusions apparently did not occur (Police reports, November 28 and 30, 1903, M6 3291, AD/BR). Provincial cities imitated the popular culture created in the Paris music halls, including its right-wing political sympathies.

101. *L'Aurore*, July 1, 1902.

moral integrity. It was a ground on which the Radicals were no longer very secure.

By the first decade of the twentieth century the nationalists had convinced the petite bourgeoisie of the capital that the Radicals no longer spoke for them and that they were *démodé* figures of ridicule. At the other end of the political spectrum, the Socialists seriously questioned if their political alliance with the Radicals benefited the working class in any way. Syndicalist revolutionaries urged workers to repudiate not only the Radicals but the Republic and the *patrie*. Despite these assaults, the Radicals were by no means bereft of supporters. Certainly the legislative elections of 1910 and 1914 demonstrated their continuing strength, especially in the provinces. Nonetheless, the mounting criticisms of both Left and Right, as well as the Radicals' difficulty in fashioning effective responses, did shake the political, social, and cultural assumptions of Radical constituents. This development especially undermined the position of left-wing Radicals in the party, the Chamber, and eventually with the electorate.

Conclusion: The Politics
of Nostalgia

The decade following the resignation of the Combes government in 1905 was one of loss and defeat for left-wing radicalism. Few dramatic confrontations or heroic battles occurred; rather, a steady, inexorable process took place in which the influence of Pelletan's vision of radical democracy diminished. This vision was never completely eliminated, however, and as a rhetorical force it continued to elicit applause and approval at sessions of party Congresses, in newspaper articles, and even during electoral campaigns. A dominant theme of this rhetoric became the frustration of left Radicals, who although victorious at the polls were unable to transform electoral success into meaningful government action. Only months after the end of the Combes government and the unraveling of the Bloc des gauches coalition, Pelletan warned the 1905 Radical Congress of the dangers in their current situation. He bitterly reviewed his own and the Radicals' history during the Third Republic. "Citizens, the nation is losing patience. . . . When I think that it has been only thirty-five years since we entered the Tuileries which the people conquered from the regime of the Second of December. . . . The disappointments have been cruel: thirty years of marching in place, of elusive or adjourned reforms."[1]

This frustration and sense of failure intensified after the 1906 elections and the actions of the Clemenceau ministry. Left Radicals identified closely with the electoral and parliamentary alliance of Radicals and Socialists. They viewed it as the necessary force to support their reform policy; it also embodied their vision of a republican society based on an interclass alliance of the "people." The war between the Clemenceau ministry and the CGT, the support this government received from a large number of moderate Radical deputies, and the continuing growth and assertiveness of the new unified Socialist party destroyed any immediate hope of a revital-

1. Le Parti radical, 5ᵉ Congrès, tenu à Paris, October, 1905, p. 186.

ized Bloc des gauches. Pelletan's disappointment was especially sharp. He had considered the 1906 electoral victory as an endorsement of a strongly reformist program.[2] At the 1907 Congress he asked how it was possible that this electoral success had not been translated into a reformist parliamentary majority and legislative action. How could the will of the people be flouted?[3] Clemenceau's position brought him only sorrow.[4] For Pelletan in particular the tension between the Left of the Radical party and Clemenceau, his comrade of the 1880s, must have been especially distressing. In a 1911 letter to Emile Combes, Pelletan reiterated his condemnation of the "domestication" of the Radical party during the Clemenceau government. The consequence, in Pelletan's view, had been to "discredit and compromise the Radical party in the Chamber."[5] During the long Clemenceau ministry, left Radicals were in a particularly untenable position. One historian of the party has described them as "paralyzed . . . simultaneously in the opposition and in the government majority."[6]

Although the bitter disillusionment and sense of personal betrayal ended with the fall of the Clemenceau ministry in July, 1909, left Radicals continued to feel stymied in their efforts to shape effective official policy. They were increasingly alienated from most of the republican governments between 1909 and 1914, although Radicals, including left Radicals, scored victories in the legislative elections of 1910 and 1914.[7] In response to this

2. Radicals received 28.5 percent of the vote and secured 241 seats in the Chamber of 581 deputies, the Socialists 10 percent of the vote and 53 deputies (Chris Cook and Jon Paxton, *European Political Facts, 1848–1918* [New York, 1978], 121).

3. "Public opinion is confused and the rush of enthusiasm which swept the country the day after our triumphant elections seems to have abated" (Le Parti radical, *7e Congrès*, tenu à Nancy, October, 1907, p. 84).

4. Le Parti radical du sud-est, *1er Congrès*, tenu à Nice, April, 1907, pp. 139–40.

5. Camille Pelletan to Emile Combes, November 8, 1911, in Combes Papers, 13537, Archives Départmentales, Charente-Maritime.

6. Berstein, *Histoire du parti radical*, I, 70.

7. In 1910 the Radicals received 20.4 percent of the vote and secured 121 seats in a Chamber of 592 deputies; the Socialists gained 13.1 percent of the vote and 78 seats. In 1914 Radicals had 18.1 percent of the vote and 140 seats in a Chamber of 592 deputies; the Socialists had 16.8 percent of the vote and 103 seats (Cook and Paxton, *European Political Facts*, 122). Pelletan, for example, denounced Aristide Briand's government as not genuinely republican in a 1910 speech at Melun. Briand, a former independent socialist, headed the government from 1909 to 1911 and

unpromising situation Pelletan repeatedly called for the revival of the Bloc alliance, a strategy widely endorsed by left Radicals. In an open letter addressed to the 1913 Congress the former premier Emile Combes urged the "reconstitution of the Bloc des gauches against the combined efforts of all the reactionary forces."[8] The parliamentary coalition could not be revived, but electoral alliances between Radicals and Socialists, especially during the second round of balloting, brought victory to the Left. But the persistence of electoral success coupled with parliamentary powerlessness only ensured the continuing frustration of left Radicals and their spokesman Camille Pelletan.

In poor health and over sixty-five years old, Pelletan was steadily losing his influence within his own jurisdiction, the party, and the Chamber. After thirty-one years he resigned his seat as a deputy in 1912, withdrawing from the heart of legislative and political life in the Third Republic. With some difficulty, he was elected to the Senate, whose very existence he had once denounced as undemocratic. During the 1913 Radical party Congress he made a bid for the party's presidency, a position he had held in 1907. It was one of the few times that there was a contest. In an unusual move, the Congress rejected Pelletan and turned to Joseph Caillaux, almost twenty years Pelletan's junior. Although Caillaux and Pelletan agreed on several key policies, such as the need for fiscal reform and alliance with the SFIO, they represented entirely different Radical styles and generations. Anger, pathos, and deep anxiety permeated Pelletan's emotional speech to the Congress.

> Did we struggle so long to arrive here? What will become of our party, what will become of the Republic, if we do not rouse ourselves? . . . [Radicalism] has been my entire life and the very reason for my existence; as a young man I received the traditions of a heroic past. . . . Ah! it took many trials and arduous efforts for us to gain the electoral majority . . . or rather to reveal to that majority the unconscious

---

then again for a few months in 1913. He took an especially hard line on syndicalist strikes and was less than enthusiastic about enforcing anticlerical laws (Police report, December 2, 1910, Dossier Pelletan, MI 25359, AN).

8. Le Parti radical, *13ᵉ Congrès*, tenu à Pau, October, 1913, p. 5.

radicalism which has always slumbered in the depth of the national consciousness. . . . [And now] after this progress . . . [comes] the beginning of a period of decline . . . toward our lamentable present condition. . . . How great our shame if we respond to this democratic majority . . . by abandoning it! . . . How great our lassitude . . . our disgrace . . . our humiliation . . . our treason, if, unlike our mighty ancestors . . . [who] brought our cause to victory, we . . . permit it to be destroyed by a sort of unconsciousness, by a weakness . . . by the habits of government domestication . . . by a deadly inability to act . . . by the failure to remain true to ourselves . . . by a paralysis of human will! . . . We will see our cause, our ideal and our very raison d'être sink to the bottom, if we cannot manage a surge of manly energy." [9]

Pelletan expressed with particular urgency the need to struggle against impotency and immobility. He was not alone in expressing concern for the party in such terms of personal decline and moral failure. A member of the party Executive Committee opened this Congress by observing that "Republican France suffers from 'sleeping sickness.' We live in a strange world. Equivocation, ambition and personal interest disfigure everything." [10] Although the 1913 Congress rejected Pelletan as president, it did incorporate his sentiments and rhetoric in the official party declaration. Most probably Pelletan himself participated in the formulation of the closing pronouncement of the Congress. The official party statement reiterated the delegates' dismay over their failure to enact reform legislation despite their electoral successes. The Radicals described themselves as immobilized, but their declaration ended with the conventional call to action: "The party must recover its role and its mission and become itself once again." Paralysis was the problem; a return to roots and traditions was the solution. Pelletan's speech also concluded with a similar appeal for a rededication to noble origins and a revival of the heroic past. "But above all . . . let us become ourselves . . . an authentic Radical party, let us recover our energy and our cohesion; let us organize ourselves, discipline ourselves . . . and raise anew

9. *Ibid.*, 43–47.
10. Debierre, *ibid.*, 15.

our old and glorious flag which, alas, has sunk low. Democracy will certainly be grateful to us."[11]

These powerful sentiments undoubtedly reflected the Radicals' political situation during the first decade and a half of the twentieth century. But the ability of many Radicals, and particularly of Camille Pelletan, to conjure up these emotions of regret, shame, and desired renewal was also related to an older tradition. Images of decline, references to a heroic past, and calls to action had appeared for decades in Radical rhetoric. At the very moment of their political debut in the early 1880s, the Radicals expressed regret for what they had lost and lamented the deterioration of political commitment. In 1895 Pelletan bemoaned "the distasteful present" so removed from "the days of heroic struggle." Precisely as he would eighteen years later, Pelletan viewed the situation of radicalism in 1895 as fraught with paradox. "Yes the hour of victory has sounded. Who would believe it today. Faced with the spectacle which the Republic now presents, I hesitate, I gather my memories, I hold my head in my hands, I ask myself: who really has triumphed at the end of this long struggle? . . . We have always been the conquerors— and we are defeated." These despairing observations also ended in a call for renewal. "Democracy has triumphed, but its victory has been stolen. She will recapture it."[12] From the beginning of the Republic to 1914 and beyond the banner of radicalism was repeatedly falling, slipping, or sinking; it was in permanent need of being taken up again, hoisted anew, or lifted aloft.[13] These recurring images of glorious pasts, stolen victories, decadent presents, and promises of better futures if only Radicals would reaffirm their essential loyalties became expected fixtures of rhetoric and ritual.

Such discourse made concrete action in the present more difficult. It often encouraged an expectation of defeat and justified the search for external enemies who had subverted what ought to have been the natural evolution of Radical triumph. These ritualistic mantras made it easy for those not sympathetic with Pelletan to dismiss him and his political agenda as mere negativity and perpetual criticism. In their obituary of Pelletan, the editors of Le Figaro, who were among his most dedicated opponents, praised his

11. *Ibid.*, 384, 50–51.

12. Camille Pelletan, Obituary for Paul Vacquerie, *Le Rappel*, February 25, 1895.

13. See, for example, Police report on meeting at Melun, December 2, 1910, Dossier Pelletan, MI 25359, AN.

brilliant journalism and oratorical skills but essentially condemned him as a man of permanent opposition. *Le Temps*, another longtime Pelletan detractor, concurred entirely, labeling Pelletan exclusively as "a man of the opposition."[14]

Radical rhetoric of dissatisfaction with current political circumstances was, however, more than merely the habit of long years in the opposition. Left radicalism from its first self-conscious organization in the 1880s was steeped in nostalgia, a desire to return to some more noble political past, one superior in all respects to the compromised and unheroic present. The inability of Radicals to shake off this nostalgia, whether for the generation of 1848 or for the Great Revolution, created a serious obstacle to their attempts to forge a modern politics. Ironically, in the early days of the Republic the Radicals seemed well aware of the need to declare their independence from the past, including earlier traditions of republican politics. Writing in *Le Rappel* in May, 1871, François-Victor Hugo criticized the revolutionary Communards for being enthralled with an out-of-date revolutionary practice. François-Victor, who must have been especially sensitive to the powerful authority of older generations, wrote: "The imitation of the past is . . . the great error of many honest and sincere patriots. In democracy, as in literature, there is a classical school which is not simply satisfied with admiring the ancients, but insists on imitating them. . . . Of course, no one venerates the French Revolution more than we do. . . . But let us remember that these ancestors were innovators. . . . They were the sons of their own actions by being men of their time. . . . Let us follow their example by not imitating them."[15] (Ironically, the very title of the Hugos' journal evoked memory and might suggest that its editors did not so easily abandon their loyalties to the past.) Ten years later, Camille Pelletan also stressed the need to escape the dangerous legacy of the past when he pleaded for amnesty for the imprisoned Communards. In his historical studies of the Commune, written in 1880, Pelletan argued that amnesty would break the deadly cycle of revolution and reaction which, in his view, had repeatedly undermined the viability of republican regimes. Yet, despite this awareness of the potentially immobilizing consequences of nostalgia,

14. *Le Figaro* and *Le Temps*, June 6, 1915.
15. *Le Rappel*, no. 701, May 15, 1871.

Camille Pelletan and his fellow left Radicals could not give up the advantages of identification with a heroic past. They failed to create themselves through their own innovations, as the younger Hugo had urged; instead, they insisted, on their legitimacy as sons of the Revolution.

The young Pelletan had certainly shared François-Victor Hugo's hope that republicanism would function as a genuinely modern political movement, responsive to new aspirations of modern men in a changing society. Nonetheless, Pelletan could not emancipate himself either from his father's generation or from the heroes of the Revolution. The political, cultural, and emotional benefits of these ties to a recognizable past were too great and the possible dangers of fundamental change in a still unstable republic too threatening. In their retreat from innovation to defend the Republic, the left Radicals were caught in the dilemma of being increasingly identified with a past of political opposition at the very time when their own growing electoral strength offered the possibility of assuming greater influence and power in the republican state. They failed to shift from the tradition of republican opposition to the creation of a democratically governing party.

Increasingly after 1900 Pelletan and his colleagues equated Radical integrity with their refusal to alter established beliefs and practices. To remain what one had always been was extolled as an important political virtue. During the 1903 Congress, Ferdinand Buisson reiterated that an essential merit of the Radical party was that it could not and would not change.[16] While Pelletan was minister of the navy, his supporters constantly noted with approval that his government policies remained entirely consistent with his concerns as an opposition deputy. This theme became a persistent refrain in his electoral platforms. Pelletan proudly opened his 1906 campaign manifesto with the assertion that neither he nor his constituents had changed in twenty-five years.[17] It was, and continues to be, easy to parody such statements and see rigidity and immobility where the Radicals claimed consistency and principles.

This link to the past persisted even after Pelletan's death in 1915. All his obituaries stressed his nineteenth-century heritage. *Le Petit Provençal*, the Marseilles paper to which Pelletan had been a regular contributor,

---

16. Le Parti radical, *3e Congrès*, tenu à Marseille, October, 1903, p. 182.
17. "Manifeste de Pelletan," *Le Petit Provençal*, May 1, 1906.

Statue of Camille Pelletan, Salon-de-Provence, Bouches-du-Rhône. Erected during the Cartel des gauches government of Edouard Herriot, 1924–1925.

(Photo by author)

underscored this inheritance and particularly the influence of his father, Eugène. The younger Pelletan had remained faithful to the "high ideals of his father." The Socialist paper *L'Humanité*, while noting that Pelletan was "not one of ours," nonetheless paid tribute to him as one of "the old republican stock, living for an ideal." Writing in the party paper, *Le Radical*, Edouard Herriot, the future interwar Radical leader, praised Pelletan as "a rock . . . a survivor of those rugged and loyal generations who carved out the Republic. He remained faithful to the ideas of his youth." Almost the exact same words, "faithful to the convictions of his youth," appeared fittingly in Le Rappel's obituary for Pelletan.[18] The nostalgia that suffused Pelletan's life and led him to look back repeatedly to the experiences of the great men of his father's generation and beyond them to the Revolution was becoming a permanent trait of the left Radicals. After World War I the Radical party, especially under Herriot's leadership, would view with nostalgia the "heroic" days of Camille Pelletan and the Bloc des gauches. As early as 1915 the new journal associated with left Radicals, Le Bonnet rouge, lamented the passing of the "good old days" of Pelletan's prime, which contrasted favorably to the unprepossessing present: "We loved you . . . a representative of a time when one fought only for ideas, when a person could love without reserve and be enthusiastic without second thoughts. . . . Modern life has planted so many weeds in our poor hearts."[19]

Critics easily portrayed this commitment to the past as a defense of the status quo. In practice, it often became just that. On no issue was this more obvious than on the question of suffrage. Commitment to popular sovereignty served as one of the defining principles of left radicalism. The regular electoral and representative processes provided the Republic its legitimacy and superiority. In the early decades of the Third Republic, however, Radicals had questioned the institution of the parliamentary system and the mechanism of its electoral procedures. They doubted if structures created by the conservative National Assembly of the 1870s would ever be capable of accurately expressing the popular will. Uncertain about how to change these structures without threatening the Republic itself and uncertain about which mechanisms would fulfill their efforts to achieve authentic

18.   Camille Ferdy in Le Petit Provençal, June 6, 1915; L'Humanité, June 6, 1915; Le Radical, June 8, 1915; Le Rappel, no. 16296, June 13, 1915, p. 2. By this time Le Rappel had become a weekly.

19.   Le Bonnet rouge, June 6, 1915. The paper was established in 1913 with connections to Caillaux in the Radical party. Pelletan had contributed to it briefly just before his death. The paper quickly gained a reputation for being very willing to accept contributions from various sources. Among the most generous were the liquor interests, always seeking to protect their legal privileges. Le Bonnet rouge was suppressed in 1916, accused of pacifism and lending support to the enemy after a long campaign against the paper by L'Action française (Bellanger et al., Histoire générale de la presse française, III, 378, 439–41).

popular representation, the Radicals tempered their criticisms and became increasingly committed to the existing parliamentary system and the established single-member electoral districts. The Boulanger Affair of the late 1880s exposed their quandary about parliamentary representation and popular sovereignty. After 1900, when both conservatives and Socialists called for the adoption of proportional representation as a more representative system, the Radicals adamantly refused any change that might jeopardize their electoral gains.

An even greater challenge was the demand of the women's rights movement to enlarge and transform the suffrage. The call to give women the vote directly countered important traditions of republicanism. In 1793 and again in 1848 republicans had specifically excluded women from the categories of citizen and individual. Republicanism functioned in a sharply defined public sphere in which masculinity was a required attribute. To have seriously endorsed women's suffrage Third Republican Radicals would have had to loosen their ties to their fathers and the Revolution; they would have had to relinquish at least partially their inheritance as "sons of the Revolution." Such a step was unthinkable. The Radical party, viewing itself as the guardian of republican traditions, refused any new definition of "universal suffrage." Its leaders explained these reactions to demands for change on suffrage issues as a defense of the Republic itself. The party and especially its left wing were trapped in a past from which they could not escape. This past offered them legitimacy and stature, as well as compensation for the contemporary situation which they could neither control nor change.

In 1914 Radicals, and even more emphatically left Radicals, did not control the French state.[20] The party—and for a time its left wing—had gained a dominant position in the critical legislative institutions of the Republic, the Chamber of Deputies and the Senate. Radicals did have considerable sway in the Ministry of Education, the important Ministry of the Interior, and increasingly in the Ministry of Agriculture, but the Foreign Affairs Ministry remained largely outside their influence. The attempts of the Combes government to republicanize the armed services, which Pelletan as minister of the navy and the parliamentary majority of the Bloc des gauches promoted, failed miserably and dramatically. The

20. Berstein, *Histoire du parti radical*, I, 17.

collapse of the Bloc government, the difficulties in reviving the left-wing parliamentary alliance, and the resurgence of nationalist sentiment in the early twentieth century were all indications of the success with which the armed services and its supporters were able to repulse Radical attempts to impose democratic reforms.

Many Radicals, particularly those who considered themselves left Radicals, were deeply uncertain about the exercise of state authority. Their tradition was one of opposition and criticism. Some had originally viewed even the republican state as a problematic legacy from authoritarian regimes. They lacked a clear agenda for how they might transform the state and were uncertain about the degree to which their republican principles endorsed such a transformation of hierarchical and authoritarian power. What precisely did it mean to republicanize the state? Camille Pelletan in particular often regarded the armed services as alien institutions within what ought to be a republican regime committed to egalitarianism. After the fall of the Bloc des gauches government, he continued to warn against the "false patriots who want to turn the army against the Republic." He supported efforts "to extend republican control over the army" and warned of the danger that "nationalists wanted to use the army as an authoritarian model."[21] But Radicals were poorly equipped to confront such threats. On one hand, they called for the transformation of the state and were suspicious of its power and authority. On the other hand, the only force Radicals could identify as able to create egalitarian institutions and practices was the power of the state itself. They remained forever caught in this ambivalence, critical of the state for restricting republican principles but seeing no other alternative than the power of the state to introduce equality and limit the consequences of hierarchy.

Views of legitimate state action varied widely among Radicals who offered diverse interpretations of state power. They wanted to be identified neither with doctrinaire laissez-faire attitudes nor with what they understood as the "étatisme" of the socialists. They debated and vàcillated between these two extremes. In 1903, during a discussion of government monopoly on education, Buisson rejected "the theory of l'Etat providence, of the state which does everything." Instead, he offered the alternative of

---

21. Le Parti radical, 5ᵉ Congrès, tenu à Paris, October, 1905, pp. 180–81.

the state that "would intervene in order to be the responsible guarantor of everyone's freedom." The state would function as "the grand liberator."[22] Pelletan had certainly viewed the state's role as one of moderate interventionism when he issued his various ministerial decrees to improve the bargaining power and working conditions of the state employees in the naval arsenals. The ultimate end of such intervention, whether in education policy or in civil service status, was to strengthen the Republic and ensure the commitment of republican citizens. But the French state was not easily forged into an instrument of political or social justice. Radicals were at constant pains to prove to their critics and to themselves that the republican regime, its bureaucratic apparatus, and its national identity were all compatible elements of a unified harmonious whole, rather than separate, conflicting structures and traditions.

Even such limited assertions of state intervention or such tempered actions aroused alarm within the Radical party. By 1910 Maurice Ajam, a moderate deputy from the Sarthe, published a pamphlet titled *Contre l'Etatisme*. He was much less concerned with Socialists than with the Radicals' adoption of "étatism" in the name of social reform. Although he claimed that he did not support "egoistic individualism," but rather "individualism combined with human solidarity," he pleaded for a "radical ideal which would reduce state action to a minimum."[23] Radicals remained divided on the issue of the appropriate role for the state, although after 1910 the left Radical position of favoring an active reform program rapidly lost ground.

How did left Radicals explain this failure to fashion a republican state and their hesitancy to reorganize the state bureaucracy? Ferdinand Buisson, in his important survey of radicalism in 1907, *La Politique radicale*, first noted the traumatic impact of the Socialist party and especially the revolutionary syndicalism of the CGT, which terrified and appalled many Radicals. In addition, he saw weaknesses among the Radicals themselves.

22. Le Parti radical, *3ᵉ Congrès*, tenu à Marseille, October, 1903, p. 181.

23. Maurice Ajam, "Contre l'Etatisme. Le Radicalisme individualiste. La Politique radicale et la politique socialiste," *Education de l'informateur parlementaire* (Paris, 1910), 85–86. Ajam had an interesting conclusion to his vision of the ideal state: "The perfect state would follow the model of good housewives accomplishing their tasks in silence. *Taccat mulier* said the less than gallant Saint Paul. Let the state then be like women and give us . . . some peace!" (*ibid.*, 86).

Paradoxically, he singled out the party's impressive electoral successes as a cause for their dilemmas. "The internal cause of the hesitation after the victory was the very number of winners. There were too many to be really sure of all of them. . . . Differences had not appeared as long as one remained at the level of campaign platform generalities. They became glaringly apparent when it was time to vote on legislative proposals."[24] Pelletan elaborated on this same theme during the 1913 Congress. The cause for what he called the party's "lamentable present situation" was inevitable: its great successes necessarily "attracted a mob of arrivistes."[25] This was hardly a satisfactory explanation for such major political disappointments. It was only a slightly modified version of the traditional republican explanation for failure: nefarious conspirators and agents of corruption were undermining the "natural" and inevitable "will of the people." Just as earlier republicans had been at a loss to explain why voters at times rejected the Republic, so in the early twentieth century left Radicals could explain the limitations of their own party and their influence within it only as a result of the action of outside forces entering the party and corrupting its "natural" inclinations. Neither Buisson nor Pelletan could consider that the paralysis of the party might rest with the contradictory principles of radicalism itself.

As important, this continuing resistance of the French state to republicanization was linked to a social order impervious to change. Only the Left of the Radical party consistently raised the issue of what type of society was necessary to sustain republican politics and a republican state. Left Radicals posed the question of how popular sovereignty could be a political reality or egalitarianism a genuine principle in a class society. They were never able to provide a satisfactory answer to this question. Ferdinand Buisson was most willing to confront this dilemma, but he too failed to resolve it. Buisson struggled with de Tocqueville's brilliant epigram, "It is a contradiction for the people to be simultaneously impoverished and sovereign [Il est contradictoire que le peuple soit à la fois misérable et souverain]."[26] For the mid-nineteenth century aristocratic commentator this observation demonstrated the utter impossibility of democratic regimes and their

24. Buisson, *Politique radicale*, 100–101.
25. Le Parti radical, *13e Congrès*, tenu à Pau, October, 1913, p. 44.
26. Quoted in Buisson, *Politique radicale*, 218.

inevitable degeneration into authoritarian states. For Ferdinand Buisson, however, in the first decade of the twentieth century this was the essential conundrum radicalism must unravel. Buisson pointed to the contradictions between the "appearance of political equality" and "the profound reality of economic inequality." This was the source of the difficult "social question." He, like Pelletan, was convinced that "democracy is not only a form of government. It is a way of organizing society."[27] But how could this modern society be created without violence and without disrupting the Republic? This question the Radicals never answered.

To some extent the left Radicals' hesitations and uncertainties in the face of this daunting task were the consequence of the ambiguous categories they used to describe society. Buisson sought to overcome class inequalities, but he identified social problems as the difficulties of "the little guys, the humble, the poor, and the disinherited."[28] Although left Radicals talked often about class and specifically the working class, their commitment was to that elusive category of "the people." Left Radicals imagined a democratic society that would promote "popular sovereignty," not advance the interests or needs of a particular class. This allegiance to "the people" was not simply rhetorical. The composition of Camille Pelletan's constituents and supporters in the Bouches-du-Rhône suggested that indeed an interclass mix of workers, rural small property owners, small town retailers, commercial employees, low-level civil servants, and some professionals supported left-wing politicians. This socially heterogeneous constituency, straddling the unstable and treacherous fault line between the working class and the petite bourgeoisie, represented both the aspirations and the justification of radicalism: to represent the "people" and thus the nation.

The left Radicals opposed the substitution of specific class interests for this more vaguely defined category, goals of "the people." They criticized the class perspective of the Socialists and also fought moderates and dissidents within their own party who were pressing hard to identify radicalism with the concrete needs of small property owners. In 1907, Camille Pelletan declared that the "decisive mission of the Radical party was social reform," but he emphatically denied that this could be a politics of class.

27. Ibid., 220–21.
28. Ibid., 219.

He identified the "glory of the French spirit" as the revolutionary tradition in which "a part of the bourgeoisie could unite with proletarians to work for the emancipation of the disinherited." The party must persist in being both "bourgeois and *peuple*."[29] In his call to revitalize the Radical party, also published in 1907, Ferdinand Buisson made a similar plea to eschew class and interest politics. In his view, both those to the Right and to the Left of the Radicals shared a perspective that identified "the problem with property . . . with the condition of things." The superiority of radicalism, according to Buisson, rested with its concern for the "condition of persons. The Declaration of the Rights of Man must remain the exclusive basis of Radical politics and sociology."[30]

By the early twentieth century Radicals like Pelletan and Buisson realized that their construction of essential, defining categories—the people, the citizen, the nation—was being challenged from a variety of directions. Socialism with its class analysis was a powerful, persuasive alternative to the traditional republican view of citizens striving to achieve full political sovereignty. Further complicating this situation, the Socialists never repudiated the concept of citizen or democratic rights. Left Radicals also employed the language of class though insisting that their political aims transcended class. Blurred and ambiguous categories permitted the Bloc des gauches to continue as an important and powerful political alliance during the first half of the twentieth century, but this same ambiguity made it impossible for the Bloc to promote a coherent social and political program. This condition paralyzed the Left of the Radical party early in the century and would eventually affect the Socialists in a similar manner. The internal shift within the party made an even greater assault on the left Radical position. Moderates now successfully argued for the abandonment of the broad representation of "the people" and the adoption of concrete measures to protect the interests of a new and more defensive petite bourgeoisie. While insisting on the dangers of socialism, these moderates fashioned their own class analysis. They envisioned a beleaguered but propertied middle class

29. Le Parti radical du sud-est, Camille Pelletan, *1er Congrès*, tenu à Nice, April, 1907, p. 144.

30. Buisson, *Politique radicale*, 237. It is perhaps not inconsequential that Georges Lefebvre in his popular history of the French Revolution, *1789*, published in 1939, made a similar, if somewhat more complex, analysis of the Declaration of the Rights of Man.

turning to a remodeled Radical party as the best defense for their acquired social positions and as the best guarantee of continuing upward social mobility. The functioning of the parliamentary system certainly encouraged such appeals to specific material interests, and the moderates found an increasing response among the Radical electorate.

Although given the least public attention, the struggle for women's suffrage was perhaps the most fundamental of the challenges to the left Radicals' conception of the citizen. The demand for an end to the exclusion of women from political life revealed the severe limitations of the principle of "universal suffrage" which provided the essential legitimacy of the Republic. This call for genuine universalism undermined the left Radicals' assertion that they represented all "the people." Citizens and people now stood as particular groups of men. The Radicals' unwillingness, or perhaps inability, to alter these gender-based definitions demonstrated the degree to which they remained tightly dependent on the masculine environment in which these categories had been created.

If the terms *citizen, individual,* and *the people* were increasingly becoming problematic and were no longer providing Radicals with an unambiguous identity and direction, the Radicals' identification with the nation, *la patrie,* was also being questioned. Right-wing nationalists competed most successfully with the Radicals as defenders of the nation. These nationalists were a new political phenomenon, some of them drawing their inspiration from nineteenth-century republican traditions. The nationalists used the Radicals' association with the Socialists, their concern for egalitarian principles, and their suspicion of military hierarchy as clear evidence that the Radicals would permit the nation to become vulnerable and that the Radicals were incapable of leadership. The Radicals countered such attacks with ever more passionate claims of their devotion to *la patrie*. As their other universalizing identities seemed to slip away, many Radicals turned with even greater fervor to their patriotism. They insisted that the state, the nation, and republicanism were all one and that they were the best representatives of this unity. A major speaker at the 1913 Congress declared, "The emotion of patriotism is especially deep on the part of the sons of the Revolution . . . the feeling of love for the fatherland, who else would have it more than you, democratic sons of republicans, sons of those who shed their blood for the Republic and the fatherland."[31] The nation was an element of their tradition which might provide the unity that no longer seemed possible when claiming the defense of citizens and the people. These outpourings of nationalist sentiment, however, drove the Radicals further from their electoral allies, the Socialists, and never put an end to the nationalists' denunciations that their patriotism was counterfeit.

By the time of World War I the nationalist aspiration for unity affected the entire political spectrum, including the Socialists. Although some on the Left still sought to make distinctions between various forms of national unity, there was a powerful drive to make all conform to the most strident nationalism. The obituaries and eulogies on the occasion of Camille Pelletan's death, one year after the war began, provided some the opportunity to demonstrate their intensified patriotic fervor. The *Petit Provençal* refashioned Pelletan into a patriot driven by desire to revenge the loss of Alsace and Lorraine in 1871. His longtime associate Camille Ferdy highlighted Pelletan's brief experience as a war correspondent during the Franco-Prussian War. He insisted that both Camille and his father had been among those "who had never forgotten" the 1870–1871 defeat and loss of territory. According to this eulogy, Pelletan had welcomed World War I as a struggle for "national liberation . . . [and] his patriotic soul quivered with enthusiasm."[32] René Viviani, the former independent socialist who in June 1915 was the premier of France, portrayed Pelletan as a soldier who had died at his post and whose memory would inspire the living to return to action.[33] But no Radical could ever go far enough in his dedication to the fatherland to satisfy the nationalists. The nationalist Right had little interest in embracing the wartime union. In its brief obituary for Camille Pelletan, *La Libre Parole* reminded readers that the Radical leader had been considered a "peril to the nation" and that his naval policies had seriously delayed the construction of large battleships.[34] Radicals could never successfully com-

31. Le Parti radical, Gaston Dumesnil, 13e *Congrès*, tenu à Pau, October, 1913, p. 68. Dumesnil (1879–1918) was a deputy from Maine et Loire from 1914 to 1918.

32. Camille Ferdy, Camille Pelletan obituary, *Le Petit Provençal*, June 6, 1915. In the summer of 1914 this Marseilles paper had added the subtitle *Quotidien d'Union national*.

33. "Obsèques Camille Pelletan," *Le Radical*, June 9, 1915.

34. *La Libre Parole*, June 6, 1915, p. 2.

pete with the nationalists in patriotic ardor without compromising their distinctive nationalism, which identified the Republic with *la patrie*.

By the 1910s the Radicals had reached a difficult moment in their development. Critics on both their Right and their Left had challenged and badly shaken the core elements of their most central identity. Radicals were unable to define precisely their commitment to popular sovereignty, egalitarianism, and the nation. Their promotion of the individual and the citizen often encountered the obstacle of class inequality, an obstacle to which they responded with much hesitation. The political clout of left Radicals declined, making it increasingly difficult to implement their program of reforms. These political defeats were often met with nostalgic regrets. Moderates gained greater practical control of the party, especially in the parliamentary arena. They gave less attention to republican universalist aims and turned instead to limited interest politics that could successfully defend the practical concerns of some provincial small property owners. Nonetheless, the rhetoric of universalism was never jettisoned. It continued to unify the Radical party until the collapse of the Third Republic in 1940.

Had the Radicals and particularly the left Radicals accomplished anything? Most emphatically yes, but rarely their intended objectives. They failed to create the democratic state and society which left Radicals regarded as essential for the success of the republican regime. They had, however, fashioned a specifically French republican political culture. They redefined the political aspirations of the lower strata of the bourgeoisie and opened new civil service careers to that social group. Radicals were a critical force in the reorganization and expansion of the republican political elite. They pioneered the development of politics as a profession, a *métier*, that could provide a few with access to considerable upward mobility, wealth, and influence.

During the Third Republic, Radical politicians gained entrée to social and political power from which their fathers had been excluded. Beginning in the 1880s, lawyers, journalists, physicians, and academics secured influential, lucrative, and prestigious careers in the parliamentary arena. Similarly, for the party rank and file the espousal of radicalism meant not only a political ideology but also the expanding possibility of state employment, which often brought tangible rewards. These material benefits of radicalism increased as Radical electoral success grew. For Radical leaders and militants, the Republic was more than a regime, more than a political ideology; it was a way of life. Satisfaction with such accomplishments was expressed in banquets such as the one held on October 14, 1906, in the Provençal town of Salon to celebrate the twenty-five years during which Camille Pelletan had represented the district. Members of the local Radical committee shared the table with departmental, regional, and national dignitaries. The Radicals had established successful networks linking electors, party rank and file, municipal officials, national deputies and senators, prefects, and even government ministers. Such prestige and influence were commemorated in albums, bronze plaques, and specially decorated tins of Sèvres biscuits.[35] The rituals surrounding this new political status appear as kitsch, but its existence had considerable social and political significance. The Radicals were instrumental in the development of a French political elite that differed from that of other major European states. A much broader range of educated bourgeois men had access to political power. In France aristocrats and the haute bourgeoisie no longer had an exclusive monopoly on state power.

The Radicals also contributed to the successful functioning of the parliamentary system. Despite their initial ambivalence toward it and despite their failure to refashion the parliamentary system into one fully compatible with their republican ideals, Radicals participated significantly in the elaboration of what has become the norm of governing in most of western Europe during much of the twentieth century. The tensions between aspirations for authentic popular representation and full sovereignty and the exigencies of parliamentary politics and state bureaucracies remained unabated. No representative government has been able to resolve this dilemma, and it continues to erode citizens' confidence in democratic regimes.

In the first two decades of the twentieth century Radicals were identified with a republican democratic regime and elicited considerable electoral support because of this identification. They became the largest party in the Chamber of Deputies and participated in the Bloc des gauches coalition, which the left Radicals enthusiastically supported. This parliamentary al-

---

35. Police report, Banquet, Salon, October 14, 1906, Dossier Pelletan, MI 25359, AN.

liance enabled the passage of a limited number of social reforms, although all supporters admitted that these laws suffered from excessive compromises. In its obituary for Camille Pelletan the Socialist daily, *L'Humanité,* underscored the significance of his introduction of the eight-hour day for state employees in the naval arsenals. Despite their many inadequacies, such reforms recognized the political principle that modern representative regimes must address the social and economic concerns of the electorate. However limited and compromised, these reforms established new relations between the state and its citizens, complex relations that included elements of greater coercion and control, as well as greater security and access to additional benefits. As important, the parliamentary and electoral coalition of the Bloc des gauches established a powerful political myth, one that corresponded to the Radical tradition of the unified force of "le peuple." At least until 1945 this attractive political symbol of the left Bloc strongly influenced the strategies and the actions of both Radicals and Socialists.

Finally, the left Radicals preserved a particular form of democratic rhetoric which influenced political discourse well into the twentieth century. Although frequently reduced to clichés, this language was available for diverse and not easily controlled purposes. Demands for equality, citizens' rights, and popular sovereignty remained and remain accessible and potent concepts that can and do effectively function as criticisms and calls for change, even within long-established parliamentary regimes.

The implementation of their democratic agenda and the creation of an authentically republican state and society had clearly eluded the left Radicals. As the essential causes of this defeat they could identify a variety of external opponents. With considerable justification, they complained of the authoritarian structure of state ministries which resisted their efforts to introduce change; they decried the resilience of antirepublican forces within the church and the armed forces and among the social elite, who retained considerable power and influence. Radicals were especially concerned with the successful reorganization of antirepublicanism under the new banners of antiparliamentarianism, nationalism, and anti-Semitism in the beginning of the twentieth century. In addition, Radicals recognized that the Socialists posed a powerful challenge, presenting their persuasive economic analysis and class politics as an alternative emancipatory movement. The movement for women's suffrage, although ignored by most

Radicals, further exposed central contradictions in the origins of Radical principles of "universal suffrage" and citizenship. Although all these elements certainly contributed to the recognized paralysis of radicalism, these external circumstances alone were not sufficient to explain the frustrations of many Radicals in the 1910s.

The repetitive and ritualistic calls for a return to origins suggest that precisely the opposite was occurring. Many in the Radical party were abandoning their original project and were redefining the party's constituency, objectives, and methods. The immediate interests of provincial small property owners were replacing attempts to maintain an inter-class electoral base. In practice, the slogan of no enemies on the Left was becoming less convincing. The principles of order and authority increasingly received the enthusiastic support of many Radicals, who viewed them as essential components in the defense of the Republic and the nation. Simultaneously, however, the electorate, the party rank and file, and even most deputies continued to expect the evocation of the heroic past, the noble actions of earlier generations, and stirring accounts of revolutionary triumphs and sacrifices. The endless, solemn, and loudly applauded repetition of these words increasingly emptied them of meaning. They were comforting and familiar, not a militant call to change. They evoked little thought and even less action; few believed that such words could have any reality. Radical rhetoric became easy to lampoon and satirize, as the nationalist Right accomplished so uproariously and successfully. Radicalism and especially the Radical Left were hopelessly old-fashioned. The cultural avant-garde, which politicians like Pelletan had been so much a part of in the 1870s, had shifted significantly by the early twentieth century, and popular democratic aspirations seemed decidedly less relevant to the creation of a modern culture and politics.

A major aim of this history has been to recapture the aspirations of those young, educated bourgeois men of the 1870s who sought to dedicate themselves to the nation, the Republic, and the people. They genuinely believed that they were engaged in the creation of a thoroughly modern politics, a democratic regime in which the people could authentically speak and govern. For some it was a moment in which politics was approached with utmost seriousness; young men especially invested great hope in the possibilities of a new state. These expectations inspired the twenty-six-year-old Pelletan and his circle of poet friends painted by Fantin-Latour in 1872. Four years later, the avant-garde poet Stéphane Mallarmé had no doubt that the impressionists' breakthrough in the visual arts was linked to a new language of poetry, which in turn was connected to the new political reality of radical democracy and universal suffrage. The special "honour" of the late nineteenth century was, in Mallarmé's view, "the participation of a hitherto ignored people in the political life of France." Writing a piece for a London art review in 1876 called "The Impressionists and Edouard Manet," Mallarmé was confident that an entirely new culture was being constructed, one that was "radical and democratic . . . in a word *Intransigeant*." It would break with the "romantic tradition of the first half of the century . . . those old imaginative artists and dreamers," and instead there would emerge the "energetic modern worker" transforming art, politics, and society. Together all these interdependent changes would, according to Mallarmé, usher in a new, genuinely modern era in which the "multitude . . . demands to see with its own eyes." In that new world nature would "express herself, calm, naked, habitual, to those newcomers of tomorrow, each one consenting to be an unknown unit in the mighty numbers of universal suffrage, and [nature would] place in their power a newer and more succinct means of observing her."[36]

Mallarmé's vision emphasized the transformation of human consciousness and the emergence of a new "worker" who perceived the world in a new way, engaged in new forms of solidarity, and acted in consort with nature. These aspirations toward total authenticity—the union of art, nature, the "multitude," and democratic institutions—were never realized. From the vantage point of the end of the twentieth century that failure may not be surprising, given the naïve and grandiose hopes of the artists and politicians of the 1870s. To ignore or dismiss these widely shared optimistic expectations, however, makes it impossible to understand the democratic movements of the nineteenth century, as well as the specific motives of the first generation of Third Republic Radicals who were committed to the modern politics of popular democracy.

36. These observations on the nature of modernity concluded an article by Stéphane Mallarmé, "The Impressionists and Edouard Manet," *Art Monthly Review*, September 30, 1876, quoted in Clark, *Painting of Modern Life*, 268.

Although naïveté may have been a handicap to realizing the republican project, certainly more fundamental was the inability to identify clearly the genuinely *modern* political objective. Republicans and especially those who claimed to be most intransigent, the Radicals, could not emancipate themselves from the past. They remained "sons of the Revolution" and thus were unable to follow Mallarmé's admonition to break with past "dreamers" and become "energetic modern workers," engaged in the transformation of consciousness. Camille Pelletan's study of Victor Hugo's political life, published in 1907, illustrated the limitations of the Radicals' attempts to elaborate a genuinely new politics. The year the work appeared coincided with a crisis in left-wing radicalism when its progress had been sharply halted. The study was to be a popular, political inspiration; for Pelletan, Hugo remained an important political mentor. Pelletan devoted a long section to the poet's involvement with the Second Republic. These were critical years when Hugo shifted from royalism to republicanism, a transformation that eventually led to his opposition to Louis Napoleon and to his exile. Even before he had definitively broken with royalism and while campaigning as a conservative for the Constituent Assembly, Hugo offered a vision of the ideal republic, which he equated with civilization itself. These descriptions offered an endless fund of metaphors that served republicans and Radicals for decades. Similar imagery reappeared in 1862 in Hugo's influential novel, *Les Misérables*, and would remain a vision which Radicals such as Pelletan found permanently compelling.

First [the Republic] will be a holy communion of all the French . . . and one day of all peoples joined in democratic principles; it will be established by liberty without usurpation or violence, ensuring equality which will permit the natural development of each individual, and creating fraternity, not of the convent, but of free men. This republic will provide education to all, as the sun gives its light, without charge. . . . It will multiply railroads, reforest some land while clearing other areas, thus increasing land values. This republic will establish the principle that every man must begin with labor and end with property. Therefore it will guarantee property as the sign of labor completed and work as the sign of future property. . . . In order to resolve the great problem of universal well-being this republic will peacefully plan the permanent growth of industry, science, art and thought. While remaining practical, it will endeavor to realize all the great dreams of the wise: establish power on the same foundation as liberty, through law; subordinate force to intelligence; abolish rebellion and war . . . make art the law of citizens and peace the law of the nations. The republic will make France flourish and it will conquer the world. In sum it will majestically embrace the entire human race and be watched over by the satisfied eye of God."[37]

In 1907 Pelletan, searching for those origins that would revitalize the party and the enthusiasm of the Radicals, had only the greatest praise for this grandiose project. It was "superb," and the elaborated social and economic reforms expressed a "marvelous richness."[38] Peace, productivity, and community characterized this ideal regime. Unlike Mallarmé, Hugo offered a ready-made regime overflowing with material plenitude. Hugo created a fiction in which the Republic already existed and then animated his world with a plethora of tangible improvements, ultimately linking railroads to God. There were no actors in Hugo's ideal republic, only recipients of a benevolent largesse, supervised by a smiling deity. Hugo ignored the perplexing contradictions surrounding the implementation of popular sovereignty, equality, and active citizenship. His heirs, the left-wing Radicals, did struggle with these central dilemmas. They never succeeded in resolving them, in part because they remained captivated by the past in which ancestors such as Hugo had promised new worlds of harmony, abundance, and benign authority.

Immediately before World War I the certainty of progress embodied in the Hugolian and Radical vision had worn thin. It exuded more than a touch of smugness which Hugo shared with his benevolent God who watched over his political fiction. After the war not only could Radicals, be ridiculed, despite their continued electoral victories and even greater parliamentary prominence, but the poetic inspiration of Victor Hugo, too, seemed shabbily out of date. In the mid-1930s a young Romanian writer with strong French connections excoriated Hugo, his romantic rhetoric,

37.   Quoted in Camille Pelletan, *Victor Hugo*, 119–20.
38.   *Ibid.*

and his democratic politics. With hilarious brilliance Eugène Ionesco denounced Hugo as an exemplary mediocrity, a man who belonged perfectly to "his historical moment and was a slave to all the historical moments of his life." An overwhelming vanity ruled this lucid buffoon, Ionesco observed. He abhorred Hugo's literary work as a "treasure house of mediocrity, stuffed with common places." His very language was a major obstacle in the struggle to create modern poetry. In Ionesco's dissection of Hugo, among the "great man's" most ridiculous and absurd characteristics were his "idealism, optimism, morality and humanism." The critic "laughed until the tears flowed at Hugo's belief in the progress of humanity, science, social life, the divine in man and other amusements of that kind." Most serious of all, Hugo talked too much; he drowned everyone and everything in a torrent of metaphors that could only signify insincerity. Ionesco was certain that a modern French poetry with unknown potential would eventually appear from the debris of the shattered Hugolian facade. Certainly contemporary defenders of Hugo, such as Edouard Herriot, literary critic and leader of the Radical party, could be dismissed as even more farcical and absurd than Hugo. For Ionesco the literary commentator and right-wing politician Charles Maurras pointed the way to modernity, which must be more disciplined and hard-edged.[39] In exposing the Hugolian rhetoric as farce, Ionesco also predicted the end of the Third Republic and with it the collapse of the left Radicals' republican project.

In the first decades of the twentieth century an ever-increasing number of French men and women viewed themselves, either with enthusiasm or dismay, as inhabiting a modern era. Many participated in a diverse range of activities seeking to create modern institutions, relations, expressions, and pleasures appropriate to their new world. These attempts to break with the past had considerable success in elite and popular culture; change was much less dramatic within social and gender hierarchies or within political structures and state institutions. Ironically, some had hoped that the Third Republic would inaugurate authentic innovations in politics and the organization of the state, which would in turn encourage even broader changes

---

39. Eugène Ionesco, *Hugoliade*, trans. Dragomir Constineanu (1935–36; rpr. Paris, 1982), 30–37, 84, 69–70.

in society and culture. No matter how serendipitous the founding of this Third Republic, the Radicals, as dedicated republicans, insisted that they would construct a democratic state and society. They and their supporters would create an appropriately modern politics in which the "people" would govern. By 1910, however, the most committed and perspicacious of the first generation of Radicals were exhausted. Camille Pelletan conceded that their efforts to implement greater equality, popular sovereignty, and universal suffrage were only partially successful. They failed to create a distinctively democratic state that would alter traditional structures and methods of state power and authority. They never resolved the tension between universal male suffrage and the workings of a parliamentary governing system. They hesitated before the different conceptions of society embodied in the categories of citizen and class. Nor were they able to respond to women's demands that universal suffrage actually become universal. Finally, Radicals were caught between their desire to speak for the people and the nation and the complex realities of a shifting and highly mutable petit bourgeois constituency. Ardent leaders, such as Pelletan, could not sever their ties with the legitimating past. They remained permanent sons of an ever more distant Revolution rather than inventors of a new twentieth-century political culture.

BIBLIOGRAPHY

PRIMARY SOURCES

Manuscript Collections

Archives Nationales, Paris

Série AP. Archives Personnelles et Familiales.
  73 Adresses de sympathie et félicitations à Combes, 1902–1904.
Série C. Archives Parlementaires, Assemblée Nationale.
  3503 Elections 1881, Bouches-du-Rhône.
  3985 Elections 1881, Bouches-du-Rhône.
  4057 Elections 1881, Seine.
  5116 Elections 1898, Bouches-du-Rhône.
  5301 Elections 1885, Bouches-du-Rhône.
  5334 Elections 1893, Bouches-du-Rhône.
  5350 Elections 1898, Bouches-du-Rhône.
  5441 Commission du budget, 1890.
  5548 Commission du budget, 1895.
  5624 Commission du budget, 1899.
  6037 Elections 1902, Bouches-du-Rhône.
  6289 Elections 1906, Bouches-du-Rhône.
  6656 Elections 1910, Bouches-du-Rhône.
  6862 Elections 1914, Bouches-du-Rhône.
  7225 Elections 1912, Bouches-du-Rhône.
  7258 Commission de la marine, 1904.
  7283 Commission du budget. Enquête sur la marine, 1904.
  7313–16 Enquête parlementaire sur l'Affaire Humbert, 1903–1904.
Série F1c I. Funérailles d'Etat.
  187–88 B Funérailles de Victor Hugo, 1885.

Série F7. Police Générale.

12541–42   Atmosphère politique, Elections 1902. Police reports.

12553   Situation politique, 1899–1905. Police reports.

12714   Groupes parlementaires avant 1914.

12794   Viticulteurs du Midi, 1907. Police reports.

13637–38   Ouvriers d'arsenaux, 1904–11.

Série F18. Beaux Arts.

407   Censor, *Le Rappel*/Barbieux, 1869–80.

1499   Inspection des théâtres, *La Revue à poivre*, 1903.

Série MI. Ministère de l'Intérieur, Notes de la Police de l'Intérieur.

25320   Dossier Edouard Drumont, 1895.

25359   Dossier Camille Pelletan, 1885–1912.

Archives de la Préfecture de la Police de Paris

Série Ba.

884   Victor Hugo, Fête, 1881, Funérailles, 1885. Police reports.

1216   Eugène Pelletan. Police reports.

1744   Cabinet de la Police, X^e arrondissement.

Archives Départmentales des Bouches-du-Rhône

Série II M2. Elections senatoriales: 10   1911.

Série II M3. Elections législatives.

30   1881.

33   1888–89.

45   1906.

Série M4. Police reports. 634 Cercle républicaine, Aix.

Série M6. Cabinet du préfet.

3291   Police reports, 1903–1904.

3305   Activités politiques, 1880–81. Police reports.

3328   Police reports, 1902.

3376   Personalités politiques et réunions politiques. Police reports.

3404   Police reports, 1909–13.

3405   Elections 1906. Police reports.

Série Z1. Monthly reports of subprefect to prefect.

28   Cercles et sociétés, autorisations, 1875–95.

32   Police reports, 1873–94.

Archives Municipales, Salon-de-Provence

Série I33: 235 Société de la jeunesse républicaine, 1887. Police report.
Série IKF: Liste des candidats, 1910. Police report.

Assemblée Nationale, Parliamentary Papers

Annales de l'Assemblée nationale. Chambre des députés. *Débats.*
————. *Programmes et professions de foi et engagements électoraux des députés.*
————. *Annexes.*
Assemblée nationale. Chambre des députés. Débats. *Journal Officiel.*

Bibliothèque Nationale, Paris

Manuscripts.
Fonds maçonniques, Loge de l'Unité, Salon, Rés FM 2 115.
Victor Hugo, NAF 24801.
Edouard Lockroy Papers, Don 24601.

Newspapers Consulted Regularly

L'Intransigeant. 1883–86.
La Justice. 1880–98.
Le Petit Provençal. 1881–1907.
Le Petit salonais. 1889.
Le Progrès de Salon. 1902–1908.
Le Rappel. 1869–1915.
Le Réveil salonais. Journal républicain organe des intérêts du commerce et de l'agriculture.
    1887–88.

Newspapers Consulted Intermittently

L'Autorité.
L'Aurore.

Le Démocrate.

L'Eclair.

L'Emancipateur. Organe de la Fédération nationale des travailleurs réunis de la Marine de l'Etat.

La Lanterne.

La Libre Parole.

Le Petit Parisien.

La Petite République.

Le Radical.

La République française.

La Revue politique et parlementaire.

Le Siècle.

La Vie politique.

La Verité.

Radical Party Congresses

Le Parti républicain radical et radical-socialiste. *1er–13e Congrès.* 1901–13.

Le Parti républicain radical et radical-socialiste du sud-est. *1er Congrès.* 1907.

Books, Pamphlets, and Articles

Adam, Juliette Lamber. *Mes Premières Armes littéraires et politique.* Paris, 1894.

Ajam, Maurice. "Contre l'Etatisme. Le Radicalisme individualiste. La Politique radicale et la politque socialiste." *Education de l'informateur parlementaire.* Paris, 1910.

Bosq, Paul. *Nos Chers Souverains, les opportunistes, les radicaux, la concentration, le dernier batteau.* Paris, 1898.

Buisson Ferdinand. *La Politique radicale. Etude sur les doctrines du Parti radical et radical-socialiste.* Paris, 1908.

———. *Le Vote des femmes.* Paris, 1911.

Champsaur, Felicien. *Victor Hugo. Les Hommes d'aujourd'hui.* Paris, 1878.

Cinna, J. *Le Parti radical et le patriotisme.* Tarn-et-Garonne, 1912.

Combes, Emile. *Mon Ministère. Mémoires, 1902–1905.* Paris, 1956.

de Champville, Georges Gabius. *Le Comité executif du Parti républicain radical et radical-socialiste de 1897 à 1907.* Paris, 1907.

Flaubert, Gustave. *Madame Bovary.* 1856; rpr. Paris, 1972.

————. *Sentimental Education*. Translated by Robert Baldick. 1869; rpr. New York, 1964.

Fournier, Marcel. "L'Organisation du parti progressiste." *Revue politique et parlementaire*, XIV (1897), 235–47.

Geffroy, Gustave. *L'Enfermée*. 2 vols. 1886; rpr. Paris, 1926.

————. *Georges Clemenceau, sa vie, son oeuvre*. Paris, 1919.

Geffroy, Gustave, and Henri de Toulouse-Lautrec. *Yvette Guilbert*. Translated by Barbara Sessions. 1894; rpr. New York, 1968.

Hugo, Victor. *Les Châtiments*. Brussels, 1853.

————. *Contemplations*. Brussels, 1856.

————. *Les Misérables*. 3 vols. 1862; rpr. Paris, 1958.

————. *Quatre-vingt treize*. Paris, 1874.

Laisant, Charles-Ange. *L'Anarchie bourgeoise. (La Politique contemporaine)*. Paris, 1887.

Lissagaray, P. O. *Histoire de la Commune de 1871*. 1896; rpr. Paris, 1983.

Lockroy, Edouard. *Au Hasard de ma vie*. Paris, 1913.

Marx, Karl. *The Civil War in France: The Paris Commune*. 1871; rpr. New York, 1940.

————. *Class Struggles in France, 1848–1850*. 1850; rpr. New York, 1964.

————. *The Eighteenth of Brumaire of Louis Bonaparte*. 1852; rpr. New York, 1963.

Michelet, Jules. *L'Amour*. Paris, 1858.

————. *La Femme*. Paris, 1860.

————. *Le Peuple*. 1846; rpr. Paris, 1974.

————. *Du Prêtre, de la femme, de la famille*. Paris, 1845.

————, and Edgar Quinet. *Des Jésuites*. Paris, 1843.

Monteil, Edgar. *Célébrités contemporaines. Edouard Lockroy*. Paris, 1886.

Pelletan, Camille. *L'Assemblée au jour de jour. Du 24 mai 1873 au 25 février 1875. Théâtre de Versailles*. Paris, 1875.

————. *Georges Clemenceau, célébrités contemporaines*. Paris, 1883.

————. *L'Impôt sur le revenu. Discours prononcé à la Chambre des députés au cours de la session générale de l'impôt sur le revenu, séance du 3 février 1908*. Paris, 1908.

————. "Mémoires (inédites)." In Paul Baquiast, "Camille Pelletan (1846–1915). Esquisse de biographie." Mémoire de maîtrise d'histoire, Université de Paris IV, 1986.

————. *Programmes et professions de foi et engagements électoraux des députés*. Paris, 1880–1910.

————. *Questions d'histoire. Le Comité central et la Commune*. Paris, 1879.

————. *La Révolution en Russie. Discours*. Paris, 1905.

————. *La Semaine de mai*. Paris, 1880.

————. *Victor Hugo. Homme politique*. Paris, 1907.

Pelletan, Eugène. *Addresse au roi coton*. New York, 1863.

————. *La Charte au foyer*. Paris, 1864.

————. *Les Droits de l'homme*. Paris, 1858.

————. *La Famille: La Mère*. Paris, 1865.

————. *La Femme au XIXe siècle*. Paris, 1869.

————. *La Nouvelle Babylone*. Paris, 1862.

————. *Le Pasteur au désert*. Paris, 1877.

Petit, Edouard. *Eugène Pelletan, 1813–1884. L'Homme et l'oeuvre d'après des documents inédits*. Paris, [1913].

Piermé, Georges. *Compte rendu du 6e Congrès du Parti radical et radical-socialiste présenté à l'Association des inséparables du progrès*. Aisne, 1906.

Reinach, Joseph. *Le "Conciones" français. L'Eloquence française depuis la Révolution jusqu'au nos jours. Textes de lecture, d'explication et d'analyse pour la classe de première (lettres)*. Paris, 1893.

Rochefort, Henri de. *Les Aventures de ma vie*. 5 vols. Paris, 1896.

SECONDARY SOURCES

Books

Abélès, Luce. *Fantin-Latour: Coin de table. Verlaine, Rimbaud, et les vilains bonshommes*. Paris, 1987.

Accampo, Elinor, Rachel Fuchs, and Mary Lynn Stewart, eds. *Gender and the Politics of Social Reform: France, 1870–1914*. Baltimore, 1995.

Agulhon, Maurice. *1848 ou l'apprentissage de la République, 1848–1852*. Paris, 1973.

————. *Marianne au combat: L'Imagerie et la symbolique républicaines de 1789 à 1880*. Paris, 1979.

————. *La République au village: Les Populations du Var de la Révolution à la Deuxième République*. Paris, 1979.

Allen, James Smith. *In the Public Eye: A History of Reading in Modern France, 1800–1940*. Princeton, 1991.

Auspitz, Katherine. *The Radical Bourgeoisie: The Ligue de l'Enseignement and the Origins of the Third Republic, 1866–1885*. Cambridge, Mass., 1982.

Baratier, Edouard, *et al. Atlas historique: Provence, comtat venaissin, principauté d'Orange, comté de Nice, principauté de Monaco*. Paris, 1969.

Bardonnet, Daniel. *Evolution de la structure du parti radical*. Paris, 1960.

Barral, Pierre. *Le Départment de l'Isère sous la Troisième République, 1870–1940*. Paris, 1962.

————, ed. *Les Fondateurs de la Troisième République*. Paris, 1968.

Barthes, Roland. *Michelet*. Translated by Richard Howard. New York, 1986.

Beau de Loménie, Emmanuel. *Les Responsabilités des dynasties bourgeoises*. 3 vols. Paris, 1943–73.

Bell, Susan Groag, and Karen M. Offen, eds. *Women, the Family and Freedom: The Debate in Documents*. 2 vols. Stanford, 1983.

Bellanger, Claude, *et al. Histoire générale de la presse française*. 5 vols. Paris, 1969–75.

Berenson, Edward. *The Trial of Madame Caillaux*. Berkeley, 1992.

Berstein, Serge. *Edouard Herriot ou la République en personne*. Paris, 1986.

———. *Histoire du parti radical*. 2 vols. Paris, 1980–82.

Berlanstein, Lenard R. *The Working People of Paris, 1871–1914*. Baltimore, 1984.

Bidelman, Patrick Kay. *Pariahs Stand Up! The Foundation of the Liberal Feminist Movement in France, 1858–1889*. Westport, Conn., 1982.

Blum, Carol. *Rousseau and the Republic of Virtue: The Language of Politics in the French Revolution*. Ithaca, N.Y., 1986.

Bonnefous, Georges. *L'Avant Guerre, 1906–14*. Vol. I of Bonnefous, *Histoire politque de la Troisième Republique*. 5 vols. Paris, 1956.

Bourgin, Georges. *La Commune*. Paris, 1953.

———. *La Troisième République, 1870–1914*. Paris, 1967.

Bouvier, Jean. *Les Deux Scandales de Panama*. Paris, 1964.

———. *Histoire économique et histoire sociale. Recherches sur le capitalisme contemporain*. Geneva, 1968.

Braudel, Fernand, and Ernest Labrousse, eds. *Histoire économique et sociale de la France*. 4 vols. Paris, 1970–82.

Bredin, Jean Denis. *L'Affaire*. Paris, 1983.

Brogan, D. W. *The Development of Modern France, 1870–1930*. 2 vols. New York, 1966.

Bron, Jean. *Histoire du mouvement ouvrier français*. 3 vols. Paris, 1968–72.

Burns, Michael. *Rural Society and French Politics: Boulangism and the Dreyfus Affair, 1886–1900*. Princeton, 1984.

Caron, François. *An Economic History of Modern France*. Translated by Barbara Bray. New York, 1989.

———. *Histoire de l'exploitation d'un grand réseau. La Compagnie du chemin de fer du Nord, 1846–1937*. Paris, 1973.

Chastenet, Jacques. *Histoire de la Troisième République*. 7 vols. Paris, 1952–63.

Chevalier, Louis. *Labouring Classes and Dangerous Classes in Paris During the First Half of the Nineteenth Century*. Translated by Frank Jellinek. Princeton, 1973.

Clark, Linda. *Schooling the Daughters of Marianne: Textbooks and the Socialization of Girls in the Modern French Primary School*. Albany, N.Y., 1984.

Clark, T. J. *The Absolute Bourgeois: Artists and Politics in France, 1848–1851*. London, 1973.

———. *The Painting of Modern Life: Paris in the Art of Manet and His Followers*. New York, 1984.

Clark, Terry N. *Prophets and Patrons: The University and the Emergence of the Social Sciences*. Cambridge, Mass.: 1973.

Cornilleau, Robert. *De Waldeck-Rousseau à Poincaré. Chronique d'une génération, (1898–1924)*. Paris, 1926.

Cross, Gary. *A Quest for Time: The Reduction of Work in Britain and France, 1840–1940*. Berkeley, 1990.

Dansette, Adrien. *Les Affaires de Panama*. Paris, 1934.

———. *Histoire religieuse de la France contemporaine de la Révolution à la Troisième République*. 2 vols. Paris, 1948–51.

Derfler, Leslie. *The Third French Republic, 1870–1940*. Princeton, 1966.

Duroselle, Jean-Baptiste. *Clemenceau*. Paris, 1988.

Earle, Edward M., ed. *Modern France: Problems of the Third and Fourth Republics*. Princeton, 1951.

Edwards, Stewart. *The Paris Commune, 1871*. London, 1971.

Ellis, Jack. *The Physician-Legislators of France: Medicine and Politics in the Early Third Republic*. New York, 1990.

Elwitt, Sanford. *The Making of the Third Republic: Class and Politics in France, 1868–1884*. Baton Rouge, 1975.

———. *The Third Republic Defended: Bourgeois Reform in France, 1880–1914*. Baton Rouge, 1986.

Estèbe, Jean. *Les Ministres de la République, 1871–1914*. Paris, 1982.

Ford, Caroline. *Creating the Nation in Provincial France: Religion and Political Identity in Brittany*. Princeton, 1993.

Fox, Edward Whiting. *History in Geographic Perspective: The Other France*. New York, 1971.

Fuchs, Rachel. *Abandoned Children: Foundlings and Child Welfare in Nineteenth-Century France*. Albany, N.Y., 1984.

———. *Poor and Pregnant in Paris: Strategies for Survival in the Nineteenth Century*. New Brunswick, N.J., 1992.

Furet, François. *La Gauche et la Révolution française au milieu du dix-neuvième siècle: Edgar Quinet et la question du jacobinisme, 1865–1870*. Paris, 1986.

———, ed. *Jules Ferry, fondateur de la République*. Paris, 1985.

Girardet, Raoul. *Le Nationalisme français, 1871–1914*. Paris, 1966.

Goguel, François. *La Politique des partis sous la Troisième République*. Paris, 1958.

Goldberg, Harvey. *The Life of Jean Jaurès*. Madison, 1968.

Gooch, R. K. *The French Parliamentary Committee System*. Charlottesville, Va., 1935.

Greenberg, Louis. *Sisters of Liberty: Marseille, Lyon, Paris, and the Reaction to a Centralized State, 1868–1871*. Cambridge, Mass., 1971.

Guiral, Pierre, and Guy Thuillier. *La Vie quotidienne des députés en France de 1871 à 1914*. Paris, 1980.

Halévy, Daniel. *The End of the Notables*. Translated by Alain Silvera and June Guicharnaud. Edited by Alain Silvera. 1930; rpr. Middletown, Conn., 1974.

———. *La République des comités. Essai d'histoire contemporaine, 1895–1934*. Paris, 1934.

Hamburger, Maurice. *Léon Bourgeois, 1851–1925: La Politique radicale-socialiste, la doctrine de la solidarité, l'arbitrage internationale et la Société des Nations*. Paris, 1932.

Harvey, David. *Consciousness and Urban Experience: Studies in the History and Theory of Capitalist Urbanization*. Baltimore, 1985.

Hause, Steven. *Hubertine Auclert: The French Suffragette*. New Haven, 1987.

Hause, Steven, and Anne Kenney. *Women's Suffrage and Social Politics in the Third Republic*. Princeton, 1984.

Hoffmann, Stanley. *In Search of France*. Cambridge, Mass., 1963.

Hood, Ronald Chalmers III. *Royal Republicans: The French Naval Dynasties*. Baton Rouge, 1985.

Howorth, Jolyon. *Edouard Vaillant: La Création de l'unité socialiste en France*. Paris, 1982.

Huard, Raymond. *Le Mouvement républicain en Bas-Languedoc, 1848–1881*. Paris, 1982.

Hunt, Lynn. *The Family Romance of the French Revolution*. Berkeley, 1992.

———. *Politics, Culture, and Class in the French Revolution*. Berkeley, 1984.

Hutton, Patrick H. *The Cult of the Revolutionary Tradition: The Blanquists in French Politics, 1864–1893*. Berkeley, 1981.

———, ed. *Historical Dictionary of the Third French Republic, 1870–1940*. 2 vols. Westport, Conn., 1986.

Ionesco, Eugène. *Hugoliade*. Translated by Dragomir Constineanu. 1935–36; rpr. Paris, 1982.

Irvine, William D. *The Boulanger Affair Reconsidered: Royalism, Boulangism, and the Origins of the Radical Right in France*. Oxford, 1989.

Joly, Jean. *Dictionnaire des parlementaires français; notices biographiques sur les parlementaires français, 1889–1940*. 8 vols. Paris, 1960–77.

Joughin, Jean T. *The Paris Commune in French Politics, 1871–1880: The History of the Amnesty of 1880*. Baltimore, 1956.

Judt, Tony. *Socialism in Provence, 1871–1914: A Study in the Origins of the Modern French Left*. New York, 1979.

Julliard, Jacques. *Clemenceau, briseur des grèves. L'Affaire de Draveil Villeneuve-St. Georges (1908)*. Paris, 1965.

Kayser, Jacques. *Les Grandes Batailles du radicalisme dès origines aux portes du pouvoir, 1820–1901*. Paris, 1962.

Landes, Joan. *Women in the Public Sphere in the Age of the French Revolution*. Ithaca, N.Y., 1988.

Larkin, Maurice. *Church and the State After the Dreyfus Affair: The Separation Issue in France*. London, 1974.

Lebovics, Herman. *The Alliance of Iron and Wheat in the Third French Republic, 1860–1914: Origins of the New Conservatism*. Baton Rouge, 1988.

Le Bras, Gabriel. *Etudes de sociologie religieuse*. 2 vols. Paris, 1955.

Lefebvre, Georges. *1789*. Paris, 1939.

Lerner, H. *La Dépêche, journal de la démocratie: Contribution à l'histoire du radicalisme sous la Troisième République*. 2 vols. Toulouse, 1978.

Levin, Miriam R. *Republican Art and Ideology in Late Nineteenth-Century France*. Ann Arbor, 1986.

Loubère, Leo. *Radicalism in Mediterranean France: Its Rise and Decline, 1848–1914*. Albany, N.Y., 1974.

Manevy, Raymond. *La Presse de la Troisième République*. Paris, 1955.

Margadant, Jo Burr. *Madame le Professeur: Women Educators in the Third Republic*. Princeton, 1990.

Martin, Benjamin F. *The Hypocrisy of Justice in the Belle Epoque*. Baton Rouge, 1984.

Maurois, André. *Olympio ou la vie de Victor Hugo*. Paris, 1954.

Mayeur, Jean-Marie. *Les Débuts de la Troisième République, 1871–1898*. Paris, 1973.

———. *La Séparation des églises et de l'état*. Paris, 1991.

———. *La Vie politique sous la Troisième République, 1870–1940*. Paris, 1984.

Mercillon, Henri, *et al. Orsay. Connaissance des Arts*. Numero spéciale. Paris, 1987.

Milhaud, Albert. *Histoire du radicalisme*. Paris, 1951.

Moses, Claire Goldberg. *French Feminism in the Nineteenth Century*. Albany, N.Y., 1984.

Néré, Jacques. *Le Boulangisme et la presse*. Paris, 1964.

Nicolet, Claude. *L'Idée républicaine en France, 1789–1924: Essai d'histoire critique*. Paris, 1982.

———. *Le Radicalisme*. 2d ed. Paris, 1957.

Nora, Pierre, ed. *Les Lieux de mémoire*. 2 vols. Paris, 1984–86.

Nord, Philip G. *Paris Shopkeepers and the Politics of Resentment*. Princeton, 1986.

Nye, Robert. *Masculinity and Male Codes of Honor in Modern France*. New York, 1993.

Oberthür, Mariel. *Le Chat Noir, 1881–1897*. Paris, 1992.

Outram, Dorinda. *The Body and the French Revolution: Sex, Class, and Political Culture*. New Haven, 1989.

Pateman, Carol. *The Disorder of Women: Democracy, Feminism, and Political Theory*. Stanford, 1989.

Pinkney, David H. *Napoleon III and the Rebuilding of Paris*. Princeton, 1958.

Price, Roger. *An Economic History of Modern France, 1730–1914*. London, 1981.

Provence historique; revue trimestrielle. Vol. XXIII, no. 93-4. Marseilles, July–December 1973.

Rearick, Charles. *Pleasures of the Belle Epoque: Entertainment and Festivity in Turn-of-the-Century France*. New Haven, 1985.

Rebérioux, Madeleine. *La République radicale? 1898–1914*. Paris, 1975.

Reid, Donald. *The Miners of Decazeville: A Genealogy of Deindustrialization*. Cambridge, Mass., 1985.

Revillon, Tony. *Camille Pelletan, 1846–1915: Quarante-cinq années de lutte pour la République*. Paris, 1930.

Rudelle, Odile. *La République absolue: Aux Origines de l'instabilité constitutionnelle de la France républicaine, 1870–1889*. Paris, 1982.

Saalman, Howard. *Haussmann: Paris Transformed*. New York, 1971.

Seigel, Jerrold. *Bohemian Paris: Culture, Politics, and the Boundaries of Bourgeois Life, 1830–1930*. New York, 1986.

Silverman, Debora L. *Art Nouveau in Fin-de-Siècle France: Politics, Psychology and Style*. Berkeley, 1989.

Singer, Barnett. *Village Notables in Nineteenth-Century France: Priests, Mayors, Schoolmasters*. Albany, N.Y., 1983.

Smith, Bonnie. *Ladies of the Leisure Class: The Bourgeoises of Northern France in the Nineteenth Century*. Princeton, 1981.

Sorlin, Pierre. *La Société française*. Vol. I, *1840–1914*. Paris, 1969.

———. *Waldeck-Rousseau*. Paris, 1966.

Soulié, Michel. *La Vie politique d'Edouard Herriot*. Paris, 1962.

Sternhell, Zeev. *La Droite révolutionnaire. Les Origines françaises du fascsime, 1885–1914*. Paris, 1978.

Stewart, Mary Lynn. *Women, Work, and the French State: Labour Protection and Social Patriarchy, 1879–1919*. Montreal, 1989.

Stone, Judith F. *The Search for Social Peace: Reform Legislation in France, 1890–1914*. Albany, N.Y., 1985.

Vizetelly, Ernest Alfred. *Paris and Her People Under the Third Republic*. 1919; rpr. New York, 1971.

————. *Republican France, 1870–1912: Her Presidents, Statesmen, Policy, Vicissitudes, and Social Life*. Boston, 1913.

Warner, Charles K. *The Winegrowers of France and the Government Since 1875*. New York, 1960.

Watson, David Robin. *Georges Clemenceau: A Political Biography*. London, 1974.

Weber, Eugen. *France, Fin de Siècle*. Cambridge, Mass., 1986.

————. *The Nationalist Revival in France, 1905–1914*. Berkeley, 1968.

Williams, Roger Lawrence. *Henri Rochefort, Prince of the Gutter Press*. New York, 1966.

Wishnia, Judith. *The Proletarianizing of the Fonctionnaires: Civil Service Workers and the Labor Movement Under the Third Republic*. Baton Rouge, 1990.

Wright, Gordon. *Notable or Notorious? A Gallery of Parisians*. Cambridge, Mass., 1991.

Zeldin, Theodore. *France: Ambition and Love*. Oxford, 1979.

Articles, Essays, and Theses

Alroy, G. "Radicalism and Modernization: The French Problem." Ph.D. dissertation, Princeton University, 1962.

Amalvi, Christian. "Le Quatorze Juillet. Du *Dies irae* à Jour de fête." In *La République*. Paris, 1984. Vol. I of *Les Lieux de mémoire*, ed. Pierre Nora. 2 vols.

Augulhon, Maurice. "Esquisses pour une archéologie de la République." *Annales: Economies, sociétés, civilisations*, XXIII (1973), 5–34.

Baal, Gérard. "Combes et la 'République des comités'." *Revue d'histoire moderne et contemporaine*, XXIV (April–June, 1977), 260–85.

————. "Le Parti radical de 1901 à 1914." Doctorat d'Etat, Université de Paris I, 1991.

————. "Un Salon dreyfusard, dès lendemains de l'Affaire à la Grande Guerre: La Marquise Arconati-Visconti et ses amis." *Revue d'histoire moderne et contemporaine*, XXVIII (July–September, 1981), 433–63.

————. "Victor Pengam et l'évolution du syndicalism révolutionnaire à Brest, 1904–1914." *Mouvement social*, LXXXII (January–March, 1973), 55–82.

Baquiast, Paul. "Camille Pelletan (1846–1915), Esquisse de biographie." Mémoire de maîtrise d'histoire, Université de Paris IV, 1986.

————. "La Jeune Ecole de la marine française, la presse et l'opinion publique." Unpublished paper, Université de Paris IV, 1987.

Ben-Amos, Anver. "Les Funérailles de Victor Hugo." In *La République*. Paris, 1984. Vol. I of *Les Lieux de mémoire*, ed. Pierre Nora. 2 vols.

Bloch, Ruth H. "The Gendered Meanings of Virtue in Revolutionary America." *Signs: Journal of Women in Culture and Society*, XIII (Autumn, 1987), 37–58.

Bouvier, Jean. "Mouvement ouvrier et conjoncture économique." *Mouvement social,* XLVIII (July–September, 1964), 3–30.

Crouzet, François. "Essai de construction d'un indice annuel de la production industrielle française au XIXe siècle." *Annales: Economies, sociétés, civilisations,* XXV (1970), 56–99.

Dogan, Mattei. "Political Ascent in a Class Society: French Deputies, 1870–1958." In *Political Decision Makers,* ed. Dwaine Marvick. Glencoe, N.Y., 1961. 57–90.

Fitch, Nancy. "Mass Culture, Mass Parliamentary Politics, and Modern Anti-Semitism: The Dreyfus Affair in Rural France." *American Historical Review,* XCVII (February, 1992), 55–95.

Ford, Caroline. "Religion and the Politics of Cultural Change in Provincial France: The Resistance of 1902 in Lower Brittany." *Journal of Modern History,* LXII (March, 1990), 1–33.

Friedman, Gerald. "Capitalism, Republicanism, Socialism, and the State: France, 1871–1914." *Social Science History,* XIV (Summer, 1990), 151–74.

Graham, James. "The French Radical and Radical Socialist Party, 1906–1914." Ph.D. dissertation, Ohio State University, 1962.

Jayot, Franz. "Les Etudiants parisiens de 1890 à 1906. Etude politique et sociale." Mémoire de maîtrise, Université de Paris X, 1973.

Kaplan, Robert. "France, 1893–98: The Fear of Revolution Among the Bourgeoisie." Ph.D. dissertation, Cornell University, 1971.

Levin, Miriam R. "The Eiffel Tower Revisited." *French Review,* LXII (May, 1989), 1052–64.

Levy-Leboyer, Maurice. "La Croissance économique en France au XIXe siècle: Résultats préliminaires." *Annales: Economies, sociétés, civilisations,* XXIII (1968), 788–807.

Loubère, Leo. "French Left-Wing Radicals and the Law as a Social Force, 1870–1900." *American Journal of Legal History,* VIII (January, 1964), 54–94.

———. "The French Left-Wing Radicals: Their Views on Trade-Unionism, 1870–98." *International Review of Social History,* VII (1962), 203–30.

———. "Left-Wing Radicals, Strikes, and the Military, 1880–1907." *French Historical Studies,* III (Spring, 1963), 93–105.

———. "Les Radicaux d'extrême gauche en France et les rapports entre patrons et ouvriers, 1871–1900." *Revue d'histoire économique et sociale,* LXII (1964), 89–103.

Mayer, Arno. "The Lower Middle Class as an Historical Problem." *Journal of Modern History,* XLVII (September, 1975), 409–36.

Moch, Leslie Page. "Government Policy and Women's Experience: The Case of Teachers in France." *Feminist Studies,* XIV (Summer, 1988), 301–24.

Morris, Peter. "The French Radical Party and the First Ministry of Georges Clemenceau." Ph.D. dissertation, Cambridge University, 1973.

Mosse, George L. "Circuses and Monuments." *Journal of Contemporary History*, VI (1971), 167–83.

Néré, Jacques. "La Crise économique de 1882 et le mouvement boulangiste." Doctorat d'Etat, Université de Paris I, 1959.

Nord, Philip G. "Manet and Radical Politics." *Journal of Interdisciplinary History*, XIX (Winter, 1989), 447–80.

————. "The Party of Conciliation and the Paris Commune." *French Historical Studies*, XV (Spring, 1987), 1–35.

Offen, Karen. "A Nineteenth Century French Feminist Rediscovered: Jenny P. d'Héricourt, 1809–1875." *Signs: Journal of Women in Culture and Society*, XIII (Autumn, 1987), 144–58.

————. "The Second Sex and the Baccalaureate in Republican France, 1880–1924." *French Historical Studies*, XIII (Fall, 1983), 252–86.

————. "Women in the Labor Force." In *Historical Dictionary of the Third French Republic, 1870–1940*, ed. Patrick Hutton. Westport, Conn., 1986. 1072–74.

Persell, Stuart M. "Jean de Lanessan and the French Positivist School of Criminal Reform, 1880–1914." *Criminal Justice Review*, XII (Fall, 1987), 1–6.

Rearick, Charles. "Festivals in Modern France: The Experience of the Third Republic." *Journal of Contemporary History*, XII (July, 1977), 435–60.

Reid, Donald. "The Third Republic as Manager: Labor Policy in the Naval Shipyards, 1892–1920." *International Review of Social History*, XXX (1985), 183–206.

Rioux, Jean Pierre. "Le Palais Bourbon." In *La Nation*. Paris, 1986. Vol. II of *Les Lieux de mémoire*, ed. Pierre Nora. 2 vols.

Sanders, Richard W. "The Labor Policies of the French Radical Party, 1901–1909." Ph.D. dissertation, Duke University, 1972.

Sewell, William H. "Le Citoyen/la citoyenne: Activity, Passivity, and the Revolutionary Concept of Citizenship." In Colin Lucas, ed., *Political Culture of the French Revolution*. New York, 1988. 105–23.

Sumler, David. "Domestic Influences on the Nationalist Revival in France." *French Historical Studies*, VI (Fall, 1970), 517–38.

Watson, David Robin. "The Nationalist Movement in Paris, 1900–1906." In *The Right in France, 1890–1919*. ed. David Shapiro. Carbondale, 1962. 49–84.

Winnacker, R. A. "The Délégation des gauches: A Successful Attempt at Managing a Parliamentary Coalition." *Journal of Modern History*, IX (December, 1937), 449–70.

Index